Governance Ethics in Organizations

MW00835574

Drawing on the findings of a series of empirical studies undertaken with boards of directors and CEOs in the United States, this groundbreaking book develops a new paradigm to provide a structured analysis of ethical healthcare governance.

Governance Ethics in Healthcare Organizations begins by presenting a clear framework for ethical analysis, designed around basic features of ethics—who we are, how we function, and what we do—before discussing the paradigm in relation to clinical, organizational, and professional ethics. It goes on to apply this framework in areas that are pivotal for effective governance in healthcare: oversight structures for trustees and executives, community benefit, community health, patient care, patient safety, and conflicted collaborative arrangements.

This book is an important read for all those interested in healthcare management, corporate governance, and healthcare ethics, including academics, students, and practitioners.

Gerard Magill holds the Vernon F. Gallagher Chair at Duquesne University in Pittsburgh, USA, where he is a tenured Professor in the Center for Healthcare Ethics.

Lawrence Prybil is the Founding Norton Professor in Healthcare Leadership at the University of Kentucky's College of Public Health, USA, where he has served as Associate Dean. He is also Professor Emeritus at the University of Iowa, USA.

Routledge Studies in Health and Social Welfare

For more information about this series, please visit: www.routledge.com/
Routledge-Studies-in-Health-and-Social-Welfare/book-series/RSHSW

Governance Ethics in Healthcare Organizations

Gerard Magill and Lawrence Prybil

LONDON AND NEW YORK

First published 2020 by Routledge

2 Park Square, Milton Park, Abingdon, Oxon OX14 4RN
605 Third Avenue, New York, NY 10017

Routledge is an imprint of the Taylor & Francis Group, an informa business

First issued in paperback 2021

Publisher's Note

The publisher has gone to great lengths to ensure the quality of this reprint but
points out that some imperfections in the original copies may be apparent.

British Library Cataloguing-in-Publication Data
A catalogue record for this book is available from the British Library

Library of Congress Cataloging-in-Publication Data
A catalog record for this book has been requested

ISBN: 978-0-367-34840-3 (hbk)
ISBN: 978-1-03-217532-4 (pbk)
DOI: 10.4324/9780429328305

Typeset in Times New Roman
by Apex CoVantage, LLC

We dedicate this book to our spouses, Marilyn Prybil and Mary Anne Campbell, whose love and support inspired us throughout this work.

Contents

4 Governance structure   46

5 Governance of community benefit   70

8 Governance of patient safety   124

9 Governance of conflicted collaborative arrangements   146

10 Governance and virtuous organizations   161

Acknowledgements

We are grateful to many people who have kindly assisted us in writing this book. We especially convey our gratitude to Ann Kelly at the University of Kentucky for her meticulous review of information on multi-sector partnerships and to Dina Siniora and Hillary Villarreal, tireless graduate assistants at Duquesne University in Pittsburgh.

1 Ethics paradigm

Introduction

This book discusses governance ethics in healthcare organizations to provide ethical guidance about trustee oversight. In addition to boards of directors and executives in healthcare, scholars, students, and professionals interested in the governance oversight of organizations will find the book to be enlightening. The analysis combines a theory perspective and an application perspective to develop a structured analysis of governance ethics.

The analysis explains that governance ethics is similar to already established fields in health ethics (clinical, organizational, and professional ethics). The general approach adopted by these established fields combines theoretical and applied perspectives to provide practical guidance. They guide their constituencies on specific issues, such as end of life care in clinical ethics, or financial propriety in organizational ethics, or conflicts of interest in professional ethics. In contrast, governance ethics deals with very different topics that relate to trustee oversight of healthcare organizations, such as with regard to patient safety or community health. Hence, governance ethics can be described as an emerging field in healthcare.

There is a considerable amount of literature on corporate governance.[1] This literature includes the relation among corporate governance, ethics (typically dealing with business ethics),[2] and corporate social responsibility.[3] However, very little has been published on the ethics of governance in healthcare organizations.[4] This significant gap in the literature is addressed by this book. To understand the importance of this discussion, it is helpful to consider the need for governance ethics, nationally and internationally.

Need for governance ethics

Over recent decades, public confidence in healthcare organizations has declined significantly. This decline has led to vigorous efforts to improve trust in health care organizations, both public and private.[5] At the same time, significant growth of large healthcare systems has occurred. The number of multi-unit health systems, both governmental and private, has increased noticeably. Also, the proportion of community hospitals becoming part of health systems continues to expand steadily.[6] This growth has stressed the crucial role of finances in a changing health economy.[7] Not surprisingly, there has emerged a greater awareness of the need for more effective governance. This means that boards of directors and executives needs to be more accountable in a manner that is evident to the populations they serve.[8] This constitutes a call for organizational transparency to the communities served by healthcare organizations.

Also, the extent of corporate fraud and abuse across the United States is well recognized. Such abuse has led to stricter government regulations. For example, the renowned Sarbanes-Oxley Act was passed with strict compliance require-ments. The act sought several goals: to diminish fraudulent financial activity; to enhance the independence of external auditing; and to emphasize the need for better oversight by boards of directors.[9] This legislation applied only to for-profit corporations. Nonetheless, the legislation also reflected concerns about the effec-tiveness of nonprofit boards. Hence, the legislation prompted trustees to provide better governance leadership. The goal here is to nurture public trust in healthcare organizations.[10]

Public trust is in large measure related to the well-known disparities in health-care access and affordability. These are exacerbated by the accompanying con-nection between quality and safety. Historically, these issues have haunted the United States,[11] and continue to do so today.[12] The loss of public trust in these sectors has been widespread and extensively documented.[13] This distrust was especially evident in nonprofit healthcare in relation to the tension between what is known as mission and margin. This tension refers to the organization's polarized commitment to serve its communities (mission) and the organization's financial success (margin).[14] For example, this tension challenges healthcare leaders to ensure the success of an organization such as with regard to ethical procurement and resourcing. However, the tension between mission and margin also requires healthcare leaders to care for employees such as with regard to remuneration across professional differences. This tension emphasizes that suc-cess should not be reduced merely to management or fiscal efficiencies. In turn, concern about this moral tension raised significant issues related to justice, such as meeting the community's health needs fairly and holding healthcare morally accountable.[15]

This widespread distrust created challenges for boards of directors in both for-profit and nonprofit sectors. These challenges highlight the need for effective governance that overlaps with but goes beyond compliance requirements. This need was especially the case in healthcare.[16] Moreover, this need for improvement was recognized in many different nations. This international awareness indicated the increasing focus on board function and trustee accountability in hospitals and healthcare systems globally.[17]

Over recent decades, continuous quality improvement became a characteris-tic of healthcare delivery. The time for continuous improvement of governance accountability in healthcare organizations has arrived. This accountability goes beyond the board's conventional responsibility for organizational oversight.

Boards of directors now need to scrutinize themselves more closely than ever. This scrutiny must seek to ensure that an organization's mission, processes, and practices will enable the organization to perform at its peak.[18] As a result, the caliber of governance in healthcare organizations is under intense examination.[19] In particular, there is an acknowledgement of the need for research-based findings to support actionable knowledge that will enhance governance in hospitals and health systems.[20] Similarly, there is a growing recognition that trustees should develop a sophisticated ethical compass to help navigate potential compromises in healthcare institutions.[21]

Obviously, boards of directors with their institutional management teams have complex responsibilities. They are responsible for overseeing a complex array of structures, processes, outcomes, and external regulations. That oversight is necessary to continuously measure, monitor, and improve organizational performance. Board effectiveness lies at the core of governance in the fast-changing environment of healthcare. It is indispensable both to identify responsibilities and to design oversight mechanisms. Without these, trust of internal and external stakeholders will be eroded. This emphasis on a sustainable approach to accountability requires the utmost transparency.[22] That is, healthcare must be resilient in the face of so many challenges. There needs to be greater oversight by trustees and executives to demonstrate organizational accountability in a manner that is evident to the populations served.

The multiple board responsibilities of trustees range from specific fiduciary duties to broader ethical obligations. All of these responsibilities require accountability to the communities served. For example, this means providing access to crucial information about the cost, price, and quality of services to achieve value. Undoubtedly, there are puzzling variations in these data. These variations contribute to widespread public concern. Such concern deals as much with the efficiency of healthcare organizations as with the effectiveness of their leadership, including governance. Hence, healthcare organizations must be increasingly accountable to their communities. Accountability of trustees means defining expectations and establishing measurement and improvement metrics of governance. This study of governance ethics in healthcare organizations seeks to engage these issues.

The ethics paradigm

The book aims to provide a structured analysis of governance ethics in healthcare organizations by presenting a new ethics paradigm that is applied to pivotal topics. The ethics paradigm provides an original framework for ethical analysis. Typically, books in the established fields of health ethics combine ethical theory with ethical principles to discuss practical topics. Discussions of ethical theory include approaches to ethics reasoning—such as deontology, utilitarianism, and communitarianism. Discussions of ethical principles include different ethical concepts—such as autonomy, beneficence, and justice. A very different approach is adopted in this book. Here, the ethics paradigm develops a more general approach that underlies ethical theories and principles, by providing a framework for an ethical analysis that does not require formal ethics training or expertise.

The framework of the paradigm guides ethical discourse by providing a structure that coalesces relevant data to interpret specific issues. The core structure of the ethics paradigm revolves around basic features of ethics: *who we are, how we function, what we do*. These features form a leitmotif throughout the study. The framework includes a focus on decision-making (concentrating on accountability vis-à-vis *how we function*). However, there is also a broader perspective that deals with stewardship (engaging identity vis-à-vis *who we are*) and quality (addressing best practices vis-à-vis *what we do*).

These basic features generate the three components of the ethics paradigm. Each component is related to specific governance contexts. The foundation component (*who we are*) operates within the context of engaging the healthcare environment. The process component (*how we function*) operates within the context of undertaking organizational oversight. The practice component (*what we do*) operates within the context of fostering organizational culture.

These basic features of ethics are indispensable for promoting leadership in governance: leadership regarding institutional identity (*who we are*); leadership regarding corporate accountability (*how we function*); and leadership regarding performance quality (*what we do*). In turn, these leadership features foster specific outcomes: the leadership focus on *identity* fosters outcomes regarding organizational stewardship of an institution's mission; the leadership focus on *accountability* fosters outcomes regarding decision-making via participative deliberation; and the leadership focus on *quality* fosters outcomes regarding best practices for standards of conduct. Here is a diagram of the ethics paradigm (Table 1.1).

The ethics paradigm is applied throughout the book to discuss topics that are pivotal for governance ethics in healthcare organizations. It can be helpful at the outset to provide an overview of these applied topics.

Applied topics

The theory perspective of the book explains the ethics paradigm (Chapters 1–3). This is complemented by the applied perspective of the book (Chapters 4–9).

Table 1.1 Ethics paradigm

Components	Foundation component	Process component	Practice component
Context	Environment of healthcare	Organizational oversight	Organizational culture
Leadership	Identity: who we are	Accountability: how we function	Quality: what we do
Outcomes	Organizational stewardship of mission	Decision-making via participative deliberation	Best practices for standards of conduct

In these applied chapters, the ethics paradigm is applied to specific topics that are crucial for governance ethics. Typically, other studies around governance in healthcare organizations focus on finance issues. In contrast, this work focuses on issues related to the healthcare of patients and communities. Naturally, this focus recognizes that finance is an indispensable aspect of board stewardship.

The applied topics begin with a discussion of governance structure for trustees. The subsequent topics consider major issues regarding effective governance in healthcare organizations: community benefit, community health, patient care, and patient safety. These topics are pivotal for governance ethics because they have contributed in no small measure to undermining public confidence in healthcare organizations, both private and public. In turn, these topics lead to an over-arching ethical problem for healthcare governance that deals with conflicted collaborative arrangements: how to distinguish wrongful complicity from legitimate cooperation with activities in other organizations. The discussion ends with a brief concluding chapter on how this approach to governance ethics can foster virtuous organizations in healthcare. Discourse on virtue ethics explains that individuals can become virtuous by connecting moral character, practical wisdom, and laudable actions. Similarly, the ethics paradigm enables an organization to become virtuous by connecting moral character (via the concept of *identity*, *who we are*), practical wisdom (via the concept of *accountability*, *how we function*), and action (via the concept of *quality*, *what we do*). In these applied chapters, the ethics paradigm is applied to identify hallmarks for governance ethics in healthcare organizations. These hallmarks are accompanied with specific ethical imperatives for boards of directors and executives. These hallmarks and accompanying ethical imperatives, along with the topics engaged in each chapter, are listed regularly, to identify them clearly in the analysis.

The topics that are discussed in the book arose from landmark research reports that have shaped the field.[23] In particular, reports by one of the co-authors of this book (with many other accompanying publications) provide critical data for the ethical analysis.[24] The reports were undertaken with boards of directors and CEOs. The focus was on assessing and improving governance performance. The process provided unprecedented access to many large health systems. This access refers to the information provided by the boards of directors and CEOs of these health systems. The research addressed their governance oversight. For example, one report engaged 14 of the 15 largest health systems in the United States.[25] The information derived from these reports indicates the priority issues identified by these trustees and CEOs for governance of their organizations.

Conclusion

This book on governance ethics in healthcare organizations deals with an emerging field that contrasts yet is consistent with the established fields of clinical, organizational, and professional ethics. Specifically, the ethics paradigm is connected with these established fields to examine governance ethics.

The originality of this study is twofold. Its first contribution lies in the way it constructs the ethics paradigm to demonstrate a consistency of ethics discourse in the well-established fields of clinical, organizational, and professional ethics in healthcare. All too often, these fields are perceived to be sufficiently different as to forgo a foundational consistency between them. Its second contribution rests in the way it presents the relatively new field of governance ethics as being consistent with these already established ethics fields in healthcare. Hence, throughout the study, the alignment between these various fields is emphasized to apply the ethics paradigm to governance ethics, thereby unpacking the accompanying moral imperatives that emerge from the topics discussed.

The book is designed to enlighten trustees and executives as well as to provide guidance for scholars, students, and professionals in healthcare. The authors hope that the ethical analysis will be of special interest internationally to boards of directors and executives in healthcare to enhance governance oversight of their organizations.

Notes

1 See: M. I. Steinberg, *The Federalization of Corporate Governance* (Oxford University Press, 2018); D. Arsalidou, *Rethinking Corporate Governance in Financial Institutions* (Routledge, 2018); S. Seifi, D. Crowther, eds., *Stakeholders, Governance and Responsibility* (United Kingdom: Emerald Publishing, 2018); T. Clarke, *International Corporate Governance: A Comparative Approach*, 2nd ed. (Routledge, 2017); N. Capaldi, et al., eds., *Dimensional Corporate Governance: An Inclusive Approach* (Springer, 2017); A. Micklethwait, P. Dimond, *Driven to the Brink: Why Corporate Governance, Board Leadership and Culture Matter* (United Kingdom: Palgrave MacMillan, 2017); M. J. Whincop, *Corporate Governance in Government Corporations* (Routledge, 2016); G. N. Bajpai, *The Essential Book of Corporate Governance* (Thousand Oaks, CA: Sage, 2016); A. Mallin, *Corporate Governance*, 5th ed. (New York: Oxford University Press, 2016); K. Emerson, T. Nabatchi (*Collaborative Governance Regimes* (Washington, DC: Georgetown University Press); M. Wright, et al., eds., *The Oxford Handbook of Corporate Governance* (Oxford University Press, 2014).

2 See: R. Upadhyay, *Ethics, Integrity, and Aptitude in Governance* (Thousand Oaks, CA: Sage, 2018); L. E. Mitchell, ed., *Corporate Governance: Values, Ethics and Leadership* (Routledge, 2018); F. Handy, A. R. Russell, *Ethics for Social Impact: Ethical Decision-Making in Nonprofit Organizations* (Palgrave MacMillan, 2018); D. G. Long, Z. Inbar, *The Ethical Kaleidoscope: Values, Ethics and Corporate Governance* (Routledge, 2017); N. Blackwell, G. Durgan. *Essential Governance, Risk & Business Ethics* (Emile Woolf International, 2017); K. V. Rao, G. N. Raju, *Business Ethics and Corporate Governance* (New Delhi: International Publishing House, 2017); R. Cressy, et al., eds., *Entrepreneurship, Finance, Governance and Ethics* (Springer, 2016); D. Hotchkiss, *Governance and Ministry: Rethinking Board Leadership*, 2nd ed. (Rowman & Littlefield, 2016); B. Tricker, G. Tricker, *Business Ethics: A Stakeholder, Governance and Risk Approach* (Routledge, 2014); J. Wieland, *Governance Ethics: Global Value Creation, Economic Organization and Normativity* (Springer, 2014); B. P. Mathur, *Ethics for Governance: Reinventing Public Services* (Routledge, 2014).

3 See: J. Weber, D. M. Wasielski, eds., *Corporate Social Responsibility* (United Kingdom: Emerald Publishing, 2018); A. Rasche, et al., eds., *Corporate Social Responsibility: Strategy, Communication, Governance* (Cambridge University Press, 2017); J. Moon, *Corporate Social Responsibility* (Oxford University Press, 2015). Also see the

series with Springer on corporate social responsibility, ethics and governance, such as: R. Altenburger, ed., *Innovation Management and Corporate Social Responsibility* (Springer, 2018); S. O. Idowu, et al., eds., *Corporate Social Responsibility in Times of Crisis* (Springer, 2019); S. O. Idowu, et al., eds., *A Standardized View on Corporate Social Responsibility* (Springer, 2018).

4 See: B. Jennings, et al., *The Ethics of Hospital Trustees* (Washington, DC: Georgetown University Press, 2004); R. A. Ritvo, et al., *Ethical Governance in Healthcare. A Board Leadership Guide for Building an Ethical Culture* (Chicago, IL: Health Forum, Inc., 2004).

5 See: Future Health Index, *Trust in Healthcare* (July 2018), at, www.futurehealthindex. com/2018/07/17/trust-healthcare-aligning-hcps-patients-long-term-partnership.

6 See: Agency for Healthcare Research and Quality, "Snapshot of U.S. Health Systems, 2016," *Comparative Health System Performance Initiative*, Data Highlight No. 1 (September 2017); B. T. Fulton, "Health Care Market Concentration Trends in the United States: Evidence and Policy Responses," *Health Affairs* 36 (9) (2017), at, https://doi.org/10.1377/hlthaff.2017.0556.

7 Deloitte, *2018 Global Healthcare Outlook: The Evolution of Smart Healthcare*, at, https://www2.deloitte.com/global/en/pages/life-sciences-and-healthcare/articles/global-health-care-sector-outlook.html

8 See: L. Prybil, et al., *The Evolving Accountability of Nonprofit Health System Boards* (Chicago, IL: AHA Center for Healthcare Governance, 2013); J. O'Brien, ed., *Governing the Corporation: Regulation and Corporate Governance in an Age of Scandal and Global Markets* (John Wiley & Sons, 2005).

9 See: *The Sarbanes-Oxley Act* (2002), at, www.soxlaw.com; J. Mead, "Confidence in the Non-Profit Sector Through Sarbanes-Oxley Style Reforms," *Michigan Law Review* 106 (2008): 881–900.

10 See: The Governance Institute, "Great Boards Need Leaders, Not Followers," *Healthcare Executive* 25 (6) (2010): 74–76.

11 See: U.S. Department of Health and Human Services, Agency for Healthcare Research and Quality, *National Healthcare Quality Report* (Washington, DC: Agency for Healthcare Research and Quality, 2013); Institute of Medicine, *Best Care at Lower Cost* (Washington, DC: National Academies Press, 2012).

12 U.S. News and World Report, *Health Care Access Rankings* (July 2018), at, www. usnews.com/news/best-states/rankings/health-care/healthcare-access

13 See: W. H. Wiist, ed., *The Bottom Line or Public Health* (New York: Oxford University Press, 2010); D. A. Shore, ed., *The Trust Crisis in Healthcare: Causes, Consequences, and Cures* (New York: Oxford University Press, 2007).

14 See: N. D. Voges, "The Ethics of Mission and Margin," *Healthcare Executive* 27 (5) (2012): 30–38; M. J. McDonough, *Can A Healthcare Market Be Moral?* (Washington, DC: Georgetown University Press, 2007); S. D. Pearson, J. E. Sabin, E. J. Emanuel, *No Margin, No Mission: Health-Care Organizations and the Quest for Ethical Excellence* (New York: Oxford University Press, 2003).

15 See: N. Daniels, *Just Health: Meeting Health Needs Fairly* (New York: Cambridge University Press, 2008); N. Daniels, J. E. Sabin, *Setting Limits Fairly* (New York: Oxford University Press, 2008); J. P. Ruger, *Health and Social Justice* (New York: Oxford University Press, 2010); E. H. Morreim, *Holding Healthcare Accountable* (New York: Oxford University Press, 2011).

16 See: W. A. Nelson, "Comparing Ethics and Compliance Programs," *Healthcare Executive* 27 (4) (2010): 46–49; R. I. Field, *Healthcare Regulation in America: Complexity, Confrontation, and Compromise* (New York: Oxford University Press, 2007).

17 For example: M. Ladikas, et al., eds., *Science and Technology Governance and Ethics: A Global Perspective from Europe, India and China* (Springer, 2016); S. Boubaker, D. K. Ngyuen, eds., *Corporate Governance in Emerging Markets* (Springer, 2014); K. S. Rajan, ed., *Lively Capital: Biotechnologies, Ethics, and Governance in Global Markets* (Duke University Press, 2012).

18 See: B. Gazley, *Transformational Governance: How Boards Achieve Extraordinary Change* (Wiley, 2015); The Governance Institute, *Intentional Governance: Advancing Boards Beyond the Conventional* (Chicago, IL: The Governance Institute, 2010).

19 N. M. Kane, et al., "The Internal Processes and Behavioral Dynamics of Hospital Boards: An Explanation of Differences Between High- and Low-Performing Hospitals," *Healthcare Management Review* 34 (1) (2009): 80–91, especially 89–90.

20 See: Independent Sector, *Principles for Good Governance and Ethical Practice: A Guide for Charities and Foundations* (Washington, DC: Independent Sector, 2015); B. Bader, et al., *Emerging Standards for Institutional Integrity: A Tipping Point for Charitable Organizations* (San Diego, CA: The Governance Institute, 2006).

21 See: E. Belmont, et al., "A New Quality Compass: Hospital Boards' Increased Role Under the Affordable Care Act," *Health Affairs* 30 (7) (2011): 1282–1288; H. Fernandez-Lynch, *Conflicts of Conscience in Healthcare: An Institutional Compromise* (Cambridge, MA: MIT Press, 2008).

22 See: D. Crowther, et al., eds., *Responsibility and Governance: The Twin Pillars of Sustainability* (Springer, 2018); H. Spitzeck, C. Lins, *Talking Sustainability in the Boardroom* (Routledge, 2018).

23 The American Hospital Association provides excellent resources for effective governance that are regularly updated, such as on its websites: American Hospital Association, Great Boards at, http://greatboards.org; American Hospital Association, Center for Healthcare Governance at, www.americangovernance.com

24 These reports listed chronologically are: L. Prybil, *The Leadership Role of Nonprofit Health Systems in Improving Community Health* (Chicago, IL: American Hospital Association, Advances in Healthcare Governance Series, 2017); L. Prybil, et al., *A Perspective on Public–Private Collaboration in the Health Sector*, Washington, DC: National Academy of Medicine, 2015); L. Prybil et al., *Improving Community Health Through Hospital–Public Health Collaboration. Insights and Lessons Learned from Successful Partnerships* (Lexington, KY: Commonwealth Center for Governance Studies, Inc., 2014); L. Prybil et al., *The Evolving Accountability of Nonprofit Health System Boards* (Chicago, IL: American Hospital Association Center for Healthcare Governance, 2013); L. Prybil et al., *Governance in Large Nonprofit Health Systems: Current Profile and Emerging Patterns* (Lexington, KY: Commonwealth Center for Governance Studies, Inc., 2012); L. Prybil et al., *Governance in High-Performing Community Health Systems: A Report on Trustees and CEO Views* (Chicago, IL: Grant Thornton LLP, 2009); L. Prybil, et al., *Governance in Nonprofit Community Health Systems: An Initial Report on CEO Perspectives* (Chicago, IL: Grant Thornton LLP, 2008); L. Prybil, et al., *Governance in High-Performing Organizations: A Comparative Study of Governing Boards in Not-for-Profit Hospitals* (Chicago, IL: Health Research and Educational Trust, 2005).

25 L. Prybil et al., *Governance in Large Nonprofit Health Systems: Current Profile and Emerging Patterns* (Lexington, KY: Commonwealth Center for Governance Studies, Inc., 2012), 3–5.

Select readings

Crowther, D., et al., eds. 2018. *Responsibility and Governance: The Twin Pillars of Sustainability*. New York: Springer.

Emerson, K., T. Nabatchi. 2015. *Collaborative Governance Regimes*. Washington, DC: Georgetown University Press.

Micklethwait, A., P. Dimond. 2017. *Driven to the Brink: Why Corporate Governance, Board Leadership and Culture Matter*. United Kingdom: Palgrave MacMillan.

Mitchell, L. E., ed. 2018. *Corporate Governance: Values, Ethics and Leadership*. United Kingdom: Routledge.

Prybil, L. 2017. *The Leadership Role of Nonprofit Health Systems in Improving Community Health*. Advances in Healthcare Governance Series. Chicago, IL: American Hospital Association.

Prybil, L., et al. 2005. *Governance in High-Performing Organizations: A Comparative Study of Governing Boards in Not-for-Profit Hospitals*. Chicago, IL: Health Research and Educational Trust.

Prybil, L., et al. 2008. *Governance in Nonprofit Community Health Systems: An Initial Report on CEO Perspectives*. Chicago, IL: Grant Thornton LLP.

Prybil, L., et al. 2009. *Governance in High-Performing Community Health Systems: A Report on Trustee and CEO Views*. Chicago, IL: Grant Thornton LLP.

Prybil, L., et al. 2012. *Governance in Large Nonprofit Health Systems: Current Profile and Emerging Patterns*. Lexington, KY: Commonwealth Center for Governance Studies, Inc.

Prybil, L., et al. 2013. *The Evolving Accountability of Nonprofit Health System Boards*. Chicago, IL: AHA Center for Healthcare Governance.

Prybil, L., et al. 2014. *Improving Community Health Through Hospital–Public Health Collaboration. Insights and Lessons Learned from Successful Partnerships*. Lexington, KY: Commonwealth Center for Governance Studies, Inc.

Prybil, L., et al. 2015. *A Perspective on Public–Private Collaboration in the Health Sector*. Washington, DC: National Academy of Medicine.

Spitzeck, H., C. Lins. 2018. *Talking Sustainability in the Boardroom*. United Kingdom: Routledge.

Upadhyay, R. 2018. *Ethics, Integrity, and Aptitude in Governance*. Thousand Oaks, CA: Sage.

2   Clinical and organizational ethics

Introduction

The analysis of governance ethics in healthcare organizations in this book is both theoretical and applied. The goal is to foster greater board oversight, focusing on the need for continuous evaluation and evidence-based improvements. This chapter engages the theoretical perspective to explain how the ethics paradigm (that is later applied to governance ethics) is aligned with clinical ethics and organizational ethics. The discussion begins with clinical ethics, which is the more usual landscape for discourse in healthcare.

Clinical ethics

Society could not function well across the spectrum of its interests, conflicts, and dilemmas without a sense of common morality as a foundation for practical decisions, such as about conscientious objection.[1] Common morality might be described as a general awareness that binds ethically serious people across cultures,[2] with human rights providing an obvious example.[3] But this awareness does not mean there is readily accessible agreement when discussing specific issues. Indeed, there is no uniformity about how to describe this basic sense of morality, especially when seeking shared solutions to build consensus.[4] Hence, various accounts of morality are provided by different ethical theories, which, in turn, develop ethical principles to guide reasoning and decision-making. These theories and principles are manifest extensively in clinical ethics.

Ethical theories and principles

There are many theories that shape the debate about ethics in healthcare. Utilitarianism is the ethical theory that ascertains whether an action is right or wrong based upon its consequences. Consequentialism is a related theory. Utility and consequences are central concepts in these approaches. Deontology or deontological ethics is the theory that ascertains whether an action is right or wrong based upon universal maxims that apply to all cases of the same kind, independent of consequences. Duty is a central concept in this approach. Liberal Individualism is a theory that is based upon rights to justify claims that individuals or groups can make upon others. The concept of rights is central in this approach. Communitarianism is a theory based upon a view of the community that celebrates the general welfare or common purposes. The concept of solidarity is central in this approach. The Ethics of Care is another ethical theory that is based upon traits of personal relationships, such as compassion, fidelity, and love. Virtue ethics combines insights from other ethical theories to connect moral character, practical wisdom, and laudable actions. Many other ethical theories have been developed, such as on Casuistry, Feminist Ethics, Natural Law, Situational Ethics, or Teleological Ethics.[5]

A consensus has emerged from these ethical theories about ethical principles to guide moral reasoning and decision-making. In healthcare, a widely adopted explanation can be found in a clustering of four principles of biomedical ethics known as "principlism." These principles are autonomy, non-maleficence, beneficence, and justice.[6] This approach has extensively influenced clinical education.[7] Hence, it is helpful to appreciate how these principles impact clinical ethics.

The ethical principle of respect for personal autonomy upholds the individual's liberty and capacity for intentional action, upon which the crucial concepts of consent, competency, and surrogacy can be based. Also, the ethical principle of non-maleficence asserts the obligation not to inflict harm on others, upon which the central concepts of negligence, standard of care, and non-treatment can be based. Furthermore, the ethical principle of beneficence emphasizes the obligation to act for the benefit of others, upon which the key concepts of paternalism, the quality of life, and balancing burdens can be based. Finally, the ethical principle of justice fosters solidarity, upon which the social concepts of fair opportunity, access to healthcare, resource allocation, and rationing can be based. Integrated with these four ethical principles in healthcare is the clinician-patient relationship, upon which are based the accountability concepts of veracity, privacy, confidentiality, and fidelity in healthcare.[8]

This link between ethical theory and principle that guide moral reasoning and decision-making provides the landscape for connecting clinical and organizational ethics as well-established fields in healthcare. Each area has developed at a very different pace. Clinical ethics has received the most attention.[9] The extensive practice of clinical ethics includes many different arenas, such as clinical research ethics,[10] transplant ethics,[11] and emerging debates over face and limb transplantation.[12] In organizational ethics, though receiving less attention, there has been substantial discourse, including on corporate morality and social responsibility,[13] as explained in the following analysis.[14] In contrast, little attention has been given to governance ethics that deals with the responsibilities of boards of directors in healthcare organizations. However, there has been a noticeable increase in ethics literature on governance issues in healthcare.[15] Furthermore, there has been growing attention to ethical issues around governance in general.[16]

The theoretical discussion in this section considers how the ethics paradigm (that is applied to governance ethics in subsequent chapters) is aligned with clinical ethics. To explain this alignment, a widely practiced aspect of clinical ethics is examined: the role of ethics consultation services that facilitate the resolution of dilemmas or value conflicts in patient care.

Ethics consultation services

Three characteristics emerged in the development of clinical ethics consultations that are consistent with the ethics paradigm: stewardship, ethics decision-making, and best practices for quality outcomes. Clinical ethics consultations, often described as ethics consultation services, are typically connected with the role of ethics committee in hospitals.[17]

One characteristic of ethics consultation services deals with stewardship. Historically ethics committees and ethics consultation services required prudent hospital stewardship, reflecting a long tradition of medical stewardship.[18] Ethics committees and ethics consultation services developed in the USA after several landmark court cases. In particular, the supreme court of New Jersey's ruling on the case of Karen Ann Quinlan in 1976 encouraged the development and use of ethics committees as being the appropriate body, rather than legal courts, to resolve treatment dilemmas in complex end-of-life cases.[19] Since 1992, The Joint Commission on Accreditation of Healthcare Organizations (known today as the Joint Commission), has had a voluntary process with which hospitals typically comply. This process mandates that accredited hospitals establish an organizational resource like an ethics committee to deal with clinical ethical concerns within the organization. In other words, the courts and the Joint Commission have encouraged healthcare to steward its organizational resources to improve ethics services. As a result, ethics consultation services for a long time have been routine in hospitals.[20] These services work closely with the ethics committee,[21] focusing increasingly upon quality,[22] such as in developing preventive approaches that try to avoid dilemmas emerging.[23]

Another characteristic of ethics consultation services deals with ethics decision-making processes. These decision-making processes are at the heart of ethics consultation services, constituting what is referred to as an ethics facilitation approach. The work of the ethicist is to facilitate an ethics consultation with other healthcare professionals and the families involved in the treatment and care of patients. Ordinarily, the ethicist is connected with the ethics committee in a hospital. This ethics facilitation role emerged over many decades of experience in healthcare. It has long been recognized that the various roles of the hospital ethics committee and the ethics consultant can overlap.[24] As these roles developed in the early decades of this specialty, there was considerable debate about these issues: what are the crucial issues in ethics consultation (e.g., its paradigms, goals, and effectiveness) and who should participate in these ethics consultations,[25] such as doctors because of their clinical training or philosophers because of their ethical reasoning skills.[26] As a result, expertise in ethics consultations was connected increasingly with giving court testimony, with clinical and social expertise, and with regulation.[27]

As experience accrued over several decades, different roles for ethics consultations were considered. For some, the ethics consultant might assume a role that is akin to being an analyst, adviser, or adversary;[28] for others, the role might be akin to being an expert, or educator, or counsellor, or advocate;[29] and for many the role might be akin to being a colleague, negotiator, case manager, or mediator to resolve conflict.[30] These role options were assembled into two broad models. On the one hand, there was a hard model that considered the ethics consultant as undertaking an independent investigation, including an interview with the patient and the issuance of a recommendation. On the other hand, there was the soft model that construed the ethics consultant in a facilitation role, bringing together the relevant parties, helping to sort out the facts, clarifying the problem at hand, raising important issues, and noting useful distinctions in the process of the ethical engagement.[31]

These roles of the ethics consultant were oriented toward an education process or toward an expert-oriented intervention leading to a practical outcome.[32] The debate revolved around the following issues.[33] On the one hand, regarding the hard model (emphasizing intervention and outcomes), the ethics consultant focuses upon knowledge and expertise to provide a practical solution. In this approach, the ethics consultant is more likely to accept responsibility for ethical decision-making. On the other hand, regarding the soft model (emphasizing an education process), the ethics consultant adopts the role of being a facilitator of ethical discourse, making no claim to superior ethical knowledge. In this approach, a good decision is reached through a process in which the relevant considerations of the stakeholders have been evaluated.

After years of debate and experience,[34] the ethics facilitation role emerged as the preferred approach. Eventually, the American Society for Bioethics and Humanities (ASBH) settled the debate by recommending the ethics facilitation approach for ethics consultation, in contrast to a more authoritarian approach. In 2006, the ASBH published voluntary guidelines called, *Core Competencies for Healthcare Ethics Consultation*.[35] The ASBH subsequently provided an education guide for training around these competencies for ethics consultation.[36] The ASBH published a revised second edition of the *Core Competencies* in 2011.[37] The revised edition continues to recommend the ethics facilitation approach and includes a major new section (13 pages in contrast to two pages in the original edition) on the quality and evaluation of ethics consultation services.[38] The focus on quality in ethics consultations is of paramount importance,[39] especially regarding empirical evaluations,[40] ongoing assessment,[41] quality improvement,[42] and cost.[43] The focus of the ASBH is upon patient-centered care.[44] Also, the ASBH approach is similar to the system of Integrated Ethics in the Veterans Health Administration.[45]

There have been many landmark studies using objective criteria that provide substantive support for the effectiveness of this approach to clinical ethics consultation. These studies include randomized controlled trials,[46] as well as pilot and longitudinal studies.[47] Also, there have been multiple surveys,[48] and many reviews have been undertaken.[49] Akin to experience in the USA, in other countries there has been a similar scrutiny of ethics consultation services.[50] This scrutiny has examined progress in different countries,[51] focusing on the variety of ethical issues involved.[52]

Because ethics consultations can occur across an extensive range of clinical environments and concerns, the ASBH provides a straightforward explanation of what is involved:

> Health care ethics consultation (HCEC or "ethics consultation") is a set of services provided by an individual or group in response to questions from patients, families, surrogates, health care professionals, or other involved parties who seek to resolve uncertainty or conflict regarding value-laden concerns that emerge in health care.[53]

As mentioned earlier, from the varying approaches to ethics consultation, the ethics facilitation approach was recommended by the ASBH, described in this way:

> The ethics facilitation approach is informed by the context in which HCEC is done and involves two core features: (1) identifying and analyzing the nature of the value uncertainty, and (2) facilitating the building of a principled ethics resolution.[54]

The ethics facilitation approach requires specific competencies. Both editions of the ASBH Core Competencies explain the need for these competencies. The ASBH identifies core skills, core knowledge, and personal attributes for proficiency in ethics consultations. Different people can perform the ethics consultation service, though debate continues over the relative advantages of an individual or a team-based approach.[55] An ethics consultation service may vary the approach adopted.[56] Hence, the different roles and responsibilities of those performing the service will require varying levels of competency, with an individual working alone (i.e., not with a team) requiring the highest level of competency.[57] The core skills for ethics consultations are assembled in three related categories.

To begin, ethical assessment and analysis skills can be basic (to deal with straightforward situations) or advanced (to deal with complex cases). The assessment competency is to identify the nature of a conflict or value uncertainty that generates the need for an ethics consultation. The analytical competency is to critically evaluate the case and identify justifiable options using relevant ethics knowledge and concepts. Next, process skills pertain to the following: overseeing an ethics consultation service; conducting a specific ethics consultation, including the facilitation of any formal meetings required; and evaluating consultations retrospectively to support ongoing improvement (this point is new in the second edition of the ASBH *Core Competencies*).[58] Finally, interpersonal skills are required to perform across the spectrum of ethics consultations, such as to listen and communicate effectively,[59] or to discern appropriate timing for an ethics consultation.[60]

In turn, the core knowledge areas can be divided into basic (an introductory sense of the topic) and advanced (a detailed understanding of the topic). These core knowledge areas, which can overlap, include the following: knowledge of moral reasoning and ethical theory; an understanding of common bioethical issues and concepts; a sense of the clinical landscape; comprehension of relevant health law and professional codes; and an awareness of the beliefs of the local patient and staff population.[61] Knowledge of these key concepts constitutes a foundation for the ASBH professional certification for ethics consultants that was initiated in 2017.[62] The discussion on professionalization has occurred for a long time,[63] including the following considerations: about requiring a code of ethics;[64] about professional qualifications needed;[65] about competencies and empirically driven standards, such as charting and documentation;[66] about credentialing requirements including the quality of ethics consultants, including prior training;[67] about certification processes including examinations;[68] and about formal accreditation of ethics consultants.[69]

In addition to core skills and core knowledge areas, there are basic attributes, attitudes, and behaviors that are required for ethics consultants. These terms are used to replace the language of character that appeared in the first edition of the ASBH *Core Competencies*.[70] However, these traits cannot be divided into basic and advanced. An example is that personal integrity should infuse the work of an ethics consultant.[71]

The discussion here has considered two characteristics of ethics consultation services, stewardship and decision-making processes. The third characteristic of ethics consultation services deals with best practices. The focus on best practices highlights quality outcomes.[72] Here, a connection is drawn between standards and quality. The basic point is that best practices can lead to improved quality.[73] Here, best practices are based on data from comprehensive research with clearly documented outcomes, adopting an evidence-based approach. When best practices result from data, they can be used to measure and increase quality by improving performance related to the identified standards. When this occurs, measures for best practices relate to quality improvement. That is, benchmarking enables an organization to measure or compare its performance against recognized best practices.[74]

In other words, best practices can be adopted as benchmarks in the sense of identifying standards of quality. Hence, the accomplishments of continuous quality improvement in healthcare generally, and more specifically in ethics consultation, are based upon objective and comprehensive research about evidence-based practice.[75] That focus is emphasized by the ASBH, explaining that its "ultimate commitment . . . is to improve and maintain the quality of HCEC" (referring to healthcare ethics consultation).[76]

To summarize, there are three characteristics of ethics consultation services: the need for stewardship of organizational resources, the focus on decision-making processes that adopts the ethics facilitation approach, and the emphasis on best practices for quality outcomes. It is important to emphasize that these distinguishing characteristics of clinical ethics in ethics consultation services are aligned with the ethics paradigm (presented in Chapter 1), as follows.

First, in ethics consultations the need for stewardship of organizational resources lies behind the legal exhortation to create ethics committee services. The legal determination in the landmark case of Karen Ann Quinlan urged hospitals to steward their resources, rather than relying on the courts, to resolve end-of-life treatment dilemmas. As a result, the Joint Commission mandated that hospitals should establish an organizational resource (such as an ethics committee) to undertake this role of ethics consultation as a basic standard of accreditation. This need for organizational stewardship reflects the foundation component of the ethics paradigm. Second, in ethics consultations the focus on decision-making processes led the ASBH to adopt an ethics facilitation approach. This focus on decision-making reflects the process component of the ethics paradigm. Third, in ethics consultations the emphasis on best practices reflects the commitment of the ASBH to improve quality outcomes. This emphasis reflects the practice component of the ethics paradigm. Finally, these characteristics of ethics consultation services that align with the ethics paradigm help clinical ethics to address the deficit of public trust in healthcare organizations, both public and private. The design of the ethics paradigm in Chapter 1 was presented in the context of addressing the loss of public trust. The widespread use of ethics consultation services nurtures the public's confidence in clinical ethics. This typically occurs at the end of life when patients and families encounter traumatic dilemmas. Another impressive testimony to public trust in ethics consultation services is the continuing requirement of them by the Joint Commission as a crucial standard of hospital accreditation. As the ethics paradigm is adopted throughout this book, each applied topic sheds light on renewing and nurturing public trust in healthcare organizations.

Organizational ethics

These three characteristics of clinical ethics (stewardship, decision-making, best practices) that are aligned with the ethics paradigm also pertain to organizational ethics in healthcare. Because the delivery of healthcare today involves a connection between of clinical and organizational issues, these distinct realms are increasingly perceived as being closely related. Recognizing these overlapping fields, the ASBH combined clinical ethics and organizational ethics in its revised edition of the *Core Competencies for Healthcare Ethics Consultation*.[77] Reflecting this close affinity, ethics committees often support both fields in a variety of models, such as the following: expanding the role of the clinical ethics committee to include organizational ethics issues; creating a distinct organizational ethics committee to address business, financial and other corporate ethics issues; or having a single ethics committee with an expanded mission to include both clinical ethics and organizational ethics subgroups.[78] This combination bolsters the rationale in this study for recognizing the affinity between organizational ethics and the more established field of clinical ethics.

Despite this connection between these fields, it remains useful to discuss organizational ethics as a distinctive area of expertise. Retaining an organizational perspective enables ethics discourse to address specific challenges that occur in the institutional environment of healthcare delivery. In other words, organizational ethics addresses value related issues linked with the institution in the broadest sense, including its business, management, corporate, and compliance interests. This broad view of organizational ethics in healthcare includes the institution's values and policies, the allocation of resources, the behavior of its personnel, and the services to its communities and constituencies.

This distinctive approach to organizational ethics recognizes these overlapping issues while acknowledging the wisdom accrued in clinical ethics. Typically, discussions of organizational ethics in the realm of business emphasize the role of stakeholders, referred to as stakeholder theory. Developed originally by R. Edward Freeman, stakeholder theory recognizes a variety of roles and values of individuals with a moral stake in an organization to present a way for resolving business and corporate conflicts.[79] However, the approach to organizational ethics in healthcare that is adopted in this analysis includes but is broader than stakeholder theory.

To understand this broader approach to organizational ethics, it is helpful to refer again to the ethics paradigm. The authors of this study developed the ethics paradigm as an organizational ethics project, while recognizing and adopting the characteristics of clinical ethics (stewardship, decision-making, best practices). A brief word on the development of the ethics paradigm can enlighten the significance of organizational ethics here.

The development of the ethics paradigm involved extensive consultation by the authors.[80] The project involved major sectors in healthcare across the USA. A wide range of leaders were consulted (representing a diversity of geographical locations and market profiles) to measure interest in organizational ethics and to clarify common themes that should shape an ethics paradigm. There were several phases in the consultation project via telephone conference calls and face-to-face interviews: undertaking telephone interviews with a number of nationally respected leaders in healthcare to inquire about their understanding of the need for an ethics paradigm in healthcare;[81] preparing an early draft of the paradigm that was sent to another group of leaders in healthcare subsequently interviewed by telephone;[82] and sending a revised draft of the paradigm to another group who then met with the authors for a roundtable discussion to finalize its format.[83]

This historical background sheds light on how the terms in the ethics paradigm adopt predominantly organizational language. The three basic features of ethics in the paradigm (*who we are, how we function, what we do*) generate its three guiding components. The foundation component (reflecting the leitmotif *who we are*) operates within the context of engaging the healthcare environment. The process component (reflecting the leitmotif *how we function*) operates within the context of undertaking organizational oversight. The practice component (reflecting the leitmotif *what we do*) operates within the context of fostering organizational culture. The three components engage three related contexts that appear regularly in the literature on organizations and governance:[84] the contexts of the healthcare environment, of organizational oversight, and of organizational culture.

In turn, these components promote leadership that fosters specific outcomes. That is, the leadership focus on institutional identity (reflecting the leitmotif *who we are*) fosters outcomes regarding organizational stewardship of an institution's mission; the leadership focus on corporate accountability (reflecting the leitmotif *how we function*) fosters outcomes regarding decision-making via participative deliberation; and the leadership focus on performance quality (reflecting the leitmotif *what we do*) fosters outcomes regarding best practices for standards of conduct. A closer look at the components of the ethics paradigm (Table 1.1) clarify the alignment of organizational ethics.

Foundation component

In the foundation component of the ethics paradigm, the healthcare environment is the context for promoting leadership regarding organizational identity (reflecting the leitmotif *who we are*) to discuss outcomes related to stewardship of an organization's mission. Here stewardship extends beyond dealing with limited resources to enhance the integration of personal and institutional integrity across the organization. This integrity is manifest in its responsibility to nurture what is received from others for future generations, thereby contributing to sustainability.[85] The institution must nurture what the community has given it to honor the past and to prepare for the future.[86] Stewardship enhances a sense of the healthcare organization's commitment to the community and thereby increases public trust in healthcare organizations, including prudent use of resources. When there are influences upon an organization that compromise its integrity, those influences can be construed as a form of institutional compromise; and when that occurs, public trust is undermined.[87] Of course, it is important to recognize that a commitment to integrity is both personal and organizational to avoid compromise for short-term gain and to nurture trust in the community.[88]

Perhaps the most basic challenge of stewardship in healthcare is to continue the organization's mission of healing patients and communities. One of the greatest dangers in healthcare today, as mentioned previously, is to focus so much upon fiscal demands that an organization's basic mission of care can be compromised. An unbalanced focus on these fiscal demands can force the organization's margin against its mission. Of course, resource management and fiscal responsibility are crucial for every organization, but they should serve the organization's core purpose. Unfortunately, organizations can mistakenly pursue a reductive understanding of corporate responsibility. That mistake can occur by focusing only on finances and resources (margin) in a manner that can ultimately undermine the

Table 1.1 Ethics paradigm

Components	Foundation component	Process component	Practice component
Context	Environment of healthcare	Organizational oversight	Organizational culture
Leadership	Identity: who we are	Accountability: how we function	Quality: what we do
Outcomes	Organizational stewardship of mission	Decision-making via participative deliberation	Best practices for standards of conduct

main goal of healthcare, healing patients and communities (mission). In contrast, the foundation component of the ethics paradigm encourages corporate morality to focus upon social responsibility from the perspective of stewardship that supports the mission of the institution.[89]

Process component

In the process component of the ethics paradigm, organizational oversight in healthcare is the context for promoting leadership regarding accountability (reflecting the leitmotif *how we function*) to discuss outcomes related to decision-making via participative deliberation. The importance of participative decision-making is widely recognized as indispensable in ethics. Standard steps in the decision-making process in clinical ethics can be readily adopted in organizational ethics, as follows.[90] The decision-making process emphasizes two related parts: the identification of a specific problem and the resolution of the problem.[91] Of course, the various steps of this process can vary depending on circumstances, so flexibility is necessary.

The identification of the problem starts with three steps. To begin, there is a recognition of the problem that includes the following: involve all the appropriate stakeholders; compile and record the appropriate data; specify the relevant aspects of the ethical dilemma regarding related values. Also, there is the description of the problem: indicate what characterizes the problem; clarify the goals that are involved; identify the basic ethical conflict. Furthermore, indicate the cause and effect relations in the problem: explain why the problem exists; distinguish the root cause from the symptoms of the problem; summarize the basic ethical issue.

Next, the process of ethical resolution involves another three steps. To begin, there is the clarification of realistic options, which includes the following: create a positive milieu for an ethical resolution to emerge; explore options that are available; investigate the ethical legitimacy of the main options. Also, there is the determination of the best ethical solution to the problem: eliminate the least likely options; weigh the viable options regarding the goals being pursued; make a rational and objective ethical decision. Furthermore, there is the implementation of the decision, including a subsequent evaluation: communicate the decision as the best ethical option in terms of risks, benefits, costs, and workability; take action to implement the decision (considering who, what, when, and how); have a quality improvement assessment of the decision-making process.

In other words, the participative decision-making process seeks to identify the relevant problem and to resolve it. This process of moral decision-making can be related to a role for the moral imagination. That is, the moral imagination can facilitate a broad awareness of complex circumstances (especially the values and narratives involved), an appreciation of the relevant ethical conflicts, and a sense of how to devise ethically acceptable solutions or alternatives.[92] When faced with complicated situations, the moral imagination can provide a capacity to intellectually grasp and ethically reason in a comprehensive manner, often involving religious perspectives or beliefs.[93] The process component of the ethics paradigm entails sophisticated decision making steps.

Practice component

In the practice component of the ethics paradigm, organizational culture is the context for promoting leadership regarding quality (reflecting the leitmotif *what we do*) to discuss outcomes related to best practices for standards of conduct. This component deals with behavior across the organization to improve the quality of healthcare, such as indicated in reports from the Institute of Medicine.[94] This practice component focuses upon behavior in a manner that develops organizational performance with objective measures of progress.[95] The practice component of the ethics paradigm functions in an integrative manner with its foundation and process components. The practice component implements the organization's deliberative processes (such as occurs with strategic planning),[96] and its stewardship of the organization's mission (such as occurs with building the public's trust).[97]

Together, the three components of the ethics paradigm provide a moral compass for the institutional integrity of healthcare organizations. This occurs by connecting *who we are* (the foundation component), *how we function* (the process component), and *what we do* (the practice component). Furthermore, the cohesive rapport between these components helps to establish a fine balance between margin and mission, thereby contributing to the renewal of public confidence in healthcare.

Conclusion

The need for and importance of organizational ethics in healthcare is supported robustly in other landmark studies on corporate morality. For example, a report by The Institute of Business Ethics in the United Kingdom, titled *Does Business Ethics Pay,*[98] adopted several measures of performance over a five-year period. The study concluded that when large corporations demonstrate a practical commitment to ethical conduct they improved financial performance in the long term.[99] Also, an influential study using five measures of performance (innovation, customer retention, turnover, quality, and profitability) provided evidence of a positive correlation between companies that try to be ethical and the organization's performance. That study explained that companies perceived as trustworthy with institutional integrity perform better with higher profits than companies perceived to be less ethical.[100] The importance of virtuous organizations is well recognized for moving institutions from crisis to exemplary leadership, and is discussed in the final chapter of this book.[101]

This chapter has presented a theoretical discussion of how the established fields of clinical ethics and organizational ethics can be aligned with the ethics paradigm as a framework for an applied ethical analysis. The consistency pertains to the focus of the framework on stewardship, ethics decision-making, and best practices. The consistency of ethics discourse in this alignment also can be shown to pertain to professional ethics, as discussed in the next chapter. Throughout this study, the alignment between these various fields is emphasized to later apply the ethics paradigm to governance ethics in healthcare organizations.

Notes

1 M. R. Wicclair, *Conscientious Objection in Health Care* (New York: Cambridge University Press, 2011).
2 See: T. L. Beauchamp, J. F. Childress, *Principles of Biomedical Ethics*, 8th ed. (New York: Oxford University Press, 2019); B. Gert, *Common Morality. Deciding What To Do* (New York: Oxford University Press, 2007); B. Gert, C. M. Culver, K. D. Clouser, *Bioethics: A Systematic Approach*, 2nd ed. (New York: Oxford University Press, 2006).
3 See: A. Gutman, J. D. Moreno, *Bioethics and the Transformation of Health Care in America* (Liveright, 2019); A. Bagheri, J. M. Moreno, S. Semplici, eds., *Global Bioethics: The Impact of the UNESCO International Bioethics Committee* (Springer, 2015); H. ten Have, M. S. Jean, *The UNESCO Declaration on Bioethics and Human Rights* (Paris: UNESCO Publishing, 2009); UNESCO, *Casebook on Human Dignity and Human Rights* (Paris: UNESCO, 2011).
4 See: N. N. Dubler, C. B. Liebman, *Bioethics Mediation: A Guide to Shaping Shared Solution* (New York: United Hospital Fund, 2004).
5 See: T. L. Beauchamp, J. F. Childress, *Principles of Biomedical Ethics*, 8th ed. (Oxford: Oxford University Press, 2019); T. L. Beauchamp, L. Walters, *Contemporary Issues in Bioethics*, 8th ed. (Belmont, CA: Wadsworth, 2013); N. S. Jecker, et al., *Bioethics: An Introduction to the History, Methods, and Practice*, 2nd ed. (Jones & Bartlett, 2007); D. F. Kelly, G. Magill, H. ten Have, *Contemporary Catholic Health Care Ethics*, 2nd ed. (Washington, DC: Georgetown University Press, 2013); H. Kuhse, et al., eds., *Bioethics: An Anthology*, 3rd ed. (Wiley-Blackwell, 2015); J. Sugarman, D. P. Sulmasy, eds., *Methods in Medical Ethics*, 2nd ed. (Washington, DC: Georgetown University Press, 2010); T. Tomlinson, *Methods in Medical Ethics* (New York: Oxford University Press, 2012).
6 T. L. Beauchamp, J. F. Childress, *Principles of Biomedical Ethics*, 8th ed. (Oxford: Oxford University Press, 2019).
7 P. C. Hébert, *Doing Right: A Practical Guide to Ethics for Medical Trainees and Physicians* (New York: Oxford University Press, 2009).
8 See: T. L. Beauchamp and J. F. Childress, *Principles of Biomedical Ethics*, 8th ed. (Oxford: Oxford University Press, 2019).
9 See: A. R. Jonsen, M. Siegler, W. J. Winslade, *Clinical Ethics*, 7th ed. (New York: McGraw-Hill, 2015); B. Lo, *Resolving Ethical Dilemmas: A Guide for Clinicians*, 5th ed. (Baltimore, MD: Lippincott Williams & Wilkins, 2013); G. E. Pence, *Medical Ethics: Accounts of Ground-Breaking Cases*, 7th ed. (McGraw-Hill, 2014).
10 See: J. F. Childress, et al., eds., *Belmont Revisited: Ethical Principles for Research with Human Subjects* (Washington, DC: Georgetown University Press, 2005); K. H. Jacobsen, *Introduction to Health Research Methods: A Practical Guide*, 2nd ed. (Jones & Bartlett, 2016); D. Koepsell, *Scientific Integrity and Research Ethics* (Springer, 2017); P. Laake, et al., eds., *Research in Medical and Biological Sciences* (London: Academic Press, 2015); S. B. Rutkove, *Biomedical Research: An Insider's Guide* (Springer, 2016); R. M. Zaner, *A Critical Examination of Ethics in Health Care and Biomedical Research* (Springer, 2015).
11 See: P. Aseni, et al., eds., *Multiorgan Procurement for Transplantation* (Springer, 2016); A. L. Caplan, J. J. McCartney, D. P. Reid, *Replacement Parts: The Ethics of Procuring and Replacing Organs in Humans* (Washington, DC: Georgetown University Press, 2015); R. A. Greenberg, et al., eds., *Ethical Issues in Pediatric Organ Transplantation* (Springer, 2016); D. Hamilton, *A History of Organ Transplantation* (Pittsburgh, PA: University of Pittsburgh Press, 2012); F. J. Miller, R. D. Truog, *Death, Dying, and Organ Transplantation: Reconstructing Medical Ethics at the End of Life* (New York: Oxford University Press, 2016); L. Territo, R. Matteson, eds., *The International Trafficking of Human Organs: A Multidisciplinary Approach* (CRC/

Taylor & Francis, 2011); R. M. Veatch, *Transplantation Ethics*, 2nd ed. (Washington, DC: Georgetown University Press, 2014); D. L. Weimer, *Medical Governance: Values, Expertise, and Interests in Organ Transplantation* (Washington, DC: Georgetown University Press, 2010).

12 See: J. P. Barret, A. V. Tomasello, *Face Transplantation: Principles, Technique and Artistry* (Springer, 2016); J. Benedict, *Covenant Consent: A Revised Consent Model for Vascularized Composite Allotransplantation* (Springer, 2017); S. Pearl, *Face/On: Face Transplants and the Ethics of the Other* (Chicago, IL: University of Chicago Press, 2017).

13 See: P. Alexander, *Corporate Social Irresponsibility* (Routledge, 2015); M. Aluchna, S. O. Idowu, eds., *The Dynamics of Corporate Social Responsibility* (Springer, 2016); A. Argenti, *Corporate Responsibility* (Sage, 2015); M. Ballard, et al., *Corporate Ethics for Big Data: A Group Project* (Amazon Digital Services, 2016); M. A. Camilieri, *Corporate Sustainability, Social Responsibility, and Environmental Management* (Springer, 2017); S. Diehl, et al., eds., *Handbook of Integrated Corporate Social Responsibility Communication* (Springer, 2016); K. Hansen, *Corporate Social Responsibility and Diversity Management* (Springer, 2016).

14 See: R. T. Hall, *An Introduction to Healthcare Organizational Ethics* (New York: Oxford University Press, 2000); C. E. Johnson, *Organizational Ethics: A Practical Approach* (Thousand Oaks, CA: Sage, 2016); E. M. Spencer, et al., *Organization Ethics in Health Care* (New York: Oxford University Press, 2000).

15 See: B. Jennings, et al., *The Ethics of Hospital Trustees* (Washington, DC: Georgetown University Press, 2004); C. Coggan, et al., *Public Health Law: Ethics, Governance, and Regulation* (Routledge, 2016); D. Mascalzoni, ed., *Ethics, Law and Governance of Biobanking* (Springer, 2016); National Academy Press, *Human Gene Editing: Science, Ethics, and Governance* (Washington, DC: National Academy Press, 2017); D. Stretch, M. Mertz, eds., *Ethics and Governance of Biomedical Research: Theory and Practice* (Springer, 2016).

16 See: R. Bhinekawati, *Corporate Social Responsibility and Sustainable Development* (Routledge, 2016); R. Cressy, et al., eds., *Entrepreneurship, Governance and Ethics* (Springer, 2016); M. Ladikas, et al., eds., *Science and Technology Governance and Ethics* (Springer, 2016); G. E. Marchant, *Emerging Technologies: Ethics, Law and Governance* (Ashgate, 2016); P. S. Renz, *Project Governance: Implementing Corporate Governance and Business Ethics in Nonprofit Organizations* (Physica-Verlag, Springer, 2009); B. Tricker, G. Tricker, *Business Ethics: A Stakeholder, Governance and Risk Approach* (Routledge, 2013); P. Uttling, J. Marques, eds., *Corporate Social Responsibility and Regulatory Governance: Towards Inclusive Development* (Palgrave-MacMillan, 2013); S. R. Vallabhaneni, *Corporate Management, Governance, and Ethics Best Practices* (Wiley, 2008); J. Wieland, *Governance Ethics: Global Value Creation, Economic Organization and Normativity* (Springer, 2014).

17 The analysis in this section of the chapter is a development of one of the co-authors previously published research, G. Magill, "Quality in Ethics Consultation," *Medicine, Health Care and Philosophy* 16 (4) (2013): 761–774.

18 M. O. Kepler, *Medical Stewardship: Fulfilling the Hippocratic Legacy* (Santa Barbara, CA: Praeger, 1981).

19 In re Quinlan. Supreme Court of New Jersey. 355 A.2d 647 (N.J. 1976). Other landmark cases that occurred subsequently were: Joseph Saikewicz in 1977, Joseph Fox in 1980, Claire Conroy in 1985, Elizabeth Bouvia in 1986, Nancy Cruzan in 1990, and Helga Wanglie in 1991.

20 See: K.-B. Celie, K. Prager, "Health Care Ethics Consultation in the United States," *AMA Journal of Ethics* 18 (5) (2016): 475–447; J. Schildmann, J. S. Gordon, J. Vollmann, eds., *Clinical Ethics Consultation: Theories and Methods, Implementation, Evaluation* (New York: Routledge, 2016); C. Bruce, et al., "Building a Vibrant Clinical Ethics Consultation Service," *The National Catholic Bioethics Quarterly* 18 (1) (Spring, 2018): 29–38;

C. Bruce, et al., *A Practical Guide to Developing & Sustaining a Clinical Ethics Consultation Service* (Baylor College of Medicine, 2015); M. P. Aulisio, R. M. Arnold, *Ethics Consultation: From Theory to Practice* (Johns Hopkins University Press, 2003).

21 See: D. M. Hester, T. Schonfeld, eds., *Guidance for Healthcare Ethics Committees* (New York: Cambridge University Press, 2012); L. F. Post, J. Blustein, *Handbook for Health Care Ethics Committees*, 2nd ed. (Baltimore, MD: Johns Hopkins University Press, 2015).

22 See: G. Magill, "Quality in Ethics Consultation," *Medicine, Health Care and Philosophy* 16 (4) (2013): 761–774.

23 See: M. R. Kenney, "A System Approach to Proactive Ethics Integration," *The National Catholic Bioethics Quarterly* 18 (1) (Spring 2018): 93–112; N. J. Kockler, K. M. Dirksen, "Integrating Ethics Services in a Catholic Health System," *The National Catholic Bioethics Quarterly* 18 (1) (Spring 2018): 113–134; J. Lesandrini, A. Muster, "Practical Steps for Integrating an Ethics Program," *The National Catholic Bioethics Quarterly* 18 (1) (Spring 2018): 39–47.

24 See: L. R. Churchill, A. W. Cross, "Moralist, Technician, Sophist, Teacher/Learner: Reflections on the Ethicist in the Clinical Setting," *Theoretical Medicine* 7 (1986): 3–12.

25 M. Fox, G. McGee, A. Caplan, "Paradigms for Clinical Ethics Consultation Practice," *Cambridge Quarterly of Healthcare Ethics* 7 (1998): 308–314.

26 See: A. Gasparetto, R. J. Jox, M. Picozzi, "The Notion of Neutrality in Clinical Ethics Consultation," *Philosophy, Ethics, and Humanities in Medicine* 13 (1) (2018): 3; M. Magelssen, R. Pedersen, R. Førde, "Four Roles of Ethical Theory in Clinical Ethics Consultation," *American Journal of Bioethics* 16 (9) (2016): 26–33, with commentary responses, pp. 34–53; G. J. Agich, "Truth in Advertising: Reasonable Versus Unreasonable Claims about Improving Ethics Consultation," *American Journal of Bioethics* 16 (3) (2016): 25–26, with commentary responses, pp. 27–57.

27 See: G. J. Agich, "Expertise in Clinical Ethics Consultation," *HEC Forum* 6 (1994): 379–383; B. Spielman, "Has Faith in Health Care Ethics Consultants Gone Too Far? Risks of an Unregulated Practice and a Model Act to Contain Them," *Marquette Law Review* 85 (2001): 161–221.

28 R. Veatch, "Clinical Ethics, Applied Ethics, and Ethical Theory," in C. Hoffmaster, B. Freedman, G. Fraser, eds., *Clinical Ethics: Theory and Practice* (Clifton, NJ: Humana Press, 1989), 7–25.

29 D. J. Self, J. D. Skeel, N. Jecker, "A Comparison of the Moral Reasoning of Physicians and Clinical Medical Ethicists," *Academic Medicine* 68 (1993): 840–855.

30 See: N. N. Dubler, C. B. Liebman, *Bioethics Mediation: A Guide to Shaping Shared Solution* (New York: United Hospital Fund, 2004); J. La Puma, D. L. Schiedermayer, "Ethics Consultation: Skills, Roles and Training," *Annals of Internal Medicine* 112 (1991): 155–160.

31 See: J. D. Moreno, *Deciding Together: Bioethics and Moral Consensus* (New York: Oxford University Press, 1995).

32 D. C. Thomasma, "Legitimate and Illegitimate Roles for the Medical Ethicist," in T. Ackerman, et al., eds., *Clinical Medical Ethics: Exploration and Assessment* (Lanham, MD: University Press of America, 1987), 83–94.

33 See: M. Yeo, "Prolegomena to any Future Code of Ethics for Bioethicists," *Cambridge Quarterly of Healthcare Ethics* 2 (1993): 403–415; T. May, "The Breadth of Bioethics: Core Areas of Bioethics Education for Hospital Ethics Committees," *Journal of Medicine and Philosophy* 26 (2001): 101–118.

34 For an account of the emergence of healthcare ethics committees in general and healthcare ethics consultation services in particular, see: R. E. Cranford, et al., *Institutional Ethics Committees and Health Care Decision-making* (Ann Arbor, MI: Health Administration Press, 1984).

35 American Society for Bioethics and Humanities (ASBH), *Core Competencies for Healthcare Ethics Consultation* (Glenview, IL: ASBH, 2006). For an explanation of

the ethics facilitation approach versus the authoritarian approach to ethics consultation, see pp. 5–6.

36 See: American Society for Bioethics and Humanities (ASBH), *Improving Competencies in Clinical Ethics Consultation. An Education Guide*, 2nd ed. (Glenview, IL: ASBH, 2015); American Society for Bioethics and Humanities, *Clinical Ethics Consultation Affairs Committee, Addressing Patient-Centered Ethical Issues in Health Care: A Case-Based Study Guide* (Glenview, IL: ASBH, 2017); American Society for Bioethics and Humanities, Clinical Ethics Consultation Affairs Committee, *Resources for Developing Advanced Skills in Ethics Consultation* (Glenview, IL: ASBH, 2017). A similar approach has been developed for Catholic healthcare, Catholic Health Association, *Striving for Excellence in Ethics: A Resource for the Catholic Health* Ministry, 2nd ed. (Washington, DC: Catholic Health Association, 2014).

37 American Society for Bioethics and Humanities (ASBH), *Core Competencies for Healthcare Ethics Consultation*, 2nd ed. (Glenview, IL: ASBH, 2011).

38 For a comparison of the two editions and an explanation of the need for greater emphasis upon quality, see: G. Magill, "Quality in Ethics Consultation," *Medicine, Health Care and Philosophy* 16 (4) (2013): 761–774.

39 G. Magill, "Quality in Ethics Consultation," *Medicine, Health Care and Philosophy* 16 (4) (2013): 761–774.

40 See: L. D. Wocial, E. Molnar, M. A. Ott, "Values, Quality, and Evaluation in Ethics Consultation," *AJOB Empirical Bioethics* 7 (4) (2016): 227–234; E. Fox, "Evaluating Ethics Quality in Health Care Organizations: Looking Back and Looking Forward," *American Journal of Bioethics* 4 (1) (2013): 71–77; R. D. Orr, et al., "Evaluation of An Ethics Consultation service: Patient and Family Perspective" *American Journal of Medicine* 101 (1996): 135–141.

41 See: R. A. Pearlman, et al., "Ethics Consultation Quality Assessment Tool," *The American Journal of Bioethics* 16 (3) (2016): 3–14, with commentary responses, pp. 25–57; D. Magnus, "Finding the Right Tools for Assessing Quality in Clinical Ethics Consultation," *American Journal of Bioethics* 16 (3) (2016): 1–2; K. Wasson, "A Call for Multiple Means of Assessing Quality in Clinical Ethics Consultation," *American Journal of Bioethics* 16 (3) (2016): 44–45; K. Wasson, et al., "Developing an Evaluation Tool for Assessing Clinical Ethics Consultation Skills in Simulation Based Education," *HEC Forum* 27 (1) (2015): 1–22.

42 See: M. Repenshek, "Examining Quality and Value in Ethics Consultation Services," *The National Catholic Bioethics Quarterly* 18 (1) (Spring, 2018): 59–68; E. Fox, "Strategies to Improve Health Care Ethics Consultation: Bridging the Knowledge Gap," *AMA Journal of Ethics* 18 (5) (May, 2016): 528–529; E. Fox, et al., "An Innovative Program to Improve Ethics Quality in Health Care," *Innovation Journal* 15 (2) (2010): 1–36.

43 See: T. N. Huynh, et al., "The Frequency and Cost of Treatment Perceived to be Futile in Critical Care," *JAMA Internal Medicine* 173 (20) (2013): 1887–1894.

44 American Society for Bioethics and Humanities (ASBH), *Addressing Patient Centered Ethical Issues in Health Care: A Case-Based Study Guide* (Glenview, IL: ASBH, 2017).

45 On the approach of Integrated Ethics, see: E. Fox, "Integrated Ethics: An Innovative Program to Improve Ethics Quality in Health Care," *Innovation Journal* 15 (2) (2010): 1–36; the National Center for Ethics in Health Care at the Veterans Health Administration, www.ethics.va.gov/integratedethics/index.asp. Also see: National Center for Ethics in Health Care, *Ethics Consultation: Responding to Ethics Questions in Health Care*, 2nd ed. (Washington, DC: U.S. Department of Veterans Affairs, 2015).

46 See: A. Rudnick, et al., "Informal Ethics Consultations in Academic Health Care Settings: A Quantitative Description and a Qualitative Analysis with a Focus on Patient Participation," *Clinical Ethics* 9 (1) (March 2014): 28–25.

47 See: C. Gorka, et al., "Growing an Ethics Consultation Service: A Longitudinal Study Examining Two Decades of Practice," *American Journal of Bioethics, Empirical Bioethics* 8 (2) (April 2017): 116–127.

48 See: A. Slowther, et al., "Development of Clinical Ethics Services in the UK: a National Survey," *Journal of Medical Ethics* 38 (4) (2012): 210–224; E. Fox, et al., "Ethics Consultation in United States Hospitals: A National Survey," *American Journal of Bioethics* 7 (2) (2007): 13–25; G. DuVal, et al., "A National Survey of US Internists' Experiences with Ethical Dilemmas and Ethics Consultation," *Journal of General Internal Medicine* 19 (3) (2004): 252–258; G. McGee, et al., "Successes and Failures of Hospital Ethics Committees: A National Survey of Ethics Committee Chairs," *Cambridge Quarterly of Healthcare Ethics* 11 (2) (2002): 87–93.

49 See: C. Gallagher, et al., "A Retrospective Review of Clinical Ethics Consultations Requested by Nurses for Oncology Patients," *Journal of Nursing* 7 (1) (2018): 1–7; J. R. Moeller, et al., "Functions and Outcomes of a Clinical Medical Ethics Committee: A Review of 100 Consults," *HEC Forum* 24 (2) (June 2012): 99–114; L. S. Johnson, et al., "Use of the Medical Ethics Consultation Service in a Busy Level 1 Trauma Center: Impact on Decision-Making and Patient Care," *American Surgeon* 78 (7) (2012): 735–740; C. Bruce, et al., "A Systematic Review of Activities at a High-Volume Ethics Consultation Service," *Journal of Clinical Ethics* 22 (2) (2011): 151–164; K. M. Swetz, et al., "Report on 255 Clinical Ethics Consultations and Review of the Literature," *Mayo Clinic Proceedings* 82 (6) (2007): 686–691.

50 E. Gefanus, "Clinical Ethics Committee and Ethics Support Infrastructure: A European Perspective," *Asian Bioethics Review* 3 (3) (2011): 293–298.

51 See: A. Slowther, et al., "Development of Clinical Ethics Services in the UK: A National Survey," *Journal of Medical Ethics* 38 (4) (2012): 210–224; L. McClimans, et al., "Can UK Clinical Ethics Committees Improve Quality of Care?" *HEC Forum* 24 (2) (2012): 139–147.

52 See: D. K. Sokol, *Doing Clinical Ethics: A Hands-on Guide for Clinicians and Others* (Dordrecht: Springer, 2012).

53 American Society for Bioethics and Humanities (ASBH), *Core Competencies for Healthcare Ethics Consultation*, 2nd ed. (Glenview, IL: ASBH, 2011), 2, section II.1.1.

54 See: American Society for Bioethics and Humanities (ASBH), *Core Competencies for Healthcare Ethics Consultation*, 2nd ed. (Glenview, IL: ASBH, 2011), 7, section II.1.1; A. J. Tarzian, "Health Care Ethics Consultation: An Update on Core Competencies and Emerging Standards from the American Society for Bioethics and Humanities' Core Competencies Update Task Force," *American Journal of Bioethics* 13 (2) (2013): 3–13, at 5; M. P. Aulisio, et al., eds., *Ethics Consultation: From Theory to Practice* (Baltimore: Johns Hopkins University Press, 2003).

55 R. Altisent, et al., "Health Care Ethics Consultation. Individual Consultant or Committee Model? Pros and Cons," *American Journal of Bioethics* 13 (2) (2013): 25–27.

56 For thorough explanations of the role of ethics committees and ethics consultants, see: D. Micah Hester et al., eds., *Guidance for Healthcare Ethics Committees* (New York: Cambridge University Press, 2012); Albert R. Jonsen, et al., *Clinical Ethics: A Practical Approach to Ethical Decisions in Clinical Medicine*, 7th ed. (New York: McGraw-Hill, 2015); L. Farber Post, et al., *Handbook for Health Care Ethics Committees*, 2nd ed. (Baltimore, MD: The Johns Hopkins University Press, 2015); M. P. Aulisio, et al., eds., *Ethics Consultation: From Theory to Practice* (Baltimore: Johns Hopkins University Press, 2003).

57 American Society for Bioethics and Humanities (ASBH), *Core Competencies for Healthcare Ethics Consultation*, 2nd ed. (Glenview, IL: ASBH, 2011), 19–21, section II.2.1.

58 American Society for Bioethics and Humanities (ASBH), *Core Competencies for Healthcare Ethics Consultation*, 2nd ed. (Glenview, IL: ASBH, 2011), 55, Appendix II, item 8.

59 American Society for Bioethics and Humanities (ASBH), *Core Competencies for Healthcare Ethics Consultation*, 2nd ed. (Glenview, IL: ASBH, 2011), pp. 22–24, section II.2.2.

60 M. E. Homan, "Factors Associated with the Timing and Patient Outcomes of Clinical Ethics Consultation in a Catholic Health System," *The National Catholic Bioethics Quarterly* 18 (1) (Spring 2018): 71–92.

61 American Society for Bioethics and Humanities (ASBH), *Core Competencies for Healthcare Ethics Consultation*, 2nd ed. (Glenview, IL: ASBH, 2011), 26–31, section II.2.3.

62 For the ASBH's Healthcare Ethics Consultant-Certified Program, at, http://asbh.org/certification/hcec-certification

63 See: B. S. Mackiewicz, "Essential Goals of Ethics Committees and the Role of Professional Ethicists," *The National Catholic Bioethics Quarterly* 18 (1) (Spring 2018): 49–57; R. Yarmolinsky, "Ethics for Ethicists? The Professionalization of Clinical Ethics Consultation," *AMA Journal of Ethics* 18 (5) (2016): 506–513.

64 See: A. J. Tarzian, et al., "A Code of Ethics for Health Care Ethics Consultants," *American Journal of Bioethics* 15 (5) (2015): 38–51; American Society for Bioethics and the Humanities (ASBH), *Code of Ethics and Professional Responsibilities for Healthcare Ethics Consultants* (Glenview, IL: ASBH, 2014).

65 See: W. S. Andereck, W. J. McGaughey, A. R. Jonsen, "The Clinical Ethics Consultant. Verifying the Qualifications of a New Type of Practitioner in a Community Hospital," *Journal of Healthcare Management* 57 (4) (2012): 264–273.

66 C. Bruce, et al., "Practical Guidance for Charting Ethics Consultation," *American Journal of Bioethics* 16 (3) (2016): 48–50.

67 See: J. J. Fins, et al., "A Pilot Evaluation of Portfolios for Quality Attestation of Clinical Ethics Consultants," *American Journal of Bioethics* 16 (3) (2016): 3–14, with commentary responses, pp. 25–57; R. Kodish, et al., "Quality Attestation for Clinical Ethics Consultants: A Two-Step Model from the American Society for Bioethics and Humanities," *Hastings Center Report* 43 (5) (2013): 26–36; H. J. Silverman, E. Bellavance, B. H. Childs, "Ensuring Quality in Clinical Ethics Consultations: Perspectives of Ethicists Regarding Process and Prior Training of Consultants," *American Journal of Bioethics* 13 (2) (2013): 29–31.

68 See: E. Fox, "The Road to Certification for Clinical Ethics Consultants: Finding Our Bearings," *American Journal of Bioethics* 16 (3) (2016): 33–35; E. Fox, "Developing a Certifying Examination for Healthcare Ethics Consultants," *American Journal of Bioethics* 14 (1) (2014): 1–4; B. D. White, et al., "Structuring a Written Examination to Asses ASBH Healthcare Ethics Consultation Core Knowledge Competencies," *American Journal of Bioethics* 14 (1) (2014): 5–17.

69 See: K. A. Berkowitz, et al., "Quality Assessment of the Ethics Consultation Service at the Organizational Level: Accrediting Ethics Consultation Services," *American Journal of Bioethics* 16 (3) (2016): 42–44; W. Shelton, B. D. White, "The Process to Accredit Clinical Ethics Fellowship Programs Should Start Now," *American Journal of Bioethics* 16 (3) (2016): 28–30; J. Spike, "Baby Steps Toward the Professionalization and Accreditation of Ethics Consultation Services," *American Journal of Bioethics* 16 (3) (2016): 52–54.

70 American Society for Bioethics and Humanities (ASBH), *Core Competencies for Healthcare Ethics Consultation*, 2nd ed. (Glenview, IL: ASBH, 2011), Appendix II, item 11.

71 American Society for Bioethics and Humanities (ASBH), *Core Competencies for Healthcare Ethics Consultation*, 2nd ed. (Glenview, IL: ASBH, 2011), 32–33, section II.2.4.

72 American Society for Bioethics and Humanities (ASBH), *Core Competencies for Healthcare Ethics Consultation*, 2nd ed. (Glenview, IL: ASBH, 2011), 34–42.

73 American Society for Bioethics and Humanities (ASBH), *Core Competencies for Healthcare Ethics Consultation*, 2nd ed. (Glenview, IL: ASBH, 2011), 44, section II.3.3.

74 C. E. Bogan, M. J. English, *Benchmarking for Best Practices* (New York: McGraw Hill, 1994).

75 Institute of Medicine, Committee on Quality of Healthcare in America, *Crossing the Quality Chasm: A New Health System for the 21st Century* (Washington, DC: National Academy Press, 2001), 157–159.

76 American Society for Bioethics and Humanities (ASBH), *Core Competencies for Healthcare Ethics Consultation*, 2nd ed. (Glenview, IL: ASBH, 2011), 51, section III. For discussion on a related issue on quality, the credentialing processes for individuals and programs, see: G. Magill, "Quality in Ethics Consultation," *Medicine, Health Care and Philosophy* 16 (4) (2013): 761–774; E. Kodish, et al., "Quality Attestation for Clinical Ethics Consultants," *Hastings Center Report* (September-October, 2013): 26–36; B. White, et al., "Structuring a Written Examination to Assess ASBH Healthcare Ethics Consultation Core Knowledge Competencies," *American Journal of* 14 (1) (2014): 5–17.

77 American Society for Bioethics and Humanities, *Core Competencies for Healthcare Ethics Consultation*, 2nd ed. (Glenview, IL, 2011), 54.

78 See: W. Nelson, "Addressing Organizational Ethics," *Healthcare Executive* 23 (2) (2008): 43–44. For a history of the development of Organizational Ethics committees in healthcare, see: S. D. Pearson, et al., *No Margin, No Mission: Health-Care Organizations and the Quest for Ethical Excellence* (New York: Oxford University Press, 2003), Chapter 3, "Organizational Ethics," 25–44.

79 See: R. E. Freeman, et al., *Stakeholder Engagement: Clinical Research* Cases (New York: Springer, 2017); R. E. Freeman, et al. *Stakeholder Theory: The State of the Art* (New York: Cambridge University Press, 2010); R. E. Freeman, *Strategic Management: A Stakeholder Approach* (New York: Cambridge University Press, 2010). Also see: P. H. Werhane, "The Healthcare Organization, Business Ethics, and Stakeholder Theory," in G. L. Filerman, et al., eds., *Managerial Ethics in Healthcare: A New Perspective* (Chicago, IL: Health Administration Press, 2014), Chapter 4; M. Bonnafous-Boucher, J. D. Rendorff, *Stakeholder Theory: A Model for Strategic Management.* Springer Briefs in Ethics (Springer, 2016); A. L. Friedman, S. Miles, *Stakeholders: Theory and Practice* (New York: Oxford University Press, 2006).

80 For an earlier explanation of the development of the ethics paradigm and the consultative process involved, see: G. Magill, L. Prybil, "Stewardship and Integrity in Health Care: A Role for Organizational Ethics," *Journal of Business Ethics* 50 (2004): 225–238; G. Magill, L. Prybil, "Guidelines for Organizational Ethics," *Health Progress* (July–August, 2001): 12–14.

81 The leaders we consulted in Phase I (with the roles and titles at the time of the interviews) were: J. Berg, Director, Academic Affairs, Institute for Ethics, American Medical Association; William Cox, President and CEO, Alliance of Catholic Healthcare Systems, Sacramento, CA; R. Davidson, President and CEO, American Hospital Association, Washington, DC; B. Halm, President and CEO, Benedictine Health System, Duluth, MN; J. King, former President and CEO, Legacy Health System, Portland, OR; W. Mason, Chair, Board of Directors, Baptist-St. Vincent Health System, Jacksonville, FL; J. Morris, III, CEO, Kootenai Medical Center, Coeur D'Alene, ID; Sr. M. R. Rocklage, RSM, Chair, Board of Directors, Sisters of Mercy Health System, St. Louis, MO; D. Russell, President and CEO, Catholic Health East, Newtown Square, PA; G. Sprenger, President and CEO, Allina Health System, Minneapolis, MN; S. Ummel, Principal and National Advisor on IDNs, Ernst & Young, Chicago, IL.

82 The leaders we consulted in Phase II (with the roles and titles at the time of the interviews) were: D. Brennan, President and CEO, Daughters of Charity National Health

System, St. Louis, MO; G. Christiansen, President and CEO, Carondelet Health System, St. Louis, MO; J. Dorsey, President and CEO, Columbia HealthOne, Denver, CO; Sr. P. Eck, CBS, Chair, Board of Directors, Bon Secours Health System, Inc., Marriottsville, MD; Rev. M. Place, President and CEO, Catholic Health Association, St. Louis, MO; C. T. Smith, President and CEO, Voluntary Hospitals of America, Inc., Irving, Texas; R. Statuto, President and CEO, St. Joseph Health System, Orange, CA; A. Yuspeh, Senior Vice President/Ethics Compliance and Corporate Responsibility, Columbia/HCA, Nashville, TN.

83   The leaders we consulted in Phase III (with the roles and titles at the time of the interviews) were: D. Brodeur, Ph.D., Senior VP, Stewardship, SSM Healthcare, St. Louis, MO; F. Brown, Vice-Chair, BJC Health System, St. Louis, MO; M. Connelly, President and CEO, Catholic Healthcare Partners, Cincinnati, OH; W. Cox, President and CEO, Alliance of Catholic Healthcare Systems, Sacramento, CA; J. S. Lore, President and CEO, Sisters of St. Joseph Health System, Ann Arbor, MI; Sr. M. R. Rocklage, RSM, President and CEO, Sisters of Mercy Health System, St. Louis, MO. The leaders we consulted after the roundtable (with affiliations listed as in Spring 1999) were: D. Berwick, M.D., President and CEO, Institute for Healthcare Improvement, Boston, MA; J. Dalton, President and CEO, Quorum Health Group, Inc., Brentwood, TN; A. Herman, Consultant to the President, Texas Health Resources, Dallas, TX. Subsequently, an early draft executive summary was published as follows: G. Magill, L. Prybil, "Guidelines for Organizational Ethics," *Health Progress* (July–August, 2001): 12–14.

84   See: E. Schein, *Organizational Culture and Leadership* (San Francisco, CA: Jossey-Bass, 2010); Craig E. Johnson, *Organizational Ethics. A Practical Approach* (Boston, MA: Sage Publications, 2016); John B. Bryson, et al., eds., *Public Value and Public Administration* (Washington, DC: Georgetown University Press, 2015).

85   L. Hartmann, J. DesJardins, C. MacDonald, *Business Ethics: Decision Making for Personal Integrity and Social Responsibility*, 3rd ed. (McGraw-Hill, 2013).

86   S. W. Goodspeed, *Community Stewardship* (Chicago, IL: AHA Press, 1998).

87   See: L. Lessig, "Institutional Corruption Defined," *Journal of Law, Medicine and Ethics* 41 (3) (Fall 2013): 553–555, at 553–554; D. Jorgensen, "Pharmaceuticals, Political Money, and Public Policy," *Journal of Law, Medicine and Ethics* 41 (3) (Fall 2013): 560. An earlier work on ethical governance made a similar association between Organizational Ethics and mission but did not pursue the relationship in a systematic manner, see: R. A. Ritvo, J. D. Ohlsen, T. P. Holland, *Ethical Governance in Healthcare. A Board Leadership Guide for Building an Ethical Culture* (Chicago, IL: Health Forum, Inc., 2004), 3–5, 66–68.

88   G. L. Filerman, et al., eds., *Managerial Ethics in Healthcare: A New Perspective* (Chicago, IL: Health Administration Press, 2014), 287.

89   W. M. Hoffman, R. E. Frederick, M. S. Schwartz, eds., *Business Ethics: Readings and Cases in Corporate Morality*, 5th ed. (Wiley-Blackwell, 2014).

90   The decision making steps listed here were initially developed by one of the authors in, B. Devlin, G. Magill, "The Process of Ethical Decision-making," in W. E. Scott, ed., *Current Ethical Thinking in Anaesthesia and Intensive Care*, special issue of the journal, *Best Practice & Research Clinical Anaesthesiology* 20 (4) (2006): 493–506. The discussion in this chapter develops the earlier analysis presented in this journal article.

91   For an expanded explanation, see: G. Magill, "Clinical Ethics: Accreditation," in H. ten Have and B. Gordijn, eds., *Encyclopedia of Global Bioethics* (Springer, 2016). The discussion in this chapter elucidates on the original analysis in this encyclopedia contribution.

92   See: G. L. Filerman, et al., eds., *Managerial Ethics in Healthcare: A New Perspective* (Chicago, IL: Health Administration Press, 2014), 274–276; P. H. Werhane, *Moral Imagination and Management Decision Making* (New York: Oxford University Press, 1999); P. H. Werhane, "Moral Imagination and Systems Thinking," *Journal of*

Business Ethics 13 (1–2) (2002): 33–42; M. Johnson, *Moral Imagination* (Chicago, IL: University of Chicago Press, 1993).

93 G. Magill, "Religious Morality," in John Henry Newman, ed., *Hermeneutics of the Imagination* (Springer, 2015), Chapter 4. A systemic explanation of the moral imagination appears in this previous publication.

94 See: Institute of Medicine, Committee on Quality of Healthcare in America, *To Err Is Human: Building a Safer Health System* (Washington, DC: National Academy Press, 2000); Institute of Medicine, Committee on Quality of Healthcare in America, *Crossing the Quality Chasm: A New Health System for the 21st Century* (Washington, DC: National Academy Press, 2001); Institute of Medicine, Committee on Enhancing Federal Healthcare Quality Programs, *Leadership by Example: Coordinating Government Roles in Improving Healthcare Quality* (Washington, DC: National Academy Press, 2002).

95 A. Forehand, "Mission and Organizational Performance in the Healthcare Industry," *Journal of Healthcare Management* 45 (4) (July–August 2000): 267–277.

96 A. M. Zuckerman, "Creating a Vision for the Twenty-First Century Healthcare Organization," *Journal of Healthcare Management* 45 (5) (September–October 2000): 294–305.

97 C. D. Kerns, "Loyalty in Managed Care: A Leadership System," *Journal of Healthcare Management* 45 (3) (May–June 2000): 158–169.

98 S. Webley, E. More, *Does Business Ethics Pay? Ethics and Financial Performance* (London: The Institute of Business Ethics, 2003).

99 C. S. Verschoor, "Ethical corporations are still more profitable," *Strategic Finance* (June 2003): 22–23.

100 K. S. Cameron, D. Bright, A. Caza, "Exploring the Relationships between Organizational Virtuousness and Performance," *American Behavioral Scientist* (February 2004); the entire issue discusses contributions to positive organizational scholarship, with theoretical and empirical studies.

101 See: G. Moore, *Virtue at Work: Ethics for Individuals, Managers, and Organizations* (Oxford University Press, 2017); P. M. Lencioni, *The Ideal Team Player: How to Recognize and Cultivate The Three Essential Virtues* (San Francisco, CA: Jossey-Bass, 2016); J. L. Badaracco, *Defining Moments: When Managers Must Choose Between Right and Right* (Harvard Business Review Press, 2016); C. Manz, et al., *The Virtuous Organization: Insights from Some of World's Leading Management Thinkers* (Singapore: World Scientific Publishing, Co., 2008); M. Jinkins, D. B. Jinkins, *The Character of Leadership: Political Realism and Public Virtue in Nonprofit Organizations* (San Francisco, CA: Jossey-Bass, 1998).

Select readings

American Society for Bioethics and Humanities. 2011. *Core Competencies for Health Care Ethics Consultation*, 2nd ed. Glenview, IL: ASBH.

American Society for Bioethics and Humanities. 2014. *Code of Ethics and Professional Responsibilities for Healthcare Ethics Consultants*. Glenview, IL: ASBH.

American Society for Bioethics and Humanities. 2015. *Improving Competencies in Clinical Ethics Consultation. An Education Guide*, 2nd ed. Glenview, IL: ASBH.

American Society for Bioethics and Humanities. 2017. *Addressing Patient Centered Ethical Issues in Health Care. A Case-Based Study Guide*. Glenview, IL: ASBH.

American Society for Bioethics and Humanities. 2017. *Resources for Developing Advanced Skills in Ethics Consultation*. Glenview, IL: ASBH.

Beauchamp, T. L., J. F. Childress. 2019. *Principles of Biomedical Ethics*, 8th ed. New York: Oxford University Press.

Devettere, R. J. 2016. *Practical Decision Making in Health Care Ethics*, 4th ed. Washington, DC: Georgetown University Press.

Farber Post, L., et al. 2007. *Handbook for Health Care Ethics Committees*. Baltimore, MD: The Johns Hopkins University Press.

Gutman, A., J. D. Moreno. 2019. *Bioethics and the Transformation of Health Care in America*. New York: Liveright.

Johnson, C. E. 2016. *Organizational Ethics: A Practical Approach*. Thousand Oaks, CA. Sage.

Jonsen, A. R., et al. 2015. *Clinical Ethics*, 7th ed. New York: McGraw-Hill.

Kelly, D. F., G. Magill, H. ten Have. 2013. *Contemporary Catholic Health Care Ethics*, 2nd ed. Washington, DC: Georgetown University Press.

Schildmann, J., et al., eds. 2016. *Clinical Ethics Consultation: Theories and Methods, Implementation, Evaluation*. New York: Routledge.

Tomlinson, T. 2012. *Methods in Medical Ethics*. New York: Oxford University Press.

3 Professional ethics

Introduction

The previous two chapters explained how the ethics paradigm provides a framework for applied analysis to foster consistency of ethics discourse across the established fields of clinical ethics and organizational ethics in healthcare. This chapter continues the theoretical discussion to apply the ethics paradigm to professional ethics. The purpose of engaging the ethics paradigm with these established fields is to later apply it to governance ethics as an emerging field in healthcare.

At the outset of this discussion it is helpful to describe professional ethics. The previous chapter offered extensive explanations of clinical ethics and organizational ethics. Briefly these fields can be described in this manner. Clinical ethics deals with values, reasoning, and responsibilities regarding treatment issues related to patients and medical providers. Organizational ethics deals with values, reasoning, and responsibilities regarding corporate issues related to institutions. Professional ethics deals with values, reasoning and responsibilities regarding professionals (e.g., nurses, physicians, social workers) with specialized practices and typically with accompanying codes of conduct.

There is a need for consistency of discourse in professional ethics because of the extensive array of topics and approaches in this large field. In general, professional ethics explores the implications of professional relations in society.[1] Typically, discussions deal with this topic either directly or implicitly by considering the role of ethics in various fields. These discussions engage on a broad perspective across the professions,[2] or within a specific profession, including behavior analysts,[3] biotechnology,[4] business,[5] computing and information technology,[6] education and teaching,[7] engineering and technology,[8] forensic science,[9] law and criminal justice,[10] media and journalism,[11] pastors,[12] police,[13] public relations,[14] public service,[15] social work,[16] and sports.[17] Moreover, there is an abundance of literature on professional ethics regarding the health professions generally,[18] and more narrowly addressing addiction care,[19] anesthesiology,[20] dentistry,[21] family therapy,[22] health information management,[23] mental health and counseling,[24] midwifery,[25] nursing,[26] pharmaceuticals,[27] pharmacy,[28] physical therapy,[29] physicians,[30] physicians' assistants,[31] and public health.[32] Not surprisingly, a concern for professional ethics has generated an abundance of codes of ethics in the various helping professions,[33] including bioethicists,[34] family counselors,[35] physicians,[36] psychologists,[37] nurses,[38] social workers.[39] Furthermore, there is extensive literature on health management that is discussed later in this chapter.

From the long list of references in the previous paragraph, it is apparent that there is an extraordinary range of issues in professional ethics. When faced with such a vast array of topics and approaches, it is daunting to traverse such an expansive terrain. Here, the ethics paradigm can be helpful to seek consistency across the myriad topics discussed in professional ethics.

The ethics paradigm revolves around the leitmotif of *who we are, how we function*, and *what we do*. These basic features of ethics are indispensable for encouraging leadership regarding *identity, accountability*, and *quality*, each promoting the following outcomes. The focus on *identity* (*who we are*) promotes the outcome of organizational stewardship of an institution's mission. The focus on *accountability* (*how we function*) promotes the outcome of decision-making via participative deliberation. The focus on *quality* (*what we do*) promotes the outcome of best practices for standards of conduct.

The previous chapter emphasized stewardship, decision-making, and best practices as aspects of clinical ethics and organizational ethics to explain their alignment with the ethics paradigm. This chapter's discussion of professional ethics focuses on the leadership concepts of *identity, accountability*, and *quality* insofar as they promote the outcomes of stewardship, decision-making, best practices. These three concepts of *identity, accountability*, and *quality* in the ethics paradigm provide a framework for applied analysis to foster consistency of ethics discourse in professional ethics. This quest for consistency occurs by using the three concepts to organize the varied topics that arise in the materials discussed. The following discussion engages many well-known approaches as representative of the diverse issues in professional ethics. The ethics paradigm (Table 1.1) guides the discussion.

Naturally, governance ethics relates to the professional work of health executives and health management. Hence, it can be helpful to explain how the ethics paradigm is consistent with discourse in these areas.

Table 1.1 Ethics paradigm

Components	Foundation component	Process component	Practice component
Context	Environment of healthcare	Organizational oversight	Organizational culture
Leadership	Identity: who we are	Accountability: how we function	Quality: what we do
Outcomes	Organizational stewardship of mission	Decision-making via participative deliberation	Best practices for standards of conduct

Code of Ethics of the American College of Healthcare Executives

To begin the conversation on professional ethics in healthcare, it can be enlighten-ing to consider the Code of Ethics of the American College of Healthcare Execu-tives (ACHE).[40] The code of ethics delineates the responsibilities of healthcare executives to its constituencies: to the profession of healthcare management (Sec-tion I); to patients or others served (Section II); to the organization (Section III); to employees (Section IV); to community and society (Section V). In addition to these sections there is an introductory Preamble. In each of these sections, the various items that are delineated lead to a considerable list of requirements. Moreover, these items recur in various ways in the ACHE's policies, including the following: the ACHE's policy statements such as on responsibility to the com-munity or ensuring quality and patient safety;[41] the ACHE's ethical policy state-ments such as on protecting confidentiality or creating an ethical culture;[42] and the ACHE commitment to social responsibility, such as on public protection or advocating for diversity.[43]

The concepts of *identity*, *accountability*, and *quality* in the ethics paradigm can provide a framework for applied analysis to organize the recurring themes in the ACHE code as being characteristic of professional ethics. These concepts are discussed briefly in the next section, with references to the various sections of the ACHE's code of ethics. First, the concept of *identity* in the ethics paradigm highlights the leitmotif of *who we are*, promoting the outcome of stewardship of an organization's mission. This concept of *identity* is evident in the focus of the code of ethics upon the mission of the ACHE as an organization (Section I). This focus emphasizes the importance of allocating limited resources as a function of organizational stewardship while respecting patient customs and practices con-sistent with the organization's philosophy (Section III). However, stewardship extends beyond financial constraints to include the organization's mission. Hence, respecting organizational identity requires the following: being truthful regarding information and communication; fostering a healthcare environment as free from harassment or coercion; and addressing mistakes effectively to minimize their recurrence (Sections III and IV).

Second, the concept of *accountability* in the ethics paradigm highlights the leitmotif of *how we function*, promoting the outcome of decision-making via par-ticipative deliberation. This concept of *accountability* is evident in the focus of the code of ethics upon cooperative activities that establish procedures to uphold patient autonomy, rights, confidentiality, and privacy (Sections II and III). These cooperative activities should support mechanisms for enlightened decisions about services, for sound management decisions that engage employee expertise, for addressing issues in clinical and organizational ethics, and for participative delib-eration in public policy (Sections III, IV, and V). This concept of *accountability* highlights the scope and function of the ACHE ethics committee (appointed by the board of directors) to review and evaluate the code of ethics, recommend action by the board including suspension or expulsion, and develop policy statements and guidelines for ethical conduct.[44] Emphasizing organizational oversight nurtures a context where there is accountability through regulatory compliance with processes to resolve conflicts of interest and avoid abuse of power (Sections I and II).

Third, the concept of *quality* in the ethics paradigm highlights the leitmotif of *what we do*, promoting the outcome of best practices for standards of conduct. This concept of *quality* is evident in the focus of the code of ethics upon standards of conduct of ethical behavior in professional relationships (Preamble). These standards advance professional activities with honesty, respect, and fairness. These activities should support the quality of care or service rendered through evidence-based clinical practices and sound management standards and business practices that avoid fraud and abuse and report negative activities promptly (Sections II and III). Highlighting quality across the organization develops an organizational culture that combines the following: protecting the reputation of management as a profession through ethical conduct; celebrating inclusivity to avoid discrimination; and respecting the needs of the community in healthcare services for all (Sections I, IV, and V).

In sum, the concepts of *identity*, *accountability*, and *quality* in the ethics paradigm provides a framework for applied analysis to organize multiple requirements in the ACHE code of ethics as being characteristic of professional ethics. The ethics paradigm is designed to have an impact on public trust and confidence in healthcare organizations. Similarly, the ACHE's code of ethics is designed to build trust and confidence regarding healthcare professionals with the public (Preamble). This impact reflects the organization's mission that healthcare executives are dedicated to improving the health of communities served and to fostering excellence in the organization's vision for healthcare management.[45] Insofar as this commitment is reflected in the ACHE's strategic plan to respond to the rapidly changing healthcare environment,[46] the ACHE's concern with public trust and confidence in healthcare organizations is robust. That is, the ethics paradigm highlights the ACHE's commitment to public trust and confidence.

Identity, accountability, and quality in healthcare management ethics

A way of illustrating the significance of the ethics paradigm for professional ethics in healthcare management is to focus individually on each of the three concepts of *identity*, *accountability*, and *quality*. This consideration of each concept individually occurs in relation to several influential books on ethics in healthcare management, as follows: *Ethics and Professionalism for Healthcare Managers*;[47] *Ethics and Management Dilemmas in Healthcare*;[48] *Managerial Ethics in Healthcare*;[49] *Ethics in Health Administration: A Practical Approach for Decision Makers*;[50] and *Ethics in Health Services Management*.[51]

First, the concept of *identity* that highlights *who we are* in the ethics paradigm is evident in the book *Ethics and Professionalism for Healthcare Managers*. The concept of *identity* can help to clarify the discussion of the profession of health-care management, professionalism, and stewardship of fiduciary duties regarding the mission of an organization. This concept of *identity* is evident in the other books, as follows: in *Ethics and Management Dilemmas in Healthcare*, in the discussion of the importance of the stewardship and mission of the healthcare organization; in *Managerial Ethics in Healthcare*, in the discussion of organizations as moral agents (related to stakeholder theory and the tension between mission and margin in organizations); in *Ethics in Health Administration: A Practical Approach for Decision Makers*, in the emphasis upon stewardship and mission in the section on organizational influences on ethics; and in *Ethics in Health Services Management*, in the focus upon the organization's mission as crucial for establishing integrity.

Second, the concept of *accountability* that highlights *how we function* in the ethics paradigm is evident in *Ethics and Professionalism for Healthcare Managers* where the book discusses ethical decision-making and interactions in healthcare organizations. This concept of *accountability* is evident in the other books, as follows: in *Ethics and Management Dilemmas in Healthcare*, in the need for ethical decision-making processes to have a consistent approach to the many challenges faced by healthcare managers; in *Managerial Ethics in Healthcare*, in the general discussion of moral decision-making throughout the book, and more specifically in encouraging organizations to foster deliberative processes in public policy; in *Ethics in Health Administration: A Practical Approach for Decision Makers*, in the discussion of ethical decision-making not only in consent but also by decision makers across the organization; and in *Ethics in Health Services Management*, in placing corporate decision-making at the center of the book's discussion of topics.

Third, the concept of *quality* that highlights *what we do* in the ethics paradigm is evident in *Ethics and Professionalism for Healthcare Managers* when considering specific issues regarding behavior and conduct to indicate best practices for standards of conduct. This concept of *quality* is evident in the other books, as follows: in *Ethics and Management Dilemmas in Healthcare*, in the discussion of the conduct and behavior of healthcare managers; in *Managerial Ethics in Healthcare*, in the discussion of on quality improvement and the need for best practices in the organization to foster an organizational culture that encourages ethical behavior; in *Ethics in Health Administration: A Practical Approach for Decision Makers*, in the need for standards of conduct in administrative practices; and in *Ethics in Health Services Management*, in highlighting the need for standards of conduct to guide a variety of ethical issues.

Furthermore, in addition to ethics in healthcare management, the related fields of organizational ethics and business ethics can illustrate the significance of the ethics paradigm. Three influential books are discussed: *Organizational Ethics*,[52] *Organizational Ethics in Health Care*,[53] and *Business & Professional Ethics*.[54] Again, the concepts of *identity*, *accountability*, and *quality* in the ethics paradigm can help to organize the multiple topics discussed in each book.

The concept of *identity* is evident in the books as follows: in *Organizational Ethics*, in the discussion of mission and servant leadership that profoundly impacts the organization's identity; in *Organizational Ethics in Health Care*, in the discussion of adopting a stakeholder theory approach related to the mission of the organization; and in *Business & Professional Ethics*, in the discussion of the reputation and credibility of organizations.

The concept of *accountability* is evident in the books, as follows: in *Organizational Ethics*, in the discussion of deliberative processes of ethical decision-making; in *Organizational Ethics in Health Care*, in the discussion of approaches to moral reasoning via participative deliberation; and in *Business & Professional Ethics*, in the discussion of ethical decision-making to resolve practical dilemmas.

The concept of *quality* is evident in the books, as follows: in *Organizational Ethics*, in the discussion of performance related concerns and of ethical practices that shape ethical culture such as in marketing, finance, accounting, and human resources; in *Organizational Ethics in Health Care*, in the discussion of discusses quality improvement programs; and in *Business & Professional Ethics*, in the discussion of accounting in the public interest and managing ethical risks.

Finally, there is a prestigious collection of essays on healthcare management that underscores the significance of the ethics paradigm. This collection of essays is from the "Healthcare Management Ethics" column in the magazine *Healthcare Executive*. The collection of essays is titled "Managing Healthcare Ethically."[55] The collection is divided into four sections: organizational ethical leadership, organizational ethics issues, clinical ethics issues, and an organization's ethics resources. Most of the essays deal with practical topics. Again, the concepts of *identity*, *accountability*, and *quality* in the ethics paradigm can help to organize the multiple topics discussed in this collection, as follows. The concept of *identity* that focuses on mission is evident in the collection's insistence that an organization's mission, vision, and value statements require conviction and action and not mere rhetoric. The concept of *accountability* is evident in the collection's insistence on the need for a systematic process of ethics reflection. The concept of *quality* is evident in the central focus of the collection on quality. The collection emphasizes that to achieve quality care there needs to be a strong commitment to fostering a leadership-driven culture that supports ethical actions and best practices across the organization.

In these books, some topics indicate the importance of the concept of *identity* in professional ethics, reflecting the focus on *who we are* in the ethics paradigm; other topics indicate the importance of the concept of *accountability* in professional ethics, reflecting the focus on *how we function* in the ethics paradigm; and yet other topics indicate the importance of the concept of *quality* in professional ethics, reflecting the focus on *what we do* in the ethics paradigm.

Identity, accountability, and quality in professional ethics

Another way of illustrating the significance of the ethics paradigm for professional ethics is to consider a variety of approaches to professional ethics. Again, the concepts of *identity*, *accountability*, and *quality* in the ethics paradigm can help to organize the multiple topics that are presented. This consideration of each concept occurs in relation to several influential books, as follows: *The Elements of Ethics for Professionals, Ethical Dimensions in the Health Professions, Ethics for Health Professionals, The Helping Professional's Guide to Ethics, Nursing Ethics and Professional Responsibility*, and *Public Value and Public Administration.*[56]

First, the concept of *identity* that highlights *who we are* in the ethics paradigm is evident in *The Elements of Ethics for Professionals* that emphasizes integrity to nurture professionalism through respect of diversity, honoring *who we are.* In the *Ethical Dimensions in the Health Professions*, the concept of *identity* is evident in the discussion of professional life to focus upon personal integrity as indispensable for being competent professionally and to highlight the centrality of moral agency that pertains to all approaches to ethics. Also, in *Ethics for Health Professionals*, the concept of *identity* is evident in the professional's concentration upon the patient as top priority at the heart of healthcare. And in *The Helping Professional's Guide to Ethics* the concept of *identity* is evident in the explanation of professional ideals to highlight *who we are* in professional life. Furthermore, the concept of *identity* is evident in *Nursing Ethics and Professional Responsibility*. Here nursing as a profession is explained in terms of the nurse-patient relationship whereby professional responsibility must provide service to individuals and communities as a basic expression of who professionals are. Finally, in the book *Public Value and Public Administration*, the concept of *identity* is evident in the emphasis on what kind of society can be identified and built by public value governance as a multisector approach.

Second, the concept of *accountability* that highlights *how we function* in the ethics paradigm is evident in this book on *Public Value and Public Administration*. The book underscores the contribution of dialogue to develop pathways for mutual efforts of persuasion, thereby building deliberative capacity to create public value. In addition, the concept of *accountability* is evident in the decision-making model that is adopted in *Ethics for Health Care Professionals*, and in the deliberative processes for making ethical decisions in *The Elements of Ethics* that requires prudence for sound judgement. Also, the concept of *accountability* is evident in *Ethical Dimensions in the Health Professions*. Here, a multi-step process of ethical decision-making is explained in section one and applied in sections two and three to elucidate deliberative processes on professional roles (e.g., student scenarios, organizational dilemmas, team decisions). Furthermore, the concept of *accountability* is evident in *The Helping Professional's Guide to Ethics* where the majority of chapters engage the importance of ethical decision-making for patient care.

Third, the concept of *quality* that highlights *what we do* in the ethics paradigm is evident in *Ethics for Health Professionals*. This book highlights the need for best practices in organizational conduct regarding vulnerable populations (e.g., minors, elderly), the workplace (e.g., regarding the Health Insurance Portability and Accountability Act—HIPAA), the medical record (e.g., Joint Commission requirements), liability issues (e.g., liability insurance), life and death issues (e.g., advance directives), and emerging controversial issues (e.g., stem cell research). Likewise, the concept of *quality* is evident in *The Helping Professional's Guide to*

Ethics that discusses the need for standards of conduct when engaging practical issues such as substance abuse. Similarly, an emphasis on the concept of *quality* is evident in the more general book, *The Elements of Ethics for Professionals*. Here, most of the chapters discuss excellence in advancing standards of conduct to ensure that professionals act prudently. This means that professionals must show respect and compassion by acting in a beneficent manner, avoiding harm or abuse and supporting social justice. Furthermore, the concept of *quality* is evident in *Nursing Ethics and Professional Responsibility*. The latter half of the book discusses best practices in advanced practice specialty areas. These areas deal with neonates, children and adolescents, women's health, adult-gerontological health, psychiatric and mental health, the anesthesia and perioperative period, palliative care and end-of-life care. Finally, the concept of *quality* is evident in the book *Public Value and Public Administration*, where measurement and assessment encourage best practices for standards of conduct.

In sum, the concepts of *identity*, *accountability*, and *quality* in the ethics paradigm provide a framework to organize the disparate issues that arise in various approaches to professional ethics.

Conclusion

This chapter concludes the theoretical perspective of the book. The discussion has considered how the ethics paradigm provides a framework for applied analysis to foster consistency of ethics discourse in clinical ethics, organizational ethics, and professional ethics. The ethics paradigm facilitates a uniform way of enlightening these established fields in a coherent manner that does not require formal ethics training or expertise. The robust framework of the ethics paradigm is now applied to the emerging field of governance ethics. The subsequent chapters present an applied perspective by addressing crucial ethical challenges for boards of directors in healthcare organizations. The book ends with a brief concluding chapter on how this approach to governance ethics can foster virtuous organizations in healthcare. Discourse on virtue ethics explains that individuals can become virtuous by connecting moral character, practical wisdom, and laudable actions. Similarly, the ethics paradigm enables an organization to become virtuous by connecting moral character (via the concept of *identity*, *who we are*), practical wisdom (via the concept of *accountability*, *how we function*), and action (via the concept of *quality*, *what we do*).

Notes

1 E. Durkeim, *Professional Ethics and Civic Morals*, 3rd ed. (New York: Routledge, 2003, originally published in 1957).
2 See: D. E. Cooper, *Ethics for Professionals in a Multicultural World* (Pearson, 2003); N. M. Crystal, *Professional Responsibility: Problems of Practice & Profession*, 5th ed. (Aspen Publishers, 2011); B. G. Fines, *Professional Responsibility: A Context and Practice Casebook* (Durham, NC: Carolina Academic Press, 2013); A. Flores, *Professional Ideals* (Wadsworth, 1987); J. Harden Fritz, *Professional Civility:*

Communicative Virtue at Work (Peter Lang, 2012); A. L. Kaufman, D. B. Wilkins, *Problems in Professional Responsibility for a Changing Profession*, 5th ed. (Durham, NC: Carolina Academic Press, 2009); C. Martin, W. Vaught, R. S. Solomon, *Ethics Across the Professions: A Reader for Professional Ethics* (New York: Oxford University Press, 2009); J. E. Moliterno, *Crunch Time: Professional Responsibility*, 5th ed. (Philadelphia, PA: Wolters Kluwer, 2016); T. Morgan, R. Rotunda, J. Dzienkowski, *Professional Responsibility*, 12th ed. (Foundation Press, 2014); R. D. Parsons, *The Ethics of Professional Practice* (Pearson, 2000); R. Pearce, et al., *Professional Responsibility: A Contemporary Approach*, 2nd ed. (West Academic Publishing, 2013); R. R. Rowan, S. Zinaich, *Ethics for the Professions* (Wadsworth Thomson Learning, 2002); K. Strom-Gottfried, *Straight Talk About Professional Ethics*, 2nd ed. (New York: Oxford University Press, 2014); W. B. Wendel, *Professional Responsibility: Examples & Explanations*, 5th ed. (Philadelphia, PA: Wolters Kluwer, 2016); P. Windt, et al., *Ethical Issues in the Professions* (Prentice Hall, Pearson), 1989); D. E. Wueste, *Professional Ethics and Social Responsibility* (Rowman & Littlefield, 1994).

3 J. S. Bailey, M. R. Burch, *Ethics for Behavior Analysts* (Routledge, 2016).

4 See: J. Bennett, ed., *The Ethics of Biotechnology* (Ashgate, 2016); J. T. Bradley, *Brutes of Angels: Human Possibility in the Age of Biotechnology* (Tucaloosa, AL: University of Alabama Press, 2013); A. Briggle, ed., *A Rich Bioethics: Public Policy, Biotechnology, and the Kass Council* (Notre Dame, IN: University of Notre Dame Press, 2010); G. Comstock, ed., *Life Sciences Ethics*, 2nd ed. (Springer, 2014); A. Dyson, J. Harris, *Ethics & Biotechnology* (Routledge, 2014); C. B. Lake, *Prophets of the Posthuman: American Fiction, Biotechnology, and the Ethics of Personhood* (Notre Dame, IN: University of Notre Dame Press, 2013); P. Murphy, *Biotechnology, Education and Life Politics* (Routledge, 2017); K. S. Rajan, ed., *Lively Capital: Biotechnologies, Ethics, and Governance in Global Markets* (Duke University Press, 2012); C. Willmott, S. Macip, *Where Science and Ethics Meet: Dilemmas at the Frontiers of Medicine and Biology* (Praeger, 2016).

5 See: G. G. Brenkert, T. L. Beauchamp, eds., *The Oxford Handbook of Business Ethics* (New York: Oxford University Press, 2012); L. J. Brooks, *Business & Professional Ethics for Directors, Executives & Accountants*, 7th ed. (Boston, MA: Cengage Learning, 2014); D. Collins, *Business Ethics: How to Design and Manage Ethical Organizations* (Oxford: Wiley, 2011); A. Crane, D. Matten, *Business Ethics: Managing Corporate Citizenship and Sustainability in the Age of Globalization*, 3rd ed. (New York: Oxford University Press, 2010); R. T. DeGeorge, *Business Ethics*, 7th ed. (Pearson, 2009); J. DesJardins, *An Introduction to Business Ethics*, 5th ed. (McGraw-Hill, 2013); R. Duska, et al., *Accounting Ethics*, 2nd ed. (Oxford: Wiley-Blackwell, 2011); O. C. Ferrell, J. Fraedrich, L. Ferrell, *Business Ethics: Ethical Decision Making and Cases*, 11th ed. (Boston, MA: Cengage Learning, 2016); D. M. Guy, D. R. Carmichael, A. A. Lach, *Ethics for CPAs: Meeting Expectations in Challenging Times* (Oxford: Wiley, 2003); T. Halbert, *Law and Ethics in the Business Environment*, 8th ed. (Boston, MA: Cengage Learning, 2014); L. Hartmann, J. DesJardins, C. MacDonald, *Business Ethics: Decision Making for Personal Integrity and Social Responsibility*, 3rd ed. (McGraw-Hill, 2013); W. M. Hoffman, R. E. Frederick, M. S. Schwartz, eds., *Business Ethics: Readings and Cases in Corporate Morality*, 5th ed. (Oxford: Wiley-Blackwell, 2014); G. Klein, *Ethics in Accounting: A Decision-Making Approach* (Oxford: Wiley, 2015); A. Lawrence, J. Weber, *Business and Society: Stakeholders, Ethics, Public Policy*, 14th ed. (McGraw-Hill, 2013); M. W. Martin, *Meaningful Work: Rethinking Professional Ethics* (New York: Oxford University Press, 2000); W. Ransome, C. Sampford, *Ethics and Socially Responsible Investment* (Routledge, 2016); J. D. Rendtorff, *Perspectives on Philosophy of Management and Business Ethics* (Springer, 2017); W. H. Shaw, *Business Ethics: A Textbook with Cases*, 9th ed. (Boston, MA: Cengage Learning, 2016); J. W. Weiss, *Business Ethics: A Stakeholder and Issues Management Approach*, 6th ed. (San Francisco, CA: Berrett-Koehler Publishers, 2014).

6 See: M. Ballard, et al., *Corporate Ethics for Big Data: A Group Project* (Amazon Digital Services, 2016); T. W. Bynum, S. Rogerson, eds., *Computer Ethics and Professional Responsibility* (Oxford: Wiley-Blackwell, 2003); K. Davis, *Ethics of Big Data: Balancing Risk and Innovation* (O'Reilly Media, 2012); M. D. Ermann, M. S. Shauf, eds., *Computers, Ethics, and Society* (New York: Oxford University Press, 2002); D. G. Johnson, *Computer Ethics*, 4th ed. (Pearson, 2009); M. J. Quinn, *Ethics for the Information Age*, 6th ed. (Pearson, 2014); G. Reynolds, *Ethics in Information Technology*, 5th ed. (Cengage, 2014).

7 See: Council for Exceptional Children, *What Every Special Educator Must Know: Ethics, Standards, and Guidelines*, 7th ed. (Council for Exceptional Children, 2016); C. Higgins, *The Good Life of Teaching: An Ethics of Professional Practice* (Oxford: Wiley-Blackwell, 2011); S. Jacob, D. M. Decker, E. T. Lugg, *Ethics and Law for School Psychologists*, 7th ed. (Oxford: Wiley, 2016); R. W. Rebore, *The Ethics of Educational Leadership*, 3nd ed. (Pearson, 2013); J. P. Shapiro, J. A. Stefkovich, *Ethical Leadership and Decision Making in Education*, 3rd ed. (Routledge, 2010); D. L. Stader, *Law and Ethics in Educational Leadership*, 2nd ed. (Pearson, 2012); K. A. Strike, E. J. Haller, J. F. Soltis, *The Ethics of School Administration*, 3rd. ed. (Teachers College Press, 2005).

8 See: C. E. Harris, et al., *Engineering Ethics: Concepts and Cases*, 5th ed. (Boston, MA: Cengage Learning, 2013); I. Van de Poel, L. Royakkers, *Ethics, Technology, and Engineering* (Wiley-Blackwell, 2011).

9 See: P. Barnett, *Ethics in Forensic Science: Professional Standards for the Practice of Criminalists* (Protocols in Forensic Science, 2001); R. T. Bowen, *Ethics and the Practice of Forensic Science* (CRC Press, 2009).

10 See: J. S. Albanese, *Professional Ethics in Criminal Justice: Being Ethical When No One Is Looking*, 4th ed. (Pearson, 2015); J. Allen, *Health Law and Medical Ethics* (Pearson, 2012); M. C. Braswell, B. L. McCarthy, B. J. McCarthy, *Justice, Crime, and Ethics*, 8th ed. (Routledge, 2014); T. A. Cannon, *Ethics and Professional Responsibility for Paralegals*, 7th ed. (Philadelphia, PA: Wolters Kluwer, 2013); K. Cheeseman, et al., eds., *Everyday Ethics for the Criminal Justice Professional*, 2nd ed. (Durham, NC: Carolina Academic Press, 2015); J. Dzienkowski, *Professional Responsibility, Standards, Rules and Statutes* (West Academic Publishing, 2016); B. F. Fremgen, *Medical Law and Ethics*, 5th ed. (Pearson, 2015); K. Judson, *Law & Ethics for Health Professionals*, 7th ed. (McGraw-Hill, 2015); L. G. Lerman, *Ethical Problems in the Practice of Law* (Philadelphia, PA: Wolters Kluwer, 2016); A. Nollkaemper, I. Plakokefalos, eds., *The Practice of Shared Responsibility in International Law* (New York: Cambridge University Press, 2017); D. K. Orlik, *Ethics for the Legal Profession*, 8th ed. (Pearson, 2013); J. M. Pollock, *Ethical Dilemmas and Decisions in Criminal Justice*, 8th ed. (Boston, MA: Cengage Learning, 2013); C. Roberson, S. Mire, *Ethics for Criminal Justice Professionals* (CRC Press, 2009); S. S. Souryai, *Ethics in Criminal Justice: In Search of the Truth*, 6th ed. (Routledge, 2014); C. R. Williams, B. A. Arrigo, *Ethics, Crime, and Criminal Justice*, 2nd ed. (Pearson, 2011).

11 See: J. Black, C. Roberts, *Doing Ethics in Media: Theories and Practical Application* (Routledge, 2011); F. Brown, ed., *Journalism Ethics: A Casebook of Professional Conduct for News Media*, 4th ed. (Marion Street Press, 2011); C. G. Christians, et al., *Media Ethics: Cases and Moral Reasoning*, 9th ed. (Routledge, 2011); L. A. Day, *Ethics in Media Communications: Cases and Controversies* (Belmont, CA: Wadsworth, 2005); K. McBride, T. Rosentiel, *The New Ethics of Journalism: Principles for the 21st Century* (CQ Press, 2013); C. Meyers, ed., *Journalism Ethics: A Philosophical Approach* (New York: Oxford University Press, 2010); P. Patterson, L. Wilkins, *Media Ethics: Issues & Cases* (McGraw-Hill, 2013); L. E. Peck, G. S. Reel, eds., *Media Ethics at Work: True Stories from Young Professionals*, 2nd ed. (CQ Press, 2016); P. L. Plaisance, *Media Ethics: Key Principles for Responsible Practice*, 2nd ed. (Sage, 2013).

12 See: R. M. Gula, *Just Ministry: Professional Ethics for Pastoral Ministers* (Paulist, 2010); K. Lebacqz, J. Driskall, *Ethics and Spiritual Care: A Guide for Pastors and Spiritual Directors* (Nashville, TN: Abingdon Press, 2000); J. E. Trull, J. E. Carter, *Ministerial Ethics: Moral Formation for Church Leaders* (Grand Rapids, MI: Baker Academic, 2014).

13 M. A. Caldero, J. P. Crank, *Police Ethics: The Corruption of Noble Cause*, 3rd. ed. (Routledge, 2010).

14 See: K. R. Fitzpatrick, *Ethics in Public Relations: responsible Advocacy* (Sage, 2006); P. J. Parsons, *Ethics in Public Relations: A Guide to Best Practice*, 3rd. ed. (Philadelphia, PA: Kogan Page, 2016).

15 See: A. W. Dutelle, *Ethics for the Public Service Professional* (CRC Press, 2011); D. Geuras, C. Garafalo, *Practical Ethics in Public Administration*, 3rd ed. (Vienna, VA: Management Concepts Inc., 2010); B. S. Sharp, G. Aguirre, K. Kicklam, *Managing in the Public Sector: A Casebook In Ethics and Leadership* (Routledge, 2010); J. H. Svara, *The Ethics Primer for Public Administrators in Government and Nonprofit Organizations*, 2nd ed. (Jones & Bartlett, 2014); K. Winstone, *Ethics in Public Life* (United Kingdom: Palgrave-MacMillan, 2015).

16 See: A. E. Barsky, *Ethics and Values in Social Work* (New York: Oxford University Press, 2009); F. G. Reamer, *Social Work Values and Ethics*, 4th ed. (New York: Columbia University Press, 2013); J. C. Rothman, *From the Front Lines: Student Cases in Social Work Ethics*, 4th ed. (Pearson, 2013).

17 See: J. L. P. Salcines, K. Babiak, G. Walters, eds. *Routledge Handbook of Sport and Corporate Social Responsibility* (Routledge Handbooks, 2015); R. C. Schneider, *Ethics of Sports and Athletics: Theory, Issues, and Application* (Philadelphia, PA: Walters Kluwer, 2008); P. K. Thornton, et al., *Sports Ethics for Sports Management Professionals* (Jones and Bartlett Learning, 2011).

18 See: V. Bryan, et al., *The Helping Professional's Guide to Ethics: A New Perspective* (New York: Oxford University Press, 2015); G. Corey, M. S. Corey, P. Callahan, *Issues and Ethics in the Helping Professions* (Boston, MA: Cengage Learning, 2014); A. Cribb, P. Duncan, eds. *Health Promotion and Professional Ethics* (Oxford: Wiley-Blackwell, 2002); Elsevier Publishing, *Legal and Ethical Issues for Health Professionals*, 3r ed. (Elsevier Saunders, 2014); K. Judson, C. Harrison, *Law and Ethics for Health Professions*, 7th ed. (McGraw-Hill, 2015); M. A. Lewis, C. D. Tamparo, B. M. Tatro, *Medical Law, Ethics & Bioethics, for the Health Professions*, 7th ed. (Philadelphia, PA: Davis Company, 2012); S. Makely, S. Badasch, D. Chesebro, *Becoming a Health Care Professional* (Pearson, 2013); S. Makely, *Professionalism in Health Care: A Primer for Career Success*, 4th ed. (Pearson, 2012); C. B. Mitchell, D. J. Riley, *Christian Bioethics: A Guide for Pastors, Health Care Professionals*, and Families (Nashville, TN: B&H Academics, 2014); E. D. Pellegrino, R. M. Veatch, J. P. Langan, eds., *Ethics, Trust, and the Professions: Philosophical and Cultural Aspects* (Washington, DC: Georgetown University Press, 2001); G. D. Pozgar, *Legal and Ethical Issues for Health Professionals*, 4th ed. (Jones & Bartlett, 2014); R. Purtilo, A. Haddad, R. Doherty, *Health Professional and Patient Interaction*, 8th ed. (St. Louis, MO: Elsevier, 2014); R. W. Scott, *Promoting Legal and Ethical Awareness: A Primer for Health Professionals* (Mosby, 2008); P. S. Stanfield, N. Cross, *Introduction to the Health Professions*, 5th ed. (Jones & Bartlett, 2008).

19 See: J. D. Berton, *Ethics for Addiction Professionals* (Oxford: Wiley, 2013); L. W. Roberts, C. Geppert, eds., *The Book of Ethics: Expert Guidance for Professionals Who Treat Addiction* (Center City, MN: Hazelden Publishing, 2008); M. J. Taleff, *Advanced Ethics for Addiction Professionals* (Springer, 2009).

20 American Society of Anesthesiologists, *Ethical Guidelines for the Anesthesia Care of Patients with do-not-resuscitate Orders* (Park Ridge, IL: American Society of Anesthesiologists, 2001).

21 See: P. L. Beemsterboer, *Ethics and Law in Dental Hygiene*, 2nd ed. (St. Louis, MO: Elsevier/Saunders, 2009); V. Kimbrough-Walls, C. Lautar, *Ethics, Jurisprudence and Practice Management in Dental Hygiene*, 3rd ed. (Pearson, 2011); D. T. Ozar, D. S. Sokol, *Dental Ethics at Chairside: Professional Principles and Practical Applications*, 2nd ed. (Washington, DC: Georgetown University Press, 2002).

22 See: L. Hecker, *Ethics and Professional Issues in Couple and Family Therapy* (Routledge, 2009); M. J. Murphy, *Ethics and Professional Issues in Couple and Family Therapy*, 2nd ed. (Routledge, 2016); A. P. Wilcoxon, et al., *Ethical, Legal, and Professional Issues in the Practice of Marriage and Family Therapy*, 5th ed. (Pearson, 2013).

23 See: L. B. Harman, *Ethical Challenges in the Management of Health Information* (Jones & Bartlett, 2006); D. C. McWay, *Legal and Ethical Aspects of Health Information Management*, 4th ed. (Clifton Park, NY: Cengage Learning, 2014); B. Mittelstadt, L. Floridi, eds., *The Ethics of Biomedical Data* (Springer, 2016).

24 See: S. K. Anderson, M. M. Handelsman, *Ethics for Psychotherapists and Counselors: A Proactive Approach* (Oxford: Wiley-Blackwell, 2009); E. Baker, *Caring for Ourselves: A Therapist's Guide to Personal and Professional Well-Being* (Washington, DC: American Psychological Association, 2003); D. N. Bersoff, *Ethical Conflicts in Psychology* (American Psychological Association, 2008); R. R. Cottone, V. M. Tarvydas, *Ethics and Decision Making in Counseling and Psychotherapy*, 4th ed. (Springer, 2016); B. T. Erford, *Orientation to the Counseling Profession: Advocacy, Ethics, and Essential Professional Foundations*, 2nd ed. (Pearson, 2013); B. Herlihy, G. Corey, *ACA Ethical Standards Casebook*, 7th ed. (American Counseling Association – ACA, 2014); R. Houser, S. J. Thoma, *Ethics in Counseling and Therapy: Developing an Ethical Identity* (London: Sage, 2012); C. Jungers, J. Gregoire, eds. *Counseling Ethics: Philosophical and Professional Foundations* (Springer, 2012); S. J. Knapp, L. VandeCreek, *Practical Ethics for Psychologists: A Positive Approach*, 2nd ed. (American Psychological Association, 2012); G. P. Koocher, P. Keith-Spiegel, *Ethics in Psychology and the Mental Health Professions: Standards and Cases*, 4th ed. (New York: Oxford University Press, 2016); M. M. Leach, et al. eds., *The Oxford Handbook of International Psychological Ethics* (New York: Oxford University Press, 2012); D. H. Levitt, H. J. Moorhead, eds., *Values and Ethics in Counseling: Real-Life Ethical Decision Making* (Routledge, 2013); T. F. Nagy, *Essential Ethics for Psychologists* (American Psychological Association, 2010); K. S. Pope, M. J. T. Vasquez, *Ethics in Psychotherapy and Counseling: A Practical Guide*, 5th ed. (Oxford: Wiley, 2016); T. P. Remley, B. P. Herlihy, *Ethical, Legal, and Professional Issues in Counseling*, 5th ed. (Pearson, 2015); L. W. Roberts, *A Clinical Guide to Psychiatric Ethics* (American Psychiatric Publishing, 2016); L. Sperry, *The Ethical and Professional Practice of Counseling and Psychotherapy* (Pearson, 2007); J. T. Thomas, *Ethics of Supervision and Consultation: Practical Guidance for Mental Health Professionals* (American Psychological Association, 2010); E. R. Welfel, *Ethics in Counseling & Psychotherapy*, 6th ed. (Boston, MA: Cengage Learning, 2015).

25 I. R. Foster, J. Lasser, *Professional Ethics in Midwifery Practice* (Jones and Bartlett, 2010).

26 See: M. Benjamin, J. Curtis, *Ethics in Nursing: Cases, Principles, and Reasoning*, 4th ed. (New York: Oxford University Press, 2010); P. B. Black, *Professional Nursing: Concepts & Challenges*, 8th ed. (St. Louis, MO: Elsevier, 2016); M. A. Burkhardt, A. Nathaniel, *Ethics and Issues in Contemporary Nursing*, 4th ed. (Boston, MA: Cengage Learning, 2013); J. B. Butts, K. L. Rich, *Nursing Ethics: Across the Curriculum and into Practice*, 4th ed. (Jones & Bartlett, 2015); E. E. Friberg, J. L. Creasia, *Conceptual Foundations: The Bridge to Professional Nursing Practice* (St. Louis, MO: Elsevier, 2016); S. T. Fry, R. M. Veatch, *Case Studies in Nursing Ethics* (Jones & Bartlett, 2010); G. W. Guido, *Legal and Ethical Issues in Nursing: Challenges and Opportunities*, 6th ed. (Pearson, 2013); C. J. Huston, *Professional Issues in Nursing*, 4th ed. (Philadelphia, PA: Wolters Kluwer, 2016); R. K. Nunnery, *Advancing Your Career: Concepts*

in Professional Nursing (Philadelphia: David Company, 2015); A. G. Peirce, J. Smith, eds., *Ethical and Legal Issues for Doctoral Nursing Students* (Lancaster, PA: Destech Publications, 2013); S. J. Westrick, *Essentials of Nursing Law and Ethics*, 2nd ed. (Jones & Bartlett, 2013).

27 See: M. N. G. Dukes, *The Law and Ethics of the Pharmaceutical Industry* (Elsevier, 2005); L. Forman, J. C. Kohler, *Access to Medicines as a Human Right: Implications for Pharmaceutical Industry Responsibility* (Toronto, Canada: University of Toronto Press, 2012); D. Ho, Philos*ophical Issues in Pharmaceuticals: Development, Dispensing, Use* (Springer, 2017); J. P. Kassirer, *On the Take: How Medicine's Complicity with Big Business Can Endanger Your Health* (New York: Oxford University Press, 2005); D. W. Light, A. F. Maturo, *Good Pharma: the Public Health Model* (Palgrave MacMillan, 2015); A. Petryana, A. Lakoff, A. Kleinman, eds., *Global Pharmaceuticals: Ethics, Markets, Practices* (Duke University Press, 2006); M. A. Rodwin, "Institutional Corruption and the Pharmaceutical Industry," *Journal of Law, Medicine and Ethics* 41 (3) (Fall 2013): 544–552; K. S. Rajan, ed., *Lively Capital: Biotechnologies, Ethics, and Governance in Global Markets* (Durham, NC: Duke University Press, 2012); S. Salek, A. Edgar, eds., *Pharmaceutical Ethics* (Wiley, 2008); M. A. Santoro, T. M. Gorrie, *Ethics and the Pharmaceutical Industry* (New York: Cambridge University Press, 2007); P. R. Vagelos, L. Galambos, *The Moral Corporation: Merck Experiences* (New York: Cambridge University Press, 2006).

28 See: R. A. Buerki, L. D. Vottero, *Pharmacy Ethics: A Foundation for Professional Practice* (American Pharmacists Association, 2013); R. A. Buerki, L. D. Vottero, *Ethical Responsibility in Pharmacy Practice*, 2nd ed. (American Institute of the History of Pharmacy, 2002); J. Moini, *Law and Ethics for Pharmacy Technicians* (Stamford, CT: Cengage Learning, 2013); K. M. Stranberg, *Essentials of Law and Ethics for Pharmacy Technicians*, 3rd ed. (CRC Press, Taylor & Francis, 2011); D. Tipton, *Professionalism, Work, and Clinical Responsibility in Pharmacy* (Jones & Bartlett, 2013); R. M. Veatch, A. Haddad, ed., *Case Studies in Pharmacy Ethics*, 2nd ed. (New York: Oxford University Press, 2008).

29 D. L. Gabard, M. W. Martin, *Physical Therapy Ethics*, 2nd ed. (Davis Company, 2011).

30 See literature cited in Chapter 2 regarding clinical ethics.

31 B. Cassidy, A. D. Blessing, E*thics and Professionalism: A Guide for the Physician Assistant* (Philadelphia, PA: Davis Company, 2007).

32 See: D. H. Barrett, et al., eds., *Public Health Ethics: Cases Spanning the Globe* (Springer, 2016); R. Bayer, L. O. Gostin, B. Jennings, B. Steinbock, eds. *Public Health Ethics: Theory, Policy, Practice* (New York: Oxford University Press, 2006); R. G. Bernheim, et al., *Essentials of Public Health Ethics* (Jones & Bartlett, 2013); C. Coggan, et al., *Public Health Law: Ethics, Governance, and Regulation* (Routledge, 2016); S. S. Coughlin, *Case Studies in Public Health Ethics*, 2nd ed. (American Public Health Association, 2009); A. Dawson, *Public Health Ethics: Key Concepts and Issues in Policy and Practice* (New York: Cambridge University Press, 2011); D. S. Goldberg, *Public Health Ethics and Social Determinants of Health* (Springer, 2017); M. Powers, R. Faden, *Social Justice: The Moral Foundations of Public Health and Health Policy* (New York: Oxford University Press, 2006); L. Gostin, *Public Health Law and Ethics: A Reader*, 2nd ed. (Berkeley, CA: University of California Press, 2010); A. Hann, *Applied Public Health Ethics: Making Ethical Decision* (United Kingdom: Routledge, 2016); S. Holland, *Public Health Ethics*, 2nd ed. (Cambridge, UK: Polity Press, 2015); B. Jennings, et al., eds., *Emergency Ethics: Public Health Preparedness and Response* (New York: Oxford University Press, 2016); D. Strech, I. Hirschberg, G. Markermann, eds., *Ethics in Public Health and Health Policy* (Springer, 2013).

33 G. Corey, M. S. Corey, *Codes of Ethics for the Helping Professions*, 5th ed. (Stamford, CT: Cengage Learning, 2015).

34 American Society for Bioethics and the Humanities, *Code of Ethics and Professional Responsibilities for Healthcare Ethics Consultants* (Glenview, IL: ASBH, 2014). Also

see: American Society for Bioethics and Humanities, *Core Competencies for Health-care Ethics Consultation*, 2nd ed. (Glenview, IL: ASBH, 2011).

35 American Association for Marriage and Family Therapy, *User's Guide to the 2015 AAMFT Code of Ethics* (Alexandria, VA: American Association for Marriage and Family Therapy, 2015).

36 American Medical Association, *The Code of Medical Ethics* (Chicago, IL: American Hospital Association, 2008), at, www.ama-assn.org/about-us/code-medical-ethics.

37 See: American Psychological Association, "Ethical Principles of Psychologists and Code of Conduct," *American Psychologist* 57 (2002): 1060–1073; L. Campbell, et al., *APA Ethics Code Commentary and Case Illustrations* (American Psychological Association, 2009); C. B. Fisher, *Decoding the Ethics Code: A Practical Guide for Psychologists* (Sage, 2012).

38 American Nurses Association, *Code of Ethics for Nurses with Interpretive Statements* (American Nurses Association, 2015); American Nurses Association, *Social Policy Statement* (Silver Spring, MD, 2010); International Council of Nurses, *Code of Ethics for Nurses* (Geneva, Switzerland: International Council of Nurses, 2012); D. M. Marsha, *Guide to the Code of Ethics for Nurses: Interpretation and Application* (American Nurses Association, 2015).

39 National Association of Social Workers, *Code of Ethics* (NASW Press, 2015); F. Reamer, *Ethical Standards in Social Work: A Review of the NASW Code of Ethics* (NASW Press, 2006).

40 ACHE, *Code of Ethics*, www.ache.org/ABT_ACHE/code.cfm

41 ACHE, *Policy Statements*, www.ache.org/policy/policy.cfm

42 ACHE, *Ethical Policy Statements*, www.ache.org/policy/index_ethics.cfm

43 ACHE, *Social Responsibility*, www.ache.org/abt_ache/socialresponsibility.cfm

44 ACHE, *Ethics Committee*, www.ache.org/abt_ache/committee_function.cfm

45 ACHE, *Mission and Vision*, www.ache.org/abt_ache/facts.cfm

46 ACHE, *Strategic Plan*, www.ache.org/abt_ache/planning.cfm

47 E. J. Forrestal, L. W. Cellucci, *Ethics and Professionalism for Healthcare Managers* (Chicago, IL: Health Administration Press, 2016).

48 F. Perry, ed., *Ethics and Management Dilemmas in Healthcare* (Chicago, IL: Health Administration Press, 2014).

49 G. L. Filerman, et al., eds., *Managerial Ethics in Healthcare: A New Perspective* (Chicago, IL: Health Administration Press, 2014).

50 E. E. Morrison, *Ethics in Health Administration: A Practical Approach for Decision Makers*, 3rd ed. (Jones & Bartlett, 2015).

51 K. Darr, *Ethics in Health Services Management*, 6th ed. (Baltimore, MD: Health Professions Press, 2018).

52 C. E. Johnson, *Organizational Ethics. A Practical Approach* (Thousand Oaks, CA: Sage Publications, 2016).

53 E. M. Spencer, et al., *Organizational Ethics in Health Care* (New York: Oxford University Press, 2000).

54 L. J. Brooks, P. Dunn, *Business & Professional Ethics for Directors, Executives & Accountants*, 7th ed. (Stamford, CT: Cengage Learning, 2015).

55 W. A. Nelson, P. B. Hofmann, *Managing Healthcare Ethically: An Executive's Guide*, 2nd ed. (Chicago, IL: Health Administration Press, 2015).

56 W. B. Johnson, C. R. Ridley, *The Elements of Ethics for Professionals* (United Kingdom: Palgrave MacMillan, 2008); R. Purtilo, *Ethical Dimensions in the Health Professions*, 4th ed. (Philadelphia, PA: Elsevier, 2005); C. C. Stanford, V. J. Connor, *Ethics for Health Professionals* (Burlington, MA: Jones & Bartlett, 2014); V. Bryan, et al., *The Helping Professional's Guide to Ethics: A New Perspective* (New York: Oxford University Press, 2015); P. M. Grace, ed., *Nursing Ethics and Professional Responsibility*, 3rd ed. (Burlington, MA: Jones and Bartlett, 2017); J. M. Bryson, et al., eds., *Public Value and Public Administration* (Washington, DC: Georgetown University Press, 2015).

Select readings

Brooks, L. J. 2015. *Business & Professional Ethics for Directors, Executives & Accountants*, 7th ed. Stamford, CT: Cengage Learning.

Bryan, V., S. Sanders, L. Kaplan. 2015. *The Helping Professional's Guide to Ethics: A New Perspective*. New York: Oxford University Press.

Bryson, J. B., et al., eds. 2015. *Public Value and Public Administration*. Washington, DC: Georgetown University Press.

Darr, K. 2018. *Ethics in Health Services Management*, 6th ed. Baltimore, MD: Health Professions Press.

Filerman, G. L., et al., eds. 2014. *Managerial Ethics in Healthcare: A New Perspective*. Chicago, IL: Health Administration Press.

Forrestal, E. J., L. W. Cellucci. 2016. *Ethics and Professionalism for Healthcare Managers*. Chicago, IL: Health Administration Press.

Grace, P. M., ed. 2014. *Nursing Ethics and Professional Responsibility*, 2nd ed. Burlington, MA: Jones and Bartlett, 3rd ed. 2017.

Hann, A. 2016. *Applied Public Health Ethics: Making Ethical Decision*. United Kingdom: Routledge.

Huston, C. J. 2016. *Professional Issues in Nursing*, 4th ed. Philadelphia, PA: Wolters Kluwer.

Morrison, E. E. 2015. *Ethics in Health Administration: A Practical Approach for Decision Makers*, 3rd ed. Burlington, MA: Jones & Bartlett.

Perry, F., ed. 2014. *Ethics and Management Dilemmas in Healthcare*. Chicago, IL: Health Administration Press.

Purtilo, R., et al. 2014. *Health Professional and Patient Interaction*, 8th ed. St. Louis, MO: Elsevier.

Stanford, C. C., V. J. Connor. 2014. *Ethics for Health Professionals*. Burlington, MA: Jones & Bartlett.

Wendel, W. B. 2016. *Professional Responsibility: Examples & Explanations*, 5th ed. Philadelphia, PA: Wolters Kluwer.

Winstone, K. 2015. *Ethics in Public Life*. United Kingdom: Palgrave-MacMillan.

4 Governance structure

Introduction

The theoretical perspective in the previous chapters presented the ethics paradigm that is used as a guide for governance ethics in the subsequent chapters. The discussion now pursues an applied perspective by considering pivotal topics to encourage greater board accountability in healthcare organizations.

There is a growing awareness among boards and CEOs of nonprofit healthcare systems of the need for a consistent approach to governance ethics. The complexity of contemporary healthcare presents intricate dilemmas that increasingly require effective governance. The treatment of applied topics here will help boards to function not merely adequately but superbly in their ethical oversight.

The analysis engages several landmark reports by one of the co-authors of this book that have shaped discourse on governance effectiveness. These reports represent unprecedented access to boards and CEOs in healthcare nationally. One report, discussed in this chapter on governance structure and in a later chapter on patient safety, is based on access to 14 of the largest 15 nonprofit health systems in the United States. That report is referred to as the *Governance Structure Report*.[1] Another report is discussed in the chapter on community benefit, referred to as the *Community Health Systems Report*.[2] Other reports are discussed in the chapter on community health, one referred to as the *Community Health Report*,[3] the other referred to as the *Leadership Report*.[4]

Each of the following chapters begins with an explanation of the need for the pivotal topic under consideration, such as the governance structure of boards in this chapter. Then the concepts of *identity*, *accountability*, and *quality* provide a framework for the applied analysis. These concepts represent the foundation component (reflecting *who we are*), the process component (reflecting *how we function*), and the practice component (reflecting *what we do*) of the ethics paradigm (Table 1.1).

In the analysis, the concepts of the ethics paradigm organize core features of effective governance from these landmark reports and the scholarly literature. The purpose is to highlight hallmarks of governance ethics that denote associated moral imperatives. Because the hallmarks represent necessary moral attributes

Table 1.1 Ethics paradigm

Components	Foundation component	Process component	Practice component
Context	Environment of healthcare	Organizational oversight	Organizational culture
Leadership	Identity: who we are	Accountability: how we function	Quality: what we do
Outcomes	Organizational stewardship of mission	Decision-making via participative deliberation	Best practices for standards of conduct

of governance ethics, they entail an obligation to be adopted by boards. In turn, the associated moral imperatives represent necessary endeavors to foster the hallmarks under consideration. The ethics paradigm organizes multiple topics on board oversight of governance structure, as follows.

First, the foundation component of the ethics paradigm deals with the *identity* of an organization, reflecting the leitmotif *who we are*, thereby highlighting board competence and board role as hallmarks of governance ethics. In turn, these hallmarks denote associated moral imperatives: board competence denotes a moral imperative regarding oversight of term limits and board composition; and board role denotes a moral imperative concerning oversight of defined responsibilities and board effectiveness.

Second, the process component of the ethics paradigm addresses the *accountability* of the organization, reflecting the leitmotif *how we function*, thereby highlighting board evaluation and succession planning as hallmarks of governance. In turn, these hallmarks denote associated moral imperatives: board evaluation denotes a moral imperative regarding oversight of fair evaluation processes; and succession planning denotes a moral imperative concerning oversight of system planning and continuous updating.

Third, the practice component of the ethics paradigm engages *quality* in an organization, reflecting the leitmotif *what we do*, thereby highlighting leadership collaboration and system-wide strategy as hallmarks of governance ethics. In turn, these hallmarks denote associated moral imperatives: leadership collaboration denotes a moral imperative regarding oversight of working relationships; and system-wide strategy denotes a moral imperative concerning oversight of transformational change and strategic planning. Before considering these hallmarks of governance ethics, it is helpful to explain the need for oversight of board structure.

Need for oversight of board structure

The governance structure of boards of directors is crucial for effective trustee oversight. Hence, the applied discussion in the book begins with this pivotal topic to prepare the groundwork for other such topics on governance ethics in the applied chapters.[5] At the heart of the discussion of board accountability in governance ethics is the need for continuous evaluation and evidence-based improvements.[6] Without a properly designed governance structure, boards will be ineffective and thereby compromise their accountability.

It is worth noting at the outset that the ethics paradigm aligns well with a major report by the Panel on the Independent Sector.[7] The panel's recommendations concentrated upon several issues that are significant for the analysis in this chapter. The panel's discussion of board commitment is akin to the foundation component in the ethics paradigm that deals with stewardship, focusing on organizational *identity*. The panel's interest in the relation between healthcare organizations and their communities is akin to the process component in the ethics paradigm concerning decision-making, focusing on organizational *accountability*. Finally, the panel's interest in practice standards is akin to the practice component in the ethics paradigm related to best practices, focusing on organizational *quality*. The applied analysis begins with discussing hallmarks of governance ethics connected with the foundation component of the ethics paradigm.

Context of foundation-related governance ethics hallmarks

The concept of *identity* in the ethics paradigm (reflecting *who we are*) emphasizes the importance of organizational stewardship. This focus on *identity* and stewardship is especially pertinent within health systems that combine evidence-based research with value-promoting practices. Boards need to develop health systems that integrate research results (such as quality improvement, comparative effectiveness research, or public health standards) with healthcare practices. There are ongoing deliberations about better integrating medical research and clinical care, presenting a leadership opportunity for boards. These deliberations reflect a trend toward health systems, urged by the Institute of Medicine, to improve the development and application of evidence in healthcare.[8] This transformation means that healthcare systems should steward research and practice to nurture institutional mission in promoting justice in healthcare while effectively addressing the surrounding environment.[9]

The complexity of the healthcare environment presents the context for discussing foundation-related governance ethics hallmarks. Boards must deal with the healthcare environment as the critical context of their oversight. This environment demands transformational changes in health systems while preserving core values to shape their organizations and the future of healthcare.[10] These changes impact the *identity* and stewardship of health systems as caring organizations. This complex environment is especially pertinent for accountable care organizations targeted by the 2010 Affordable Care Act and its continuing evolution focusing on patient-centered care.[11] An example of this change is the shift from care focused primarily on individuals to care that is attuned to the health of the community.[12] These transformational changes will require health systems to address the needs of aging populations, to provide a greater emphasis on preventing illness, and to promote the health of the communities served. As a result, organizations increasingly will be concerned with the well-being of their communities rather than treating healthcare merely as a business transaction, thereby underscoring the organizational tension between mission and margin.[13]

Because of the increasing need for services and the demanding constraints on resources, healthcare leaders must improve in evidence-based and measurable ways. Boards must comprehend how the healthcare environment impacts their communities and influences their duties and responsibilities. The topics discussed in the following sections continue to be prevalent in the American Hospital Association's 2019 *National Healthcare Governance Survey Report*.[14]

Within this context of the challenging healthcare environment, the foundation component of the ethics paradigm focuses on the concept of *identity*, reflecting the leitmotif *who we are*. This concept emphasizes stewardship to enhance an organization's mission in healthcare. Here, the ethics paradigm organizes core features of effective governance from one of the landmark reports mentioned earlier, the *Governance Structure Report*, to highlight hallmarks of governance ethics and their associated moral imperatives.

The concept of *identity* focuses on *who the board is*, thereby highlighting board competence and board role as hallmarks of governance ethics. In turn, these hallmarks denote associated moral imperatives: oversight of board competence denotes a moral imperative regarding oversight of term limits and board composition; and oversight of the board role denotes a moral imperative concerning oversight of defined responsibilities and board effectiveness. These are discussed in what follows.

Board competence: foundation-related governance ethics hallmark

Board competence is the first hallmark of governance ethics regarding the foundation component of the ethics paradigm. To situate the significance of this hallmark, it is worth referring to the Blue Ribbon Panel on Healthcare Governance. This panel published an historic report on governance to explore ways of enhancing board effectiveness. The Panel emphasized the increasing interest in competency-based governance. Specifically, the panel flagged competencies of individual members and competencies of the board as a team and provided guidance for educational resources in the field.[15] In a similar manner, the landmark *Governance Structure Report* (that guides this chapter) emphasized the importance of boards insisting on governance design and policies that enable them to perform their responsibilities. To achieve this, boards also must have independence, diversity, and ideally the involvement of clinicians.[16]

The concept of *identity* in the ethics paradigm highlights board competence as a governance ethics hallmark by drawing attention to *who we are* (as a board that serves a health system). In turn, this hallmark denotes an associated moral imperative regarding oversight of term limits and board composition.

Moral imperative: board oversight of term limits and board composition

On the one hand, there should be formal limits on terms served and on the number of voting members. The number of consecutive terms for board members should be restricted to encourage the development of expertise and different perspectives.[17] Naturally, staggered terms and transition planning are needed to minimize losing too many experienced members in a short time. Frequently, terms are three years with a limit of three consecutive terms. In the *Governance Structure Report*, 79 percent of the large health systems adopted term limits.[18] At the same time, the number of voting members on the board should be restricted to meet the specific needs of the organization. On this point, the Internal Revenue Service (IRS) has an interesting perspective. That is, the IRS states that nonprofit boards should be large enough to represent a sufficiently broad public interest with appropriate skills and resources, while not being so large as to hinder decision-making.[19]

In the *Governance Structure Report*, there was 100 percent support regarding limits on the number of voting members of their boards; the voting terms and voting members reflected the size of the board.[20] A range of 9–17 voting members for hospital and health system boards was recommended in a 2007 Blue Ribbon Panel report.[21] Most of the system boards (72 percent) in the *Governance Structure Report* were in line with the recommendations of this Blue Ribbon Panel, but some were significantly larger: three of the 14 ranged from 18 to 28 voting members, with one outlier having 60 voting members. Excluding the outlier, the median size of these health systems was 15 voting members. In contrast, at that time there were 12 or fewer voting members in America's Standard and Poor's 500 boards.[22]

On the other hand, board size impacts the composition of the board which includes its independence, diversity, and engagement with clinicians. The importance of these for board and organizational performance is well recognized.[23] Each of these topics is worth closer scrutiny.

To begin, on independence, the board charter (establishing its independence) has been identified as a significant factor in good governance in publicly traded companies for some time.[24] To maintain integrity, the critical nature of independence requires the board to avoid so-called groupthink that can arise out of mistaken allegiance to fellow board members or groups rather than the organization's best interests.[25] On the issue of board independence, the *Governance Structure Report* indicated general agreement that from two-thirds to a majority of board members should be independent. The report explained that 60 percent of the members of the system boards were independent board members. However, the six secular health systems in the study had 82 percent of independent membership in contrast to 49 percent of independent membership among the faith-based systems. The faith-based percentage seems to have reflected a substantial proportion of board members being affiliated with previous or current religious sponsors.[26]

Next, on the issue of board diversity, the *Governance Structure Report* indicated there should be appropriate experience and skills to perform the fiduciary duties effectively. This observation included members with diverse backgrounds including ethnic, racial, and gender perspectives. Diversity can significantly improve the ethical reputation of the organization within the community, not least because a multi-cultural society needs multi-cultural leaders.[27] Diversity also can result in better care insofar as individuals from diverse communities can represent the beliefs and preferences of those communities. There is an obvious obligation to narrow the gaps that appears to persist.[28] Increasing diversity in leadership is a core element in a national effort to eliminate healthcare disparities: the other elements are increasing the collection of race, ethnicity, and language data as well as increasing cultural competency training.[29] The *Governance Structure Report* documented the following outcomes: 17 percent of the systems' board members were non-Caucasian, with similar proportions in the secular and faith-based systems.[30] The proportion of women on boards of the faith-based systems was 40 percent, with only 21 percent of women serving on the boards of the secular systems.[31]

Furthermore, the *Governance Structure Report* emphasized the significance of clinician engagement by the board. The participation of physician leaders is as an effective executive and governance practice with approximately 20 percent of hospital and health system boards being physicians.[32] As physicians serve on boards, it is important to note the need for ethical scrutiny of potential conflicts of interest that unfortunately characterize the medical profession internationally.[33] The role of clinicians in healthcare governance is widely accepted.[34] This role help proactively align hospitals and community physicians in long-term partnerships; these partnerships can cultivate an ethical culture of relationship building to improve patient care and outcomes.[35]

Also, clinician engagement should include nurses. For example, a critical report of the Institute of Medicine encourages the engagement of nurses on healthcare boards.[36] There is a growing realization of the need to increase the professional representation of nurses on boards, especially given the focus by boards on clinical issues like quality care and patient safety.[37] At the time of the *Governance Structure Report*, national studies indicated that nurses comprised only about 6 percent of nonprofit hospital and community health system boards.[38] In this report, 14 percent of the board members were physicians, and 6 percent of the board members were nurses. However, on the secular boards, physicians comprised 18 percent of the board compared to 11 percent of faith-based boards, whereas nurses comprised 9 percent of faith-based boards compared to 2 percent of the secular boards. Thirteen percent of the CEOs and boards in this study group indicated that their board composition was about right, whereas 28 percent indicated that more clinical expertise would be beneficial. Subsequent studies have indicated that the proportion of nurses as voting board members has ranged from 2 to 6 percent.[39]

Board role: foundation-related governance ethics hallmark

Board role is the second hallmark of governance ethics regarding the foundation component of the ethics paradigm. The concept of *identity* (with its focus on stewardship) in the ethics paradigm highlights board role as a governance ethics hallmark by drawing attention to *who we are* (as a board that serves a health system). In turn, this hallmark denotes an associated moral imperative regarding board oversight of defined responsibilities and board effectiveness.[40] The topics discussed here are consistent with recent national surveys.[41]

Moral imperative: board oversight of defined responsibilities and board effectiveness

On the one hand, defined responsibilities are indispensable for efficient governance. The governance functions of nonprofit boards of hospitals and health systems are widely documented and accepted.[42] There remains considerable concern about board effectiveness in performing these functions.[43] To bolster effective governance, there is general recognition that boards need to be proactive,[44] well organized and engaged,[45] with a clearly delineated committee design.[46] In the *Governance Structure Report*, significant consistency in board roles emerged: all the systems' boards should have clearly defined responsibilities described in a written document (e.g., in a bylaws provision or a policy statement), formally adopted by the system board.[47] In contrast, a study of 114 nonprofit community health systems published in 2009 reported only 72 percent of boards meeting this standard.[48]

On the other hand, board effectiveness requires boards to have an executive committee as part of their governance. In this report, 13 of the 14 systems had an executive committee of their board, with 82 percent reporting that executive committees have two principal functions: to act between board meetings on routine, non-strategic matters that require formal board action; and to be a sounding board for the CEO who seeks informal governance counsel, such as on board meeting priorities. However, these executive committees do not serve as a decision-making body on substantive issues.[49]

In the *Governance Structure Report*, 64 percent of the health systems reported holding executive sessions as part of every board meeting, with the remaining 36 percent having executive sessions at some board meeting but not always. Moreover, all the systems' boards in this report had standing board committees to deal with audit and compliance, executive compensation, and financial matters.[50] Also, this report indicated that nearly all the systems' boards assigned clear oversight responsibilities to standing board committees on patient care quality and safety, board education and development, and system-wide strategy and planning functions. However, only 43 percent of the systems' boards had standing committees with clear oversight responsibility for system-wide community benefit policies. Finally, when CEOs and board members in this report were asked about the perceived effectiveness of the board committees, a strong majority perceived their board committees as well organized and effective, though approximately a third of the board members indicated there was room for improvement.[51]

In sum, the foundation component of the ethics paradigm highlights board competence and board role as hallmarks of governance ethics. By focusing on

identity in the ethics paradigm, these hallmarks denote associated moral imperatives: board competence denotes a moral imperative regarding board oversight
of term limits and board composition; and board role denotes a moral imperative concerning oversight of defined responsibilities and board effectiveness. The
next section considers the process component of the ethics paradigm that focuses
on the concept of *accountability* to highlight process-related hallmarks of governance ethics.

Context of process-related governance ethics hallmarks

The concept of *accountability* in the ethics paradigm (reflecting *how we function*) emphasizes the importance of decision-making via participative deliberation. This focus on *accountability* requires boards to be attentive to organizational
oversight as the context for assessing their responsibilities.

Organizational oversight in healthcare institutions presents the context for
considering decision-making processes that engage all relevant stakeholders.
These stakeholders include system-level relations with the local operating units.
There should be a constructive relationship between stakeholders and large-scale
organizations. Hence, accountability is crucial for corporate responsibility and
effective governance. Not surprisingly, the concept of *accountability* has elicited
significant professional and government scrutiny that is likely to increase.[52] This
increased interest occurs in part because the internal processes of boards vary significantly between high- and low-performing hospitals nationally.[53] The process
component of the ethics paradigm highlights the importance of *accountability*. At
the heart of board accountability in governance ethics is the need for continuous
evaluation and evidence-based improvements.

An important aspect of organizational oversight in healthcare institutions is
the relationship that organizations have with the communities they serve. Nonprofit hospitals and health systems are created and exist principally to serve communities by providing services to those in need. The board, in concert with the
organization's management team, acts to ensure that the organization's resources
are employed prudently. After all, board holds these resources in trust for the
community and other stakeholders. Being accountable to this trust is at the core
of the mission of healthcare organizations. The challenge is that communities
typically have not established formal requirements or expectations for nonprofit
health organizations. Hence, solid mechanisms or procedures typically are not
in place to demonstrate the healthcare organization's accountability to the community. This contrasts noticeably with the formal requirements or expectations of
regulatory agencies, accrediting bodies, payers, and other organizational entities
to which nonprofit hospitals and systems are accountable. The increasing need for
protocols to respond to the communities or populations served by healthcare organizations underscores the importance of participative decision-making aligned
with the concept of *accountability* in the process component of the ethics paradigm. The board's approach to participative decision-making is indispensable for
an organization's performance.[54] In the *Governance Structure Report*, 63 percent

of board members and 57 percent of CEOs indicated that boards were actively engaged in decision-making processes, with the board and the management team being willing to challenge each other constructively.[55]

Within this context of organizational oversight in healthcare institutions, the process component of the ethics paradigm focuses on the concept of *accountability*, reflecting the leitmotif *how we function*. This concept emphasizes decision-making via participative deliberation in the healthcare organization. Here, the ethics paradigm organizes core features of effective governance from the *Governance Structure Report* to highlight hallmarks of governance ethics and their associated moral imperatives.

The concept of *accountability* focuses on *how the board functions*, thereby highlighting board evaluation and succession planning as hallmarks of governance ethics. In turn, these hallmarks denote associated moral imperatives: board evaluation denotes a moral imperative regarding board oversight of fair evaluation processes; and succession planning denotes a moral imperative concerning board oversight of system planning and continuous updating. These are discussed in subsequent sections.

Board evaluation: process-related governance ethics hallmark

Board evaluation is the first hallmark of governance ethics regarding the process component of the ethics paradigm. The concept of *accountability* in the ethics paradigm highlights board evaluation as a governance ethics hallmark by drawing attention to *how we function* (as a board). In turn, this hallmark denotes an associated moral imperative regarding board oversight of fair evaluation processes.

Moral imperative: board oversight of fair evaluation processes

To undertake an effective evaluation process requires clear-mindedness regarding the different levels of accountability that boards must honor. As social institutions chartered to serve the needs of their patients and communities, the boards of non-profit health systems have multiple fiduciary duties. Boards have a responsibility to understand these accountabilities and ensure they are met. There are three broad categories of these accountabilities that hospital and health system boards must ensure are fulfilled.[56]

One category includes accountabilities that are mandated by parties with financial, ownership, and/or regulatory authority. These parties (some in the private sector, some governmental) have the power to specify requirements and standards that healthcare organizations must meet. These parties must apply sanctions if they fail to do so. One form of mandated accountability involves healthcare institutions with a parent organization that holds ultimate legal control. For instance, in many faith-based health systems, the boards of local or "market-based" organizations are accountable to and controlled by a parent system, which, in turn, may be directly accountable to a sponsoring body such as a religious congregation or federation. Other examples of parties to whom hospitals and health systems have mandated accountability include the following: the Center for Medicare and Medicaid Services (CMS) establishes "Conditions for Participation" in the Medicare program and payment rules; state agencies engage licensure and regulatory authority; and the IRS has the authority to prescribe requirements that nonprofit hospitals and systems must meet for tax-exempt status. Revisions made in 2007 to the IRS Form 990, "Return of Organizations Exempt from Income Tax," and related schedules have expanded the information that must be submitted by nonprofit healthcare institutions and now is publicly available.[57]

Another category of accountabilities, while important and often essential, includes those that are voluntary in nature. For example, to be accredited by the Joint Commission (until 2007 known as the Joint Commission on Accreditation of Healthcare Organizations), hospitals must meet the prescribed requirements and standards, provide extensive information, and submit to review processes, all of which can consume substantial resources. However, the vast majority of nonprofit hospitals conclude that the benefits of accreditation outweigh the costs and, therefore, elect to be accountable to the accrediting body for meeting its requirements. Similarly, hospitals that want to offer medical residencies, advanced nursing certification, and/or other formal educational programs must accept accountability to the various bodies that review and certify these programs. In the healthcare field, there are numerous voluntary programs of this nature, each with its own requirements, standards, and accountability protocols.[58]

A further category of board accountabilities deals with relationships with the communities served. Nonprofit health systems exist primarily to serve communities. Hence, governing boards, along with management, have a stewardship role to address these healthcare needs.[59]

For nonprofit hospitals and health systems, these categories of accountability involve the following: (1) complying with many sets of requirements and standards, often duplicative and sometimes contradictory; (2) submitting large amounts of information to numerous external parties; and (3) dealing with formal sanctions, penalties, and/or criticism when any of these parties believe the hospital or health system has not fully met their requirements or standards. Further, these accountabilities are often fulfilled separately without any coordinating mechanism that would provide a clear picture of the full range of accountabilities and their influence on healthcare cost and quality or impact on community needs. Few hospital or health system boards have ready access to a complete list of the external parties to whom the organization they govern has some form of accountability, much less a solid understanding of the multiplicity of requirements those parties expect the organization to meet. Boards must fulfill their responsibility for the communities their healthcare organizations serve. Hence, boards need to understand the range of voluntary accountabilities and requirements their organizations have agreed to meet. This board responsibility is to ensure that organizational resources are being allocated and used prudently and effectively in a manner that supports the healthcare mission of their organizations.[60]

However, there must be fair evaluation processes. The concept of *accountability* in the ethics paradigm emphasizes the importance of board evaluation. There have been notable achievements resulting from board evaluations.[61] A national study of public companies in 2011 reported 91 percent of companies regularly conduct full board evaluations with 83 percent undertaking evaluations of board committees.[62] Also, a survey of 81 health systems reported that 92 percent of the system boards had a formal evaluation process of performance at least every two years.[63] There remain significant challenges. A board can claim compliance by merely using a formulaic checklist that adopts general assessment processes that are not organization specific. But such compliance with generic evaluation expectations is unlikely to improve its effectiveness significantly. Rather, assessment processes need to emphasize an ongoing evaluation of board performance. This performance includes the board's commitment to specific action or change resulting from the process. In other words, an ongoing objective evaluation must be combined with follow-up actions to improve board performance.[64]

The *Governance Structure Report* emphasizes these points. In the report, around 86 percent of the boards conduct some formal board evaluation every year or every two years. However, the results were lower concerning the more stringent standard of implementing follow-up action after formal board evaluation. Only 52 percent of the board members and CEOs reported that their board evaluations resulted in actions that substantially changed the board. Approximately 32 percent reported the board evaluations did not result in substantial changes and the others being unsure. Moreover, only 30 percent of system leaders (boards and CEOs) considered their current board evaluation processes to be "excellent," with 54 percent indicating the evaluation process in place currently was "somewhat beneficial."[65] The *Governance Structure Report* emphasizes that effective governance requires a thorough assessment of board evaluation processes and practices. Such a rigorous approach will improve the effectiveness of boards, board committees, and board leadership.[66] This emphasis upon board evaluation reflects the focus on *accountability* in the process component of the ethics paradigm.

A required board duty is to have an objective evaluation of the CEO's performance. This process includes making the original appointment and establishing performance expectations in advance with clearly defined goals. For example, a national survey of public companies reported that 70 percent of boards collaborate with their CEOs to establish both financial and non-financial goals. Studies of hospital and health system boards report that most boards use a formal process for evaluating CEO performance.[67] However, a study by the American Hospital Association's Center for Healthcare Governance had more gloomy news. The study indicates that 82 percent of CEOs did not receive at their appointment clear performance expectations, and 66 percent reported that no formal evaluation process occurred at the end of the first year.[68] This study illustrates why there are serious concerns about the rigor and efficacy of CEO evaluation.[69]

In contrast, the *Governance Structure Report* mentions signs of effectiveness that can be a model for others. This report found that boards regularly evaluated their CEO's performance in relation to pre-established criteria. And 75 percent of system leaders (boards and CEOs) reported that the board CEO evaluation process produced clear performance expectations and assessed CEO performance fairly. Interestingly, the report also mentioned that for 50 percent of the systems the board compensation committee led the evaluation process, with the board chair either serving on this committee or working closely with it in the evaluation process.[70]

Succession planning: process-related governance ethics hallmark

Succession planning is the second hallmark of governance ethics regarding the process component of the ethics paradigm. The concept of *accountability* in the ethics paradigm highlights succession planning as a governance ethics hallmark by drawing attention to *how we function* (as a board). In turn, this hallmark denotes an associated moral imperative regarding board oversight of system planning and continuous updating. Succession planning is construed as comprising the board, board leadership positions, and senior management positions including clinical positions.

Moral imperative: board oversight of system planning and continuous updating

On the one hand, effective succession planning needs to be cognizant of the crucial relation between system-level and local planning. Board accountability requires the allocation of roles, responsibility, and authority to local units or organizations in the health system: this distribution between system-level and local leadership is crucial for effective governance.[71] In the *Governance Structure Report*, approximately 85 percent of the systems had adopted an organizational model with overall governance assigned to a system-level board and local boards with limited decision-making authority. All these systems have a board document that allocated governance responsibility and decision-making authority between the system and local units. Nearly all the boards and CEOs agreed that such an allocation requires continuous efforts to improve accountability. For example, if hospital-level boards are replaced with regional boards, the traditional linkages hospital boards had with their communities can be diminished. As a result, there could be potential communications and accountability issues. However, typically the accountability of boards (including accountability mechanisms) to the communities served are not expressed or codified in detail. This suggests a significant arena for further governance effectiveness.[72]

On the other hand, effective succession planning at the system and local levels needs to have continuous updating. This involves defining leadership needs (especially as they evolve to fit the internal and external environmental changes), assessing current talent, implementing a leadership development program, and systematic planning to identify individuals for future leadership roles. Not surprisingly, major organizations dedicate considerable scrutiny to leadership succession planning as a crucial component of effective governance.[73] However, there are serious issues.[74] For example, in 2011 the National Association of Corporate Directors undertook a survey of public companies, reporting that only one-third had a formal CEO succession plan.[75] Also in 2011, a survey of CEOs reported only 44 percent of hospitals with a succession plan for their CEO.[76] Also, in 2011 a study by the Governance Institute identified only 41 percent of participating hospitals and health systems have an explicit process for board leadership succession planning for board officers and committee chairs.[77] In the *Governance Structure Report*, 43 percent of the systems have some form of succession planning for board leadership and senior management positions including the CEO. Undoubtedly, succession planning in the healthcare field needs improvement. The *Governance Structure Report* indicates that most CEOs and board leaders recognize that developing and sustaining succession plans in a systematic manner is indispensable for effective governance. Leadership succession planning for boards, board leadership, and senior management should be a system-wide strategic priority.[78]

In sum, the process component of the ethics paradigm highlights board evaluation and succession planning as hallmarks of governance ethics. By focusing on *accountability* in the ethics paradigm, these hallmarks denote associated moral imperatives: board evaluation denotes a moral imperative regarding board oversight of fair evaluation processes; and succession planning denotes a moral imperative concerning board oversight of system planning and continuous updating. The next section considers the practice component of the ethics paradigm that focuses on the concept of *quality* to highlight practice-related hallmarks of governance ethics.

Context of practice-related governance ethics hallmarks

The concept of *quality* in the ethics paradigm (reflecting *what we do*) emphasizes the importance of best practices for standards of conduct. This focus on *quality* requires boards to be attentive to organizational culture as the context for assessing their responsibilities. For example, just as healthy organizational culture requires trust and confidence between the CEO and the board,[79] that same culture can reinvigorate the public's trust. This relationship between governance oversight and improved hospital performance is emerging as an internationally prominent issue.[80]

Organizational culture reflects a pattern of beliefs and traditions that have shaped practices and prevail when the board convenes to carry out its duties.[81] Board culture distinguishes an effective board from an ineffective board. For example, the unfortunate but well-known case of Enron indicates the damage of a passive management-driven board culture with low expectations and standards. This passive environment fails to ask hard questions or detect egregious irregularities or unethical conduct.[82] Another example of the negative impact that a passive board culture can have on an organization is the fallout over falsified emission standards in cars manufactured by different companies.[83]

Organizational culture provides the crucial context for an organization's success.[84] A healthy culture, nurtured by board practices, will result in an ethical climate or ethical tone that integrates ethics across the organization.[85] This ethical climate should be just and fair, requiring the organizational leadership's engagement.[86] This culture also should integrate core values with organizational well-being.[87] Organizational culture has a significant impact on strengthening ethical behavior.[88] That is, organizational culture is necessarily grounded in ethics: boards need to ensure that an ethical climate permeates the organization. Board improvement of the ethical culture requires the board's support of an effective ethics program across the entire organization. To cultivate this culture also requires the board to openly discuss ethics and the use of ethics resources across the organization. In this manner, as the board promotes organizational culture it will also nurture an ethics-driven atmosphere throughout the organization.[89] In turn, this creates a pervasive caring tone.[90]

Organizational culture provides the context for effective performance through best practices for standards of conduct.[91] To nurture a healthy culture there need to be a board commitment to high-performance standards and a willingness to take decisive action.[92] Of course, each board is responsible for creating its own culture. The *Governance Structure Report* emphasizes that boards should undertake an objective appraisal to determine practical steps to improve their organizational culture as a crucial part of board performance.[93]

Within this context of organizational culture, the practice component of the ethics paradigm focuses on the concept of *quality*, reflecting the leitmotif *what we do*. This concept emphasizes best practices for standards of conduct. Here, the ethics paradigm organizes core features of effective governance from the *Governance Structure Report* to highlight hallmarks of governance ethics and their associated moral imperatives.

The concept of *quality* focuses on what boards do, thereby highlighting leadership collaboration and system-wide strategy as hallmarks of governance ethics. In turn, these hallmarks denote associated moral imperatives: board oversight of leadership collaboration denotes a moral imperative regarding oversight of working relationships; and board oversight of system-wide strategy denotes a moral imperative concerning oversight of transformational change and strategic planning. These are discussed in the following sections.

Leadership collaboration: practice-related governance ethics hallmark

Leadership collaboration is the first hallmark of governance ethics regarding the practice component of the ethics paradigm. This hallmark includes the respective responsibilities of the CEO and the board. Also, the hallmark includes executive support for organizational culture in a trust based reciprocal relationship. The concept of *quality* in the ethics paradigm highlights leadership collaboration as a governance ethics hallmark by drawing attention to *what we do* (as a board). In turn, this hallmark denotes an associated moral imperative regarding board oversight of working relationships.

Moral imperative: board oversight of working relationships

On the one hand, a robust organizational culture indicates the importance of leadership collaboration between the CEO and the board that contributes to other leadership roles in the organization. This entails, according to the *Governance Structure Report*, having a CEO with exceptional leadership and management skills who works in tandem with board leadership. That is, there must be a mutual understanding about the respective roles of governance and management, especially to develop excellent board-management relations.[94] Formal written descriptions of the respective duties of the CEO and the board chair help immensely. These should be approved by the board and updated regularly. In the *Governance Structure Report*, 100 percent of the systems had formal, written descriptions (adopted by the board) of the CEOs position, and 85 percent of the boards had adopted formal position descriptions for the board chair. Also, 91 percent of board members and 86 percent of CEOs indicated there was solid agreement among board members of the distinctions between the CEO's role and the board chair's role. Furthermore, the same number indicated an excellent relationship between the CEO and the board chair.[95]

On the other hand, CEOs should provide strong support for good working relationships regarding governance, manifested directly in the caliber of staff support provided for the board. How boards are supported by senior staff provides an interesting insight into the CEOs commitment to strong governance by cultivating a healthy board culture. In the *Governance Structure Report*, 91 percent of the boards and 100 percent of the CEOs reported that standing committees of the board have senior staff support.[96] A high level of CEO support is needed not only for the role of governance in general but also to build trust-based board-CEO relationships. Again, in the *Governance Structure Report* nearly all board members indicated CEO support as being consistently high. The report indicated 90 percent of the boards having working relationships with the CEO as being excellent, with the following insights concerning board culture. Nearly all the boards and CEOs considered their boards as demonstrating a commitment to their system's mission (93 percent) and honoring their conflict of interest and confidentiality policies (board members, 93 percent; CEOs, 86 percent). The report indicated 75 percent of board members and 71 percent of CEOs perceived an atmosphere of mutual trust among board members. Moreover, 74 percent of board members and 93 percent of CEOs reported that the board closely tracks the health system's clinical and financial performance taking appropriate action when performance does not meet targets. However, only 57 percent reported board leadership holding board members to high standards of performance, and around 50 percent indicated that robust engagement and respectful disagreement was encouraged.[97] Clearly, these are issues that warrant concerted board attention.

System-wide strategy: practice-related governance ethics hallmark

System-wide strategy is the second hallmark of governance ethics regarding the practice component of the ethics paradigm. System-wide strategy includes

approaches that result in continuous performance improvement across the organization. The concept of *quality* in the ethics paradigm highlights system-wide
strategy as a governance ethics hallmark by drawing attention to what we do (as
a board). In turn, this hallmark denotes an associated moral imperative regarding
board oversight of transformational change and strategic planning.

Moral imperative: board oversight of transformational change and strategic planning

On the one hand, focusing upon transformational change as a key characteristic of system-wide strategy has been a required aspect of corporate governance
theory.[98] Of course, transformational change must be consistent with an organization's mission.[99] Effective boards focus careful attention on system-wide
strategies and key priorities. Focusing on possibilities that will generate transformational change will require the use of board time and effort wisely. The *Governance Structure Report* indicates that the way board meetings are organized and
how time is allocated, such as on transformational matters, are indicative of board
effectiveness.[100] Moreover, boards with broader expertise have been correlated
with responding better not only to the complex environment that hospitals face
but also to their strategic focus.[101] Globally, the transformational role of the board
will significantly influence its capability for strategic action.[102]

On the other hand, transformational change cannot occur without strategic
planning. Boards are often criticized for concentrating on short-term issues such
as current operating performance and not on strategic issues confronting the
organization.[103] Surveys of boards in public companies and nonprofit organizations often rank strategic planning and oversight as one of the top priorities of the
board.[104] Recent research indicates that the shift of boards to strategic approaches
is not occurring sufficiently.[105] Healthcare organizations, especially via their
boards, should be accountable with appropriate transparency to the communities
they are chartered to serve.[106] The *Governance Structure Report* is attentive to the
time and energy that boards devote to strategic issues. The effectiveness of the
changes should be evaluated with a commitment to best practices for continual
quality improvement. Some examples of mechanisms to improve the strategic
focus of the board include the following: using a consent agenda format for board
meetings; having board retreats; dedicating time at every board meeting to a specific challenge concerning the organization's future direction; and placing board
discussion on strategic issues as the first segment in every board meeting.[107]

Furthermore, strategic planning is a crucial aspect of effective governance.
In the *Governance Structure Report*, all the health system boards were engaged
in a process of reforming board practices to accelerate a shift to a strategic focus
addressing system-wide concerns. The combined estimate of boards and CEOs
about the amount of board time dedicated to strategic thinking and planning at the
time of this study varied in different health systems from a low of 15 percent to
a high of 53 percent with a mean estimate of 30 percent. Of course, boards must
provide oversight of system operations and performance. They need to increase
their engagement with system-wide strategy with related strategic challenges

and opportunities. As boards dedicate more time and energy to strategic changes (which will be crucial for organizational survival and success), there will be an increased need for forthright assessment regarding continuous quality improvement of board performance. For example, there should be a standing board committee with oversight responsibility for system-wide policies and programs on priorities in the realm of population health.[108] Also, the *Governance Structure Report* indicated that only one-third of boards and CEOs in the 14 systems felt their system board meetings were well organized in a consistent manner and strategically focused. However, all these health systems expressed commitment to increase energy and time devoted to strategic issues.[109]

In sum, the practice component of the ethics paradigm highlights leadership collaboration and system-wide strategy as hallmarks of governance ethics. By focusing on *quality* in the ethics paradigm, these hallmarks denote associated moral imperatives: leadership collaboration denotes a moral imperative regarding board oversight of working relationships; and system-wide strategy denotes a moral imperative concerning board oversight of transformational change and strategic planning.

Conclusion

The chapter has highlighted hallmarks of governance ethics with associated moral imperatives regarding governance structure of boards in healthcare organizations. The contribution of the ethics paradigm can be summarized in this manner.

First, in the context of the challenging healthcare environment, the foundation component of the ethics paradigm focuses on stewardship to enhance an organization's mission in healthcare as crucial for effective governance. This component deals with the *identity* of an organization, reflecting the leitmotif *who we are*, thereby highlighting board competence and board role as hallmarks of governance ethics. In turn, these hallmarks denote associated moral imperatives: board competence denotes a moral imperative regarding board oversight of Term limits and board composition; and board role denotes a moral imperative concerning board oversight of defined responsibilities and board effectiveness.

Second, in the context of organizational oversight in healthcare institutions, the process component of the ethics paradigm focuses upon decision-making to encourage participative deliberation in organizations. This component addresses the *accountability* of the organization, reflecting the leitmotif *how we function*, thereby highlighting board evaluation and succession planning as hallmarks of governance. In turn, these hallmarks denote associated moral imperatives: board evaluation denotes a moral imperative regarding board oversight of fair evaluation processes; and succession planning denotes a moral imperative concerning board oversight of system planning and continuous updating.

Third, in the context of organizational culture in healthcare, the practice component of the ethics paradigm focuses on best practices to develop standards of conduct. This component engages *quality* in an organization, reflecting the leitmotif *what we do*, thereby identifying leadership collaboration and system-wide strategy as hallmarks of governance ethics. In turn, these hallmarks denote associated moral imperatives: leadership collaboration denotes a moral imperative regarding board oversight of working relationships; and system-wide strategy denotes a moral imperative concerning board oversight of transformational change and strategic planning.

This chapter has applied the ethics paradigm to highlight hallmarks of governance ethics regarding board structure, denoting associated moral imperatives. The next chapter adopts the same approach to discuss hallmarks of governance ethics concerning community benefit.

Notes

1 L. Prybil, et al., *Governance in Large Nonprofit Health Systems: Current Profile and Emerging Patterns* (Lexington, KY: Commonwealth Center for Governance Studies, Inc., 2012). Referred to in this book as the *Governance Structure Report*.

2 L. Prybil, et al., *Governance in High-Performing Community Health Systems: A Report on Trustee and CEO Views* (Chicago, IL: Grant Thornton LLP, 2009). Referred to in this book as the *Community Health Systems Report*.

3 L. Prybil, et al. *Improving Community Health Through Hospital–Public Health Collaboration. Insights and Lessons Learned from Successful Partnerships* (Lexington, KY: Commonwealth Center for Governance Studies, Inc., 2014). Referred to in this book as the *Community Health Report*.

4 L. Prybil, *The Leadership Role of Nonprofit Health Systems in Improving Community Health* (Chicago, IL: American Hospital Association, Advances in Healthcare Governance Series, 2017). Referred to in this book as the *Leadership Report*.

5 Previous research on governance in nonprofit hospitals and community health systems contributed to the design of this study. For previous research data, see: L. Prybil, et al., *Governance in High-Performing Organizations: A Comparative Study of Governing Boards in Not-for-Profit Hospitals* (Chicago, IL: Health Research and Educational Trust, 2005); L. Prybil, et al., *Governance in Nonprofit Community Health Systems: An Initial Report on CEO Perspectives* (Chicago, IL: Grant Thornton LLP, 2008); L. Prybil, et al., *Governance in High-Performing Community Health Systems* (Chicago, IL: Grant Thornton LLP, 2009).

6 L. Prybil et al., *The Evolving Accountability of Nonprofit Health System Boards* (Chicago, IL: AHA Center for Healthcare Governance, 2013).

7 Independent Sector, *Principles for Good Governance and Ethical Practice: A Guide for Charities and Foundations* (Washington, DC: Independent Sector, 2015), Preamble.

8 The Institute of Medicine, L. Olsen, D. Aisner, J. M. McGinnis, eds., *The Learning Healthcare System: Workshop Summary* (Washington, DC: National Academies Press, 2007); E. M. Largent, S. Joffe, F. G. Miller, "Can Research and Care Be Ethically Integrated?" *Hastings Center Report* 41 (4) (2011): 37–46.

9 R. R. Faden, T. L. Beauchamp, N. E. Kass, "Learning Healthcare Systems and Justice," *Hastings Center Report* 41 (4) (2011): 3.

10 F. D. Squazzo, "Today's Leader: Committed to Core Values," *Healthcare Executive* 25 (6) (2010): 8–18.

11 See: A. R. Bennett, "Accountable Care Organizations," *Journal of Healthcare Management* 57 (4) (2012): 244–254; B. Cliff, "Patient-Centered Care: The Role of Healthcare Leadership," *The Journal of Healthcare Management* 57 (6) (2012): 381–383; M. K. Totten, "Transforming Healthcare: The Board's Role," *Healthcare Executive* 27 (1) (2012): 74–77; S. Frampton, P. Charmel, eds., *Putting Patients First: Best Practices in Patient Centered Care*, 2nd ed. (San Francisco, CA: Jossey-Bass, 2009).

12 See: American Hospital Association, *Blue Ribbon Panel Report: Learnings on Governance from Partnerships that Improve Community Health* (Chicago, IL: American Hospital Association, 2016); American Hospital Association, Center for Healthcare Governance, *Blue Ribbon Panel Report: Governance Practices in an Era of Healthcare Transformation* (Chicago, IL: American Hospital Association, 2012).

13 M. A. Hall, "A Corporate Ethics of 'Care' in Healthcare," *Seattle Journal for Social Justice* 3 (1) (2004): 417–428.

14 The American Hospital Association, *2019 National Health Care Governance Survey Report* (Washington, DC: Center for Healthcare Governance, 2019).

15 See: The Center for Healthcare Governance, *Blue Ribbon Panel on Healthcare Governance, Building an Exceptional Board: Effective Practices for Healthcare Governance* (Chicago, IL: Center for Healthcare Governance, 2007); Center for Healthcare Governance, *Competency-Based Governance: A Foundation for Board and Organizational Effectiveness* (Chicago, IL: Center for Healthcare Governance, 2009); Center for Healthcare Governance, "Board Member Evaluation Incorporates Core Competencies," *Healthcare Executive* 25 (5) (2010): 70–71.

16 *Governance Structure Report*, 6, 9–12.

17 D. Anning, F. Entin, M. Totten, *The Guide to Good Governance for Hospital Boards* (Chicago, IL: Center for Healthcare Governance, 2010), 91.

18 *Governance Structure Report*, 6.

19 The Internal Revenue Service, "Governance and Related Topics: 501(c)(3) Organizations," (February 4, 2008), 2–3, at www.irs.gov/pub/irs-tege/governance_practices.pdf.

20 *Governance Structure Report*, 7–8.

21 The Center for Healthcare Governance, *Blue Ribbon Panel on Healthcare Governance, Building an Exceptional Board: Effective Practices for Healthcare Governance* (Chicago, IL: Center for Healthcare Governance, 2007), 13. One study recommends seven voting board members devoting at least two days a month beyond regular board meeting; see: R. Pozen, "The Case for Professional Boards," *Harvard Business Review* 88 (2010): 52.

22 Spencer Stuart, "Vision Statement. Corporate Boards: Now and Then," *Harvard Business Review* 89 (2011): 39.

23 See: H. Kang, M. Cheng, S. J. Gray, "Corporate Governance and Board Composition: Diversity and Independence of Australian Boards," *Corporate Governance: An International Review* 15 (2) (2007): 194–207; J. A. Alexander, S. Y. Lee, "Does Governance Matter? Board Configuration and Performance in Non-Profit Hospitals," *The Milbank Quarterly* 84 (4) (2006): 733–758.

24 C. Bart, "An Empirical Examination of the Content and Composition of Board Charters," *International Journal of Business Governance and Ethics* 2 (3/4) (2006): 198–216.

25 See: M. B. Leslie, "The Wisdom of Crowds? Groupthink and Nonprofit Governance," *Florida Law Review* 62 (2010): 1179–1226; A. Page, "Unconscious Bias and the Limits of Director Independence," *University of Illinois Law Review* 1 (2009): 237–294; M. A. O'Connor, "The Enron Board: The Perils of Groupthink," *University of Cincinnati Law Review* 71 (2003): 1233–1320; S. M. Brainbridge, "Why a Board? Group Decisionmaking in Corporate Governance," *Vanderbilt Law Review* 55 (1) (2002): 1–55.

26 *Governance Structure Report*, 6, 9–10. Also see: Independent Sector, *Principles for Good Governance and Ethical Practice: A Guide for Charities and Foundations* (Washington, DC: Independent Sector, 2015). The IRS recommends a majority of independent board members, see the IRS Revenue Ruling 69–545 (1969–2 C.B. 117).

27 *Governance Structure Report*, 6, 10–12. Also see: T. C. Dolan, "Increasing Diversity in Governance and Management," *Journal of Healthcare Management* 58 (2) (2013): 84–86; T. Miller, M. Triana, "Demographic Diversity in the Boardroom: Mediators of the Board Diversity – Firm Performance Relationship," *Journal of Management*

Studies 46 (5) (2009): 755–786; L. L. Dallas, "The New Managerialism and Diversity on Corporate Boards of Directors," *Tulane Law Review* 76 (2002): 1363–1391.

28 See: P. B. Hofmann, "Addressing Racial and Ethnic Disparities in Healthcare," *Healthcare Executive* 25 (5) (2010): 46–50; P. A. Weil, "A Racial/Ethnic Comparison of Career Attainments in Healthcare Management," *Healthcare Executive* 24 (6) (2009): 22–31.

29 A coalition of healthcare associations is involved in this initiative, Equity of Care, including the American Association of Medical Colleges, the American College of Healthcare Executives, the American Hospital Association, and the Catholic Health Association. See: www.equityofcare.org.

30 *Governance Structure Report*, 6, 10–12.

31 *Governance Structure Report*, 6, 10–12.

32 *Governance Structure Report*, 6, 12–13. Also see: L. Prybil et al., *Governance in High-Performing Community Health Systems* (Chicago, IL: Grant Thornton LLP, 2009), 8; J. Oliva, M. Totten, *A Seat at the Power Table: The Physician's Role on the Hospital Board* (Chicago, IL: Center for Healthcare Governance, 2007), 3; The Governance Institute, *Dynamic Governance: An Analysis of Board Structure and Practices in a Shifting Industry* (San Diego, CA: The Governance Institute, 2011), 5.

33 M. A. Rodwin, *Conflicts of Interest and the Future of Medicine* (New York: Oxford University Press, 2011).

34 R. McSherry, P. Pearce, *Clinical Governance. A Guide to Implementation for Healthcare Professionals*, 2nd ed. (London: Blackwell Publishing, 2007).

35 See: K. E. Mack, L. J. Voyten, R. V. Hausrod, "The Search for Quality and Outcomes: Strategic Physician Alignment is Key to Improving Care While Reducing Costs," *Healthcare Executive* 28 (3) (2013): 86–88.

36 Institute of Medicine, *The Future of Nursing: Leading Change, Advancing Health* (Washington, DC: The National Academies Press, 2011).

37 L. Prybil, et al., "Building the Case for Including Nurse Leaders on Healthcare Organization Boards," *Nursing Economics$* 37 (4) (July 2019): 169–197; L. Prybil, et al., "Involving Nurse Leaders in Governance Roles," *BoardRoom Press* 30 (4) (2019): 4 and 14; L. Sundean, K. White, L. Thompson, L. Prybil. 2019. "Governance Education for Nurses: Preparing Nurses for the Future," *Journal of Professional Nursing* 35 (Sept–Oct, 2019): 346–352.

38 L. Prybil, "Nurses in Healthcare Governance: Is the Picture Changing?" *Journal of Nursing Care Quality* 28 (2012): 103–107; C. M. Khoury, et al., "Nursing Leadership from Bedside to Boardroom: A Gallup National Survey of Opinion Leaders," *Journal of Nursing Administration* 41 (7–8) (2011): 299–305; J. Greene, "A New Voice at the Table," *Trustee* 65 (3) (2012): 8–12.

39 See: L. Prybil, "Nursing Engagement in Governing Health Care Organizations: Past, Present, and Future," *Journal of Nursing Care Quality* 31 (4) (2016): 299–303; L. Prybil, et al., "Nurses on Boards: the Time has Come," *Nurse Leader* 12 (4) (2014): 48–52; L. Prybil, "Nurses in Health Care Governance: Is the Picture Changing?" *Journal of Nursing Care Quality* 28 (2) (2103): 103–107; L. Prybil, "Engaging Nurses in Governing Hospitals and Health Systems," *Journal of Nursing Care Quality* 24 (1) (2009): 5–9; L. Prybil, "Nursing Involvement in Hospital Governance," *Journal of Nursing Care Quality* 22 (1) (2007): 1–3; M. Szekendi, L. Prybil, et al., "Governance Practices and Performance in U.S. Academic Medical Centers," *American Journal of Medical Quality* 30 (6) (2015): 520–525.

40 *Governance Structure Report*, 6, 14.

41 See: American Hospital Association, *2019 National Health Care Governance Survey Report* (Washington, DC: Center for Healthcare Governance, 2019); Governance Institute, *2017 Governance Institute Biennial Survey Shows Positive Governance Evolution* (San Diego, CA: The Governance Institute, 2017).

42 See: F. Entin, J. Anderson, K. O'Brien, *The Board's Fiduciary Role: Legal Responsibilities of Healthcare Governing Boards* (Chicago, IL: The Center for Healthcare

Governance, 2006); L. Prybil, "A Perspective on Local-Level Governance in Multi-Unit Systems," *Hospital and Health Services Administration* 36 (1) (1991): 3–12.

43 D. Culica, E. Prezio, "Hospital Board Infrastructure and Functions: The Role of Governance in Financial Performance," *International Journal of Environmental Research and Public Health* 6 (3) (2009): 862–873.

44 See: J. D. Blum, "Great Boards Need Leaders, Not Followers. Turn Good Boards into High Performers," *Healthcare Executive* 25 (2010): 74–76; J. D. Blum, "The Quagmire of Hospital Governance," *Journal of Legal Medicine* 31 (2010): 35–57, esp. 49–51.

45 Center for Healthcare Governance, *Building an Exceptional Board: Effective Practices for Healthcare Governance* (Chicago, IL: Center for Healthcare Governance, 2007) 22–23.

46 See: L. L. Walker, "The Supporting Cast. Strong, Focused Committees and Task Forces are Essential to Overall Governance Excellence," *Trustee* 65 (2012): 67; B. Bader, E. Zablocki, "Evaluating and Improving Board Committees," *Great Boards* VIII (2) (2008): 1–19.

47 *Governance Structure Report*, 14–15.

48 See: L. Prybil et al., *Governance in High-Performing Community Health Systems* (Chicago, IL: Grant Thornton LLP, 2009), 12–13; G. Magill, L. Prybil, "Board Oversight of Community Benefit: A Moral Imperative," *Kennedy Institute of Ethics Journal* 21 (1) (2011): 38–40.

49 *Governance Structure Report*, 16. Also see: R. LeBlanc, ed., *The Handbook of Board Governance: Public, Private, and Not-for-Profit Board Members* (Wiley, 2016); Grant Thornton, *2009 National Board Governance Survey for Not-for-Profit Organizations* (Chicago, IL: Grant Thornton, LLP, 2009), 2.

50 *Governance Structure Report*, 6, 14–15.

51 *Governance Structure Report*, 17.

52 See: L. B. Miller, *Boards Under Fire: Are Not-for-Profit Institutions Being Held to a New Standard of Accountability* (Washington, DC: Volunteer Trustee Foundation and the Governance Institute, 2001); and L. A. Bebchuk, "The Case for Increasing Shareholder Power," *Harvard Law Review* 118 (3) (2005): 835–914.

53 N. M. Kane, et al., "The Internal Processes and Behavioral Dynamics of Hospital Boards: An Exploration of Differences between High- and Low-Performing Hospitals," *Healthcare Management Review* 34 (1) (2009): 80–91.

54 M. Useem, "How Well-Run Boards Make Decisions," *Harvard Business Review* 84 (11) (2006): 130–138.

55 *Governance Structure Report*, 38–39.

56 L. Prybil et al., *The Evolving Accountability of Nonprofit Health System Boards* (Chicago, IL: AHA Center for Healthcare Governance, 2013), section on "Categories of Board Accountabilities," 7–9.

57 L. Prybil, R. Killian, "Community Benefit Needs Board Oversight," *Health Progress* 94 (July–August, 2013): 90–94.

58 L. Prybil, et al., *The Evolving Accountability of Nonprofit Health System Boards*. Monograph Series (Chicago, IL: AHA Center for Healthcare Governance, 2013), 8.

59 L. Prybil, et al., *The Evolving Accountability of Nonprofit Health System Boards*. Monograph Series (Chicago, IL: AHA Center for Healthcare Governance, 2013(, 8.

60 See: L. Prybil, R. Killian, "Community Benefit Needs Board Oversight," *Health Progress* 94 (July–August, 2013): 90–94; L. Prybil, et al., *The Evolving Accountability of Nonprofit Health System Boards*. Monograph Series (Chicago, IL: AHA Center for Healthcare Governance, 2013), 8–9.

61 D. A. Nadler, B. A. Behan, M. B. Nadler, eds., *Building Better Boards: A Blueprint for Effective Governance* (San Francisco, CA: Jossey-Bass, 2006).

62 National Association of Corporate Directors, *NACD Public Company Governance Survey* (Washington, DC: National Association of Corporate Directors, 2011), 15.

63 The Governance Institute, *Dynamic Governance: An Analysis of Board Structure and Practices in a Shifting Industry* (San Diego, CA: The Governance Institute, 2011), 98.

64 See: Alliance for Advancing Nonprofit Healthcare, *Great Governance. A Practical Guide for Busy Board Leaders and Executives of Nonprofit Healthcare Organizations* (Washington, DC: Alliance for Advancing Nonprofit Healthcare, 2011), 9; J. Swiecicki, "Trends in Board Performance," *Trustee* 64 (4) (2011): 24–27.

65 *Governance Structure Report*, 22–24.

66 *Governance Structure Report*, 56.

67 See: National Association of Corporate Directors, *NACD Public Company Governance Survey* (Washington, DC: National Association of Corporate Directors, 2011), 79; The Governance Institute, *Dynamic Governance: An Analysis of Board Structure and Practices in a Shifting Industry* (San Diego, CA: The Governance Institute, 2011), 99.

68 K. R. Cohen, *Best Practices for Developing Effective and Enduring Board/CEO Relationships* (Chicago, IL: Center for Healthcare Governance, 2008), 12.

69 L. Prybil, W. Murray, T. Cotter, E. Bryant, "Transforming CEO Evaluation in a Multi-Unit Organization," in A. R. Kovner, et al., eds., *Evidence-Based Management in Healthcare* (Chicago, IL: Health Administration Press, 2009), 153–159.

70 *Governance Structure Report*, 18, 25–26.

71 The Center for Healthcare Governance, *Blue Ribbon Panel on Healthcare Governance, Building an Exceptional Board: Effective Practices for Healthcare Governance* (Chicago, IL: Center for Healthcare Governance, 2007), 22–24.

72 *Governance Structure Report*, 18–20, 44.

73 See: K. McDonagh, L. Prybil, L., M. Totten, "Leadership Succession Planning: A Governance Imperative," *Trustee* 66 (April, 2013): 15–18; Grant Thornton, Succeeding at Succession (Chicago, IL: Grant Thornton LLP, January 2010); Grant Thornton, *Succeeding at Succession: Establishing Your Goals and Objectives* (Chicago, IL: Grant Thornton LLP, May 2010).

74 T. C. Dolan, "The CEO Turnover and Succession Planning Crisis," *Healthcare Executive* 26 (5) (2011): 6.

75 National Association of Corporate Directors, *NACD Public Company Governance Survey* (Washington, DC: National Association of Corporate Directors, 2011), 21.

76 See: "CEO Survey, Board Role and Succession Plans," *Healthcare Executive* 25 (6) (2010): 92.

77 The Governance Institute, *Dynamic Governance: An Analysis of Board Structure and Practices in a Shifting Industry* (San Diego, CA: The Governance Institute, 2011), 99.

78 *Governance Structure Report*, 45, 57–58 (also, 6, 18, 27–28).

79 J. M. Buell, "Trust & Confidence: Does Your Board Have These in You?" *Healthcare Executive* 25 (5) (2010): 18–25.

80 S. S. Haniyeh, et al., "Does Transfer of Hospital Governance to Board of Trustees per se Lead to Improved Hospital Performance?" *International Journal of Hospital Research* 1 (2) (2012): 97–102.

81 L. Prybil, "What's Your Board's Culture," *Trustee* 61 (6) (2008): 16–24; A. Kabcenell, Creating a Culture of Excellence," *Healthcare Executive* 27 (4) (2012): 68–71.

82 On the impact of a weak board culture on the Enron case, see: B. Bader, Culture: The Critical But Elusive Component of Great Governance," in *Governance Structure and Practices: Results, Analysis, and Evaluation: 2009 Biennial Survey of Hospitals and Healthcare Systems* (San Diego, CA: The Governance Institute, 2009), 19. Also see: N. B. Rapoport, B. G. Dharan, eds., *Enron: Corporate Fiascos and Their Implications* (New York: Foundation Press, 2004).

83 Jack Ewing, "A Few Dirty Tricks: Documents Show Audi's Role in the Volkswagen Emissions Scandal," *New York Times* (July 26. 2019), at www.nytimes.com/2019/07/26/business/audi-vw-emissions-scandal.html?smid=nytcore-ios-share.

84 P. R. Knecht, K. Bass, "Why Board Culture Matters. Interpersonal and Group Dynamics Can Affect the Entire Organization," *Trustee* 65 (5) (2012): 21–24.

85 See: L. L. Dallas, "Corporate Ethics in the Healthcare Marketplace," *Seattle Journal for Social Justice* 3 (1) (2004): 213–227.

86 See: I. R. Lazarus, "On the Road to Find Out . . . Transparency and Just Culture Offer Significant Return on Investment," *Journal of Healthcare Management* 56 (4) (2012): 223–228; A. S. Frankel, et al., "Fair and Just Culture, Team Behavior, and Leadership Engagement: The Tools to Achieve High Reliability," *Health Services Research* 41 (4) (2006): 1690–1709.

87 E. M. Spencer, et al., *Organization Ethics in Healthcare* (New York: Oxford University Press, 2000), Chapter 8, "Developing a Positive Ethical Climate in the Healthcare Organization," 136–150.

88 J. A. Gilbert, "A Reflection on Everyday Ethics," *Healthcare Executive* 28 (1) (2013): 60–63, referring to the nonprofit Ethics Resource Center results from its 2011 National Business Ethics Survey spanning more than a decade.

89 W. A. Nelson, J. Donnellan, "An Executive-Driven Ethical Culture," *Healthcare Executive* 24 (6) (2009): 44–46.

90 M. A. Hall, "A Corporate Ethics of 'Care' in Healthcare," *Seattle Journal for Social Justice* 3 (1) (2004): 417–428.

91 See: N. Chambers, C. Cornforth, "The Role of Corporate Governance and Boards in Organizational Performance," in K. Walsh, G. Harvey, P. Jas, eds., *Connecting Knowledge and Performance in Public Service: From Knowing to Doing* (New York: Cambridge University Press, 2010), 99–127; C. Cornforth, ed., *The Governance of Public and Non-Profit Organizations: What Do Boards Do?* (London: Routledge, 2003).

92 See: J. Yonek, S. Hines, M. Joshi, *A Guide to Achieving High Performance in Multi-Hospital Health Systems* (Chicago, IL: Hospital Research and Educational Trust, 2010), 1; L. Prybil et al., *Governance in High-Performing Community Health Systems* (Chicago, IL: Grant Thornton LLP, 2009), 28–29.

93 *Governance Structure Report*, 37–38, 45, 58.

94 *Governance Structure Report*, 18, 21. Also see: K. R. Cohen, *Best Practices for Developing Effective and Enduing Board/CEO Relationships* (Chicago, IL: American Hospital Association, Center for Healthcare Governance, 2008), 15–18.

95 *Governance Structure Report*, 18, 21.

96 *Governance Structure Report*, 37, 40.

97 *Governance Structure Report*, 37–38, 45.

98 J. Sarra, ed., *Corporate Governance in Global Capital Markets* (British Columbia, Canada: University of British Columbia Press, 2005).

99 See: Center for Healthcare Governance, "Governance in Transformational Times," *Healthcare Executive* 28 (1) (2013): 80–83; L. Gage, *Transformational Governance: The Challenges Facing Trustees of Nonprofits and Public Hospitals* (Chicago, IL: Center for Healthcare Governance, 2012).

100 *Governance Structure Report*, 18, 35, 42–43.

101 K. Ford-Eickhoff, et al., "Hospital Boards and Hospital Strategic Focus: The Impact of Board Involvement in Strategic Decision-making," *Healthcare Management Review* 36 (2) (2011): 145–154.

102 B. Kim, M. L. Burns, J. E. Prescott, "The Strategic Role of the Board," *Corporate Governance: An International Review* 17 (6) (2009): 728–743.

103 C. Bhagat, M. Hirt, C. Kehoe, "Governance Since the Economic Crisis: McKinsey Global Survey Results," *McKinsey Quarterly* (July 2011): 1–9.

104 National Association of Corporate Directors, *NACD Public Company Governance Survey* (Washington, DC: National Association of Corporate Directors, 2011), 5.

105 The Governance Institute, *Dynamic Governance: An Analysis of Board Structure and Practices in a Shifting Industry* (San Diego, CA: The Governance Institute, 2011), 24.

106 L. Prybil et al., *The Evolving Accountability of Nonprofit Health System Boards* (Chicago, IL: AHA Center for Healthcare Governance, 2013), section on "Board Accountability in a Changing Environment," 5–7, and section on "Enhancing Board Accountability to the Communities They Serve," 9–12.
107 *Governance Structure Report*, 42–43, 56–57.
108 *Governance Structure Report*, 55–57.
109 *Governance Structure Report*, 37, 55.

Select readings

American Hospital Association. 2016. *Blue Ribbon Panel Report: Learnings on Governance from Partnerships that Improve Community Health*. Chicago, IL: American Hospital Association.

American Hospital Association. 2019. *2019 National Health Care Governance Survey Report*. Washington, DC: Center for Healthcare Governance.

Center for Healthcare Governance. 2012. *Governance Practices in an Era of Healthcare Transformation*. Chicago, IL American Hospital Association.

Gage, L. 2012. *Transformational Governance: The Challenges Facing Trustees of Nonprofits and Public Hospitals*. Chicago, IL: Center for Healthcare Governance.

Governance Institute. 2017. *2017 Governance Institute Biennial Survey Shows Positive Governance Evolution*. San Diego, CA: The Governance Institute.

Prybil, L. 2017. *The Leadership Role of Nonprofit Health Systems in Improving Community Health*. Chicago, IL: American Hospital Association, Advances in Healthcare Governance Series.

Prybil, L., et al. 2005. *Governance in High-Performing Organizations: A Comparative Study of Governing Boards in Not-for-Profit Hospitals*. Chicago, IL: Health Research and Educational Trust.

Prybil, L., et al. 2008. *Governance in Nonprofit Community Health Systems: An Initial Report on CEO Perspectives*. Chicago, IL: Grant Thornton LLP.

Prybil, L., et al. 2009. *Governance in High-Performing Community Health Systems: A Report on Trustee and CEO Views*. Chicago, IL: Grant Thornton LLP.

Prybil, L., et al. 2012. *Governance in Large Nonprofit Health Systems: Current Profile and Emerging Patterns*. Lexington, KY: Commonwealth Center for Governance Studies, Inc.

Prybil, L., et al. 2013. *The Evolving Accountability of Nonprofit Health System Boards*. Chicago, IL: AHA Center for Healthcare Governance.

Prybil, L., et al. 2014. *Improving Community Health Through Hospital–Public Health Collaboration. Insights and Lessons Learned from Successful Partnerships*. Lexington, KY: Commonwealth Center for Governance Studies, Inc.

Prybil, L., et al. 2015. *A Perspective on Public–Private Collaboration in the Health Sector*. Washington, DC: National Academy of Medicine.

5   Governance of community benefit

Introduction

This chapter applies the ethics paradigm to discuss hallmarks of governance ethics regarding board oversight of community benefit.[1] Community benefit is a pivotal issue for governance ethics. Dealing properly with community benefit advances the health of many but dealing poorly with it undermines public confidence in healthcare organizations.

In the analysis of the applied chapters, the concepts of the ethics paradigm organize core features of effective governance from landmark reports and the scholarly literature. The landmark report by one of the co-authors of this book that shapes the discussion in this chapter is referred to as the *Community Health Systems Report*.[2] The purpose is to highlight hallmarks of governance ethics that denote associated moral imperatives. Because the hallmarks represent necessary moral attributes of governance ethics, they entail an obligation to be adopted by boards. In turn, the associated moral imperatives represent necessary endeavors to foster the hallmarks under consideration.

The ethics paradigm organizes multiple topics on board oversight of community benefit, as follows. First, the foundation component of the ethics paradigm deals with the *identity* of an organization, reflecting the leitmotif *who we are*, thereby highlighting board engagement as a hallmark of governance ethics for community benefit. In turn, this hallmark denotes an associated moral imperative of board oversight of the standing committee structure. Second, the process component of the ethics paradigm addresses the *accountability* of the organization, reflecting the leitmotif *how we function*, thereby highlighting effective communication as a hallmark of governance ethics for community benefit. In turn, this hallmark denotes an associated moral imperative regarding board oversight of community needs assessment. Third, the practice component of the ethics paradigm engages *quality* in an organization, reflecting the leitmotif *what we do*, thereby highlighting board oversight of organizational performance as a hallmark of governance ethics. In turn, this hallmark denotes an associated moral imperative regarding board oversight of continuous improvement.

Each of the applied chapters begins with an explanation of the need for the pivotal topic under consideration, such as governance of community benefit here.

Table 1.1 Ethics paradigm

Components	Foundation component	Process component	Practice component
Context	Environment of healthcare	Organizational oversight	Organizational culture
Leadership	Identity: who we are	Accountability: how we function	Quality: what we do
Outcomes	Organizational stewardship of mission	Decision-making via participative deliberation	Best practices for standards of conduct

Again, the concepts of *identity*, *accountability*, and *quality* provide a framework for the applied analysis. These concepts represent the foundation component (reflecting *who we are*), the process component (reflecting *how we function*), and the practice component (reflecting *what we do*) of the ethics paradigm (Table 1.1).

The interest in community benefit from the perspective of board oversight has been discussed for many years in national healthcare organizations. Hence, before considering hallmarks of governance ethics regarding this topic, it is helpful to explain the need for the community benefit standard.

Need for board oversight of community benefit

Community benefit can be described as a form of public trust that is linked with nonprofit hospitals obtaining tax-exempt status. The community benefit standard includes a provision of care for the poor (charity care) but also must be thought of in larger terms to include the promotion of health.[3] This is a significant ethical issue.[4] The need for board oversight of community benefit is a subject of continuing scrutiny.[5] For example, in the absence of strong federal regulation regarding community benefit programs in nonprofit hospitals, states are intervening to raise standards other than merely meeting Internal Revenue Service (IRS) requirements (discussed later).[6] This need for board oversight of community benefit reflects an indispensable obligation of governance in healthcare organizations. This obligation in part reflects the history of providing charitable care in healthcare in the USA and in part reflects the role of healthcare organizations being good corporate citizens.[7]

Not surprisingly, ethical discourse on this need highlights the strain between altruistic service to the community being served (community solidarity) and the fiduciary duty for the healthcare organization to stewardship of its resources (resource allocation).[8] This strain recalls the tension between mission and margin that is at the heart of governance ethics.

There are many IRS guidelines related to tax-exempt status. Notably, in 1969, the IRS issued Revenue Ruling 69–545. The purpose was to justify an organization's tax-exempt status by creating the community benefit standard regarding nonprofit hospitals being exempt from federal income tax under section 501(c)(3) of the IRS Code. The determination of this status changed from providing charity care to providing community benefit. The ruling provided the context for establishing the community benefit standard that continues today.[9]

This ruling let hospitals qualify for tax-exempt status if they engaged in the promotion of health. The standard could be met through a variety of measures including the following: if a hospital operates an emergency room that is available for all irrespective of the ability to pay; or, if a hospital uses surplus funds to advance education, training, and research or make improvements in patient care. In 1992, the IRS issued hospital audit guidelines to monitor the implementation of this expanded interpretation. This ongoing monitoring by the IRS was accompanied by scrutiny from voluntary healthcare organizations, local governments, and different states. The *Community Health Systems Report* suggested that cumulatively this scrutiny created a growing sense of consternation with what was occurring.[10]

In 2007 there were substantial revisions to the IRS Form 990, specifically Schedule H for hospitals. According to the IRS, Schedule H was intended to "combat the lack of transparency surrounding the activities of tax-exempt organizations that provide hospital or medical care."[11] For nonprofit healthcare institutions, the revised Form 990 and Schedule H required much more extensive information about charity care (referred to in Schedule H as "financial assistance") and other aspects of community benefit than in the past. The redesigned form consisted of a common document to be completed by all tax-exempt organizations with a series of schedules to combat lack of transparency and encourage consistency in reporting. These revisions phased in during 2008 and 2009.[12] The revision required tax-exempt organizations to submit reports annually with more information about community benefit services including charity care. The American Hospital Association provides a Schedule H community benefit report.[13]

Subsequently, the Patient Protection and Affordable Care Act of March 2010 amended the IRS code by adding Section 501(r)(3). This section required every hospital facility operated by a 501(c)(3) organization to undertake a community health needs assessment. This had to occur at least every three years. The hospitals were required to develop an implementation strategy to address the identified community needs making the results available to the public.[14] These new requirements had substantial impact on nonprofit hospitals and healthcare systems.[15] Moreover, the Patient Protection and Affordable Care Act promoted the development of Accountable Care Organizations (ACOs) to improve the health status and the care efficiency of a defined population.[16] The goal of community assessment was to address population health, specifically to bridge the well-documented quality chasm between individual patient care and public health.[17] Naturally, this endeavor required a lot better communication and coordination between healthcare providers and public health agencies.[18]

Over the following years there emerged an increasing need for data to support community benefit investment in nonprofit healthcare.[19] Robust oversight and clear direction for community benefit programs have become an essential component of effective governance.[20] In light of the provisions of IRS Code Section 501(r)(3), especially regarding community benefit programs, it became urgent for governing boards to make further progress regarding community benefit plans in nonprofit health systems.[21]

That is why the *Community Health Systems Report* (that is discussed further in this chapter) highlighted the need for an increased focus by boards. This focus should be on system-wide community benefit programs and community health needs to be properly accountable to the communities and populations they serve.[22] The report recommends focusing on "meeting the emerging benchmarks for good governance with respect to their systems' community benefit responsibilities."[23] By comparing the structures, practices, and cultures of boards with established benchmarks for good governance, the report contributed in a pivotal manner to assessing and enhancing board effectiveness.[24] A significant outcome of the report is that community benefit requires improved board oversight: "concerted board-level attention to this area is necessary and important."[25] In the report, several critical differences were identified as being statistically significant between boards in high-performing community health systems and both mid-range and low-performing systems.[26]

The discussion now applies the ethics paradigm to organize core features of effective governance regarding community benefit. This discussion focuses on the *Community Health Systems Report* and the scholarly literature. The relevance of ethics for board oversight of community benefit has been longstanding.[27] The purpose is to highlight hallmarks of governance ethics that denote associated moral imperatives. The applied analysis begins with discussing hallmarks of governance ethics connected with the foundation component of the ethics paradigm.

Board engagement: foundation-related governance ethics hallmark

The foundation component of the ethics paradigm, in the context of the challenging environment of healthcare, focuses on stewardship to enhance an organization's mission as crucial for effective governance. This component depicts the *identity* of an organization, reflecting the leitmotif *who we are*. That is, the concept of *identity* in the ethics paradigm emphasizes the importance of organizational stewardship.

The principle of stewardship connected with an organization's mission requires the organization to respect the trust it receives from the community. This highlights the trust relation between communities and hospitals. A guiding principle to increase trust and confidence is to "be who we say we are" in terms of reflecting and implementing the hospital's mission.[28] Stewardship protects and enhances the integrity of the organization, ensuring that mission responsiveness permeates the organization to meet actual needs, such as should occur in community benefit programs.[29]

It is crucial to interpret the principle of stewardship as a foundation for an organization's mission rather than construing the principle as merely providing operational directions for management functions. If the principle of stewardship is reduced merely to management functions related to fiscal responsibility, as important as these functions are, the organization can lose sight of its core mission of healing patients and building trusting communities. Of course, effective implementation of these management functions as enactments of stewardship are necessary for the success of an organization. However, that implementation should always reflect the more basic mission that the principle highlights. In other words, when management functions are detached from the underlying organizational mission, a reductive understanding of these functions can compromise the trust in the communities served.

Improvement of community benefit services and programs via more effective board oversight should not be reduced to merely being a matter of better accounting or more efficient management, far less being merely a matter of legal compliance. Rather, community benefit is an essentially ethical endeavor insofar as it reveals the core commitment of the board to steward the organization's fundamental mission as a tax-exempt organization that is committed to serving its community. Hence, boards must effectively discharge their governance oversight of community benefit practices. Healthcare mission includes the commitment to heal patients, to build trust with communities, and to improve quality of lives by decreasing health disparities, enhancing health status, and assuring healthcare access. In this mission, health systems and hospitals have an inherent responsibility to assess and improve the health of their communities as well as providing care and treatment for their patients. A good example of this connection between organizational mission and community benefit is articulated by the Catholic Health Association: "sustaining community benefit programs requires that healthcare organizations have a clear mission to serve their communities and a solid community benefit program infrastructure."[30]

The concept of *identity* in the ethics paradigm (reflecting the leitmotif *who we are*) emphasizes the importance of organizational stewardship. This focus requires boards to be attentive to the challenging healthcare environment as the context for considering their responsibilities. The concept of *identity* highlights board engagement as a hallmark of governance ethics for community benefit. This concept draws attention to who the board is in relation with its organization. In turn, this hallmark denotes an associated moral imperative regarding board oversight of the standing committee structure. These are discussed later.

To understand board engagement as a hallmark of governance ethics regarding community benefit, it is important to underscore the role of the board in non-profit governance.[31] Board engagement includes having a well-organized structure with defined duties to routinely scrutinize community benefit issues. The *Community Health Systems Report* highlighted gaps with regard to established benchmarks for good governance.[32] The report indicated that only 70 percent of all community health system boards in the report have formal discussions on a regular basis about community benefit responsibilities and programs. However, 90 percent of high-performing system CEOs indicated that their boards engage in such discussions. This information indicated a gap in the mid-range systems (of which 72 percent reported such discussions) and a more significant gap in low-performing systems (of which only 36 percent reported such discussions).[33]

There is need for robust board engagement regarding community benefit responsibilities. Highlighting board engagement as a hallmark of governance eth ics underscores a mission-related duty of the board: that is, to inspire its health-care organization to serve its communities. This focus upon robust engagement enables boards to clarify their responsibilities and to develop strategies for effec-tive governance. Board engagement understood in this manner should provide excellence in leadership with specific oversight of community benefit. This gov-ernance responsibility has been widely recognized. For example, from early in the debate on community benefit, the Catholic Health Association emphasized this responsibility of the board. That is, the board's must ensure that the organiza-tion's community benefit mission is fulfilled, upholding the community's interest as being paramount.[34]

Moral imperative: board oversight of the standing committee structure

Oversight of board engagement is a hallmark of governance ethics. This hallmark denotes an associated moral imperative regarding board oversight of the standing committee structure. Committee structure helps to clarify the board's *identity* (who the board is) in the face of community benefit challenges. The responsibilities of nonprofit governing boards in healthcare organizations are widely recognized,[35] and there are established expectations for the design of boards.[36] Despite this well-established knowledge about effective governance regarding the make-up of a board, there remain serious concerns about board effectiveness.[37] As a result, public dismay over board oversight continues, especially with regard to nonprofit healthcare.[38] A proactive role in governance is generally evident in the committee structure and yields more effective boards, connecting the caliber of governance with organizational success.[39] Hence, board oversight in its committee structure constitutes a standard of good governance.[40] In other words, board engagement that is manifest in its committee structure leads to governance effectiveness.[41]

A well-organized committee structure with clearly defined duties is one of the keys to effective governance.[42] Hence, board engagement typically should require a standing committee for effective oversight, working with the entire board appro-priately. This committee oversight can guarantee that community benefit remains a high priority aligned with the organization's mission. In this sense, boards must ensure the organization's fidelity to its nonprofit healthcare mission.[43]

The *Community Health Systems Report* indicated that only 40 percent of com-munity health systems had standing board committees with clearly assigned oversight responsibility for community benefit policies and programs (50 per-cent in high-performing systems; 42 percent in mid-range systems; and 18 per-cent in low-performing systems).[44] Such a surprisingly low figure reflects poorly on organizational stewardship. The low figure appears to be connected with the report's findings that many boards did not routinely deliberate about community benefit issues. Also, the low figure suggests that boards did not have a board-adopted policy and plan for community benefit. The absence of a standing com-mittee to serve as a governance focal point had an obvious impact. That is, there was not sufficient advocacy or championing for community benefit, potentially preventing this pivotal topic from being included in the board's ongoing agenda.

In sum, the foundation component of the ethics paradigm highlights board engagement as a hallmark of governance ethics. By focusing on *identity* in the ethics paradigm (dealing with who the board is), this hallmark denotes an associated moral imperative regarding board oversight of the standing committee structure.

Effective communication: process-related governance ethics hallmark

The concept of *accountability* in the ethics paradigm (reflecting the leitmotif *how we function*) emphasizes the importance of decision-making via participative deliberation. This focus requires boards to be attentive to organizational oversight as the context for assessing their responsibilities. The concept of *accountability* highlights effective communication as a hallmark of governance ethics for community benefit. To meet this charge, boards should be designed to have processes for communication with diversity of thinking. The concept draws attention to how the board functions in the organization. In turn, this hallmark denotes an associated moral imperative regarding board oversight of community needs assessment to plan appropriate resource allocation and program development. These are discussed in the following sections.

Regarding effective communication as a hallmark of governance ethics, board oversight is needed internally and externally. The *Community Health Systems Report* highlighted the need for boards to actively collaborate both internally (such as with system management teams) and externally with other organizations and constituencies to undertake a reliable and ongoing community needs assessment.[45] Internally, board oversight must ensure that, through effective communication, community benefit programs are integrated across the organization. Community benefit staff typically integrate and coordinate their activities across the organization to properly serve its communities. Externally, relevant community members and agencies need to be included in communication about services.[46] Increased board accountability can occur by reinforcing effective communication between nonprofit organizations and their communities. This focus on effective communication will foster robust responses to expectations regarding community benefit.[47]

Moral imperative: board oversight of community needs assessment

Board oversight of effective communication is a hallmark of governance ethics. This hallmark denotes an associated moral imperative regarding board oversight of community needs assessment. This imperative reflects the concept of *accountability* in the ethics paradigm. Professional associations have urged healthcare organizations to develop formal processes that deal with community needs assessment.[48] Yet the *Community Health Systems Report* indicated that only 29 percent of all community health systems collaborate on an ongoing basis with other local organizations in this regard. This collaboration refers to formal assessment processes designed to determine community needs to which systems resources should be allocated. However, 70 percent of the high-performing system CEOs reported that their health systems collaborate with other local organizations in assessing community needs on a regular basis. This information indicated a significant gap in the mid-range systems (of which only 27 percent reported undertaking such a needs assessment) and low-performing systems (of which only 9 percent reported undertaking such a needs assessment).[49]

As legal fiduciaries of the community, boards must conduct and communicate their governance activities to ensure that community interests are being protected. This concern is especially pertinent for unmet health needs and vulnerable populations,[50] such as typically occurs in community benefit practices. Deliberating on community needs is a distinguishing aspect of this hallmark of governance ethics, consistent with longstanding expectations of national associations. For example, the Catholic Health Association emphasized that "Community benefit programs are designed to address specific community health needs."[51] Hence, community needs assessment constitutes an ethical imperative as a defining feature of the decision-making processes in effective communication.

In sum, the process component of the ethics paradigm highlights board engagement as a hallmark of governance ethics. By focusing on *accountability* in the ethics paradigm (dealing with how the board functions), this hallmark denotes an associated moral imperative regarding board oversight of community needs assessment.

Organizational performance: practice-related governance ethics hallmark

The concept of *quality* in the ethics paradigm (reflecting the leitmotif *what we do*) emphasizes the importance of best practices for standards of conduct. This focus requires boards to be attentive to organizational culture as the context for assessing their responsibilities. The concept of *quality* highlights organizational performance as a hallmark of governance ethics for community benefit. In turn, this hallmark denotes an associated moral imperative regarding board oversight of continuous improvement. These are discussed later.

The purpose of focusing upon best practices in this component of the ethics paradigm is to shed light on the need to weave policy and planning with performance for effective board oversight of community benefit. This oversight constitutes a threshold responsibility that reveals the ethical caliber of the organization and of the board. The reason for this threshold responsibility is that community benefit is not just one item among a litany of other competing demands in a healthcare organization. Rather, community benefit practices are at the foundation of the mission of nonprofit healthcare. They are required by state statutes and IRS revenue rulings and they are ethically obligatory from the perspective of social responsibility.

Regarding organizational performance as a hallmark of governance ethics, board oversight is needed to combine policy and action planning. The *Community*

Health Systems Report highlighted the need for boards to develop a specific strategy for oversight of community benefit. This strategy should combine policy and planning with action, including measurable objectives for effective reporting. There should be clear measurement tools to both collect and analyze relevant data. This undertaking should identify the organizational objectives in clear and measurable terms. The goal is to ensure that reporting and accountability mechanisms are in place both to track progress and to provide reports on a regular basis. Such conduct demonstrates that boards are committed to governance effectiveness regarding community benefit.[52] Despite this obvious need for a board strategy to develop a policy and plan with performance reports, the data identified worrisome gaps, as follows.

To begin, the *Community Health Systems Report* indicated that only 60 percent of community health system boards had adopted a formal written policy to define guidelines for their community benefit programs. However, 90 percent of high-performing system CEOs reported that they had a formal written policy. This information indicated a gap in the mid-range systems (of which only 60 percent report having such a policy) and a more significant gap in low-performing systems (of which only 27 percent report having such a policy).[53]

Next, the *Community Health Systems Report* indicated that only 34 percent of community health system boards had adopted a formal community benefit plan with measurable system wide objectives. However, 50 percent of high-performing system CEOs reported that they had a formal community benefit plan. This information indicated a gap in the mid-range systems (of which only 36 percent report having a specific plan) and a more significant gap in low-performing systems (of which only 9 percent report having a specific plan).[54]

Furthermore, the *Community Health Systems Report* indicated that only 68 percent of community health system boards were presented regularly with performance data on community benefit. The data referred to measurable system wide objectives regarding its community benefit program. However, 90 percent of high-performing system CEOs reported that they regularly receive this performance data. This information indicated a gap in the mid-range systems (of which 70 percent report regularly receiving such performance data) and a more significant gap in low-performing systems (of which only 36 percent report regularly receiving such performance data).[55]

This hallmark of governance ethics focuses on the ethical conduct of the board's oversight of organizational performance with accompanying measurable objectives. This hallmark engages the responsibility of the board to provide adequate programs and services for community benefit. The endeavor here is to plan and monitor outcomes toward established goals and objectives with periodic reports.

This need for board oversight is consistent with longstanding expectations among professional associations. For example, the Catholic Health Association has focused on planning for performance reports: "We believe that vigilance in how we plan, evaluate, and report community benefit is more important than ever;" to assist its members, the association provided a detailed guide by adopting a public health approach to program evaluation.[56] Also, the association has encouraged the development of evidence-based community benefit endeavors.[57] Dashboard technology provided an example of the emphasis upon assessing and monitoring. Regarding community benefit program outcomes, dashboard technology has been adopted to consolidate data from disparate systems in meaningful ways in a consistent and accessible manner.[58]

Board oversight of organizational performance requires measurement outcomes for the community.[59] It is indispensable to provide thorough reports to communities on a regular basis.[60] As boards adopt this approach, performance evaluations need to apply to the boards themselves just as other occurs with other responsibility reviews (such as on governance structures). These best practices and standards of conduct contribute to high quality board oversight.[61]

Moral imperative: board oversight of continuous improvement

Board oversight of organizational performance is a hallmark of governance ethics. This hallmark denotes an associated moral imperative regarding board oversight of continuous improvement. This imperative reflects the concept of *quality* in the ethics paradigm. To understand the moral imperative of continuous improvement regarding community benefit, it can be helpful to return to the *Governance Structure Report* (undertaken several years after the *Community Health Systems Report*).[62] The *Governance Structure Report* highlights the need for board oversight of continuous improvement regarding community benefit by focusing on the following threshold items: the need to improve oversight of (1) standing board committees for community benefit programs; (2) formal goals and planning guidelines for community benefit programs; (3) collaboration with local public healthcare organizations concerning community benefit programs; and (4) local organizations.

To begin, there is a clear need for a practical policy about board oversight of community benefit programs. A well-organized committee structure having clearly defined duties with knowledgeable and engaged members is a key to effective governance.[63] The *Governance Structure Report* highlighted the need to assign oversight responsibility for governance functions to standing board committees. The report recorded the number and proportion of boards in its study population that assigned oversight responsibility for seven core governance functions to standing board committees. Across the board, large health systems were more likely than hospitals to have standing committees with oversight responsibility for these important functions. For several functions, this practice was virtually universal among these large systems. However, less than a majority had standing board committees with oversight responsibility for system-wide community benefit policies and programs.[64] This information indicated the need for continuous improvement of board oversight.

Also, the *Governance Structure Report* emphasized that board planning must adopt formal goals and guidelines for community benefit programs. The interviews with board leaders and CEOs in the report included several questions regarding their system's community benefit policies and programs. A pivotal issue was if a board adopted a formal, written statement that defines overall goals and guidelines for the system's community benefit program. Comparing the findings for Catholic systems to the other large systems, the report indicated that boards in most of the Catholic systems had adopted a formal policy as compared to only a few of the other systems. Moreover, the report indicated that most of the system boards had adopted a written, formal statement defining overall goals and guidelines for the system's community benefit program. However, only half of the systems required their local organizations to adopt formal community benefit plans that identified specific priorities and strategies.[65] This information indicated the need for continuous improvement of board oversight.

Furthermore, the *Governance Structure Report* underscored the need for collaboration with local public healthcare organizations. For example, in the report only 6 percent of boards and CEOs reported that their board requires collaboration between the system's facilities and local public health agencies. One way was mentioned to gauge the participating systems' stance on coordination between their local delivery organizations and public health agencies. That is, the board members and CEOs were asked if their system's board required their local organization to collaborate with local public healthcare organizations in their vicinities. The information shows that such requirements were quite uncommon. Only one of the 14 large systems, a secular organization, had established a policy requiring all of its local organizations to collaborate with local public healthcare organizations in assessing community needs and setting community benefit program priorities. However, there was recognition of the nationwide need for greater focus on prevention and population health. In light of this recognition, many board members and CEOs expressed support for the idea of promoting stronger coordination and between their local leadership teams and public healthcare organizations.[66] Again, this information indicated the need for continuous improvement of board oversight.

Finally, formal community benefit plans could be adopted by the local organizations of health systems, if that would provide value depending on arrangements with the parent system. In the foreseeable future, public and private organizations in nearly all sectors of American society face serious financial constraints. Hence, these organizations must establish resource allocation priorities very carefully. Over many years, uncompensated care (charity care and bad debt, but not Medicaid or Medicare underpayment costs) in hospitals across the USA increased significantly. This trend affected the availability of resources for other community benefit activities.[67] As a result, developing formal plans and setting clear priorities for community benefit programs emerged as indicators of effective governance and management in healthcare organizations.[68] In the *Governance Structure Report*, CEOs and board leaders were asked this crucial question: if their system's board required their local organizations to develop and adopt a formal community benefit plan that identifies specific priorities for its program. The report indicated that 67 percent of these large systems directed their local leadership teams to develop formal plans with priorities, strategies, and metrics for their community benefit programs. In several instances, they specified that local plans must address certain system-wide priorities.[69] Once more, this information indicated the need for continuous improvement of board oversight.

The outcome of this analysis is to emphasize ethical imperative of continuous improvement regarding community benefit. Pressure will increase upon nonprofit healthcare organizations. The provisions of IRS Code Section 501(r)(3) will continue, and resources will become further constrained. Hence, continuous improvement regarding community benefit programs will be indispensable for governance ethics. Specifically, there will be an increased need for ongoing assessment of community health needs, careful prioritization of those needs, and adoption of formal community benefit plans. These plans must be part of board oversight at both the local and system levels of nonprofit health systems.

In sum, the practice component of the ethics paradigm highlights organizational performance as a hallmark of governance ethics. By focusing on *quality* in the ethics paradigm (dealing with what the board does), this hallmark denotes an associated moral imperative regarding board oversight of continuous improvement.

Conclusion

The chapter has highlighted hallmarks of governance ethics with associated moral imperatives regarding community benefit. The contribution of the ethics paradigm can be summarized in this manner.

First, in the context of the challenging healthcare environment, the foundation component of the ethics paradigm focuses on stewardship to enhance an organization's mission as crucial for effective governance. This component deals with the *identity* of an organization, reflecting the leitmotif *who we are*, thereby highlighting board engagement as a hallmark of governance ethics for community benefit. In turn, this hallmark denotes an associated moral imperative of board oversight of the standing committee structure.

Second, in the context of organizational oversight in healthcare institutions, the process component of the ethics paradigm focuses upon decision-making to encourage participative deliberation in organizations. This component addresses the *accountability* of the organization, reflecting the leitmotif *how we function*, thereby highlighting effective communication as a hallmark of governance ethics for community benefit. In turn, this hallmark denotes an associated moral imperative regarding board oversight of community needs assessment.

Third, in the context of organizational culture in healthcare, the practice component of the ethics paradigm focuses on best practices to develop standards of conduct. This component engages *quality* in an organization, reflecting the leitmotif *what we do*, thereby highlighting board oversight of organizational performance as a hallmark of governance ethics. In turn, this hallmark denotes an associated moral imperative regarding board oversight of continuous improvement.

This chapter has applied the ethics paradigm to highlight hallmarks of governance ethics regarding community benefit, denoting associated moral imperatives. The next chapter adopts the same approach to discuss hallmarks of governance ethics concerning community health.

Notes

1 The analysis in this chapter is a development of an earlier published study by the authors. See: G. Magill and L. Prybil, "Board Oversight of Community Benefit: A Moral Imperative," *Kennedy Institute of Ethics Journal* 21 (1) (March 2011): 25–50.

2 L. Prybil, et al., *Governance in High-Performing Community Health Systems. A Report on Trustee and CEO Views* (Chicago, IL: Grant Thornton LLP, 2009). Referred to as the *Community Health Systems Report*.

3 See: M. King, *A Spirit of Charity: Restoring the Bond Between America and its Public Hospitals* (Salisbury, MD: Secant Publishing, 2017). Also see: R. Pollack, *Community Benefits Go Far Beyond Charity Care* (American Hospital Association, 2018), at www.aha.org/news/blog/2018-01-16-community-benefits-go-far-beyond-charity-care.

4 See: M. Rozier, "How Should Nonprofit Hospitals' Community Benefit Be More Responsive to Health Disparities?" *AMA Journal of Ethics* 21 (3) (2019): E273–280.

5 See: D. Dranove, et al., *A Floor-and-Trade Proposal to Improve the Delivery of Charity-Care by U.S. Nonprofit Hospitals* (Washington, DC: The Hamilton Project at the Brookings Institute, 2015); D. B. Rubin, et al., "Tax-Exempt Hospitals and Community Benefit: New Directions in Policy and Practice," *Annual Review of Public Health* 36 (1) (2015): 545–557; S. Rosenbaum, et al., "The Value of the Nonprofit Tax Exemption," *Health Affairs* 34 (7) (2015): 1225–1233.

6 T. Bannow, "States Step in to Fill Regulatory Void Over Community Benefit," *Modern Healthcare* (August 5, 2019): 21–23; C. J. Evashwick, *Hospitals & Community Benefit: New Demands and New Approaches* (Chicago, IL: Health Administration Press, 2013); M. G. Reyes, ed., *Nonprofit Hospitals and the Community Benefit Standard* (Hauppauga, NY: Nova Science Publications, 2011).

7 L. Prybil, R. Killian, "Community Benefit Needs Board Oversight," *Health Progress* (July–August, 2013): 90–94.

8 S. D. Pearson, et al., *No Margin, No Mission: Health-Care Organizations and the Quest for Ethical Excellence* (New York: Oxford University Press, 2003), Chapter 7, "Community Benefits," 117–138.

9 IRS, Revenue Ruling 69–545, 1969–2, C.B 117, at www.irs.gov/charities-non-profits/charitable-hospitals-general-requirements-for-tax-exemption-under-section-501c3. A subsequent IRS ruling (Revenue Ruling 83–157, 1983–2, C.B. 94) clarified that hospitals did not need to operate an emergency room to quality for tax exempt status if adequate emergency services were provided elsewhere in the community and the hospital otherwise met the community benefit standard.

10 *Community Health Systems Report*, 20–21.

11 See: D. Folkemer et al., "Hospital Community Benefits After the ACA: The Emerging Federal Framework," *The Hilltop Institute-Issue Brief* (January, 2011): 3; Alliance for Advancing Nonprofit Healthcare, *Maximizing Community Benefit: A Six-Point Program* (Washington, DC, April 2009); P. McCruden, "The Affordable Care Act and Community Benefit: A Mandate Catholic Health Care Can (Partly) Embrace," *Kennedy Institute of Ethics Journal* 23 (3) (2012): 229–248; R. I. Field, *Healthcare Regulation in America. Complexity, Confrontation, and Compromise* (New York: Oxford University Press, 2007, 192.

12 See: IRS, *Instructions for Schedule H* (Form 990), 2009, at www.irs.gov/instructions/i990sh. Also see: IRS, Form 990, Return of Organization Exempt from Income Tax, at www.irs.gov/pub/irs-pdf/i990.pdf; IRS, IRS Exempt Organizations Hospital Study. Final Report (2009), at, www.irs.gov/pub/irs-tege/execsum_hospprojrept.pdf.

13 American Hospital Association, *Tax-Exempt Hospitals' Schedule H Community Benefit Report* (Chicago, IL: American Hospital Association, 2019).

14 See: www.irs.gov/pub/irs-drop/n-10-39.pdf. Also see: S. R. Singh, et al., "Analysis of Hospital Community Benefit Expenditures' Alignment with Community Health Needs: Evidence from a National Investigation of Tax-Exempt Hospitals," *American Journal*

of Public Health 105 (5) (2015): 914–921; S. R. Singh, et al., "Hospital Community Benefit in the Context of the Larger Public Health System: A State-Level Analysis of Hospital and Governmental Public Health Spending Across the United States," *Journal of Public Health Management and Practice* 22 (2) (2015): 164–174; J. Corrigan, et al., "Hospital Community Benefit Programs: Increasing Benefits to Communities," *JAMA* 313 (12) (2015): 1211–1212.

15 IRS, New Requirements for 501(c)3 Hospitals Under the Affordable Care Act, at, www.irs.gov/charities-non-profits/charitable-organizations/new-requirements-for-501c3-hospitals-under-the-affordable-care-act.

16 S. DeVore, R. W. Champion, "Driving Population Health Through Accountable Care Organizations," *Health Affairs* 30 (1) (2011): 41–50.

17 P. Honore, D. Wright, H. Koh, "Bridging the Quality Chasm between Health Care and Public Health," *Journal of Public Health Management and Practice* 18 (1) (2012): 1–2.

18 See: Institute of Medicine of the National Academies, *Primary Care and Public Health: Exploring Integration to Improve Population Health* (Washington, DC: The National Academies Press, 2012).

19 A. Baehr, et al., "Developing Data to Support Effective Coordination of Nonprofit Hospital Community Benefit Investment," *Journal of Healthcare Management* 63 (4) (July–August 2018): 271–280.

20 See: G. Magill, L. Prybil, "Board Oversight of Community Benefit: A Moral Imperative," *Kennedy Institute of Ethics Journal* 21 (1) (2011): 25–50; L. Prybil, J. Benton, "Community Benefit: The Nonprofit Community Health Perspective," in D. B. Nash, et al., eds., *Governance for Healthcare Providers: The Call to Leadership* (Boca Raton, FL: CRC Press, Taylor and Francis Group, 2009), 267–283.

21 See: American Hospital Association, *Managing Population Health: The Role of the Hospital* (Chicago, IL: Health Research and Educational Trust, 2012), 1–19.

22 *Community Health Systems Report*, 18, 31–35, 44–45, 56–57. Also see: L. Prybil et al., *Governance in Nonprofit Community Health Systems. An Initial Report on CEO Perspectives* (Chicago, IL: Grant Thornton LLP, 2008).

23 *Community Health Systems Report*, 42.

24 *Community Health Systems Report*, foreword. Also see an earlier summary of this data in, L. Prybil, "Community Benefit: The Nonprofit Community Health System Perspective," in D. B. Nash, et al., *Governance for Healthcare Providers. The Call to Leadership* (Boca Raton, FL: CRC Press, Taylor & Francis Group, 2009), 267–283.

25 *Community Health Systems Report*, 12.

26 *Community Health Systems Report*, 39–40.

27 See: B. Jennings, et al., *The Ethics of Hospital Trustees* (Washington, DC: Georgetown University Press, 2004); J. Horwitz, "Nonprofit Ownership, Private Property, and Public Accountability," *Health Affairs* (2006): W308–W311; J. R. Horwitz, "Why We Need the Independent Sector: The Behavior, Law, and Ethics of Not-for-Profit Hospitals," *UCLA Law Review* 50 (6) (2003).

28 J. G. King, E. Moran, *Trust Counts Now: Hospitals and their Communities: A Report to the American Hospital Association* (American Hospital Association, 2006), 7.

29 G. Magill, L. Prybil, "Stewardship and Integrity in Health Care: A Role for Organizational Ethics," *Journal of Business Ethics* 50 (2004): 225–238.

30 See: Catholic Health Association, *A Guide for Planning & Reporting Community Benefit*, 2008 edition (St. Louis, MO: Catholic Health Association, 2008), 9; Catholic Health Association, *Assessing and Addressing Community Health Needs* (Washington, DC: Catholic Health Association, 2013); Catholic Health Association, *Striving for Excellence in Ethics: A Resource for the Catholic Health Ministry*, 2nd ed. (Washington, DC: Catholic Health Association, 2014).

31 *ABA Coordinating Committee on Nonprofit Governance, Guide to Nonprofit Corporate Governance in the Wake of Sarbanes-Oxley* (Chicago, IL: American Bar Association, 2007).

32 *Community Health Systems Report*, 41–42.

33 *Community Health Systems Report*, 21, table 17.

34 See: Catholic Health Association, *A Guide for Planning & Reporting Community Benefit* (2017); Catholic Health Association, "What Board members Should Know about the Organization's Community Benefit Program," in Catholic Health Association, ed., *The IRS Form 990, Schedule H* (St. Louis, MO: Catholic Health Association, 2009), 12.

35 See: F. Entin, et al., *The Board's Fiduciary Role: Legal Responsibilities of Health Care Governing Boards* (Chicago, IL: Center for Healthcare Governance, 2006); Independent Sector, *Principles for Good Governance and Ethical Practice: A Guide for Charities and Foundations* (Washington, DC: Independent Sector, 2015); Congressional Budget Office, *Nonprofit Hospitals and the Provision of Community Benefit* (Washington, DC, December 2006).

36 C. Sundaramurthy, M. Lewis, "Control and Collaboration: Paradoxes of Governance," *Academy of Management Review* 28 (July 2003): 397–415.

37 R. Hamilton, "Corporate Governance in America: Major Changes But Uncertain Benefits," *Journal of Corporate Law* (Winter 2000): 349–373.

38 L. Prybil, et al., *Governance in High-Performing Organizations: A Comparative Study of Governing Boards in Not-for-Profit Hospitals* (Chicago, IL: Health Research and Educational Trust, 2005).

39 N. Bradley, "Corporate Governance Scoring and the Link Between Corporate Governance and Performance Indicators: In Search of the Holy Grail," *Corporate Governance* 12 (January, 2004): 8–10.

40 B. Bader, E. Zablocki, "Evaluating and Improving Board Committees," *Great Boards* 2 (Summer 2008): 1–19.

41 Governance Institute, *Striving for Excellence: Health System Governance at the Dawn of the New Millennium* (The Governance Institute, 2002), 28–29.

42 Center for Healthcare Governance, *Building An Exceptional Board: Effective Practices for Healthcare Governance* (Chicago, IL: Center for Healthcare Governance, 2007).

43 T. L. Greaney, K. M. Boozang, "Mission, Margin, and Trust in the Nonprofit Healthcare Enterprise," *Yale Journal of Health Policy, Law and Ethics* V (1) (Winter 2005): 1–87.

44 *Community Health Systems Report*, 10–12, table 8.

45 *Community Health Systems Report*, 42.

46 See: Catholic Health Association, *A Guide for Planning & Reporting Community Benefit* (St. Louis, MO: Catholic Health Association, 2008), 20–21; American Hospital Association, *Community Accountability and Transparency: Helping Hospitals Better Serve their Communities* 3 (November 2007), 5.

47 See: M. Schlesinger, B. H. Gray, "How Nonprofits Matter In American Medicine, and What to Do About It," *Health Affairs* (20 June 2006): W300; P. Sasso, "Searching for Trust in the Not-for-Profit Boardroom: Looking Beyond Duty of Obedience to Ensure Accountability," *UCLA Law Review* 50 (6) (2003).

48 See: American Hospital Association, *Strengthening Community Trust: Strategies for CEOs* (Chicago, IL: AHA, 2006), 1–9; Catholic Health Association, *A Guide for Planning & Reporting Community Benefit* (St. Louis, MO: Catholic Health Association, 2008), 65–78; Public Health Institute, *Advancing the State of the Art of Community Benefit* (Oakland, CA: Public Health Institute, November, 2004), 15.

49 *Community Health Systems Report*, 22–23, table 19.

50 C. J. Evashwick, K. Gautam, "Governance and Management of Community Benefit," 89 (5) (2008): 10–15.

51 Catholic Health Association, *A Guide for Planning & Reporting Community Benefit* (St. Louis, MO: Catholic Health Association, 2008), 8.

52 *Community Health Systems Report*, 42.

53 *Community Health Systems Report*, 23–24, table 19.

54 *Community Health Systems Report*, 24, table 20.

55 *Community Health Systems Report*, 2, table 21.

56 See: Catholic Health Association, *A Guide for Planning & Reporting Community Benefit* (St. Louis, MO: Catholic Health Association, 2008), 5, 10–11; Catholic Health Association, *Evaluating Community Benefits Programs* (St. Louis, MO: Catholic Health Association, 2009), adopting a systematic approach to evaluating and improving programs that applies public health program evaluation to community benefit programs.

57 J. Trochio, C. Evashwick, "The Future of Evidence-Based Community Benefit," *Health Progress* 89 (5) (September–October, 2009): 9.

58 See: L. Baskett, et al., "Using the Dashboard Technology Properly," *Health Progress* 89 (5) (September–October, 2008): 16–23. Interestingly, this essay also aligns the conduct of monitoring programs with decision-making processes and with the ethical principle of stewardship, but the alignment is not explained or pursued in a systematic manner. Also see: K. N. Gillespie, et al., "Measuring the Impact of Community Benefit," *Health Progress* 89 (5) (September–October, 2008): 29–33.

59 L. Minich, et al., "Can Community Change Be Measured for Outcome-Based Initiative?" *American Journal of Community Psychology* 38 (2006): 182–190.

60 *Community Health Systems Report*, 42. Also see: "'Community Connections' Helps Keep Health System Close to Those It Serves," *AHA News* 45 (13) (June 22, 2009): 7.

61 Independent Sector, *Principles for Good Governance and Ethical Practice: A Guide for Charities and Foundations* (Washington, DC: Independent Sector), Preamble, 2–6, and 13–19 for the principles on effective governance.

62 L. Prybil, et al., *Governance in Large Nonprofit Health Systems: Current Profile and Emerging Patterns* (Lexington, KY: Commonwealth Center for Governance Studies, Inc., 2012). Referred to as the *Governance Structure Report*.

63 L. Walker, "The Supporting Cast: Strong, Focused Committees and Task Forces are Essential to Overall Governance Excellence," *Trustee* 65 (March, 2012): 6–7.

64 *Governance Structure Report*, 14.

65 *Governance Structure Report*, 18, 31–35.

66 *Governance Structure Report*, 34.

67 For example, uncompensated care increased from $21.6 billion in 2000 to $39.3 billion in 2010, an increase of 82%. See: American Hospital Association, "AHA: Hospitals' Uncompensated Care Increased 82% Since 2000," *AHA News* (January 9, 2012): 7.

68 See: L. Prybil, J. Benton, "Community Benefit: The Nonprofit Community Health Perspective," in D. Nash et al., eds., *Governance for Healthcare Providers: The Call to Leadership* (Boca Raton, FL: CRC Press, Taylor and Francis Group, 2009), 267–283; C. Evashwick and K. Gautam, "Governance and Management of Community Benefit," *Health Progress* 89 (September–October, 2008): 12.

69 *Governance Structure Report*, 35.

Select readings

American Hospital Association. 2012. *Managing Population Health: The Role of the Hospital*. Chicago, IL: Health Research and Educational Trust.

American Hospital Association. 2019. *Tax-Exempt Hospitals' Schedule H Community Benefit Report*. Chicago, IL: American Hospital Association.

Dranove, D., et al. 2015. *A Floor-and-Trade Proposal to Improve the Delivery of Charity-Care by U.S. Nonprofit Hospitals*. Washington, DC: The Hamilton Project at the Brookings Institute.

Evashwick, C. J. 2013. *Hospitals & Community Benefit: New Demands and New Approaches*. Chicago, IL: Health Administration Press.

Independent Sector. 2015. *Principles for Good Governance and Ethical Practice: A Guide for Charities and Foundations*. Washington, DC: Independent Sector.

King, M. 2017. *A Spirit of Charity: Restoring the Bond Between America and its Public Hospitals*. Salisbury, MD: Secant Publishing.

Nash, D. B., et al., eds. 2009. *Governance for Healthcare Providers: The Call to Leadership*. Boca Raton, FL: CRC Press, Taylor and Francis Group.

Prybil, L. 2017. *The Leadership Role of Nonprofit Health Systems in Improving Community Health*. Chicago, IL: American Hospital Association, Advances in Healthcare Governance Series

Prybil, L., et al. 2008. *Governance in Nonprofit Community Health Systems. An Initial Report on CEO Perspectives*. Chicago, IL: Grant Thornton LLP.

Prybil, L., et al. 2009. *Governance in High-Performing Community Health Systems: A Report on Trustee and CEO Views*. Chicago, IL: Grant Thornton LLP.

Prybil, L., et al. 2014. *Improving Community Health Through Hospital: Public Health Collaboration. Insights and Lessons Learned from Successful Partnerships*. Lexington, KY: Commonwealth Center for Governance Studies, Inc

6   Governance of community health

Introduction

This chapter applies the ethics paradigm to discuss hallmarks of governance ethics regarding community health. The previous chapter on community benefit stressed that community needs assessment is an indispensable ethical imperative. This chapter discusses the much broader issue of community health that similarly requires an ongoing needs assessment.

There is an abundance of literature on public health ethics. Typically, the literature discusses generic approaches to ethics (such as on norms, codes, autonomy, consent, equity, fairness, justice and social value), or considers the political and legal context (authority, constraints, public/individual tensions), to discuss issues about public health. The issues have a vast spectrum including these topics: addiction, biosecurity, behavior, conflicting interests, disease, disability, disadvantage, environmental and occupational health, epidemiology, genetics, global health, health promotion, health communication, health evaluation, health inequities, population health, harm reduction, immunization, infectious disease, reproduction, research, risk reduction, safety, screening, setting priorities, surveillance, vaccinations, violence, vulnerability, welfare.[1] However, the focus that occurs in this chapter is gaining increased attention—the collaboration between hospitals, health systems, and public health agencies to enhance community health as part of a multi-sector effort that is needed. This multi-sector approach should include a broad range of stakeholders, including the business sector, educational institutions, and social service organizations, in addition to healthcare organizations and public health agencies.[2] This multi-sector approach is advocated strenuously in a 2019 report from the National Academies of Science, seeking health improvement through public and private efforts in cross-sector collaborative action.[3] Also, a 2019 report from the US Surgeon General on community health encourages multi-sector collaboration so that businesses can be community change-makers and forces for health.[4] Community health is a governance priority.[5]

In the analysis of the applied chapters, the concepts of the ethics paradigm organize core features of effective governance from landmark reports and the scholarly literature. There are two pivotal reports by one of the co-authors of this book that shape the discussion in this chapter regarding community health. The reports focus on hospital and public health collaboration, the first is referred to as the *Community Health Report*,[6] and the second is referred to as the *Leadership Report*.[7] These reports deal with cooperative endeavors to improve community health with outcomes that have significant implications for governance ethics. The reports call for boards and executive leadership in nonprofit health systems to assume a substantial role in multi-sector initiatives to measure and improve community health across the nation. There is substantial evidence that hospitals play a crucial role in successful multi-sector partnerships focused upon improving community health.[8]

The purpose is to highlight hallmarks of governance ethics that denote associated moral imperatives. Because the hallmarks represent necessary moral attributes of governance ethics, they entail an obligation to be adopted by boards. In turn, the associated moral imperatives represent necessary endeavors to foster the hallmarks under consideration.

The ethics paradigm organizes multiple topics on board oversight of community health, as follows. First, the foundation component of the ethics paradigm deals with the *identity* of an organization, reflecting the leitmotif *who we are*, thereby highlighting board oversight of partnership engagement as a hallmark of governance ethics for community health. In turn, this hallmark denotes an associated moral imperative of board oversight of the mission and structure of community health partnerships. Second, the process component of the ethics paradigm addresses the *accountability* of the organization, reflecting the leitmotif *how we function*, thereby highlighting partnership consensus as a hallmark of governance ethics for community health. In turn, this hallmark denotes an associated moral imperative regarding board oversight of collaboration within community health partnerships. Third, the practice component of the ethics paradigm engages *quality* in an organization, reflecting the leitmotif *what we do*, thereby highlighting partnership performance as a hallmark of governance ethics for community health. In turn, this hallmark denotes an associated moral imperative regarding board oversight of performance improvement in community health partnerships.

Each of the applied chapters begins with an explanation of the need for the pivotal topic under consideration, such as governance of community health here. Again, the concepts of *identity, accountability*, and *quality* provide a framework for the applied analysis. These concepts represent the foundation component (reflecting *who we are*), the process component (reflecting *how we function*), and the practice component (reflecting *what we do*) of the ethics paradigm (Table 1.1).

Table 1.1 Ethics paradigm

Components	Foundation component	Process component	Practice component
Context	Environment of healthcare	Organizational oversight	Organizational culture
Leadership	Identity: who we are	Accountability: how we function	Quality: what we do
Outcomes	Organizational stewardship of mission	Decision-making via participative deliberation	Best practices for standards of conduct

The interest in partnerships that improve community health has become a major concern for nonprofit healthcare systems.[9] Hence, before considering hallmarks of governance ethics regarding this topic, it is helpful to explain the need to advance community health partnerships.

Need to advance community health partnerships

The context of this discussion is the disconcerting paradox that the USA spends nearly 18 percent of the nation's gross domestic product on healthcare, much more than other developed nations.[10] The *Community Health Report* and the *Leadership Report* noted how much the USA lags on many metrics of population health, having extensive disparities in healthcare services.[11] To improve the health status of communities and society, it is inadequate to concentrate only on access to medical services and quality patient care. Rather, the delivery of healthcare services needs to go beyond treating individuals to being better integrated with well-established principles of public health. This approach involves more attention being given to the environment, lifestyles, prevention, early detection and treatment, and reliable determinants of health. Collectively, these factors have approximately a 90 percent greater impact in determining the health status of individuals and population groups. There needs to be considerable improvement in cooperation between health delivery, public health, and community stakeholders. Above all, governing boards have a critical role in reflecting their commitment to community health improvement in their organizations' strategic plan, priorities, and resource allocation.[12]

The Patient Protection and Affordable Care Act (ACA) of 2010 included a provision that led to action by the Internal Revenue Service (IRS). The ACA amended the IRS Code by adding Section 501(r). The new IRS requirement mandates every hospital operated by a 501(c)(3) organization to conduct a needs assessment regarding community health, with an implementation strategy to address priorities. Occurring at least every three years, this assessment may involve multiple hospitals working together to yield a joint report. In other words, the IRS provisions encourage relationships between hospitals, public health agencies, and others to assess these needs, to set priorities, and develop implementation strategies. This requirement of the IRS can help hospitals strengthen the justification of maintaining their tax-exempt status.[13] Also, Public Health Accreditation Board standards encourage multi-sector collaboration in health needs assessment.[14]

There is an increasing awareness of the need for effective communication and collaboration among health delivery organizations, the public health sector, and other multi-sector initiatives interested in the improvement of community health.[15] This awareness is a rediscovery of an insight articulated in 1932, nearly a century ago, by the Committee on the Costs of Medical Care when it emphasized that it is a folly to deal in a separate manner with medical services and public health.[16] The inherent difficulty of achieving successful collaborative arrangements probably contributed to the schism between the sectors of healthcare and public health from the 1930s. Also, there were many other factors that contributed to this schism, including the following: the dominance of employer-sponsored health insurance plans during World War II (e.g., Blue Cross/Blue Shield) focusing almost entirely on medical and hospital services; the infusion of enormous resources by the creation of Medicare and Medicaid into the medical and hospital sectors; progress in medical science and technology that generated an increasing demand for new procedures; and the asymmetry in funding and prestige of private-sector medicine and hospitals in relation to public health. Not surprisingly, there resulted differences in priorities, lack of mutual understanding, and cultural rifts.[17]

Fortunately, since the 1990s there has been increased awareness of significance of collaboration in the health arena, especially regarding community health.[18] This awareness is apparent in groups working together in a voluntary manner for a mutual interest. By illustration, in 1994 two major associations created a joint endeavor: the American Medical Association and the American Public Health Association established the Medicine/Public Health Initiative. While this initiative did not endure, the purpose was to consider why medicine and public health functioned so separately and independently and to explore opportunities for closer working relationships.[19] Subsequently, many reports by prominent organizations advocated for collaborative models to create a collective impact in medicine and public health.[20]

There are multiple rationales to support this shift from a narrow focus on individual patients to a broader focus that integrates communities into the nation's health agenda. Concentrating on the medical needs of individuals should be expanded to include population health approaches, as discussed in the *Community Health Report* and the *Leadership Report*. Reflecting this paradigm shift from treating individuals to engaging communities, there could be an acceleration of new alliances focused upon community health.[21] There are many studies that indicate an urgency to align improving community health with restraining healthcare expenditures.[22] Efforts over the long term to restrain the nation's health expenditures while improving community health will require much more comprehensive strategies that address behavior, education, the environment, and so forth.[23] This scenario led the Institute for Healthcare Improvement to establish a triple aim in healthcare: simultaneously to address the quality of patient care, to improve population health, and to reduce per capita costs of care across the public and private sectors of society. To achieve these aims, there are significant challenges that require integrating the measurement of population health status with the design of long-term multi-sector collaboration and the development of value-based payment systems focused on outcomes.[24] To address these aims by concerted efforts that recognize the multiple determinants of health outcomes, there needs to be better communication and coordination across all related public and private sectors.[25]

From the outset, it should be noted that failure occurs with almost half of the alliances, coalitions, and partnerships with two or more organizations. The *Community Health Report* and the *Leadership Report* indicate that in studying cross-sector collaborative initiatives for community health across the nation, only about half succeeded.[26] The success rate can increase significantly, up to 80 percent, when these collaborative arrangements incorporate a set of core characteristics and related indicators. The characteristics are delineated in terms of these categories: vision, mission, values; goals and objectives; partners; organizational structure; leadership; partnership operations; program success and sustainability; and performance evaluation and improvement.[27]

These reports considered successful partnerships between hospitals, public health agencies, and community stakeholders committed to improving the health of their communities. In the *Community Health Report*, the selected alliances were required to have been in operation for two years with successful performance and with diversity in location, form, and focus. Using qualitative analysis, the report determined findings and patterns from which it developed recommendations that are discussed later.[28] In the *Leadership Report*, the study examined five nonprofit health systems committed to community health improvement. The report engaged with multi-sector efforts to measure and improve the health of the communities they serve. The recommendations are discussed in the following sections.[29]

The discussion now applies the ethics paradigm to organize core features of effective governance regarding community health. The discussion focuses on the *Community Health Report*, the *Leadership Report*, and the scholarly literature. The purpose is to highlight hallmarks of governance ethics that denote associated moral imperatives. The applied analysis begins with discussing hallmarks of governance ethics connected with the foundation component of the ethics paradigm.

It is useful to note that the hallmarks of governance ethics regarding community health are designed in connection with the hallmarks of governance ethics regarding community benefit. That is, the focus in the previous chapter was on board engagement, effective communication, and organizational performance. The focus continues in this chapter's discussion of partnership engagement, partnership consensus, and partnership performance as hallmarks of governance ethics.

Partnership engagement: foundation-related governance ethics hallmark

The foundation component of the ethics paradigm, in the context of the challenging environment of healthcare, focuses on stewardship to enhance an organization's mission as crucial for effective governance. This component depicts the *identity* of an organization, reflecting the leitmotif *who we are*. The concept of *identity* highlights partnership engagement as a hallmark of governance ethics for community health. This concept draws attention to who the board is. In turn, this hallmark denotes an associated moral imperative regarding board oversight of the mission and structure of community partnerships. These are discussed later.

To understand partnership engagement as a hallmark of governance ethics, it is helpful to note that often crises in the community spark concerted action. Such action is designed to address needs that instigate different community health coalitions via partnership engagement.[30] The *Community Health Report* and the *Leadership Report* explained that these coalitions can provide guidance for other organizations and communities interested in developing their own out-reach. Addressing population health constitutes a moral imperative at local, state, and national levels.[31] These partnership efforts should be ongoing, not just a one-time occurrence.[32] When faced with urgent need in the health of a community, visionary and inspirational leaders are sought to generate collective action via partnership engagement. These individuals can provide instrumental leadership in founding an alliance and in contributing to its success insofar as well-qualified and dedicated personnel are designated to manage partnerships.[33] To create a cohesive coalition, these leaders need to articulate and communicate around a common understanding of the concepts, definitions, and principles of popula-tion health.[34] Effective communication requires mutual understanding of key concepts and terms. A significant obstacle to multi-sector collaboration in part-nership engagement has been the differences in respective interpretations of the concept of population health, using the same words with different meanings. For the public health sector, the concept refers to health outcomes of a group and their distribution within the group. From this perspective, the impact of education, the environment and socioeconomic influences affect the health status of a population in addition to their access to quality medical services. In contrast, the medical and hospital sectors all too often understood population health in relation to patients served by their organizations.[35]

The *Community Health Report* and the *Leadership Report* emphasized that hav-ing a trust-based relationship grounded in honesty and respect among the found-ing institutions is critical for a successful alliance.[36] Collective action has become increasingly productive for community development.[37] Often a tradition of com-munity cooperation lies behind new partnership engagement to foster community health. These types of established relations must be preserved through excellent communications and assessment as the group moves from planning to operations. To nurture this rapport new groups must have a culture and values that are sub-stantively compatible and congruent, even though they typically will not be iden-tical. In contrast, a primary cause for failure can be lack of trust.[38] These leaders and relationships cultivate a growing awareness of a fundamental change that recognizes the need for prevention, early diagnosis and treatment, and the promo-tion of wellness. This shift has created an emerging pattern that acknowledges the need for more attention to population health by engaging the following: improved understanding; better communication with the public health community; and coordinated action to improve community health with cooperation between pri-vate and public sectors.[39] Partnership engagement brings communities and orga-nizations together in programs and activities can generate collective interest while building community spirit and social capital. These efforts to improve community health serve an important social role by enabling group action aimed at population health improvement.[40]

Board oversight of partnership engagement is a hallmark of governance eth-ics. This hallmark denotes an associated moral imperative regarding board over-sight of the mission and structure of community partnerships. The mission and the structure of these partnerships can be distinct, though typically are closely related.

Moral imperative: board oversight of mission and structure of community partnerships

Board oversight of the mission of community partnerships is indispensable. The *Community Health Report* and the *Leadership Report* acknowledged the daunting challenges that must be faced both in the start-up years and in on-going operations of community partnerships. To address these challenges effectively they must emphasize the importance of mission, vision, and values, including their alignment with clear goals and objectives. These must focus on improving community health with firm support of the partnering organizations, be clearly stated, and be communicated widely. The identity of each collaboration helps to connect its mission with accompanying problems, while seeking to build community recognition, credibility, and respect. In the *Leadership Report* and the *Community Health Report*, the coalitions were generally relatively small entities without much history in community service. However, they had well-known organizational partners in the community, such as hospitals. This experience highlights the need to find ways to inform communities (such as by formal reports and community presentations) about these transformational endeavors that impact them all.[41] A clear mission statement is decisive for engaging the scope of these alliances, driving direction, strategies, and services, and bolstering community support with effective outreach. The mission statement is amplified by a strategic plan that guides a tangible course of action. Of course, these require ongoing review and improvement in content and format, especially regarding goals, objectives, and evaluation protocols.[42] However, because of the combination of health needs in communities and limited organizational capabilities, efforts to improve community health should have a defined mission, strategically and pragmatically indicating priority needs to inspire interest, engagement, and support. There can be a mission dissonance between coalition members when some may be traditionally focused on individual patients or related patient groups, whereas others may primarily address community health. Here, it is pivotal to sustain fidelity to population health outreach.[43] Well-designed coalitions with multiple stakeholders can be a catalyst for collective action regarding community health needs, using evidence-based experience to build on success. That is, community-powered problem solving creates synergy for a collective impact addressing complexity.[44] But having an unrealistic purpose that is not sufficiently pragmatic can compromise progress toward maintaining momentum and sustaining commitment.[45]

Also, board oversight of the structure of community partnerships is crucial. In the *Leadership Report* and the *Community Health Report*, it is evident that the mission of the coalition should shape its organizational structure, which in turn impacts the likelihood of success. A durable structure is crucial for carrying out the mission and goals of these coalitions. Typically, organizational models have a comparatively informal structure in contrast to corporate structures such as those with 501(c)(3) status. Generally, most appear to be open-ended regarding future possibilities to accommodate emerging needs.[46] Of course, there are many forms of collaboration with varying purposes, ranging from informal and non-binding to formal and legal arrangements. The organization's documents should articulate the key features of the partnership, especially its mission, goals, and core policies.[47] Two observations can be made generally about the structure of these partnerships.

On the one hand, the *Community Health Report* and the *Leadership Report* explained that having one or more anchor institutions to build multi-sector participation with common interests in community health can contribute to long-term survival and success.[48] Working together on programs and initiatives around a common cause is not necessarily contrary to competition in other areas.[49] Several examples can be highlighted. A coalition of big ten institutions was established in 1958. It was called the Committee on Institutional Cooperation and is now referred to as the Big Ten Academic Alliance (BTAA). The alliance has undertaken a number of initiatives. One purpose of this collaboration was to seek interventions that improve health equity. This partnership with these universities illustrates the role of educational institutions regarding population health. In 2013, a public-private learning collaborative was established by the Association of State and Territorial Health Officials (ASTHO). This alliance sought to improve hypertension control, contributing to a national goal of the Department of Health and Human Services of preventing 1 million heart attacks and strokes.[50] Another example is a multi-state collaborative, founded in 2009 with many states working together. With the Millbank Memorial Fund as an anchor institution providing support, the principal focus of collaborative efforts has been multi-payer primary care transformation.[51] Yet another example is MaineHealth, a nonprofit health system based in Portland that supports extensive Healthy Community programs.[52] Anchor institutions should be able to offer stable support, economic and otherwise. Successful collaborative partnerships for community health can be inspiring.[53] These collaboratives emphasize the importance of not relying only on health sector organizations to meet the enormous challenges facing community health. The leadership of business, education, and government sectors is indispensable.[54] On the other hand, the *Community Health Report* and the *Leadership Report* urged that antecedent informal connections should develop a formal affiliation agreement to address the complex issues involved around policies, strategy, budget, etc. Examples of these formal agreements are creating a steering committee or a leadership council. It is very helpful to establish a designated body that is empowered by the leading institutions with a succinct and simple written charter that is updated regularly to deal with these core functions: the coalition's vision, mission, and values with accompanying goals and objectives; the composition, responsibilities, and authority of the policy-setting body; and the powers and decisions that are restricted to the main institutions in the alliance. The charter should define the leadership role and responsibilities with regular updating.[55] The designated body, such as a partnership board, has the responsibility and authority to adopt policies and approve initiatives supporting the coalition's mission. This oversight will enable a coalition to be more robustly engaged in identifying priorities and strategies focused on action for community health improvement. The board should be comprised of individuals who have demonstrated interest and expertise in population health, can provide effective direction, monitor progress and adopt action plans to ensure ongoing progress. Also, standing committees for oversight of the coalition should be established by the participating health departments or hospitals. Tax exempt status is not required, but certainly preferred. This is because the tax-exempt status of nonprofit hospitals requires the provision of community benefit to provide measurable contributions that improve the populations served. Similarly, public health departments have statutory authority and accountability for community health in the populations that they serve.[56]

Hence, the governing boards and executives in nonprofit hospitals, health systems, and local health departments could establish standing board committees with oversight responsibility for their respective organization's role in population health improvement. Of course, it may not be necessary to have a standing committee for each partnership, with oversight responsibility being assigned to a board with a broader charge. The committees can address high-priority health needs, honor the social roles of their constituent organizations, and work together to improve the health of the populations they serve.[57]

In sum, the foundation component of the ethics paradigm highlights partnership engagement as a hallmark of governance ethics. By focusing on *identity* in the ethics paradigm (dealing with who the board is), this hallmark denotes an associated moral imperative regarding board oversight of the mission and structure of community partnerships.

Partnership consensus: process-related governance ethics hallmark

The concept of *accountability* in the ethics paradigm (reflecting the leitmotif *how we function*) emphasizes the importance of decision-making via participative deliberation. This focus requires boards to be attentive to organizational oversight as the context for assessing their responsibilities. The concept of *accountability* highlights partnership consensus as a hallmark of governance ethics for community health. To meet this charge, boards should be designed to have processes for consensus building. The concept draws attention to how the board functions in the organization. In turn, this hallmark denotes an associated moral imperative regarding board oversight of collaboration within community partnerships. These are discussed in what follows.

To understand partnership consensus as a hallmark of governance ethics, it is helpful to note that excellent communication channels are required among the partners, staff and community. The *Community Health Report* and the *Leadership Report* explained that consensus-building efforts must focus on substantive community engagement, support, and input to identify all relevant needs. These channels need to be clear, transparent, and effective to foster consensus about the work of the coalition. This culture requires mutual respect and trust, with the members having compatible values and dedication to build the coalition together.[58] This requires all involved, especially staff, to share ownership of the partnership, be open and transparent with each other, and demonstrate long-term commitment to its vision, mission, and values. In this environment, the alliance should focus on programs in which they have expertise or can efficiently secure required talent externally. Naturally, conflicts can occur. In an environment of decision-making in these consensus-oriented coalitions, there must be well-established mechanisms to proactively identify and resolve concerns.[59]

The *Community Health Report* and the *Leadership Report* emphasized that the coalition needs to have someone in charge of partnership operations to lead the deliberative processes required for action. Typically, the title of executive director (or similar names) devotes a considerable amount of work time to management of the coalition. This occurs either with or without significant technical support depending on each arrangement. A significant challenge is that the director usually has limited or no formal authority over the coalition members or over others who are affiliated and upon whom the alliance depends. Hence, the director relies on influence or persuasion for managing programs and personnel who are classically volunteers. This is similar to the challenges that a director encounters in managing nonprofit associations with many volunteers.[60] Although some coalitions have a strong anchor institution, most involve a much looser model that adopts a consensus style of direction, even though they may evolve into a more structured approach.[61] Because the director is essential for success, deliberative processes need to be adopted that reflect a model of servant leadership that makes progress through consensus-building. There is a significant amount of literature on this topic of servant leadership that centers around character, empathy, moral authority, systems thinking, and skilled communication.[62] In building a partnership consensus for community health, leaders have substantive responsibility but limited decision-making authority. Here, autocratic or hierarchic approaches are replaced with an approach based on teamwork and consensus-building, involving many in decision-making, and supporting workers while developing the institution.[63]

Moral imperative: board oversight of collaboration within community partnerships

Board oversight of partnership consensus is a hallmark of governance ethics. This hallmark denotes an associated moral imperative regarding board oversight of collaboration within community partnerships. Collaboration can flourish by adopting decision-making processes that foster participative deliberation. Unfortunately, a substantial proportion of organizational alliances are not successful, especially when there are many members accompanied with diffuse and complex decision-making processes. Hence, there is significant need for board oversight of decision-making processes to foster collaboration.

This collaborative approach can enable community partnerships to have an enduring impact over time for engaging a range of other parties from both public and private sectors. In other words, collaborative decision-making via participative deliberation can encourage the participation of many different sectors in partnerships for community health. Certainly, hospitals and public health departments and related stakeholders should typically be among the principal partners.

However, many other community organizations should be engaged insofar as they share a commonality of interest for the health of the community, such as school systems, health plans, and the business community. Also, including local, state, and federal government agencies can be productive by incorporating health considerations in their decision-making processes. Similarly, in the private sector professional associations at state and national levels should encourage these collaborative partnerships.

The *Community Health Report* and the *Leadership Report* showed that successful collaborative partnerships for community health require broad-based and multi-sector support.[64] For example, there is a solid body of evidence that hospitals and health systems are a key component of successful multi-sector partnerships for community health.[65] Also, there is extensive literature on multi-sector collaboration within community health partnerships.[66] These alliances can be very effective in addressing community health needs, serving the public interest and well-being. In other words, cooperation between professions can develop relational collaboration through organizational partnerships for the public good.[67] Adopting decision-making processes that encourage participative deliberation enables these collaborations to flourish.

In sum, the process component of the ethics paradigm highlights partnership consensus as a hallmark of governance ethics. By focusing on *accountability* in the ethics paradigm (dealing with how the board functions), this hallmark denotes an associated moral imperative regarding board oversight of collaboration within community partnerships.

Partnership performance: practice-related governance ethics hallmark

The concept of *quality* in the ethics paradigm (reflecting the leitmotif *what we do*) emphasizes the importance of best practices for standards of conduct. This focus requires boards to be attentive to organizational culture as the context for assessing their responsibilities. The concept of *quality* highlights partnership performance as a hallmark of governance ethics for community health. In turn, this hallmark denotes an associated moral imperative regarding board oversight of performance improvement in community partnerships. These are discussed in what follows.

To understand partnership performance as a hallmark of governance ethics, it is helpful to recognize the need for best practices. That is, collaborations for community health must relate to established best practices. The *Community Health Report* and the *Leadership Report* urged that partnership performance should be reviewed using evidence-based assessment. Successful coalitions must regularly monitor and measure outcomes in relation to their organizational goals and objectives using reliable metrics with a timeline for achievement. This should be a recurring process whereby progress reports are provided to the partners, community and key stakeholders. These reports should have accompanying actions that contribute to assessing partnership performance.[68] Recurring assessments should be based on the best science available to review the following: community health measures to be addressed, objectives and targets to be achieved, and metrics and tools to monitor progress.[69]

The *Community Health Report* and the *Leadership Report* explained that demonstrating successful partnership performance requires an expansive review of issues, including the following: engaging the support of the community; considering the length of time in operation; prioritizing community needs combined with strategies to address them; and examining evidence of long-term impact on community health.[70] All of this requires a wide-reaching perspective of the health landscape. Of course, access to quality services is indispensable and accounts for the major share of health expenditures in the USA. However, the economic, physical, and social environment must also be addressed.[71] Hence, efforts to develop community health must combine multiple facets: selecting from the broad range of interacting influences; establishing priorities; developing approaches for implementation; and designing standards to assess organizational performance. Each community's needs should be instrumental in shaping the focus and functions of a coalition and in guiding coalition outcomes.[72]

Moral imperative: board oversight of performance improvement in community partnerships

Board oversight of partnership performance is a hallmark of governance ethics. This hallmark denotes an associated moral imperative regarding board oversight of performance improvement in community partnerships. From the *Community Health Report* and the *Leadership Report* there emerges two critical requirements for performance improvement that meets the needs of coalitions: the metrics selected to monitor progress by considering measurable impacts; and the resources to meet the needs identified. Naturally, there are considerable challenges when considering these together.[73] It is crucial to scientifically connect health yardsticks with evidence-based strategies and sufficient resources. Fortunately, there is reliable information to gauge the burden of disease, injuries, and risk that can guide allocating assets and efforts. Aligning impacts and resources is indispensable.[74]

One critical requirement for performance improvement deals with impact. On this topic, the issue of effective assessment measures, using benchmarks of quality to improve population health, has been acknowledged for a long time.[75] However, objective evidence of the impact of collaborative arrangements for community health appears all too thin.[76] To be effective it is crucial to have a common understanding of population health to facilitate benchmarking, comparative evaluation, and mutual understanding.[77] In the *Community Health Report* and the *Leadership Report*, an agreed perspective enables participants to clarify how health status is assessed in a realistic manner.[78] To achieve these, it can be helpful to adopt leading health indicators presented in a ten-year plan by the US Department of Health and Human Services. Some of these indicators examined include the following: access to health services; clinical and preventive services; environmental quality; injury and violence; maternal, infant, and child health; mental health; nutrition, physical activity, and obesity; oral health; reproductive and sexual health; social determinants; substance abuse; and tobacco.[79]

In the *Community Health Report* and the *Leadership Report*, performance improvement in community health coalitions presents a serious challenge. The challenge is evident when considering infant mortality or the prevalence of cardiovascular disease where advances require a lot of time and effort.[80] There must be well-reasoned priorities in selecting determinants and measures (intermediate and long-term) to track improvements in community health. Of course, it is challenging to select specific community needs when assessing them means examining flawed linkages between determinants and measures of population health, perceptions of health needs, and intervention efficacy.[81] However, performance improvement reviews require evidence-based strategies to compile pertinent data as a basis for factual evaluation. Sound data will contribute to addressing significant gaps in evaluating achievements in community health.[82]

An example of a successful multi-sector approach is the Health of New Ulm Project in Minnesota on cardiovascular risk factors. In this project, the electronic health record system in the town's medical center provided an ideal repository for surveillance and registry data on community-wide cardiovascular disease.[83]

Despite the widely recognized difficulty in generating data for sustained improvement, especially on mortality and morbidity, several features have shown themselves to provide reliable information. Partnerships with a focus on a single community health need (such as reducing heart attacks), or on a narrow set of needs, can perform better than affiliations with more comprehensive, far-reaching missions. Such coalitions have a relatively less difficult challenge and they can more easily demonstrate positive results. Second, coalitions tend to be successful when they adopt benchmarks for performance improvement, approaches to achieve them, and ways to make assessments. Third, alliances can flourish when they recognize that a complex collection of issues contribute to performance improvement in community health. This recognition enables organizations to connect basic determinants, intermediate steps, and outcomes (even though more research on these links is needed).[84] Through performance improvement reports, community health partnerships can gain credibility and earn respect of key stakeholders. This credibility and respect can be nurtured by developing, regularly updating, and disseminating impact statements using evidence to present the effect of the partnership in relation to its available resources and incurred costs. Doing so highlights for partners, funders, the community and other stakeholders the value proposition of the partnership. These efforts demonstrate the benefits being provided and the progress being made and offers a compelling case for further investment and inspires community interest and support.[85]

The other critical requirement for performance improvement deals with resources. The *Community Health Report* and the *Leadership Report* underscore that the long-term survival of a coalition for community health requires financial sustainability. Different funding levels for collaborative partnerships significantly influence how community health initiatives can advance. This influence includes the design and operation of a coalition, the volume and intensity of supported activities with associated costs, the size of the population served, and the mix of other in-kind support. Significant attention needs to be dedicated to finances, including the value of in-kind contributions within a coalition's organizations, to avoid becoming vulnerable to financial instability.[86] Deliberate plans are needed to broaden and diversify sources for funding support with the partners identifying resource requirements (regarding both personnel and funding), building sufficient capital and operating budgets, and securing those resources.[87] Unfortunately, there is limited financial support for multi-sector collaborative initiatives focusing on community health. Moreover, health departments tend to be lightly funded even as they encounter great challenges. Faced with this disconcerting reality, leaders in hospitals and public health must develop their own funding strategies for multi-sector collaboration to improve community health. Fundraising is a major challenge for most of these endeavors.[88]

The *Community Health Report* and the *Leadership Report* suggest that a key strategy to financial stability deals with involving anchor institutions. Large healthcare organizations or robust health departments, and indeed many other organizations can be anchor institutions for multi-sector partnerships focused on improving community health. These partnerships could benefit greatly by more participation of business organizations. Various forms of support can be very helpful for these multi-sector partnerships. However, financial resources from the business community, health plans, and healthcare providers is necessary to sustain the partnerships.

These institutions can provide long-term commitment to a coalition's mission with solid long-term financial (but not necessarily complete funding) and in-kind support for community health initiatives. By illustration, hospitals and health systems have in the past directed community benefit funds, required by their tax-exempt status, to support services for uninsured or under-insured patients. Increasingly, they tend to apply a considerable portion of these funds to support affiliated multi-sector community health partners. This increase has been influenced by the Affordable Care Act and the Public Health Accreditation Board standards that call for collaborative efforts to engage community health needs.[89] Or, there could be other resources for ongoing financial support. These resources include the following: health plans with leaders who appreciate the need to focus resources on population health; local employers who recognize the value of a coalition for their community; and local government's investment in the welfare of the community.[90] Major local employers and health plans can provide robust support for community health initiatives. However, when there is low level of engagement by them as principal partners or major funders, concern is justified.[91] Having one or more organizational partners make a commitment in this manner is a fundamental strategy for sustainability. Of course, this sort of continuing support will depend upon continuous performance improvement by partnerships to demonstrate a measurable and compelling impact on community health.[92]

Even in these scenarios, the *Community Health Report* and the *Leadership Report* recognize that additional financial support is typically necessary such as grants from local, state, and national sources, both private and governmental. The availability of federal or foundation grant programs can provide a catalyst for a partnership to address community health initiative. This catalyst support can focus on a start-up or provide short-term support, but rarely does it provide durable support.[93] The upside is that personnel are highly dedicated with lots of talent. Personnel also contribute significantly to creating social capital by making connections between the coalition members and the community. However, reliance on grant support can constrain a coalition, restricting long-term plans as well as the stabilization of staff support. Coalitions for community health ordinarily rely extensively on volunteers and staff from the organizational members. Nonetheless, heavy reliance on volunteers can cause substantial turnover, thereby stressing full-time staff and requiring continuing recruitment efforts for succession planning.[94] Without grant renewal or securing an equivalent funding source, the future of a coalition will be in jeopardy. Because resources are crucial for performance improvement of coalitions for community health, it is time for government agencies via public policy and many others to establish more public-private alliances. From the policy perspective, examples might be local and state government funding, state-level policies supporting hospital and public health cooperation, and federal-level programs that stimulate successful public-private partnerships. Perhaps more sustainably, financial resources from the business community, health plans, and healthcare providers are indispensable if these alliances are to be sustained and flourish.[95]

In sum, the practice component of the ethics paradigm highlights partnership performance as a hallmark of governance ethics. By focusing on *quality* in the ethics paradigm (dealing with what the board does), this hallmark denotes an associated moral imperative regarding board oversight of performance improvement in community partnerships.

Conclusion

The chapter has indicated hallmarks of governance ethics with associated moral imperatives regarding the community health. The contribution of the ethics paradigm can be summarized in this manner.

First, in the context of the challenging healthcare environment, the foundation component of the ethics paradigm focuses on stewardship to enhance an organization's mission as crucial for effective governance. This component deals with the *identity* of an organization, reflecting the leitmotif *who we are*, thereby highlighting board oversight of partnership engagement as a hallmark of governance ethics for community health. This hallmark connects with the hallmark of board engagement in the previous chapter. In turn, this hallmark denotes an associated moral imperative of board oversight of the mission and structure of community health partnerships.

Second, in the context of organizational oversight in healthcare organizations, the process component of the ethics paradigm focuses upon decision-making to foster participative deliberation in organizations. This component addresses the *accountability* of the organization, reflecting the leitmotif *how we function*, thereby highlighting partnership consensus as a hallmark of governance ethics for community health. This hallmark connects with the hallmark of effective communication in the previous chapter. In turn, this hallmark denotes an associated moral imperative regarding board oversight of collaboration within community health partnerships.

Third, in the context of organizational culture in healthcare, the practice component of the ethics paradigm is to focus on best practices to develop standards of conduct. This component engages *quality* in an organization, reflecting the leitmotif *what we do*, thereby highlighting partnership performance as a hallmark of governance ethics for community health. This hallmark connects with the hallmark of organizational performance in the previous chapter. In turn, this hallmark denotes an associated moral imperative regarding board oversight of performance improvement in community health partnerships.

This chapter has applied the ethics paradigm to identify hallmarks of governance ethics regarding community health, denoting associated moral imperatives. The next chapter adopts the same approach to discuss hallmarks of governance ethics concerning patient care.

Notes

1 See: D. H. Barrett, et al., eds., *Public Health Ethics: Cases Spanning the Globe* (Springer, 2016); Richard Bonnie, Ruth Gaare Bernheim, *Public Health Law, Ethics, and Policy*, University Casebook Series (St. Paul, MN: West Academic, 2015); R. G. Bernheim, et al., *Essentials of Public Health Ethics* (Burlington, MA: Jones & Bartlett Learning, 2015); S. Holland, *Public Health Ethics*, 2nd ed. (Malden, MA: Polity, 2015); Angus Dawson, ed., *Public Health Ethics: Key Concepts and Issues in Policy and Practice* (New York: Cambridge University Press, 2011); L. O. Gostin, ed., *Public Health and Law Ethics: A Reader*, 2nd ed. (Berkeley, CA: University of California Press, 2010).
2 L. Prybil, et al., *A Perspective on Public–Private Collaboration in the Health Sector* (Washington, DC: National Academy of Medicine, 2015), 9–10.
3 See: National Academies of Science, Engineering, and Medicine, *Criteria for Selecting the Leading Health Indicators for Healthy People 2030* (Washington, DC: The National Academies Press, 2019); National Academies of Science, Engineering, and Medicine, *Vital Signs: Core Metrics for Health and Health Care Progress* (Washington, DC: The National Academies Press, 2015); National Academies of Science, Engineering, and Medicine, *Toward Quality Measures for Population Health and the Leading Health Indicators* (Washington, DC: The National Academies Press, 2013).
4 Department of Health and Human Services, Office of the Surgeon General, *Surgeon General Priority: Community Health and Economic Prosperity* (2019), at www.hhs. gov/surgeongeneral/priorities/community-health-economic-security/index.html.
5 M. Connelly, L. Prybil, "Charting a Course to Community Health: A Governance Priority," *Health Progress* 98 (September–October, 2017): 71–72; M. Totten, L. Prybil, "Building Community Health," *Trustee* 70 (February, 2017): 26–27.
6 L. Prybil, et al. *Improving Community Health Through Hospital–Public Health Collaboration. Insights and Lessons Learned from Successful Partnerships* (Lexington, KY: Commonwealth Center for Governance Studies, Inc., 2014). Referred to as the *Community Health Report*.
7 L. Prybil, *The Leadership Role of Nonprofit Health Systems in Improving Community Health* (Chicago, IL: American Hospital Association, Advances in Healthcare Governance Series, 2017). Referred to as the *Leadership Report*.

8 *Leadership Report*, 5. Also see: F. Scutchfield, L. Prybil, L., R. Dixon, "Entering a New Era in Hospital and Public Health Collaboration for Community Benefit," in R. Bialek, L. Beitsch, J. Moran, Solving Population Health Through Collaboration (London: Routledge, Taylor & Francis Group, 2017), Chapter 25; L. Prybil, L., et al., "The Evolution of Public Health – Hospital Collaboration in the United States," *Public Health Reports* 131 (July–August, 2016): 522–525; L. Prybil, M. Totten, "Better Community Health: Hospital, Health System Boards Need to Find, Work with Multiple Partners to Achieve Their Goals," *Trustee* 69 (March, 2016): 26–27; F. D. Scutchfield, et al., "Public Health and Hospitals: Lessons Learned from Partnerships in a Changing Healthcare Environment," *American Journal of Public Health* 106 (January 2016): 45–48; R. Killian, L. Prybil, "Improving Community Health through Multi-Sector Partnerships," *Governance Institute Boardroom Press* 26 (August, 2015): 5–11; G. Mays, F. D. Scutchfield, "Improving Public Health System Performance Through Multiorganizational Partnerships," *Preventing Chronic Disease* 7 (November 2010): 1–8.

9 American Hospital Association, *2016 Blue Ribbon Panel Report, Learnings on Governance from Partnerships that Improve Community Health* (Chicago, IL: American Hospital Association, 2016).

10 See: Centers for Medicare & Medicaid Services, *National Health Expenditure Data* (2019), at, www.cms.gov/research-statistics-data-and-systems/statistics-trends-and-reports/nationalhealthexpenddata/nationalhealthaccountshistorical.html; Statista, National per capita health expenditures in the United States from 1960–2019, at www.statista.com/statistics/184955/us-national-health-expenditures-per-capita-since-1960/; Peterson-Kaiser, Health Care Tracker, *How Does Health Spending in the US Compare to Other Countries?* (2019), at www.healthsystemtracker.org/chart-collection/health-spending-u-s-compare-countries/#item-start.

11 *Leadership Report*, 4; *Community Health Report*, 3. Also see: S. Glied, et al., "Where the Money Goes: The Evolving Expenses of the US Healthcare System," *Health Affairs* 35 (2016): 1197–1203; H. J. Heiman, S. Artiga, *Beyond Health Care: The Role of Social Determinants in Promoting Health and Health Equity* (Menlo Park, CA: The Henry J. Kaiser Family Foundation, 2014); K. Davis, et al., *Mirror, Mirror on the Wall: How the Performance of the U.S. Health Care Systems Compares Internationally* (New York: The Commonwealth Fund, 2014).

12 *Leadership Report*, 4; *Community Health Report*, 3–4, 38. Also see: M. Soto, *Population Health in the Accountable Care Era* (Washington, DC: AcademyHealth, 2013); Association for Community Health Improvement, *Trends in Hospital-Based Population Health Infrastructure* (Chicago, IL: Health Research and Educational Trust, 2013).

13 *Leadership Report*, 5; *Community Health Report*, 3, 37. Also see: IRS Section 1.501(r)-3(b)(1) & (5), Federal Register 78 (66) (April 5, 2013); S. Rosenbaum, et al., "The Value of the Nonprofit Hospital Tax Exemption Was $24.6 Billion in 2011," *Health Affairs* 34 (2015): 1–9.

14 *Community Health Report*, 39. Also see: A. Carman, L. Prybil, M. Totten, "Partners for Public Health: Hospitals and Health Departments Can Collaborate on Community Health Needs Assessments," *Trustee* 66 (May 2013): 26–27; Public Health Accreditation Board, *Standards and Measures for Initial Accreditation* (2019), at www.phaboard.org/standards-and-measures-for-initial-accreditation/; Public Health Accreditation Board, *Standards: An Overview* (2013), at www.phaboard.org/wp-content/uploads/2019/01/PHAB-Standards-Overview-Version-1.5.pdf.

15 L. Prybil, et al., *A Perspective on Public–Private Collaboration in the Health Sector* (Washington, DC: National Academy of Medicine, 2015), 9–10.

16 L. Prybil, et al., *A Perspective on Public–Private Collaboration in the Health Sector* (Washington, DC: National Academy of Medicine, 2015), 1, referring to: The Committee on the Costs of Medical Care, *Medical Care for the American People* (Chicago, IL: The University of Chicago Press, 1932), 47.

17 L. Prybil, et al., *A Perspective on Public–Private Collaboration in the Health Sector* (Washington, DC: National Academy of Medicine, 2015), 2. See: National Quality Forum, *Multistakeholder Input on a National Priority: Improving Population Health by Working with Communities* (Washington, DC: National Quality Forum, 2016).

18 L. Prybil, et al., *A Perspective on Public–Private Collaboration in the Health Sector* (Washington, DC: National Academy of Medicine, 2015), 2.

19 L. Prybil, et al., *A Perspective on Public–Private Collaboration in the Health Sector* (Washington, DC: National Academy of Medicine, 2015), 3. See: R. Lasker and the Committee on Medicine and Public Health, *Medicine and Public Health: The Power of Collaboration* (New York: New York Academy of Medicine, 1997).

20 L. Prybil, et al., *A Perspective on Public–Private Collaboration in the Health Sector* (Washington, DC: National Academy of Medicine, 2015), 3. See: Institute of Medicine, *Collaboration Between Health Care and Public Health* (Washington, DC: The National Academies Press, 2015); Robert Wood Johnson, *Collaborations to Build Healthier Communities* (Princeton, NJ: Robert Wood Johnson Foundation, 2013); Institute of Medicine, *Primary Care and Public Health: Exploring Integration to Improve Population Health* (Washington, DC: The National Academies Press, 2012).

21 *Leadership Report*, 33; *Community Health Report*, 5, 38, 45. See also: Robert Wood Johnson, *Building a Culture of Health: 2014 President's Message* (Princeton, NJ: Robert Wood Johnson Foundation, 2014); Health Research and Educational Trust, *Hospital-Based Strategies for Creating a Culture of Health* (Chicago, IL: Health Research and Educational Trust, 2014).

22 *Community Health Report*, 4, referring to: Institute of Medicine, *For the Public's Health: Investing in a Healthy Future* (Washington, DC: National Academy of Sciences, 2012; Institute of Medicine, *Primary Care and Public Health: Exploring Integration to Improve Community Health* (Washington, DC: National Academy of Sciences, 2012); Robert Wood Johnson, *Time to Act: Investing in the Health of our Children and Communities* (Princeton, NJ: Robert Wood Johnson Foundation, 2014).

23 L. Prybil, et al., *A Perspective on Public–Private Collaboration in the Health Sector* (Washington, DC: National Academy of Medicine, 2015), 3. See: L. Taylor, et al., *Leveraging the Social Determinants of Health* (New Haven, CT: Yale Global Health Leadership Institute, 2015); M. Stoto, *Population Health in the Accountable Care Era* (Washington, DC: AcademyHealth, 2013).

24 *Leadership Report*, 6, *Community Health Report*, 4 and L. Prybil, et al., *A Perspective on Public–Private Collaboration in the Health Sector* (Washington, DC: National Academy of Medicine, 2015), 3. Also see: American Hospital Association, *Triple Aim Strategies to Improve Behavioral Health Care* (Chicago, IL: American Hospital Association, 2016).

25 *Leadership Report*, 5, *Community Health Report*, 4 and L. Prybil, et al., *A Perspective on Public–Private Collaboration in the Health Sector* (Washington, DC: National Academy of Medicine, 2015), 3. Also see: A. Weil, "It Takes a Community," *Health Affairs* 33 (2014): 1886; R. Letourneau, "Partnering for Better Population Health Management," *HealthLeaders* 17 (May 2014): 48–51.

26 *Community Health Report*, 23 and L. Prybil, et al., *A Perspective on Public–Private Collaboration in the Health Sector* (Washington, DC: National Academy of Medicine, 2015), 5. Also see: J. Forrer, *Governing Cross-Sector Collaboration* (Wiley, 2014).

27 *Community Health Report*, 6. Also see: L. Herald, et al., "Decision-making Fairness and Consensus-Building in Multisector Community Alliances," *Nonprofit Management and Leadership* 24 (Winter 2013): 159–161; J. Kania, M. Kramer, "Collective Impact," *Stanford Social Innovation Review* 54 (Winter 2011): 36–41.

28 *Community Health Report*, 38–44.

29 *Leadership Report*, 32–34.

30 *Community Health Report*, 10, 16, 29.

31 *Community Health Report*, 28, 30, 38.

32 *Leadership Report*, 34; *Community Health Report*, 42.

33 *Community Health Report*, 10–11, 29, and Appendix A, 49; also, L. Prybil, et al., *A Perspective on Public–Private Collaboration in the Health Sector* (Washington, DC: National Academy of Medicine, 2015), 6.

34 *Community Health Report*, 30–31, 42. Also see: R. A. Goodman, et al., What is "Community Health"? Examining the Meaning of an Evolving Field in Public Health," *Preventive Medicine* 67 (Suppl. 1) (October 2014): S58–S61; N. Adler, et al., *Building the Science for a Population Health Movement* (Washington, DC: National Academy of Sciences, 2013).

35 L. Prybil, et al., *A Perspective on Public–Private Collaboration in the Health Sector* (Washington, DC: National Academy of Medicine, 2015), 4–5. See: L. Casalino, et al., "Accountable Care Organizations and Population Health Organizations," *Journal of Health Politics, Policy, and Law* 40 (2015): 819–821.

36 *Leadership Report*, 33; *Community Health Report*, 6, Appendix A, 49; Appendix C, 65–66.

37 See: L. Gram, et al., "Understanding Participation Dilemmas in Community Mobilization: Can Collective Action Theory Help?" *Journal of Epidemiology and Community Health* (2018): 1–7, at, https://jech.bmj.com/content/73/1/90; A. Cigarini, et al., "Quantitative Account of Social Interactions in a Mental Health Care Ecosystem: Cooperation, Trust and Collective Action," *Nature: Scientific Reports* 28 (8) (2018): 3794, at www.nature.com/articles/s41598-018-21900-1; G. Chiarenza, ed., "Embracing a Collective Action Approach to Community Development," *Community Investments* 26 (1) (Spring 2014): 2–4.

38 *Leadership Report*, 33; *Community Health Report*, 11, 29, 40. See: R. Kaplan, et al., "Managing Alliances with the Balanced Scorecard," *Harvard Business Review* 88 (January 2010): 114–120; J. Chao, et al., "Avoiding Blind Spots in Your Next Joint Venture," *McKinsey on Finance* 48 (Autumn 2013): 25–30.

39 *Leadership Report*, 4–5; *Community Health Report*, 28–29, 38. See also: R. Tio, "Moving Towards Population Health," *Hospitals and Health Networks* 88 (May 2014); A. Garcia, et al., "U.S. Health Care is Moving Upstream," *Health Progress* 94 (January–February, 2013): 7–13.

40 *Leadership Report*, 32–33; *Community Health Report*, 39. See: U.S. Centers for Disease Control and Prevention, *Community Health Assessment for Population Health Improvement: Resource of Most Frequently Recommended Health Outcomes and Determinants* (Atlanta, GA: Office of Surveillance, Epidemiology, and Laboratory Service, 2013).

41 *Leadership Report*, 5; *Community Health Report*, 16, 23–25, Appendix A, 48, and L. Prybil, et al., *A Perspective on Public–Private Collaboration in the Health Sector* (Washington, DC: National Academy of Medicine, 2015), 5–6.

42 *Leadership Report*, 32; *Community Health Report*, 16–17, 30.

43 *Leadership Report*, 32; *Community Health Report*, 23. See: Trust for America's Health, *A Healthier America 2013: Strategies to Move from Sick Care to Health Care* (Washington, DC: Trust for America's Health, 2013); H. Sox, Resolving the Tension Between Population and Individual Health," *Journal of the American Medical Association* 310 (November 12, 2013): 1933–1934; J. Resnik, "Leading the Way to Population Health," *Hospitals and Health Network* 88 (September, 2014): 14; Health Research and Educational Trust, "The Second Curve of Population Health," *Trustee* 67 (May 12, 2014): 17–20.

44 *Community Health Report*, 5. Also see: F. Gouillart, D. Billings, "Community-Powered Problem Solving," *Harvard Business Review* 19 (April 2013): 71–77; R. Nidumolo, et al., "The Collaboration Imperative," *Harvard Business Review* 92 (April 2014): 77–84; J. Kanie, et al., "Embracing Emergence: How Collective Impact Addresses Complexity," *Stanford Social Innovation Review* 6 (January 21, 2013).

45 *Leadership Report*, 33; *Community Health Report*, 40.

46 *Leadership Report*, 33; *Community Health Report*, 13.

47 *Leadership Report*, 33; *Community Health Report*, Appendix A, 48, and L. Prybil, P. et al., *A Perspective on Public–Private Collaboration in the Health Sector* (Washington, DC: National Academy of Medicine, 2015), 2, 6. See: Beatty, K., et al., "Collaboration Among Missouri Nonprofit Hospitals and Local Health Departments," *American Journal of Public Health* 105 (2015): S237–S344; Pestronk, R., et al., "Public Health's Role: Collaborating for Healthy Communities," *Health Progress* 94 (2013): 21–25.

48 *Leadership Report*, 33; *Community Health Report*, 13. See: D. Zuckerman, *Hospitals Building Healthier Communities: Embracing the Anchor Mission* (Takoma Park, MD: The Democracy Collaborative, 2013).

49 *Community Health Report*, 30–31, Appendix C, 81–84. Also see: D. Nygren. "Competitors as Collaborators," *Trustee* 66 (September 2013): 13–27; M. Brainerd, et al., "Doing Well by Doing Good: A Leader's Guide," *McKinsey Quarterly* (September 2013).

50 L. Prybil, et al., *A Perspective on Public–Private Collaboration in the Health Sector* (Washington, DC: National Academy of Medicine, 2015), 7–8, at www.btaa.org/about/news-and-publications/news/2016/06/30/the-committee-on-institutional-cooperation-is-now-the-big-ten-academic-alliance.

51 *Community Health Report*, Appendix C, 74–75. Also see: www.milbank.org/programs/primary-care-transformation.

52 *Community Health Report*, Appendix C, 74–75. Also see: MaineHealth Healthy Communities; MaineHealth Health Index.

53 *Community Health Report*, 36–37. Also see: G. Nelson, et al., *Hospital Community Benefits after the ACA: Addressing Social and Economic Factors that Shape Health* (Baltimore, MD: The Hilltop Institute, 2014).

54 *Leadership Report*, 33; *Community Health Report*, 41 and *Community Health Report*, Appendix C, 63–64. Also see: L. Prybil, et al., *A Perspective on Public–Private Collaboration in the Health Sector* (Washington, DC: National Academy of Medicine, 2015), 9; R. Schulz, *A New Model for Private Sector Partnerships to Improve Economic Well-being and Community Outcomes* (Washington, DC: Institute of Medicine, 2015).

55 *Leadership Report*, 32; *Community Health Report*, 14, 41, Appendix A, 48–49. See: K. Peisert, *Governing the Value Journey: A Profile of Structure, Culture, and Practices of Boards in Transition* (San Diego, CA: The Governance Institute, 2013).

56 See: L. H. Mayer, "The Rising of the States in Nonprofit Oversight," *Nonprofit Quarterly* (August 11, 2016); S. Rosenbaum, et al., "The Value of the Nonprofit Hospital Tax Exemption was $24.6 Billion in 2011," *Health Affairs* 34 (2015): 1–9.

57 *Leadership Report*, 4; *Community Health Report*, 43–44; Appendix A, 48; Appendix C, 69–70.

58 Health Research and Educational Trust, *Creating Effective Partnerships to Build a Culture of Trust* (Chicago, IL: Health Research and Educational Trust, 2016).

59 *Community Health Report*, 6, and Appendix A, 49.

60 *Community Health Report*, 17–18.

61 *Leadership Report*, 5; *Community Health Report*, 32.

62 For example, see: J. W. Sipe, D. M. Frick, *Seven Pillars of Servant Leadership* (Mahwah: NJ: Paulist Press, 2015); R. K. Greenleaf, *The Servant as Leader* (Atlanta, GA: Greenleaf Center, 2015); K. M. Keith, *The Case for Servant Leadership* (Atlanta, GA: Greenleaf Center, 2015); D. Wheeler, *Servant Leadership for Higher Education: Principles and Practice* (San Francisco, CA: Jossey-Bass, 2012).

63 *Leadership Report*, 5; *Community Health Report*, 32. See: L. Spears, "Tracing the Growing Impact of Servant-Leadership," in L. Spears, ed., *Insights on Leadership: Service, Stewardship, Spirit, and Servant Leadership* (New York: John Wiley and Sons, Inc., 1998).

64 *Leadership Report*, 4; *Community Health Report*, 31, 39, 44. See: L. Rudolf, J. Caplan, *Health in All Policies: A Guide to State and Local Government* (Oakland, CA: Public Health Institute, 2014).

65 See: American Hospital Association, *Triple Aim Strategies to Improve Behavioral Health Care* (Chicago, IL: American Hospital Association, 2016); Health Research and Educational Trust, *Creating Effective Hospital–Community Partnerships to Build a Culture of Health* (Chicago, IL: Health Research and Educational Trust, 2016); Health Research & Educational Trust, *Engaging Patients and Communities in the Community Health Needs Assessment Process* (Chicago, IL, 2016); M. Chen, et al., *The Role of Hospitals in Improving Non-Medical Determinants of Community Population Health* (New York, NY: New York State Health Foundation, 2016); D. Radley, et al., *Rising to the Challenge: The Commonwealth Fund Scoreboard on Local Health System Performance, 2016* (New York, NY: The Commonwealth Fund, 2016); T. Norris, T. Howard, *Can Hospitals Heal America's Communities?* (Cleveland, OH: Democracy Collaborative, 2015).

66 *Community Health Report*, 6. See: P. Barnes et al., "Measures of Highly Functioning Health Coalitions," *Frontiers in Public Health Services and Systems Research* 3 (August, 2014): 1–5.

67 *Community Health Report*, 5; Appendix C, 72–73. Also see: J. Gittell, et al., "Interprofessional Collaborative Practice and Relational Coordination," *Journal of Interprofessional Care* 27 (2013): 210–213; G. Mays, F. D. Scutchfield, "Improving Public Health System Performance Through Multiorganizational Partnerships," *Preventing Chronic Disease* 7 (November 2010): 1–8.

68 *Leadership Report*, 32; *Community Health Report*, 16; Appendix A, 48–49; Appendix C, 94–96. Also see: L. Prybil, et al., *A Perspective on Public–Private Collaboration in the Health Sector* (Washington, DC: National Academy of Medicine, 2015), 6.

69 *Community Health Report*, Appendix C, 89–93.

70 *Leadership Report*, 32; *Community Health Report*, Appendix A, 49.

71 *Community Health Report*, 18. See: S. Teutsch, J. Fielding, "Applying Comparative Effectiveness Research to Public and Population Health Initiatives," *Health Affairs* 30 (February, 2011): 349–355.

72 *Leadership Report*, 32; *Community Health Report*, 18.

73 *Leadership Report*, 32; *Community Health Report*, 20–21.

74 *Community Health Report*, 24. See: C. Murray, A. Lopez, "Measuring the Global Burden of Disease," *New England Journal of Medicine* 369 (August 1, 2013): 448–457.

75 *Community Health Report*, 21, referring to the Institute of Medicine, *Toward Quality Measures for Population Health and the Leading Indicators* (Washington, DC: National Academy of Sciences, 2013).

76 See: L. Prybil, et al., *A Perspective on Public–Private Collaboration in the Health Sector* (Washington, DC: National Academy of Medicine, 2015), 9; R. Porterfield, et al., "Measuring Public Health Practice and Outcomes in Chronic Disease: A Call for Coordination," *American Journal of Public Health* 105 (Suppl. 2) (2015): S180–S188.

77 L. Prybil, P et al., *A Perspective on Public–Private Collaboration in the Health Sector* (Washington, DC: National Academy of Medicine, 2015), 5. See: Institute of Medicine, *Vital Signs: Core Metrics for Health and Health Care Progress* (Washington, DC: The National Academies Press, 2015); Robert Wood Johnson Foundation, *From Vision to Action: A Framework and Measures to Mobilize a Culture of Health* (Princeton, NJ: Robert Wood Johnson Foundation, 2015).

78 *Leadership Report*, 32; *Community Health Report*, 30.

79 *Community Health Report*, 22, Table 14, "Leading Health Indicators." See: Federal Interagency Workgroup, *Healthy People 2020*, at www.healthypeople.gov/2020.

80 *Community Health Report*, 23–24. See: U.S. Centers for Disease and Prevention, *Community Health Assessment for Population Health Improvement: Resources of Most Frequently Recommended Health Outcomes and Determinants* (Atlanta, GA: Office of Surveillance, Epidemiology, and Laboratory Services, 2013).

81 *Leadership Report*, 6; *Community Health Report*, 20.

82 *Leadership Report*, 32; *Community Health Report*, 32, Appendix C, 85–88.

83 See: A. C. Sidebottom, et al., "Assessing the Impact of the Health of New Ulm Project on Cardiovascular Risk Factors: A Population-Based Program to Reduce Cardiovascular

Disease," *Preventive Medicine* 112 (July 2018): 216–221; L. Prybil, et al., *A Perspective on Public–Private Collaboration in the Health Sector* (Washington, DC: National Academy of Medicine, 2015); National Quality Forum, *Multistakeholder Input on a National Priority: Improving Population Health by Working with Communities* (Washington, DC: National Quality Forum, 2016); National Quality Forum. 2016. *Improving Population Health by Working with Communities* (Washington, DC: National Quality Forum, 2016).

84 *Community Health Report*, 21, 34.

85 *Leadership Report*, 33; *Community Health Report*, 42–43.

86 *Leadership Report*, 33; *Community Health Report*, 26, 28.

87 *Leadership Report*, 33; *Community Health Report*, 43; Appendix A, 49.

88 L. Prybil, et al., *A Perspective on Public–Private Collaboration in the Health Sector* (Washington, DC: National Academy of Medicine, 2015), 6. See: Institute of Medicine, *Spread, Scale, and Sustainability in Population Health* (Washington, DC: The National Academies Press, 2015); K. Wilson, et al., "Describing the Continuum of Collaboration Among Local Health Departments With Hospitals Around the Community Health Assessments," *Journal of Public Health Management and Practice* 20 (2014): 617–624.

89 *Community Health Report*, 27, 30 and L. Prybil, et al., *A Perspective on Public–Private Collaboration in the Health Sector* (Washington, DC: National Academy of Medicine, 2015), 6–7. See: S. Johnson, "Diagnosing a Community Health Needs: Non-For-Profit Hospitals Target Health Improvement Efforts Under Reform Law," *Modern Healthcare* 44 (June 16, 2014): 14–16; G. Young, et al., "Provision of Community Benefits by Tax-Exempt U.S. Hospitals," *New England Journal of Medicine* 368 (April 18, 2013): 1519–1527.

90 L. Prybil, et al., *A Perspective on Public–Private Collaboration in the Health Sector* (Washington, DC: National Academy of Medicine, 2015), 6–7. See: P. McDonald, et al., "The Employer-led Health Care Revolution," *Harvard Business Review* 93 (2015): 39–50.

91 *Community Health Report*, 31. See: J. McGuire, *Population Health Investments by Health Plans and Large Provider Organizations: Exploring the Business Case* (Boston, MA: Northeastern University, 2016).

92 *Community Health Report*, 43 and L. Prybil, P et al., *A Perspective on Public–Private Collaboration in the Health Sector* (Washington, DC: National Academy of Medicine, 2015), 6.

93 *Community Health Report*, 10, 29, Appendix C, 97–98.

94 *Community Health Report*, 24–25.

95 *Leadership Report*, 33; *Community Health Report*, 45, and L. Prybil, et al., *A Perspective on Public–Private Collaboration in the Health Sector* (Washington, DC: National Academy of Medicine, 2015), 6.

Select readings

American Hospital Association. 2016. *2016 Blue Ribbon Panel Report, Learnings on Governance from Partnerships that Improve Community Health.* Chicago, IL: American Hospital Association.

American Hospital Association. 2016. *Triple Aim Strategies to Improve Behavioral Health Care.* Chicago, IL: American Hospital Association.

Chen, M., et al. 2016. *The Role of Hospitals in Improving Non-Medical Determinants of Community Population Health.* New York, NY: New York State Health foundation.

Health Research and Educational Trust. 2016. *Creating Effective Partnerships to Build a Culture of Trust.* Chicago, IL: Health Research and Educational Trust.

Health Research and Educational Trust. 2016. *Engaging Patients and Communities in the Community Health Needs Assessment Process*. Chicago, IL: Health Research and Educational Trust.

Institute of Medicine. 2015. *Collaboration Between Health Care and Public Health*. Washington, DC: The National Academies Press.

National Quality Forum. 2016. *Improving Population Health by Working with Communities*. Washington, DC: National Quality Forum.

Prybil, L. 2017. *The Leadership Role of Nonprofit Health Systems in Improving Community Health*. Chicago, IL: American Hospital Association, Advances in Healthcare Governance Series.

Prybil, L., et al. 2014. *Improving Community Health Through Hospital–Public Health Collaboration. Insights and Lessons Learned from Successful Partnerships*. Lexington, KY: Commonwealth Center for Governance Studies, Inc.

Prybil, L., et al. 2015. *A Perspective on Public–Private Collaboration in the Health Sector*. Washington, DC: National Academy of Medicine.

Radley, D., et al. 2016. *Rising to the Challenge: The Commonwealth Fund Scoreboard on Local Health System Performance*. New York: The Commonwealth Fund.

Robert Wood Johnson Foundation. 2015. *From Vision to Action: A Framework and Measures to Mobilize a Culture of Health*. Princeton, NJ: Robert Wood Johnson Foundation.

Schulz, R. 2015. *A New Model for Private Sector Partnerships to Improve Economic Well-Being and Community Outcomes*. Washington, DC: Institute of Medicine.

Taylor, L., et al. 2015. *Leveraging the Social Determinants of Health*. New Haven, CT: Yale Global Health Leadership Institute.

7 Governance of patient care quality

Introduction

The previous two applied chapters addressed community-related topics (community benefit and community health). This chapter and the next chapter apply the ethics paradigm to discuss hallmarks of governance ethics regarding patient care quality and patient safety. The significance of board oversight of quality and safety is widely recognized. For example, the Joint Commission provides guidelines on what boards need to know about these pivotal issues.[1] Also, the Agency for Healthcare Research and Quality and the Institute for Healthcare Improvement provide ongoing resources.[2] In ethics studies just over a decade ago, board oversight of patient care quality and patient safety was not prominent,[3] but now they are recognized as essential governance responsibilities.[4] Although patient care quality and patient safety are discussed together in the literature, this chapter and the next deal with them separately to focus on their distinctive issues related to governance ethics.

In the analysis in the applied chapters, the concepts of the ethics paradigm organize core features of effective governance from landmark reports and the scholarly literature. Instead of a formal report, there is a study by one of the co-authors of this book that shapes the discussion in this chapter. The study is referred to as the *Accountability Study*.[5] The purpose is to highlight hallmarks of governance ethics that denote associated moral imperatives. Because the hallmarks represent necessary moral attributes of governance ethics, they entail an obligation to be adopted by boards. In turn, the associated moral imperatives represent necessary endeavors to foster the hallmarks under consideration.

The ethics paradigm organizes multiple topics on board oversight of patient care quality as follows. First, the foundation component of the ethics paradigm deals with the *identity* of an organization, reflecting the leitmotif *who we are*, thereby indicating board transparency as a hallmark of governance ethics. In turn, this hallmark denotes an associated moral imperative concerning board oversight of the development of trust to support patient care quality. Second, the process component of the ethics paradigm addresses the *accountability* of the organization, reflecting the leitmotif *how we function*, thereby indicating board responsiveness as a hallmark of governance ethics. In turn, this hallmark denotes an

Table 1.1 Ethics paradigm

Components	Foundation component	Process component	Practice component
Context	Environment of healthcare	Organizational oversight	Organizational culture
Leadership	Identity: who we are	Accountability: how we function	Quality: what we do
Outcomes	Organizational stewardship of mission	Decision-making via participative deliberation	Best practices for standards of conduct

associated moral imperative concerning board oversight of factors contributing to support patient care quality. Third, the practice component of the ethics paradigm engages *quality* in an organization, reflecting the leitmotif *what we do*, thereby indicating board oversight of mechanisms for patient care quality as a hallmark of governance ethics. In turn, this hallmark denotes an associated moral imperative concerning board oversight of the social contract for patient care quality.

Each of the applied chapters begins with an explanation of the need for the pivotal topic under consideration, such as governance of patient care quality here. Again, the concepts of *identity*, *accountability*, and *quality* provide a framework for the applied analysis. These concepts represent the foundation component (reflecting *who we are*), the process component (reflecting *how we function*), and the practice component (reflecting *what we do*) of the ethics paradigm (Table 1.1).

Before discussing hallmarks of governance ethics, it is helpful to explain the need for board oversight of patient care quality.

Need for board oversight of patient care quality

It is widely recognized, as indicated in the *Governance Structure Report* (discussed in previous chapters), that board oversight of patient care quality is an indispensable feature of effective governance.[6] Nonetheless, the level of clinical services in hospitals and health systems needs to be improved, especially from the perspective of monitoring and improving clinical services.[7] It has long been recognized that board oversight of patient care quality is crucial for effective governance, especially regarding system-wide measures and standards.[8] A survey of 1,000 board chairs indicated that less than half rated oversight of patient care quality as a top priority, with only a minority of board member having any formal training in this area.[9] There is a longstanding acknowledgment that enhancing board oversight of patient care quality nurtures the trust of communities served,[10] with that trust reflecting improvements in care.[11]

Over the past decade, there has been a recognition of the urgency for board oversight concerning poor performance indicators in US healthcare. Now, nearly 18 percent of the US gross domestic product is devoted to healthcare, far more than other industrialized countries for which the median figure is less than 10 percent. Healthcare spending in the USA is nearly $11,000 per person, over twice the median figure for other industrialized nations.[12] But the USA lags on many indicators of population health such as infant mortality and life expectancy, and there is abundant evidence of wide disparities in healthcare services.[13]

A broad array of factors contributes to this scenario, including economic, lifestyle, political, and social issues. In this regard, the *Governance Structure Report* emphasized the performance of non-governmental, nonprofit health systems, which are growing in numbers, providing a large proportion of inpatient and outpatient services.[14] Nonprofit hospitals and health systems in the private sector are regulated and/or influenced by local, state, and federal government requirements, accrediting commissions, bond rating agencies, payers, and many other external parties.[15] Governing boards, with the assistance of their management teams, must remain updated regarding ever-changing expectations and must oversee compliance with them.[16] As the number and size of health systems continue to grow, an increasing share of overall governance responsibility deals with system or parent boards of these health systems.[17] The numbers in the USA are large: in 2019, the American Hospital Association indicated there are 2,968 community hospitals (of the 6,210 total of hospitals in the USA) that are part of non-government, nonprofit health systems.[18]

Governance of large and complex healthcare organizations poses many challenges and requires high levels of expertise. To meet these challenges, there are multiple accountabilities for health system boards. There needs to be greater transparency, better responsiveness, and specific accountability mechanisms. The components of the ethics paradigm emphasize the significance of these elements regarding board oversight as being crucial for governance ethics.

The discussion now applies the ethics paradigm to organize core features of effective governance regarding patient care quality. This discussion focuses on the *Accountability Study* and the scholarly literature. The purpose is to highlight hallmarks of governance ethics that denote associated moral imperatives. The applied analysis begins with discussing hallmarks of governance ethics connected with the foundation component of the ethics paradigm.

Board transparency: foundation-related governance ethics hallmark

The foundation component of the ethics paradigm, in the context of the challenging environment of healthcare, focuses on stewardship to enhance an organization's mission as crucial for effective governance. This component depicts the *identity* of an organization, reflecting the leitmotif *who we are*. The concept of *identity* highlights board transparency as a hallmark of governance ethics for patient care quality. This concept draws attention to *who the board is* in relation with its organization. Here, transparency showcases the stewardship of the organization regarding its mission. In turn, this hallmark denotes an associated moral imperative regarding board oversight of the development of trust to support patient care quality. These are discussed in the next section.

To understand board transparency as a hallmark of governance ethics, it is crucial to recognize accountability as an indispensable characteristic of board effectiveness regarding its fiduciary duties, as discussed in the *Accountability Study*.[19] The necessity for and significance of transparency is widely recognized. For example, the state statutes under which both investor-owned and nonprofit corporations are chartered call for their governing boards to have overall responsibility for the organization and the services and/or products it provides. There is increasing interest by regulators and the public in how effectively boards are performing their fiduciary duties and fulfilling their broader responsibility to owners, stakeholders, and society at large.[20]

In the healthcare field, the call for more robust board oversight is not new, as discussed in the *Accountability Study*. In 1918, as the number and social roles of hospitals were expanding, the American College of Surgeons stated, "All hospitals are accountable to the public for their degree of success . . . if the initiative is not taken by the medical profession, it will be taken by the lay public."[21] In today's environment, oversight is crucially connected with transparency by governing boards of nonprofit healthcare organizations. One reason has been the large variations in healthcare services from community to community and from institution to institution. The variation is substantial, well documented, and challenging.[22]

The existence of these problems is increasingly visible to state and federal regulators, payers, the media, and the public. Many events have brightened the spotlight on the performance of hospitals and health systems and on those who are responsible for them. Not surprisingly, there are significant concerns about the transparency of healthcare organizations.[23] All hospital and health system boards, in concert with their clinical and executive leadership teams, must scrutinize the performance of the organization for which they are responsible to create greater transparency for board oversight of patient care quality.

Moral imperative: board oversight of the development of trust to support patient care quality

Oversight of board transparency is a hallmark of governance ethics. This hallmark denotes an associated moral imperative regarding board oversight of the development of trust to support patient care quality. This support includes the assessment and continuous improvement of patient care quality. There is a growing public interest in healthcare organizations. This interest is part of a wider public concern about the development of trust in communities that are served. This concern about trust pertains to large institutions in all sectors, such as banking, the federal government, and others. The declining trust in large institutions has created new challenges for boards.[24] A decade ago, federal legislation and regulations tried to address this issue. For example, the Dodd-Frank Wall Street Reform and Consumer Protection Act of 2010 encouraged placing more power in the hands of shareholders: the purpose was to influence the election of board members, levels of executive compensation, and other corporate decisions.[25]

Similarly, in healthcare, calls for greater board responsiveness have become more frequent and explicit, as emphasized in the *Accountability Study*. For example, the National Association for Healthcare Quality, in conjunction with several other national associations, urged leaders of healthcare organizations to implement structures to assure integrity in the evaluation of patient care quality. That evaluation should occur via "comprehensive, transparent, accurate data collection and reporting to internal and external oversight bodies."[26] Also, the Patient Protection and Affordable Care Act prompted hospital boards and their parent systems to heighten their focus on their responsiveness for developing and maintaining effective patient care quality control processes.[27]

Failure to address these issues regarding the public's trust is likely to result in closer scrutiny of nonprofit hospitals and health systems and could result in additional regulatory controls. This erosion of trust increasingly threatens the practice of medicine.[28] These trust-related concerns could increase review of the benefits they are providing to the communities they serve, ultimately leading to increasing challenges to tax-exempt status or pressures to establish "payment in lieu of taxes" requirements.[29]

Furthermore, the *Accountability Study* explained that developing trust requires effective oversight as an ongoing requirement for boards and executive leaders to perform their responsibilities. Board transparency is crucial for this oversight. Boards should provide information regarding the extent to which their responsibilities have been accomplished and an explanation when they have not.[30] Clarity about responsibilities is essential for sound organizational governance and management. Lack of clarity in defining responsibilities and/or demonstrating how they have been fulfilled leads to an erosion of trust on the part of the internal and external stakeholders that healthcare boards and management serve.[31]

In sum, the foundation component of the ethics paradigm indicates board transparency as a hallmark of governance ethics. By focusing on *identity* in the ethics paradigm (dealing with *who the board is*), this hallmark denotes an associated moral imperative concerning board oversight of the development of trust to support patient care quality.

Board responsiveness: process-related governance ethics hallmark

The concept of *accountability* in the ethics paradigm (reflecting the leitmotif *how we function*) emphasizes the importance of decision-making via participative deliberation. This focus requires boards to be attentive to organizational oversight as the context for assessing their responsibilities. The concept of *accountability* highlights board responsiveness as a hallmark of governance ethics for community health. The concept draws attention to *how the board functions* in the organization. In turn, this hallmark denotes an associated moral imperative regarding board oversight of factors contributing to support patient care quality. These are discussed in the next section.

To understand board responsiveness as a hallmark of governance ethics, it is helpful to note the growing significance of shareholder voices. In the world of investor-owned companies, there is an ongoing discussion of the role of shareholders, the investors who hold an ownership position. The crucial issues that are being addressed deal with the following: how should shareholder voices be heard by those who govern and manage these organizations; what level of influence should shareholders have in the appointment and re-appointment of board members, the selection and retention of CEOs and other corporate decisions; and what are the merits of quarterly earnings and current stock prices for judging board and CEO effectiveness in relation to longer-term performance metrics.[32] In the large and growing sector of non-governmental, nonprofit organizations, similar questions about participative decision-making are being raised.[33]

The *Accountability Study* acknowledges that the public wants more board responsiveness from large institutions, both public and private. In the healthcare field the availability of information about the cost, price, and quality of services is growing.[34] Several developments are dramatically expanding the volume of information available to the public at large, including the following: the public availability of the increasingly detailed IRS form 990 and related schedules; the release of extensive Medicare pricing data by the Center for Medicare and Medicaid Services; and investigative reporting by media. This deluge of publicly available information requires greater attention in board oversight.

Moral imperative: board oversight of factors contributing to support patient care quality

Oversight of board responsiveness is a hallmark of governance ethics. This hallmark denotes an associated moral imperative regarding board oversight of factors contributing to support patient care quality. As discussed in the *Governance Structure Report*, it is advisable for nonprofit hospitals and health system boards to have a standing committee with oversight responsibility for the organization's community benefit policies and programs.[35] This is a good example of the need for greater board responsiveness to the community as a matter of governance accountability. This trend toward greater transparency through accountability will continue. Transparency must center on the consumer who should be empowered to inquire about treatment options, risks, outcomes, and costs. Healthcare providers must respond accordingly to ensure appropriate care is delivered, with quality of care being foremost.[36]

However, the *Accountability Study* also emphasized that the mere availability of more information is insufficient. Information alone cannot build public understanding or provide a solid basis for organizational accountability to the communities served. This particularly deals with information about complex subjects around healthcare services, the impact these services are having on population health, and the community benefit provided by healthcare organizations. For many citizens, this information can be difficult to interpret and comprehend without advice and assistance. The mere availability of information does not readily translate into board responsiveness about that information, especially in terms of involving patients and the community.[37] A growing body of evidence demonstrates a wide variation in access, cost, and quality of healthcare services. Hence, there are significant public concerns about the efficiency of healthcare organizations and the accountability of their clinical, executive, and governance leadership.[38]

It is well known that a substantial portion of USA healthcare expenditures is spent on services that are unneeded and/or inappropriate, leading to overtreatment, waste, and preventable harm. Also, there are well known critical reports on access, cost, and quality of healthcare services.[39] Naturally, this information contributes to public concerns about healthcare institutions. No one can understand why prices for the same procedures for similar patients, adjusted for differences in cost of living in various locations, should vary considerably.[40] To address these public concerns and accompanying distrust, there is an urgent need for greater responsiveness by governing boards regarding the communities they serve.[41]

In sum, the process component of the ethics paradigm highlights board responsiveness as a hallmark of governance ethics. By focusing on *accountability* in the ethics paradigm, this hallmark denotes an associated moral imperative concerning board oversight of factors contributing to support patient care quality.

Board mechanisms for patient care quality: practice-related governance ethics hallmark

The concept of *quality* in the ethics paradigm (reflecting the leitmotif *what we do*) emphasizes the importance of best practices for standards of conduct. This focus requires boards to be attentive to organizational culture as the context for assessing their responsibilities. The concept of *quality* highlights oversight of board mechanisms for patient care quality as a hallmark of governance ethics for community health. In turn, this hallmark denotes an associated moral imperative regarding board oversight of the social contract for patient care quality. These are discussed in what follows.

To understand what is meant by board mechanisms for patient care quality as a hallmark of governance ethics, it is important to appreciate how boards can shape organizational culture. There are many opportunities for the governing boards of nonprofit health systems to cultivate a board culture that develops best practices for standards of conduct. Cultivating board culture entails boards understanding quality measurements that are critical in healthcare, such as those promoted by the Agency for Healthcare Quality and Research, by the Centers for Medicare & Medicaid Services, and by the World Health Organization.[42] The practical mechanisms can be illustrated in relation to the hallmarks of transparency and responsiveness for governance ethics, as discussed in the previous sections.

On the one hand, boards must strategically increase their level of transparency with their constituencies, both internal and external, as discussed in the *Accountability Study*. Here, transparency means that boards should develop practical mechanisms for quality care related to sharing information with the communities they serve. These mechanisms would be manifest in the organization's policies and programs designed to build their stakeholders' understanding, support, and trust.[43] Health systems that do not offer board transparency expose themselves to danger. The danger is to allow the media and others to assume leadership for informing and educating key stakeholders and the community. Giving the media this leeway is a risky strategy.[44] Nonetheless, effective use of media in healthcare, including social media, can be helpful.[45]

On the other hand, the *Accountability Study* emphasizes the importance of board responsiveness. That is, boards of nonprofit health systems need to examine how they develop deliberative processes with the communities their institutions serve with accompanying quality care mechanisms. For years, it has been customary for many, perhaps most, nonprofit hospitals and health systems to declare that they are accountable to the communities and populations they serve in their bylaws, mission statements, and other corporate documents.[46] Boards must work to realize these claims.

For boards to be appropriately responsive to the communities they serve, they need to realize these claims. To do so, boards have to remain updated with the fast-moving developments around patient care quality. Much progress has been made on developing methods for defining and implementing patient-centered care, including the following: access to care; respect for patient preferences; coordination and integration of care; information and education; continuity and transition.[47] Considerable work has been undertaken on the theory, methods, and tools regarding patient care quality to enlighten boards on mechanisms for quality of care from medical, nursing and legal perspectives.[48] Board oversight of patient care quality is crucial for success in high reliability organizations.[49] In particular, boards must be attentive to the increasing focus on diversity and inclusion regarding patient care quality.[50] Quality care mechanisms for board responsiveness as effective measures of their oversight accountability are crucial,[51] such as for communicating about quality care issues across the organization.[52]

The *Accountability Study* also explains that for geographically dispersed health systems, growth and structural changes can complicate the challenges inherent in board accountability.[53] For effective governance, board responsiveness requires appropriate quality care mechanisms to address these challenges.[54] Expansion into new locations through acquisition or start-ups creates a need to establish communication channels, identify and address the community's concerns and expectations, and build mutual understanding and trust.[55] Subsidiary or local boards must meet these challenges to be appropriately responsive to their communities by cooperating with their health system and its governing practices.[56]

Also, the *Accountability Study* notes that systems may choose to allow boards at the local level to retain some decision-making authority. These boards, especially when including community members, can serve as an important source of community input and linkage to the community. Board responsiveness requires building communications and trust between healthcare organizations and the communities they serve. To foster this responsiveness, some examples are as follows: having a governing board composed of community members; establishing advisory councils; and conducting community forums for two-way communication.[57]

Moral imperative: board oversight of the social contract for patient care quality

With robust board responsiveness, board mechanisms for patient care quality will continue to foster effective governance for the communities served by healthcare organizations.[58] Oversight of board mechanisms for patient care quality is a hallmark of governance ethics. This hallmark denotes an associated moral imperative regarding board oversight of the social contract for patient care quality.

The concept of the social contract expresses a traditional idea in healthcare.[59] There is a broad understanding of what the social contract entails, including being an advocacy-oriented call to action,[60] referring to the relation between patients and providers,[61] or broadly describing the role of medicine in society.[62] Discussions about the social contract have been connected with policy around healthcare reform.[63] The concept of social contract is being adopted increasingly to identify the duties and responsibilities between health organizations and care recipients, between providers and patients. For example, the Institute for Healthcare Improvement emphasizes the partnership between patients and providers.[64]

The *Accountability Study* mentioned another example of this social contract in reference to quality care. There can be a formal, written commitment signed by the CEO, the board chair, the medical staff president, and the chief nurse executive. This expresses a commitment to the community regarding actions that will be taken to improve the institution's performance with respect to patient care quality.[65] This constitutes a practical mechanism to share the institution's targets and performance with the community the institution serves.[66]

The *Accountability Study* explains that the significance of board oversight of the social contract for patient care quality should not be underestimated. This issue highlights the need for nonprofit health systems to review, renew, and strengthen their bonds with the communities they exist to serve. This approach relies on effective mechanisms for quality care to demonstrate how boards are in practice meeting these responsibilities, especially regarding continuous evaluation and improvement. Also, this approach can establish best practices to foster trust between patients and providers. The practical mechanisms of transparency and responsiveness discussed in this chapter can provide a sturdy platform to build loyalty and to counter any erosion of public confidence in healthcare organizations. That is, these mechanisms can foster public understanding, a culture of trust, and support for the health system, its mission, and its leadership.[67]

In sum, the practice component of the ethics paradigm suggests that board oversight of mechanisms for patient care quality is a hallmark of governance ethics. By focusing on leadership regarding *quality* in the ethics paradigm, this hallmark denotes associated moral imperatives concerning board oversight of the social contract for patient care quality.

Conclusion

The chapter has indicated hallmarks of governance ethics with associated moral imperatives regarding patient care quality. The contribution of the ethics paradigm can be summarized in this manner.

First, in the context of the challenging healthcare environment, the foundation component of the ethics paradigm focuses on stewardship to enhance an organization's mission in healthcare as crucial for effective governance. This component deals with the *identity* of an organization, reflecting the leitmotif *who we are*, thereby indicating board transparency as a hallmark of governance ethics. In turn, this hallmark denotes an associated moral imperative of board oversight of the development of trust to support patient care quality.

Second, in the context of organizational oversight in healthcare, the process component of the ethics paradigm is to focus upon decision-making to foster participative deliberation in institutions. This component addresses the *accountability* of the organization, reflecting the leitmotif *how we function*, thereby indicating board responsiveness as a hallmark of governance ethics. In turn, this hallmark denotes an associated moral imperative of board oversight of factors contributing to support patient care quality.

Third, in the context of organizational culture in healthcare, the practice component of the ethics paradigm is to focus on best practices to develop standards of conduct. This component engages *quality* in an organization, reflecting the leitmotif *what we do*, thereby indicating board oversight of mechanisms for patient care quality as a hallmark of governance ethics. In turn, this hallmark denotes an associated moral imperative of board oversight of the social contract for patient care quality.

This chapter has applied the ethics paradigm to identify hallmarks of governance ethics regarding patient care quality, denoting associated moral imperatives. The next chapter adopts the same approach to discuss hallmarks of governance ethics concerning the closely related topic of patient safety.

Notes

1 See: Joint Commission, Patient Safety, *Joint Commission Fact Sheet* (Oakbrook, IL: Joint Commission Resources, 2018); Joint Commission, *Getting the Board on Board: What Your Board Needs to Know About Quality and Patient Safety*, 3rd ed. (Oakbrook, IL: Joint Commission Resources, 2016); Joint Commission, 2019 *National Patient Safety Goals* (Oakbrook, IL: Joint Commission Resources), at www.jointcommission.org/hap_2017_ npsgs/; Joint Commission, Inspiring Health Care Excellence (Oakbrook Terrace, IL: Joint Commission Resources, 2019), at www.jointcommission.org/assets/1/6/General_ brochure.pdf.

2 Agency for Healthcare Research and Quality, *Quality and Patient Safety* (2019), at, www.ahrq.gov/professionals/quality-patient-safety/index.html; Institute for Healthcare Improvement, *CPPS, Certified Professional in Patient Safety* (2019), at www. ihi.org/education/cpps-certified-professional-in-patient-safety/Pages/default.aspx; Institute for Healthcare Improvement, *Quality, Cost and Value* (2019) at www.ihi.org/ Topics/QualityCostValue/Pages/default.aspx.

3 See: R. A. Ritvo, et al., *Ethical Governance in Healthcare. A Board Leadership Guide for Building an Ethical Culture* (Chicago, IL: Health Forum, Inc., 2004). In this book, just a few pages were dedicated to the problem of medical mistakes (pp. 60–63) and quality of care (pp. 61, 63).

4 L. Prybil, et al., *Governance in Large Nonprofit Health Systems: Current Profile and Emerging Patterns* (Lexington, KY: Commonwealth Center for Governance Studies, Inc., 2012), 28–31 (referred to as the *Governance Structure Report*). Also see: L. Prybil, et al., "Board Oversight of Patient Care Quality in Large Nonprofit Health Systems," *American Journal of Medical Quality* 29 (1) (2014): 39–43; "Strategies

to Govern Quality," in NEJM Catalyst, *Taking Healthcare Governance to the Next Level* (2018), at, https://catalyst.nejm.org/healthcare-governance-next-level-quality-committee/; HealthCatalyst, *Engaging Health System Boards of Trustees in Quality and Safety: Six Must-Know Guidelines* (2019), at www.healthcatalyst.com/insights/healthcare-boards-quality-safety-pivotal-role.

5 L. Prybil, et al., *The Evolving Accountability of Nonprofit Health System Boards* (Chicago, IL: AHA Center for Healthcare Governance, Monograph Series, 2013, referred to as the *Accountability Study*.

6 *Governance Structure Report*, 28–31. Also see: L. Prybil, et al., "Board Oversight of Patient Care Quality in Community Health Systems," *American Journal of Medical Quality* 25 (1) (2012): 34–41.

7 *Governance Structure Report*, 29. Also see: J. Cowan, "Good Medical Practice Should Improve Patient safety," *Clinical Governance: An International Journal* 12 (2) (2007): 136–141; J. L. Reinersten, *Hospital Boards and Clinical Quality: A Practical Guide* (Toronto, ON: Ontario Hospital Association, 2007), 1–12. Also see: D. J. Mason, et al., "The Representation of Health Professionals on Governing Boards of Healthcare Organizations in New York City," *Journal of Urban Health* 90 (5) (2012): 888–901.

8 *Governance Structure Report*, 30. Also see: The Governance Institute, "Enhancing Quality Oversight," *Healthcare Executive* 25 (2) (2010): 80–81.

9 M. K. Totten, "Transforming Care Delivery to Focus on Patient Outcomes," *Healthcare Executive* 27 (5) (2012): 68–69, referring to, A. K. Jha, A. Epstein, "Hospital Governance and the Quality of Care," *Health Affairs* 29 (1) (2010): 182–187.

10 D. M. Berwick, "Building Quality in the Healthcare Environment," *Quality and Safety in Healthcare* 12 (2003): 12–16, reprinted in, D. A. Shore, *The Trust Crisis in Healthcare* (New York: Oxford University Press, 2007), 49–59.

11 See: L. L. Leape, "Medical Errors and Patient Safety," in D. A. Shore, ed., *The Trust Crisis in Healthcare* (New York: Oxford University Press, 2007), 60–69; R. M. Wachter, *Understanding Patient Safety*, 2nd ed. (New York: McGraw Hill, 2017).

12 Centers for Medicare & Medicaid Services, *National Health Expenditure Data* (2017), at www.cms.gov/research-statistics-data-and-systems/statistics-trends-and-reports/nationalhealthexpenddata/nationalhealthaccountshistorical.html.

13 *Accountability Study*, 5; Centers for Disease Control and Prevention, *Infant Mortality*, at www.cdc.gov/reproductivehealth/maternalinfanthealth/infantmortality.htm.

14 *Accountability Study*, 5.

15 *Accountability Study*, 5.

16 *Accountability Study*, 5.

17 *Accountability Study*, 5.

18 American Hospital Association, *2019 AHA Hospital Statistics* (Chicago, IL: American Hospital Association, 2019), at www.aha.org/statistics/fast-facts-us-hospitals.

19 *Accountability Study*, 7.

20 National Council of Nonprofits, *Finding the Right Board Member for your Nonprofit* (2019), at www.councilofnonprofits.org/tools-resources/finding-the-right-board-members-your-nonprofit. Also see: R. Pozen, "The Case for Professional Boards," *Harvard Business Review* 88 (2010): 51–58; C. Bhagat, et al., "Tapping the Potential of Boards," *McKinsey Quarterly* 1 (2013): 91–98.

21 American College of Surgeons, "Standard of Efficiency for the First Hospital Survey of the College," *Bulletin of the American College of Surgeons* 3 (1918): 1–4.

22 *Accountability Study*, 6. Also see: Institute of Medicine, *Best Care at Lower Cost* (Washington, DC: National Academies Press, 2012); Agency for Healthcare Research and Quality, *National Healthcare Quality Report* (Washington, DC: Agency for Healthcare Research and Quality, 2013, updated in 2017).

23 M. Makary, *Unaccountable: What Hospitals Won't Tell You and How Transparency Can Revolutionize Healthcare* (New York: Bloomberg Press, 2012); L. Gage, *Transformational Governance: The Challenges Facing Trustees of Nonprofit and Public Hospitals* (Chicago, IL: Center for Healthcare Governance, 2012).

24 National Association of Corporate Directors, *2018–2019 NACD Public Company Governance Survey* (2019), at www.nacdonline.org/analytics/survey.cfm?ItemNumber= 63801. For earlier data, see: National Association of Corporate Directors, *Governance Challenges-2012 and Beyond* (Washington, DC: NACD, 2012); J. Kirby, "Trust in the Age of Transparency," *Harvard Business Review* 89 (2012): 158–159.

25 See: www.congress.gov/bill/111th-congress/house-bill/4173/text.

26 *Accountability Study*, 7. Also see: National Association for Healthcare Quality, *Call to Action: Safeguarding the Integrity of Healthcare Quality and Safety Systems* (Washington, DC: NAHQ, 2012).

27 *Accountability Study*, 7. Also see: E. Belmont, et al., "A New Quality Compass: Hospital Boards' Increased Role Under the Affordable Care Act," *Health Affairs* 30 (2011): 1282–1283.

28 D. Wolfson, Commentary: Erosion of Trust Threatens Essential Element of Practicing Medicine," *Modern Healthcare* (March 9, 2019), at www.modernhealthcare.com/ opinion-editorial/commentary-erosion-trust-threatens-essential-element-practicing-medicine.

29 Editorial, "Profit Motive: The City's UPMC Suit will Turn on One Key Factor," *Pittsburg Post Gazette* (March 27, 2013).

30 *Accountability Study*, 5.

31 *Accountability Study*, 6.

32 National Association of Corporate Directors, *NACD Directorship 2020: Dynamics and Culture in the Boardroom* (2019), at www.nacdonline.org/insights/publications. cfm?ItemNumber=8838.

33 See: T. Verulava, et al., "The Role of Non-Profit Organizations in Health Care Systems," *Georgian Medical News* 274 (2018): 174–178; M. Wynland, "The Role of Nonprofits in Healthcare: A Trends Summary," *Nonprofit Quarterly* (February 7, 2014), at, https:// nonprofitquarterly.org/the-role-of-nonprofits-in-health-care-a-trends-summary/.

34 *Accountability Study*, 9. Also see: H.-K. Fleming, "Improving Quality and Lowering Cost Through Community Care Teams," *Journal of Healthcare Management* 63 (4) (2018): 242–250.

35 *Governance Structure Report*, 17.

36 G. S. Kaplan, "Building a Culture of Transparency in Health Care," *Harvard Business Review* (November 9, 2018), at, https://hbr.org/2018/11/building-a-culture-of-transparency-in-health-care. Also see: S. Rivkin, F. Seitel, *Transparency: How Much of a Good Thing?* (Chicago, IL: Center for Healthcare Governance, 2011).

37 *Accountability Study*, 10. Also see: R. Islam, et al., "Clinical Complexity in Medicine: A Measurement Model of Task and Patient Complexity," *Methods of Information in Medicine* 55 (1) (2016): 14–22.

38 *Accountability Study*, 10.

39 See: H. Lyu, et al., "Overtreatment in the United States," *PLos One* 12 (9) (September 6, 2017), at, https://doi.org/10.1371/journal.pone.0181970; A. E. Carroll, "The High Costs of Unnecessary Care," *JAMA Forum* (November 14, 2017): 1748–1749, at, https://doi.org/10.1001/jama.2017.16193; Institute of Medicine, *Best Care at Lower Cost* (Washington, DC: National Academies Press, 2013).

40 Health Care Cost Institute, *2017 Health Care Cost and Utilization Report*, at, www. healthcostinstitute.org/images/easyblog_articles/276/HCCI-2017-Health-Care-Cost-and-Utilization-Report-02.12.19.pdf.

41 M. Bismark, et al., "The Role of Governing Boards in Improving Patient Experience," *Patient Experience Journal* 1 (1) (2014): 144–152.

42 Agency for Healthcare Quality and Research, Understanding Quality Measurement (2019), at www.ahrq.gov/professionals/quality-patient-safety/quality-resources/tools/ chtoolbx/understand/index.html; Centers for Medicare & Medicaid Services, *Quality Measure and Quality Improvement* (2019), at www.cms.gov/Medicare/Quality-Initiatives-Patient-Assessment-Instruments/MMS/Quality-Measure-and-Quality-Improvement-. html; J. Hanefield, et al., "Understanding and Measuring Quality of Care: Dealing with

Complexity," *Bulletin of the World Health Organization* 95 (2017): 368–374, at, http://doi.org/10.2471/BLT.16.179309.

43 *Accountability Study*, 11.

44 *Accountability Study*, 11. See: S. Rivkin, F. Seitel, *Transparency: How Much of a Good Thing?* (Chicago, IL: Center for Healthcare Governance, 2011).

45 See: L. Yingjie, et al., "Understanding Health Care Social Media Use from Different Stakeholder Perspectives: A Content Analysis of an Online Health Community," *Journal of Medical Internet Research* 19 (4) (April 2017): e109, at, https://doi.org/10.2196/jmir.7087; L. Bou-Karroum, et al., "Using Media to Impact Health Policy-Making: An Integrative Systematic Review," *Implementation Science* 12 (52) (April 18, 2017), at, https://implementationscience.biomedcentral.com/articles/10.1186/s13012-017-0581-0.

46 *Accountability Study*, 11.

47 Oneview, *Principles of Patient-Centered Care* (2015), at www.oneviewhealthcare.com/the-eight-principles-of-patient-centered-care.

48 See: B. Furrow, et al., *Law and Health Care Quality, Patient Safety, and Liability* (St. Paul, MN: West Academic Publishing, 2018); Y. D. Dlugacz, *Introduction to Health Care Quality: Theory, Methods, and Tools* (Plano, TX: Jossey-Bass, 2017); R. Lloyd, *Quality Health Care: A Guide to Developing and Using Indicators* (Burlington, MA: Jones and Bartlett, 2017); E. Murray, *Nursing Leadership and Management for Patient Safety and Quality Care* (Philadelphia, PA: F. A. Davis Company, 2017).

49 See: C. Oster, J. Braaten, *High Reliability Organizations: A Healthcare Handbook for Patient Safety and Quality* (Nursing Knowledge, 2016); R. Barry, *High-Reliability Healthcare: Improving Patient Safety and Outcomes with Six Sigma* (Chicago, IL: Health Administration Press, 2017).

50 M. L. Martin, et al., eds., *Diversity and Inclusion in Quality Patient Care Quality: A Case-Based Compendium* (Springer, 2018).

51 *Accountability Study*, 11. Also see: R. Mannion, et al., "Do Hospital Boards Matter for Better, Safer, Patient Care Quality?" *Social Science & Medicine* 177 (March 2017): 278–287; R. Miller, et al., "Hospital Board Oversight of Quality and Safety: A Stakeholder Analysis," *BMC Health Services Research* 15: (June 16, 2015): 196, at, https://doi.org/10.1186/s12913-015-0771-x.

52 R. Iedema, et al., *Communicating Quality and Safety in Health Care* (New York: Cambridge University Press, 2015).

53 *Accountability Study*, 11.

54 U.S. Department of Health and Human Services, *Practical Guidelines for Health Care Governing Boards on Compliance Oversight* (U.S. Department of Health and Human Services, 2015).

55 *Accountability Study*, 11.

56 Governance Institute, *Subsidiary and Local Boards* (2019), at www.governanceinstitute.com/page/SubLocalBoards.

57 *Accountability Study*, 11–12.

58 *Accountability Study*, 12. Also see: S. E. Sondheim, et al., "Governance Practices in an Era of Healthcare Transformation," *Journal of Healthcare Management* 62 (5) (2017): 316–326. Also see: AHA's Center for Healthcare Governance, *Governance Practices in an Era of Healthcare Transformation* (AHA's Center for Healthcare Governance, 2012).

59 A. L. Wells, "Reevaluating the Social Contract in American Medicine," *AMA Journal of Ethics* (April 2004), at, https://journalofethics.ama-assn.org/article/reevaluating-social-contract-american-medicine/2004-04.

60 K. Senthil, et al., "Preserving the Social Contract in Health Care: A Call to Action," *American Journal of Public Health* 105 (12) (2015): 2404.

61 L. Nimita, I. B. Carol, "The Modern Social Contract between the Patient, the Healthcare Provider, and Digital Medicine," *Journal of Socialomics* 3 (1) (2014), at, https://doi.org/10.4172/2167-0358.1000105.

62 D. Bhugra, "Medicine's Contract with Society," *Journal of the Royal Society of Medicine* 107 (4) (2014): 144–147.

63 A. Carroll, "The Social Contract and Health Care Reform," *The Incidental Economist* (July 18, 2014), at, https://theincidentaleconomist.com/wordpress/more-on-the-social-contract-and-health-care-reform/.

64 Institute for Healthcare Improvement, *Universal Patient Compact* (2019), at www.npsf.org/page/patientcompact.

65 *Accountability Study*, 12.

66 *Accountability Study*, 12.

67 *Accountability Study*, 12–13. Also see: Health Research and Educational Trust, *Creating Effective Partnerships to Build a Culture of Trust* (Chicago, IL: Health Research and Educational Trust, 2016).

Select readings

Barry, R. 2017. *High-Reliability Healthcare*. Chicago, IL: Health Administration Press.

Dlugacz, Y. D. 2017. *Introduction to Health Care Quality: Theory, Methods, and Tools*. Plano, TX: Jossey-Bass.

Furrow, B., et al. 2018. *Law and Health Care Quality, Patient Safety, and Liability*. St. Paul, MN: West Academic Publishing.

Iedema, R., et al. 2015. *Communicating Quality and Safety in Health Care*. New York: Cambridge University Press, 2015.

Joint Commission. 2016. *Getting the Board on Board. What Your Boards Need to Know About Quality and Patient Safety*, 3rd ed. Oakbrook, IL: Joint Commission Resources.

Joint Commission. 2019. *Inspiring Health Care Excellence*. Oakbrook Terrace, IL: Joint Commission Resources.

Lloyd, R. 2017. *Quality Health Care: A Guide to Developing and Using Indicators*. Burlington, MA: Jones and Bartlett.

Martin, M. L. et al., eds. 2018. *Diversity and Inclusion in Quality Patient Care: A Case-Based Compendium*. New York: Springer.

Murray, E. 2017. *Nursing Leadership and Management for Patient Safety and Quality Care*. Philadelphia, PA: F. A. Davis Company.

Prybil, L., et al. 2012. *Governance in Large Nonprofit Health Systems: Current Profile and Emerging Patterns*. Lexington, KY: Commonwealth Center for Governance Studies, Inc.

Prybil, L., et al. 2013. *The Evolving Accountability of Nonprofit Health System Boards*. Chicago, IL: American Hospital Association Center for Healthcare Governance.

8 Governance of patient safety

Introduction

This chapter applies the ethics paradigm to discuss hallmarks of governance ethics regarding patient safety, a pivotal topic closely connected with the discussion in the previous chapter on patient care quality. Just as there are two chapters in the book on community-related issues (community benefit and community health), there are two chapters on patient-related issues.

The connection between patient care quality and patient safety has been acknowledged for a long time.[1] More specifically, there has been longstanding pressure in healthcare to strengthen board oversight of safety as a quality concern,[2] requiring ethical scrutiny.[3] In addition to safety of patients, boards have responsibility to ensure the safety of those who work in the organization and others present in the organization for other reasons. However, this chapter focuses on board oversight of patient safety.[4] Oversight of patient safety has generated policy debates and led to enhancing self-regulation and governance responsibility, including shared responsibility between boards and medical staffs.[5] A closer alignment emerged between hospital and medical staff leadership, connecting executive performance with safety and quality.[6] The Joint Commission publishes requirements annually for hospital accreditation that mandate sound practices in patient safety.[7] Despite a lot of progress regarding this alignment, patient safety, as an ethical issue related to patient care quality, continues to present significant oversight challenges for boards.

In the analysis of the previous applied chapters, the concepts of the ethics paradigm organize core features of effective governance from landmark reports and the scholarly literature. The analysis in this chapter emphasizes the scholarly literature that has developed significantly in recent years. The purpose is to highlight hallmarks of governance ethics that denote associated moral imperatives. Because the hallmarks represent necessary moral attributes of governance ethics, they entail an obligation to be adopted by boards. In turn, the associated moral imperatives represent necessary endeavors to foster the hallmarks under consideration.

The ethics paradigm organizes multiple topics on board oversight of patient safety, as follows. First, the foundation component of the ethics paradigm deals with the *identity* of an organization, reflecting the leitmotif *who we are*, thereby highlighting board oversight of error prevention as a hallmark of governance ethics for patient safety. In turn, this hallmark denotes an associated moral imperative of board oversight of a systems approach for patient safety. Second, the process component of the ethics paradigm addresses the *accountability* of the organization, reflecting the leitmotif *how we function*, thereby highlighting board oversight of deliberative processes for patient safety as a hallmark of governance ethics. In turn, this hallmark denotes an associated moral imperative regarding board oversight of proactive deliberations for patient safety. Third, the practice component of the ethics paradigm engages *quality* in an organization, reflecting the leitmotif *what we do*, thereby highlighting board oversight of practical mechanisms for patient safety as a hallmark of governance ethics. In turn, this hallmark denotes an associated moral imperative regarding board oversight of a patient safety culture.

Each of the applied chapters begins with an explanation of the need for the pivotal topic under consideration, such as governance of patient safety here. Again, the concepts of *identity, accountability*, and *quality* provide a framework for the applied analysis. These concepts represent the foundation component (reflecting *who we are*), the process component (reflecting *how we function*), and the practice component (reflecting *what we do*) of the ethics paradigm (Table 1.1).

The significance of patient safety is now well established in medical care.[8] However, patient safety also shapes the caliber of high-reliability organizations,[9] including management and administration,[10] related regulation,[11] and ethics.[12] All of these require continuous clinical governance and board oversight across the different areas of health.[13] Not surprisingly, the federal government quickly developed a keen interest in this complex issue,[14] as did the World Health Organization, establishing the World Alliance for Patient Safety.[15] To begin the discussion, it is helpful to explain the need for board oversight of patient safety.

Need for board oversight of patient safety

Nearly a decade ago, national surveys indicated that only half of nonprofit hospital board chairs identified clinical quality as one of the board's top two priorities and only 74 percent of health system boards had standing committees on safety as a quality concern.[16] At that time, the US Department of Health

Table 1.1 Ethics paradigm

Components	Foundation component	Process component	Practice component
Context	Environment of healthcare	Organizational oversight	Organizational culture
Leadership	Identity: who we are	Accountability: how we function	Quality: what we do
Outcomes	Organizational stewardship of mission	Decision-making via participative deliberation	Best practices for standards of conduct

and Human Services presented a national quality strategy to focus on meeting the needs of patients, including patient safety.[17] Also, the National Quality Forum included patient safety among its "National Priorities and Goals," urging healthcare leaders to be intolerant of safety defects in care.[18] In 2009, the Joint Commission established the Center for Transforming Healthcare to seek quality solutions for the most critical and complicated safety problems. It combined a process called *Robust Process Improvement* (integrating statistical models and change management principles) with the center's *Targeted Solution Tool* to generate confidential reporting on its extranet, *Joint Commission Connect*. The purpose was to compile data from organizations with solutions for resolving safety issues, through processes such as the "Lean" methodology (advancing safety through risk reduction processes).[19] The Joint Commission and the National Quality Forum strenuously encouraged board oversight of patient safety. Similarly, the Patient Protection and Affordable Care Act of 2010 urged boards to provide oversight for safety as a quality care issue.[20] From that time onwards it was widely recognized that governing boards hold the ultimate responsibility for patient safety. Hence, boards need to have a continuous commitment to healthcare structures, deliberative processes, and professional practices that support safe and reliable care.[21] These items (structures, processes, practices) are discussed later in relation to the concepts of *identity*, *accountability*, and *quality* in the ethics paradigm.

The *Governance Structure Report*, discussed in previous chapters, also considered the topic of patient safety. The report explained that 93 percent of the boards studied indicated a standing committee with oversight responsibility for patient safety as a quality concern, with approximately 80 percent adopting system-wide measures and standards. All of the system CEOs and all of board members who were interviewed responded independently that their system board regularly received written reports on system-wide and hospital-specific performance to established measures and standards. Also, approximately 80 percent of board members and CEOs reported their system board as having adopted specific action plans in the previous 12 months to improve system performance regarding patient safety as an issue for patient care quality. Moreover, board members and CEOs reported that they devoted a substantial portion of board meeting time (median estimate of 22 percent) to strategic deliberations regarding patient safety as quality issues. Nonetheless, the report noted a significant need to clarify board roles regarding patient safety. An example was the need to better manage the enormous amount of safety data to facilitate board members to understand and perform their duties in this complex area.[22]

It is abundantly clear today that patient safety as a quality issue in healthcare requires board oversight for effective governance. To merit the status of being a high performing healthcare system or hospital, it is expected as a matter of effective governance to have board oversight of their organization's patient safety programs. The discussion now applies the ethics paradigm to organize core features of effective governance regarding patient safety. The purpose is to highlight hallmarks of governance ethics that denote associated moral imperatives. The applied analysis begins with discussing hallmarks of governance ethics connected with the foundation component of the ethics paradigm.

Error prevention: foundation-related governance ethics hallmark

The foundation component of the ethics paradigm, in the context of the challenging environment of healthcare, focuses on stewardship to enhance an organization's mission as crucial for effective governance. This focus requires boards to be attentive to the healthcare environment as the context for engaging their responsibilities. This component depicts the identity of an organization, reflecting the leitmotif *who we are*. The concept of *identity* highlights board oversight of error prevention as a hallmark of governance ethics for patient safety. This concept draws attention to who the board is in relation with its organization. In turn, this hallmark denotes an associated moral imperative regarding board oversight of a systems approach for patient safety. These are discussed in what follows.

To understand board oversight of error prevention as a hallmark of governance ethics, it is helpful to emphasize that there has been extensive discourse on the causes and potential solutions for medical error.[23] A variety of approaches emerged to prevent errors in healthcare generally,[24] as well as in specialized settings such as in acute care, in the intensive care unit, in the emergency department, in clinical oncology, regarding anesthesia.[25] And, clinicians quickly recognized the need to discuss medical error issues with their patients.[26] Also, interest emerged around medical errors in clinical research trials.[27] In particular, high profile cases of errors caught the public's attention. There were two critical cases of error in medical treatment and medical research, each leading to death, that caused controversy: the death of Jesica Santillan after a transplant,[28] and the death of Jesse Gelsinger in a research protocol, the first gene therapy death in the USA.[29]

Because many cases of error resulted in litigation (such as in the Santillan and Gelsinger cases),[30] organizational compliance measures became increasingly influential.[31] There is an awkward paradox in healthcare in which the trained expertise of the profession, even from the best medical schools in the world, regularly encounter the reality of healthcare being error-provoking by its nature.[32] As boards began to focus on avoiding error, the challenges for governance oversight were unambiguous.[33]

The need to have a governance focus on medical error was spotlighted by a report from the Institute of Medicine (IOM) in 2000.[34] The IOM report was the result of many years of scholarly studies.[35] T. A. Brennan, L. L. Leape, and others published a threshold study in 1991, known as the Harvard Medical Practice Study, reporting data on medical error from 1984. Other studies followed, such as on the prevention of medical errors and on the liability of organizations.[36] The publicity from many such studies on medical errors in the 1990s[37] focused attention on the issues of who should be responsible for avoiding medical errors.

In 1997 a prestigious commission on quality was established, the President's Advisory Commission on Consumer Protection and Quality in the Healthcare

Industry. In 1998, the IOM formed the Quality of Healthcare in America Committee to review an emerging problem, the extent of medical error in USA healthcare. In 1999 the National Quality Forum was established as a nonprofit organization to develop a national strategy for healthcare quality (it merged in 2006 with the National Committee for Quality Healthcare). And, in 2000, a list of Fortune 500 companies combined to establish The Leapfrog Group to seek improvements in healthcare. Then, also in 2000, the IOM issued its report extrapolating from results of the Harvard Medical Practice Study and from a study in Colorado and Utah in the early 1990s, to identify the estimated high number of patient deaths in USA healthcare each year as a result of medical error.[38] Naturally, such astounding figures were disputed.[39] But in July 2004 Health Grades Inc. (a Colorado consulting firm) suggested that the numbers of US deaths from medical error could be more than twice as high as projected by the 2000 IOM report.[40] Most accept that the IOM figures at least indicated a very serious problem for medical care and public health alike. The IOM report wanted to invigorate a national agenda to reduce errors in healthcare. It certainly precipitated a firestorm as it sought to engage ethics with policy.[41]

The IOM report defined medical error as the failure of a planned action to be completed as intended or the use of a wrong plan to achieve an aim. However, not all errors result in harm to the patient. Following this line of analysis, scholars subsequently referred to errors that cause patient injury as preventable adverse events.[42] An adverse event is an injury resulting from a medical intervention; it is not due to the original condition of the patient. For example, at the time of the IOM report some estimated that as many as one third of adverse drug events among outpatients were preventable or ameliorable.[43]

Another study in 2002, in the *Archives of Internal Medicine*, reported that drug errors occurred daily in one out of five doses in a typical 300-bed hospital. The study was based on an analysis of 36 hospitals in Colorado and Georgia. The analysis focused on the problems arising from administering errors after a physician had properly prescribed for the patient. The data was shocking insofar as the study focused on properly prescribed medications; it did not deal with errors linked with the wrong prescription of a drug by a physician or the wrong filling of a prescription in the pharmacy.[44]

The IOM report explained that medical errors can occur in any stage of care, including diagnosis, treatment and preventive care.[45] Diagnostic errors can occur when there is a mistake or delay in clinical diagnosis, or when there is a failure to provide relevant or indicated tests, or when there is a failure to act on the results of monitoring or testing, or when there is a use of outmoded tests. Treatment errors can occur in administering a procedure or in a surgical intervention, or in avoidable delay in treatment, or in the dose or method of using a drug, or in inappropriate care for a disease. Preventative errors can occur when there is inadequate monitoring or follow-up or by not providing prophylactic treatment. Also, scholars at that time explained there could be many other forms of medical error such as can be caused by communication failure or equipment malfunction, or resulting from fatigue among clinicians, or due to infection control, arising from using information technology, and management mistakes, etc. Moreover, medication errors could occur in the processes of prescribing, dispensing, administering, monitoring, and system and management control.[46]

To effectively address medical error, there needs to be a firm grasp of the types and causes of the problem. To explain the various types of medical error, the original IOM report adopted the theory of errors in the work of James Reason.[47] The IOM report adopted the important distinction of Reason between latent errors and active errors. Active errors occur with frontline operators and their effects are felt more or less immediately. Latent errors typically are removed from the operator's control, such as by poor design. It is latent error that presents the greatest threat. However, typical responses to errors tend to dwell on active errors insofar as they focus upon the individuals responsible. Adopting this distinction, the IOM differentiated between mistakes and slips or lapses. A slip or lapse occurs when the action is not what was originally intended—that constitutes an error of execution. This does not mean that a slip or lapse is minor or unimportant—patients can die from them too. Also, in a mistake the action happens as planned but does not accomplish its intended outcome because the original, intended action was mistaken or wrong—that constitutes an error of planning. Hence, in a mistake or error the intention is not adequate, and a failure of planning is involved.[48]

The main controversy of the IOM report centered around the claim that up to 98,000 patients died each year in USA healthcare resulting from medical error. Many of those patients may have been very sick upon admission to the hospitals, but they were not dying. The IOM report carried a soothing title, *To Err is Human: Building a Safer Health System.*[49] In 2011, the Joint Commission estimated that approximately 10 percent of patients in acute care hospitals were likely to be seriously harmed or killed caused by iatrogenic errors.[50] At that time, estimates for adverse events in hospitals were significantly higher than previously estimated.[51]

The IOM followed up on its report with other important studies. The original IOM report in 2000 focused upon the main causes of medical error. In 2001, the IOM published a related report, *Crossing the Quality Chasm.*[52] This report focused the lack of coordination in healthcare that prevents the provision of many medical interventions already recognized and established as benefiting patients. That is, the report addressed the environment of healthcare delivery to highlight the problem of medical error. This report criticized the quality and delivery of care because they can increase the probability of error.[53] The study urged a reconfiguration of healthcare delivery in a manner that would decrease medical error.

Then, in 2002 the IOM issued another follow-up report, *Leadership by Example.*[54] This report again focused upon medical error, arguing for urgent improvement in the nation's healthcare services, and emphasizing improvement processes for about one third of Americans in six different government programs: Medicare (40 million), Medicaid (42.3 million), the State Children's Health Insurance Program (4.6 million), the Department of Defense (8.4 million), the Veterans Health Administration program (4 million), and the Indian Health Services program (1.4 million). The report took the opportunity of dealing with federally funded government programs in healthcare as an obvious starting point in the national agenda for reducing medical error. That is, the report exhorted the government in its federal programs to establish better quality standards in reporting requirements for clinical data and in purchasing standards to reward and promote higher levels of quality. Moreover, the report encouraged the development of updated delivery models in healthcare and the expansion of applied health services research to support improvement.

The IOM published further studies to update previous research and to suggest new standards of care on preventing medication errors.[55] For example, in 2004 the IOM released another report,[56] further confirming its initial report. The report focused on the workload of staff nurses who care for an increased numbers of patients while fighting fatigue from long working hours.[57] Subsequent studies suggested that deaths from medical error annually in the USA are much higher than originally estimated by the IOM report, reaching to over 250,000.[58] In 2016, a study from Johns Hopkins University estimated that more than 250,000 people die annually from medical errors in the USA, being the third leading cause of death after heart disease and cancer.[59] Today, the estimates hover between 250,000 to 440,000 deaths caused by medical error annually in the USA.[60] Furthermore, in 2017 the Institute for Healthcare Improvement reported that 21 percent of patients report a personal experience with medical error in the USA.[61]

In light of this extensive reporting, board oversight of error prevention can be construed as a hallmark of governance ethics. The foundation component of the ethics paradigm, in the context of the challenging environment of healthcare, focuses on stewardship to enhance an organization's mission as crucial for effective governance. The concept of *identity* in the ethics paradigm draws attention to *who the board is* in relation with its organization, emphasizing the need to steward the challenging reality of medical error.

Moral imperative: board oversight of a systems approach for patient safety

Board oversight of error prevention is a hallmark of governance ethics. This hallmark denotes an associated moral imperative regarding board oversight of a systems approach to patient safety. The original IOM report emphasized the need for systems to resolve underlying problems. The IOM report was widely recognized and well received.

In borrowing insights from the work of Reason, the IOM sought to address the basic problem. The report highlighted the role of systems in accidents and explained that a system can be understood as a set of interdependent elements that interact to achieve a common aim. Here, a system can refer to many different entities, such as an integrated delivery system, a multi-hospital system, a system with many partners over a wide geographical area. Also, a system can refer to a smaller unit such as an operating room or an obstetrical unit. The compromise of systems is more associated with latent failures, mentioned earlier. So, identifying and fixing latent failures contributes more substantively to creating safer systems. In other words, for the IOM report, adopting the scholarship of Reason, safety typically results from the interacting components of a system.[62] Hence, the IOM reports argued that only remedying the underlying systems (for example, improving quality standards in clinical data reporting requirements) will effectively accomplish the goals of patient safety. Accompanying the IOM reports, there emerged widespread interest in a systems approach to patient safety, such as by the National Coalition on Healthcare and the Institute for Healthcare Improvement.[63] Similarly, the systems approach led the Agency for Healthcare Research and Quality to develop indicators for patient safety that enable healthcare organizations to track problems.[64]

Subsequently, the shift of emphasis from individuals to systems was pursued extensively to better engage the relation between human reliability and complex systems.[65] In particular, the impact of human factors in crisis management received considerable attention.[66] This focus on systems led to a keen focus upon the role of human factors, such as in using medical devices,[67] including the psychology of human cognition and action and the processes of human perception.[68] Not surprisingly, the increased interest in a systems approach to patient safety generated concerns among clinicians and health managers, such as regarding professional liability,[69] disclosure and apologies,[70] no-fault reporting.[71] Yet, the focus on a systems approach to patient safety has increased significantly in healthcare.[72]

In sum, the foundation component of the ethics paradigm highlights board oversight of error prevention as a hallmark of governance ethics. By focusing on *identity* in the ethics paradigm (dealing with *who the board is*), this hallmark denotes an associated moral imperative regarding board oversight of a systems approach for patient safety.

Deliberative processes for patient safety: process-related governance ethics hallmark

The concept of *accountability* in the ethics paradigm (reflecting the leitmotif *how we function*) emphasizes the importance of decision-making via participative deliberation. This focus requires boards to be attentive to organizational oversight as the context for overseeing their responsibilities. The concept of *accountability* highlights board oversight of deliberative approaches for patient safety as a hallmark of governance ethics for community health. The concept draws attention to *how the board functions* in the organization. In turn, this hallmark denotes an associated moral imperative regarding board oversight of proactive deliberations for patient safety. These are discussed in the following section.

To understand board oversight of deliberative approaches as a hallmark of governance ethics, it is helpful to be aware that the dominant model for addressing medical error was referred to as the *professional sanctions model*, emphasizes individual culpability.[73] This model continues to be relevant for board oversight, but mainly from the perspective of malpractice. The model tends to punish individuals for their medical errors to prevent future recurrence. However, this model can be linked with the surge of lawsuits for medical malpractice.[74] Yet, despite hefty penalties and personal shame in using this model, the extent of medical errors did not diminish. This sanctions-oriented model blamed the professional for carelessness or incompetence, focusing upon the individual rather than the problem and its cause. The malpractice system in US healthcare deals with this model to deter future medical mistakes. However, with this model, resistance to open reporting of medical error has created a serious problem for quality care.[75] That is because a malpractice environment deters open reporting by professionals because of the climate of fear and shame. Of course, tort law through compensation of victims can shed light on the need for improvements in patient safety.[76]

By engaging the concept of *accountability* in the process component in the ethics paradigm, there emerges a different model for addressing medical error. This is called the *patient safety model* that adopts a more deliberative approach to medical error. This model addresses medical error by seeking changes in the causes of individuals making medical mistakes. By clarifying what caused the error, safeguards can be implemented to prevent recurrence. This model develops quality improvement and encourages reporting to address underlying issues that cause error. This deliberative process for patient safety (in contrast to pursuing the *professional sanctions model*) constitutes a hallmark of governance ethics.

Moral imperative: board oversight of proactive deliberations for patient safety

Board oversight of deliberative processes for patient safety is a hallmark of governance ethics. This hallmark denotes an associated moral imperative regarding board oversight of proactive deliberations for patient safety. That is, a process that is sufficiently deliberative must be proactive in its design and implementation. Some analogies can help understand this proactive characteristic. The basic issue here is to shift from fixing blame upon individual professionals to proactively fixing the systems to prevent error and promote safety.

One analogue occurs in road safety. When a specific site is associated with several car accidents, safety rails are built to prevent future crashes. Likewise, deliberative processes for safety seek to design system fixes when medical errors arise. Another well-known analogy is that of airline safety to shed light on the *patient safety model*. As early as the 1950s safety centers for military aviation began to focus on human factors. Likewise, drawing upon military aviation experience, civilian aviation adopted more comprehensive approaches to safety. Civilian aviation began to implement accident investigations, incident reporting, and research for continuous quality improvement. Consequently, the Federal Aviation Administration (FAA) assumed regulatory oversight with the responsibility of ensuring flight safety. It became the task of an independent federal agency, the National Transportation Safety Board (NTSB), to conduct accident investigations, making recommendations to the FAA for regulatory action. At the heart of its success is the process of confidential incident reporting that is conducted through the National Aeronautics and Space Administration (NASA) Safety Reporting System

(ASRS).[77] Hence, after civilian airlines were freed from regulatory reprisals for reporting pilot error and near misses, pilot cooperation soared. The extensive, confidential reporting and subsequent remedies in the airline industry resulted in much improved safety for passengers, as has been extensively documented since the IOM report.[78]

A similar system in healthcare could encourage self-reporting of mistakes and close calls with confidential assurances. In 2010 the Joint Commission explained the importance of close calls and sentinel events: they provide information about active or latent mistakes; they yield data about contributing factors; they highlight points of failure. This approach facilitates investigations with less anxiety about liability claims. Such an approach is likely to encourage system implementation of preventative measures and appropriate compensation for victims.[79]

Another analogy is occupational health to exemplify how an industry can become safer over time. The Occupational Safety and Health Act of 1970 created the Occupational Safety and Health Administration (OSHA) and its research arm, the National Institute for Occupational Safety and Health. The purpose of OSHA is to encourage the reduction of workplace hazards and to implement new or existing safety and health programs by undertaking the following: providing research in occupational health and safety; maintaining record-keeping systems; developing training programs; and enforcing mandatory standards for job safety and health.[80]

These analogies provide valuable lessons for safety in healthcare from the perspective of governance ethics. There needs to be better board oversight of relating safety concerns with the need to improve performance. Patient safety strategies need to include a focus on appropriate organizational and national leadership, development of a relevant knowledge base, and dissemination of knowledge in a timely manner throughout the industry. The FAA and OSHA dedicated government agencies with regulatory responsibility for safety that is separate from the agencies responsible for research. The research entities can generate reports that are useful to the regulatory authorities as they set standards. Also, aviation and occupational health recognized the need to expand the knowledge base on safety as well as to establish dissemination processes for this new knowledge. And substantial resources were provided to support these initiatives in aviation and occupational health. Adequate resources were indispensable for steady improvement over time. In other words, safety improvements were not the result of a one-time effort; rather, results occurred through an ongoing commitment of resources and leadership.

A similarly cohesive effort is needed by governance boards to foster a proactive process. This what is meant here by proactive deliberations for patient safety. The lessons in other industries suggest that to decrease medical errors a *patient safety model* designed around proactive deliberations may have more success than a reactive and punitive *professional sanctions model*. The basic problem with the *professional sanctions model* is that it tends to be reactive by blaming individuals for medical error. In such a mindset, medical mistakes tend to be hidden from families and patients to minimize the threat of litigation, and risk management focuses on reducing pecuniary penalties rather than reducing risks to the patient of future error. These are not the paving stones for sound governance in healthcare organizations. There is a distinction between risk management and patient safety. The distinction reflects the difference between responding to errors versus creating a safe environment that explores past failure to create defenses against future failure. Of course, because of human frailty, there will continue to be medical mistakes that result from malice or malpractice, deserving of appropriate lawsuits and penalties. In contrast, a *patient safety model* focuses on proactive deliberations to create systems that prevent medical errors.

In sum, the process component of the ethics paradigm highlights board oversight of deliberative processes for patient safety as a hallmark of governance ethics. By focusing on *accountability* in the ethics paradigm (dealing with *how the board functions*), this hallmark denotes an associated moral imperative regarding board oversight of proactive deliberations for patient safety.

Practical mechanisms for patient safety: practice-related governance ethics hallmark

The concept of *quality* in the ethics paradigm (reflecting the leitmotif *what we do*) emphasizes the importance of best practices for standards of conduct. This focus requires boards to be attentive to organizational culture as the context for implementing their responsibilities. The concept of *quality* highlights board oversight of practical mechanisms for patient safety as a hallmark of governance ethics. In turn, this hallmark denotes an associated moral imperative regarding board oversight of a patient safety culture. These are discussed in the next section.

To understand board oversight of practical mechanisms for patient safety as a hallmark of governance ethics, it is helpful to emphasize the significance of root cause analysis. This approach has elicited extensive discussion,[81] being adopted in many different fields,[82] as well as in healthcare.[83] The approach has been adopted by the Joint Commission as part of its efforts to develop mechanisms for patient safety.[84] One step in the process of root cause analysis is assigning a team to assess the causal factors that underlie (actual or potential) sentinel events. The Joint Commission describes a sentinel event as an unexpected occurrence involving death or serious injury (physical or psychological), or the risk thereof,[85] as explored in its publication.[86] Another step in the process is to study the problem comprehensively by integrating these steps: identifying relevant risk reduction strategies; evaluating proposed actions and designing a plan for improvement; ensuring acceptability of the action plan; implementing the improvement plan; developing measures of effectiveness and ensuring their success; and effectively communicating the results.[87]

Not surprisingly, root cause analysis has become a well-established and widely adopted mechanism to improve patient safety. This emphasizes why board oversight of practical mechanisms for patient safety is a hallmark of governance ethics. In turn, this hallmark denotes an associated moral imperative regarding board oversight of patient safety culture.

Moral imperative: board oversight of a patient safety culture

Developing a culture of patient safety is indispensable for the improvement of organizational culture in healthcare.[88] Similarly, organizational culture has a significant impact on patient safety, as it does on the workplace in healthcare generally.[89] The IOM report (*To Err Is Human*) explained this organizational culture as including the following: provide leadership; respect human limits in the design process; promote effective team functioning and communication; anticipate the unexpected; and create a learning environment.[90] Each of these is considered as necessary for governance ethics.

To begin, the role of leadership—clinical, executive, and governance—is crucial for cultivating a healthy culture of safety.[91] The respective roles of clinical leaders, executive leaders, and the board should be clear, mutually understood, and closely coordinated in order to be effective. Effective leadership for patient safety necessarily includes team building that includes the following: making patient safety a priority corporate objective; making patient safety the responsibility of everyone, such as by endorsing non-punitive solutions; making clear assignments for and expectation of safety oversight; providing human and financial resources for systems redesign; and developing mechanisms for identifying and dealing with unsafe practitioners, emphasizing the new focus of safety upon systems. When assigning a team, several items must be addressed: staff should be assured of the objectivity of any organizational improvement that occurs, such as the identification and reduction of risks instead of any assignment of blame to individuals; and leaders should empower their teams to make recommendations for change, providing appropriate practical resources. These issues enable team work to improve patient safety.[92]

Also, it is necessary to respect human limits in the design process, such as by the following: designing jobs for safety, including being attentive to work hours and loads, staffing ratios, and sources of distraction, fatigue or sleep deprivation; avoiding reliance on memory, such as by adopting the use of protocols and checklists whenever appropriate; using constraints and forcing functions to guide users to the next action or decision and to structure critical tasks; avoiding reliance on vigilance (because attention spans are limited), simplifying key processes (to minimize problem solving), and standardizing work processes (to reduce reliance on memory and enabling newcomers to use devices safely).[93]

Furthermore, designing processes of care to anticipate the unexpected is indispensable for a culture of safety. Designing processes of care require the following: adopting a proactive approach that anticipates threats to safety; planning before accidents occur, such as via the automation of tasks that are repetitive and time consuming; and anticipating recovery, such as by making mistakes visible when possible, making it easy to reverse operations, and making it difficult to perform non-reversible operations.[94]

Finally, an organizational culture of safety requires the creation of an effective learning culture, including data technology and machine learning, that includes the following: using simulations whenever possible, such as for training, for problem solving and for crisis management; encouraging reporting of mistakes and hazardous conditions to collaborate in problem solving and ensure there are no reprisals for reporting failures; and ensuring that communication flows freely. In an effective learning-culture there should appropriate feedback about mistakes, such as via reporting of events, understanding what occurred and why it occurred, developing and implementing recommendations for improvements, and tracking changes for subsequent assessment of their effectiveness.[95]

In a manner that is complementary to the original IOM report's approach to developing a culture of safety, the Joint Commission provides ongoing guidance to cultivate a culture of safety through its national patient safety goals, its *Journal on Quality and Patient Safety*, its publication *The Source* for accreditation and certification compliance, its official newsletter, *The Joint Commission Perspectives*, and other resources.[96] Most significantly, the Joint Commission has emphasized the importance of board oversight of patient safety.[97]

In sum, the practice component of the ethics paradigm highlights board oversight of practical mechanisms for patient safety as a hallmark of governance ethics. By focusing on *quality* in the ethics paradigm (dealing with *what the board does*), this hallmark denotes an associated moral imperative regarding board oversight of patient safety culture.

Conclusion

This chapter has highlighted hallmarks of governance ethics with associated moral imperatives regarding patient safety. The contribution of the ethics paradigm can be summarized in this manner.

First, in the context of the challenging healthcare environment, the foundation component of the ethics paradigm focuses on stewardship to enhance an organization's mission in healthcare as crucial for effective governance. This component deals the *identity* of an organization, reflecting the leitmotif *who we are*, thereby indicating board oversight of error prevention as a hallmark of governance ethics for patient safety. In turn, this hallmark denotes an associated moral imperative concerning board oversight of a systems approach for patient safety.

Second, in the context of organizational oversight in healthcare, the process component of the ethics paradigm is to focus upon decision-making to foster participative deliberation in organizations. This component addresses the *accountability* of the organization, reflecting the leitmotif *how we function*, thereby indicating board oversight of deliberative processes for patient safety as a hallmark of governance ethics. In turn, this hallmark denotes an associated moral imperative concerning board oversight of proactive deliberations for patient safety.

Third, in the context of organizational culture in healthcare, the practice component of the ethics paradigm is to focus on best practices to develop standards of conduct. This component engages *quality* in an organization, reflecting the leitmotif *what we do*, thereby indicating board oversight of practical mechanisms for patient safety as a hallmark of governance ethics. In turn, this hallmark denotes an associated moral imperative concerning board oversight of a patient safety culture.

This chapter has applied the ethics paradigm to identify hallmarks of governance ethics regarding patient safety, denoting associated moral imperatives. As boards pursue their governance responsibilities for communities (community benefit and community health) and for patients (patient care quality and patient safety), scenarios can arise in which partnership arrangements can conflict with an organization's mission. The next chapter considers these problems that boards encounter regarding conflicted collaborative arrangements in healthcare organizations.

Notes

1 See: L. Prybil, et al., "Board Oversight of Patient Care in Community Health Systems," *American Journal of Medical Quality* 25 (1) (2012): 34–41.

2 See: H. J. Jiang, et al., "Enhancing Board Oversight on Quality of Hospital Care: An Agency Theory Approach," *Healthcare Management Review* 37 (2) (2012): 144–153.

3 See: N. Dixon, *Review of Ethical Issues Related to Clinical Audit and Quality Improvement Activities: A Guide for NHS Organisations* (United Kingdom: Healthcare Quality Improvement Partnership, 2009), 1–41; W. A. Nelson, "Ethics: A Foundation for Quality," *Healthcare Executive* 26 (6) (2011): 46–49; H. A. Taylor, et al., *The Ethical Review of Healthcare Quality Improvement Initiatives: Findings from the Field* (New York: The Commonwealth Fund, 2010), 1–9; H. A. Taylor, et al., "Ethics, Oversight and Quality Improvement Initiatives," *Quality and Safety in Healthcare* 19 (4) (2010): 271–274.

4 The analysis in this chapter develops previous publications by one of the authors on patient safety. See: G. Magill, "Ethical and Policy Issues Related to Medical Error and Patient Safety," in S. A. M. McLean, ed., *First Do No Harm: Law, Ethics, and Healthcare* (London: Ashgate, 2006), Chapter 7, 101–116; D. F. Kelly, G. Magill, H. ten Have, *Contemporary Catholic Healthcare Ethics* (Washington, DC: Georgetown University Press, 2014), Chapter 24, at 274–278; G. Magill, "Patient Safety," in H. ten Have, B. Gordijn, eds., *Encyclopedia of Global Bioethics* (Springer, 2016).

5 C. A. Goeschel, *Quality, Patient Safety, and Boards of Trustees: Implications for Creating Safer Healthcare* (Dr. Sci Dissertation, Tulane University School of Public Health and Tropical Medicine, 2010).

6 See: F. J. Crosson, L. A. Tollen, *Partners in Health: How Physicians and Hospitals Can be Accountable Together* (San Francisco, CA: Jossey-Bass, 2010).

7 See: Joint Commission, *Comprehensive Accreditation Manual. CAMH for Hospitals*, effective January 1, 2019 (Oakbrook, IL: Joint Commission Resources, December 2018); Joint Commission, *2019 Hospital Accreditation Standards* (Oakbrook, IL: Joint Commission Resources, December 2018).

8 See: J. Howard, *Cognitive Errors and Diagnostic Mistakes: A Case-based Guide to Critical Thinking in Medicine* (New York: Springer, 2019); R. M. Wachter, *Understanding Patient Safety*, 2nd ed. (New York: McGraw Medical, 2017).

9 See: J. Byrnes, S. Teman, *The Safety Playbook. A Healthcare Leader's Guide to Building a High-Reliability Organization* (Chicago, IL: Health Administration Press, 2017); R. Barry, *High-Reliability Healthcare: Improving Patient Safety and Outcomes with Six Sigma* (Chicago, IL: Health Administration Press, 2017).

10 See: R. Wears, K. Sutcliffe, *Still Not Safe: Patient Safety and the Middle-Managing of American Medicine* (New York: Oxford University Press, 2019); K. Z. Pederson, *Organizing Patient Safety* (United Kingdom: Palgrave MacMillan, 2017); A. Rosiek-Kryszweska, ed., *Healthcare Administration for Patient Safety and Engagement* (Open Library: Medical Information Science References, 2017).

11 See: O. Quick, *Regulating Patient Safety* (New York: Cambridge University Press, 2017); J. Tingle, et al., eds., *Global Patient Safety: Law, Policy and Practice* (United Kingdom: Routledge, 2018).

12 J. D. Banja, *Patient Safety Ethics: How Vigilance, Mindfulness, Compliance, and Humility Can Make Healthcare Safer* (Baltimore, MD: Johns Hopkins University Press, 2019).

13 See: A. G. Al Hasmi, *Environment, Health and Safety Governance and Leadership* (United Kingdom: Routledge, 2017).

14 See: Department of Health and Human Services, *HHS Data Shows Major Strides Made in Patient Safety* (2014), at, https://innovation.cms.gov/files/reports/patient-safety-results. pdf; Department of Health and Human Services, Office of the Inspector General, *Adverse Events in Hospitals. National Incidence Among Medicare Beneficiaries* (Washington, DC: DHHS, 2010); United States Congress, *Medical Errors* (BiblioGov, 2010). The Bib-lioGov project is an effort to expand awareness of public documents and records.

15 World Health Organization, *World Alliance for Patient Safety* (2004), at www.who.int/ patientsafety/worldalliance/en/.

16 See: A. K. Jha, A. Epstein, "Hospital Governance and the Quality of Care," *Health Affairs* 29 (1) (2010): 182–187; The Governance Institute, *Dynamic Governance: An Analysis of Board Structure and Practices in a Shifting Industry* (San Diego, CA: The Governance Institute, 2011), 42.

17 U.S. Department of Health and Human Services, *2012 Annual Progress Report to Congress, National Strategy for Quality Improvement in Healthcare* (August 2012), at www.ahrq.gov/workingforquality/nqs/nqs2012annlrpt.pdf.

18 National Quality Forum, *Aligning Our Efforts to Transform America's Healthcare. National Priorities and Goals* (Washington, DC: National Quality Forum, 2008).

19 See: Joint Commission, *Getting the Board on Board. What Your Boards Need to Know About Quality and Patient Safety*, 3rd ed. (Oakbrook, IL: Joint Commission Resources, 2016), 5. To access the Center for Transforming HealthCare, see: www.centerfortrans forminghealthcare.org. On change management, see: Institute for Healthcare Improve-ment, *How to Improve* (Cambridge, MA: Institute for Healthcare Improvement, 2011). On Lean methodology, see: Joint Commission, *Advanced Lean Thinking: Proven Methods to Reduce Waste and Improve Quality in Healthcare* (Oakbrook, IL: Joint Commission Resources, 2008).

20 See: E. Belmont, et al., "A New Quality Compass: Hospital Boards' Increased Role under the Affordable Care Act," *Health Affairs* 30 (2011): 1281; B. Ide, "Moving Beyond Quality: Growing Regulations and Enforcement Are Expanding Trustees' Oversight Responsibilities," *Trustee* 64 (6) (2011): 29.

21 See: Joint Commission, *The Essential Guide for Patient Safety Officers*, 2nd ed. (Oak-brook, IL: Joint Commission Resources, 2013), Chapter One, "The Role of Leader-ship," 1–12; Institute for Healthcare Improvement, *The Power of Having the Board on Board* (Cambridge, MA: Institute for Healthcare Improvement, 2012); Joint Commis-sion, *From the Front Office to the Front Line. Essential Issues for Healthcare Leaders*, 2nd ed. (Oakbrook, IL: Joint Commission Resource, 2011).

22 L. Prybil, et al., *Governance in Large Nonprofit Health Systems: Current Profile and Emerging Patterns* (Lexington, KY: Commonwealth Center for Governance Studies, Inc., 2012), 14, 28–31, 43–44, 57 (referred to as the *Governance Structure Report*).

23 See: F. Allhoff, S. L. Borden, eds., *Ethics and Error in Medicine* (United Kingdom: Routledge, 2019); M. C. Allen, J. Norman, *Medical Error Prevention* (CME Resource/ NetCE, 2013); S. McIver, S., R. Wyndham, *After the Error: Speaking out About Patient Safety to Save Lives* (Toronto: ECW Press, 2013); W. Charney, *Epidemic of Medi-cal Errors and Hospital-Acquired Infections: Systemic and Social Causes* (Taylor and Francis, CRC Press, 2012); B. J. Lawner, et al., *Avoiding Common Prehospital Errors* (Philadelphia, PA: Wolters Kluwer, 2012).

24 See: Abha Agrawal, ed., *Patient Safety: A Case-Based Comprehensive Guide* (New York: Springer, 2014).

25 See: M. St. Pierre, et al., eds., *Crisis Management in Acute Care Settings: Human Factors, Team Psychology, and Patient Safety in a High Stakes Environment* (New York: Springer, 2011); Joint Commission, *Patient Safety in the Intensive Care Unit* (Oakbrook, IL: Joint Commission Resources, 2010); Joint Commission, *Pediatric Patient Safety in the Emergency Department* (Oakbrook, IL: Joint Commission Resources, 2010); P. Croskerry, ed., *Patient Safety in Emergency Medicine* (Philadelphia, PA: Wolters Kluwer, 2009); A. P. Dicker, *Quality and Safety in Radiation Oncology* (Springer, 2016); A. Surbone, M. Rowe, *Clinical Oncology and Errror Reduction* (Wiley-Blackwell, 2015); C. Marcucci, et al., eds, *Avoiding Common Anesthesia Errors* (Philadelphia, PA: Wolters Kluwer, 2007).

26 See: R. D. Truog, et al., *Talking with Patients and Families about Medical Error: A Guide for Education and Practice* (Baltimore MD: Johns Hopkins University Press, 2011); Joint Commission, *Speak Up: Help Prevent Errors in Your Care* (Oakbrook, IL: Joint Commission Resources, 2011).

27 See: A. M. Capron, "When Experiments go Wrong: the U.S. Perspective," *Journal of Clinical Ethics* 15 (1) (2004): 22–29.

28 See: D. Resnick, "The Jesica Santillan Tragedy: Lessons Learned," *Hastings Center Report* 33 (4) (2003): 12–20; A. Camarow, "Jesica's Story: One Mistake Didn't Kill Her – The Organ Donor System was Fatally Flawed," *US News & World Report* (July 28–August 4, 2003): 51–54.

29 G. Magill, "Science, Ethics and Policy," in G. Magill, et al., eds., *Genetics and Ethics. An Interdisciplinary Study* (Saint Louis, MO: Saint Louis University Press, 2004), 253–283, at 259–260.

30 See: J. Tingle, et al., eds., *Global Patient Safety: Law, Policy and Practice* (Routledge, 2018); J. R. Abele, ed., *Medical Errors and Litigation* (Tucson, AR: Lawyers & Judges Publishing, 2011).

31 See: J. D. Banja, *Patient Safety Ethics: How Vigilance, Mindfulness, Compliance, and Humility Can Make Healthcare Safer* (Johns Hopkins University Press, 2019).

32 See: J. Howard, *Cognitive Errors and Diagnostic Mistakes: A Case-based Guide to Critical Thinking in Medicine* (Springer, 2019).

33 See: Joint Commission, *Getting the Board on Board: What Your Board Needs to Know About Quality and Patient Safety*, 3rd ed. (Oakbrook, IL: Joint Commission Resources, 2016).

34 The Institute of Medicine, *To Err is Human: Building a Safer Health System* (Washington, DC, National Academies Press, 2000).

35 For a brief history of studies over the decades preceding the IOM report, see: C. Vincent, *Patient Safety*, 2nd ed. (Wiley-Blackwell, 2010), Chapter 1, "Medical Harm: A Brief History," 3–13; Chapter 2, "The Emergence of Patient Safety," 14–30; V. A. Sharpe, A. I. Faden, *Medical Harm. Historical, Conceptual, and Ethical Dimensions of Iatrogenic Illness* (New York: Cambridge University Press, 1998), "Introduction," 1–14.

36 T. A. Brennan, et al., "Incidence of Adverse Events and Negligence in Hospitalized Patients: Results of the Harvard Medical Practice Study," *New England Journal of Medicine* 324 (1991): 370–376; L. L. Leape, et al., "Preventing Medical Injury," *Quality Review Bulletin* 19 (1993): 144–149; L. L. Leape, et al., "Systems Anlysis of Adverse Drug Events," *Journal of the American Medical Association* 274 (1995): 35–43; A. A. Noble, T. A. Brennan, "Managing Care in the Era of Systems-Think: Organizational Liability and Patient Safety," *Journal of Law, Medicine, & Ethics* 29 (2001): 290–304.

37 See: L. L. Leape, "Error in Medicine," *Journal of the American Medical Association* 272 (1994): 1851–1857; L. L. Leape, et al., "Promoting Patient Safety by Preventing Medical Error," *Journal of the American Medical Association* 280 (1998): 1444–1447. For data on systems that reduce medical error, see: www.leapfroggroup.org

38 E. J. Thomas, et al., "Incidence and Types of Adverse Events and Negligent Care in Utah and Colorado," *Medical Care* 38 (2000): 261–271.

39 C. J. McDonald, et al., "Deaths Due to Medical Errors are Exaggerated in Institute of Medicine Report," *Journal of the American Medical Association* 284 (2000): 93–95.

40 Health Grades Quality Study, *Patient Safety in American Hospitals* (Denver, CO: Health Grades Inc., 2004).

41 See: T. A. Brennan, "The IOM Report on Medical Error – Could it Do Harm?" *New England Journal of Medicine* 342 (2000): 1123–1125.

42 See: K. Weeks, et al., *Reducing Medical Errors and Adverse Events* (Amazon Digital Services, 2012).

43 T. K. Ghandi, et al., "Adverse Drug Events in Ambulatory Care," *New England Journal of Medicine* 348 (16) (2003): 1556–1564; W. M. Tierney, "Adverse Outpatient Drug Events – A Problem and an Opportunity," *New England Journal of Medicine* 348 (16) (2003): 1587–1589.

44 See: K. N. Barker, et al., "Medication Errors Observed in 36 Healthcare Facilities," *Archives of Internal Medicine* 162 (16) (2002): 1897–1903; S. B. Haga, W. Burke, "Using Pharmacogenetics to Improve Drug Safety and Efficacy," *Journal of the American Medical Association* 291 (23) (2004): 2869–2871.

45 The Institute of Medicine, *To Err is Human: Building a Safer Health System* (Washington, DC: National Academies Press, 2000), "Errors in Healthcare: A Leading Cause of Death and Injury," 26–48.

46 See: Institute of Medicine, Committee on Patient Safety and Health Information Technology, *Health IT and Patient Safety: Building Better Systems for Better Care* (Washington, DC: National Academies Press, 2011); S. B. Rubin, L. Zoloth, eds., *Margin of Error: The Ethics of Mistakes in the Practice of Medicine* (Hagerstown, MD: University Publishing Group, 2000).

47 See: The Institute of Medicine, *To Err is Human: Building a Safer Health System* (Washington, DC, National Academies Press, 2000), 1–16; J. T. Reason, *Human Error* (Cambridge: Cambridge University Press, 1990); and J. T. Reason, *Managing the Risk of Organizational Accidents* (Aldershot: Ashgate, 1997).

48 See: J. T. Reason, *Human Error* (Cambridge: Cambridge University Press, 1990); and J. T. Reason, *Managing the Risk of Organizational Accidents* (Aldershot: Ashgate, 1997). On latent and active errors, see: K. G. M. Volpp, D. Grande, "Residents' Suggestions for Reducing Errors in Teaching Hospitals," *New England Journal of Medicine* 348 (9) (2003): 851–855.

49 The Institute of Medicine, *To Err is Human: Building a Safer Health System* (Washington, DC: National Academies Press, 2000).

50 Joint Commission, *The Value of Close Calls in Improving Patient Care. Learning How to Avoid and Mitigate Patient Harm* (Oakbrook Terrace, IL: Joint Commission Resources, 2011), Foreword.

51 See: D. C. Classen, et al., "'Global Trigger Tool' Shows that Adverse Events in Hospitals May Be Ten Times Higher than Previously Measured," *Health Affairs* 30 (3) (2011): 581–589.

52 Institute of Medicine, *Crossing the Quality Chasm: A New Health System for the 21st Century* (Washington, DC: National Academy Press, 2001).

53 For a commentary on the first two IOM reports, see: B. J. McNeil, "Shattuck Lecture-Hidden Barriers to Improvement in the Quality of Care," *New England Journal of Medicine* 345 (22) (2001): 1612–1620.

54 Institute of Medicine, *Leadership by Example: Coordinating Government Roles in Improving Healthcare Quality* (Washington, DC: National Academy Press, 2002).

55 Institute of Medicine, *Preventing Medication Errors* (Washington, DC: National Academies Press, 2006); Institute of Medicine, *Patient Safety: Achieving a New Standard of Care* (Washington, DC: National Academies Press, 2004).

56 See: Institute of Medicine, Healthcare Quality Initiative, *Keeping Patients Safe: Transforming the Work Environment of Nurses* (Washington, DC: National Academy Press, 2004); Institute of Medicine, *Healthcare Quality Initiative, Patient Safety: Achieving a New Standard for Care* (Washington, DC: National Academy Press, 2004).

57 See: J. Morrissey, "Quality vs. Quantity. IOM Report: Hospitals Must Cut Back Workload and Hours of Nurses to Maintain Patient Safety," *Modern Healthcare* (November 10, 2003): 8, 11; J. F. Quinn, "Revisioning the Nursing Shortage: A Call to Caring for healing the Healthcare System," *Frontiers of Health Services Management* 19 (2) (2002): 3–21.

58 J. John, "A New, Evidence-based Estimate of Patient Harms Associated with Hospital Care," *Journal of Patient Safety* 9 (3) (2013): 122–128.

59 Johns Hopkins Medicine, *Study Suggests Medical Errors Now Third Leading Cause of Death in the U.S.* (2016), at, www.hopkinsmedicine.org/news/media/releases/study_suggests_medical_errors_now_third_leading_cause_of_death_in_the_us.

60 Cureatr, *There's Much Work to be Done: 8 Medical Error Statistics to Know* (2019), at, https://blog.cureatr.com/theres-much-work-to-be-done-8-medical-errors-statistics-to-know.

61 Institute for Healthcare Improvement, *New Survey Finds 21 Percent of Americans Report Personal Experience with Medical Errors* (September 28, 2017), at, www.ihi.org/about/news/Documents/IHIPressRelease_Patient_Safety_Survey_Sept28_17.pdf.

62 Institute of Medicine, *To Err is Human: Building a Safer Health System* (Washington, DC: National Academies Press, 2000), 49–68.

63 See: National Coalition on Healthcare and the Institute for Healthcare Improvement, *Reducing Medical Errors and Improving Patient Safety* (Washington, DC: National Coalition on Healthcare, 2000), 1–31.

64 See: Agency for Healthcare Research and Quality, *Patient Safety Indicators Overview* (2019), at www.qualityindicators.ahrq.gov/Modules/psi_overview.aspx; Agency for Healthcare Research and Quality, *Quality and Patient Safety* (2019), at www.ahrq.gov/professionals/quality-patient-safety/index.html; Agency for Healthcare Research and Quality, *Hospital Survey on Patient Mechanisms for Safety* (Rockville, MD: Agency for Healthcare Research and Quality, 2012).

65 See: D. S. Dhillon, *Human Reliability and Error in Medical System* (Hackensack, NJ: World Scientific Publishing, 2003).

66 See: Y. Donchin, D. Gopher, eds., *Around the Patient Bed: Human Factors and Safety in Healthcare* (Taylor and Francis, CRC Press, 2013); M. St. Pierre, et al. eds., *Crisis Management in Acute Care Settings: Human Factors, Team Psychology, and Patient Safety in a High Stakes Environment* (New York: Springer, 2011), especially Chapters 3–6.

67 D. Feigal, et al., "Ensuring Safe and Effective Medical Devices," *New England Journal of Medicine* 348 (3) (2003): 191–192.

68 See: S. Decker, *Patient Safety: A Human Factors Approach* (Taylor and Francis, CRC Press, 2011); S. Decker, *Drift into Failure: From Hunting Broken Components to Understanding Complex Systems* (Farnham, UK: Ashgate, 2011); J. W. Gosbee, L. L. Gosbee, eds., *Using Human Factors Engineering to Improve Patient Safety*, 2nd ed. (Oakbrook, IL: Joint Commission Resources, 2010).

69 See: Agency for Healthcare Research and Quality, *Medical Liability Reform and Patient Safety Initiative* (Rockville, MD: Agency for Healthcare Research and Quality, 2010).

70 See: L. L. Leape, *Disclosing Medical Errors: A Guide to an Effective Explanation and Apology* (Chicago, IL: Joint Commission Resources, 2006); W. Levinson, et al., "Disclosure of Medical Error," *JAMA Professional* (August 16, 2016): 764–765, at, https://doi.org/10.1001/jama.2016.9136.

71 See: Joint Commission, *The Essential Guide for Patient Safety Officers*, 2nd ed. (Oakbrook, IL: Joint Commission Resources, 2013), Chapter Eight, "Disclosure," 81–89;

Joint Commission, *Understanding and Preventing Sentinel and Adverse Events in your Healthcare Organization* (Oakbrook, IL: Joint Commission Resources, 2008), Chapter 6, "Ethics and Disclosure of Events," 173–194.

72 See: Agency for Healthcare Research and Quality, *Systems Approach, Patient Safety Network* (January 2019), at, https://psnet.ahrq.gov/primers/primer/21/systems-approach; G. Caplea, "Taking a Systems Approach to Patient Safety," *Health IT & CEO Report* (March 11, 2019), at, www.beckershospitalreview.com/ehrs/taking-a-systems-approach-to-improve-patient-safety.html.

73 See: G. Magill, "Ethical and Policy Issues Related to Medical Error and Patient Safety," in S. A. M. McLean, ed., *First Do No Harm: Law, Ethics, and Healthcare* (London: Ashgate, 2006), Chapter 7, 101–116; D. F. Kelly, G. Magill, H. ten Have, *Contemporary Catholic Healthcare Ethics* (Washington, DC: Georgetown University Press, 2014), Chapter 24, at 274–278; G. Magill, "Patient Safety," in H. ten Have & B. Gordijn, eds., *Encyclopedia of Global Bioethics* (Springer, 2016).

74 See: D. M. Studdart, et al., "Medical Malpractice," *New England Journal of Medicine* 350 (3) (2004): 283–292, at 287; W. M. Sage, "Medical Liability and Patient Safety," *Health Affairs* 22 (4) (2003): 26–36.

75 See: L. L. Leape, "Patient Safety: Reporting of Adverse Events," *New England Journal of Medicine* 347 (2002): 1633–1638; J. R. Cohen, "Future Research on Disclosure of Medical Errors," *Annals of Internal Medicine* 141 (6) (2004): 481; K. M. Mazor, et al., "Communicating with Patients about Medical Errors: A Review of the Literature," *Archives of Internal Medicine* 164 (15) (2004): 1690–1697.

76 E. B. Weeks, et al., "Tort Claims Analysis in the VHA for Quality Improvement," *Journal of Law, Medicine, & Ethics* 29 (2001): 335–345.

77 See: National Research Council, *Aviation Safety and Pilot Control: Understanding and Preventing Unfavorable Pilot/Vehicle Interactions* (National Academies Press, 1997); The Institute of Medicine, *To Err Is Human: Building a Safer Health System* (Washington, DC, National Academies Press, 2000), "Building Leadership and Knowledge for Patient Safety," 69–85.

78 See: S. Gordon, P et al., *Beyond the Checklist: What Else Healthcare Can Learn Beyond Teamwork and Safety* (Ithaca, NY: Cornell University Press, 2013); D. Marshall, *Crew Resource Management: From Patient Safety to High Reliability* (Littleton, CO: SaferHealthcare, 2010).

79 See: The Joint Commission, *Front Line of Defense: The Role of Nurses in Preventing Sentinel Events* (Oakbrook Terrace, IL: Joint Commission Resources, 2018); Joint Commission, *The Value of Close Calls in Improving Patient Care. Learning How to Avoid and Mitigate Patient Harm* (Oakbrook Terrace, IL: Joint Commission Resources, 2011).

80 See: U.S. Department of Labor, *OSH Act of 1970*, at www.osha.gov/laws-regs/oshact/completeoshact; J. MacLaury, *The Job Safety Law of 1970: Its Passage Was Perilous* (U.S. Department of Labor), at www.dol.gov/general/aboutdol/history/osha.

81 See: R. J. Latino, et al., *Root Cause Analysis: Improving Performance for Bottom-Line Results*, 4th ed. (CRC Press/Taylor & Francis, 2011); B. Anderson, et al., *Root Cause Analysis and Improvement in the Healthcare Sector* (Quality Press, 2010); D. Okes, *Root Cause Analysis: The Core Problem of Solving and Corrective Action* (Milwaukee, WI: ASQ Quality Press, 2009).

82 See: D. Okes, *Root Cause Analysis: The Core of Problem Solving and Corrective Action*, 2nd ed. (ASQ Press, 2019); M. A. Latino, et al., *Root Cause Analysis: Improving Performance for Bottom-Line Results* (CRC Press, 2016); L. N. Vanden Heuvel, et al., *Root Cause Analysis Handbook* (Rothstein Publishing, 2014); M. A. Barslou, *Root Cause Analysis: A Step-by-Step Guide* (Productivity Press, 2014).

83 See: B. Anderson, T. N. Fagerhaug, *The ASQ Pocket Guide to Root Cause Analysis* (ASQ Press, 2013); Anderson, B., et al., *Root Cause Analysis and Improvement in the Healthcare Sector* (Quality Press, 2010).

84 See: Joint Commission, *Root Cause Analysis in Healthcare*, 6th ed. (Oakbrook Terrace, IL: Joint Commission Resources, 2017); Joint Commission, *The Essential Guide for Patient Safety Officers*, 2nd ed. (Oakbrook, IL: Joint Commission Resources, 2013), Chapter Two, "Assessing and Improving Mechanisms for Safety," 13–21.

85 See: Joint Commission, *Front Line of Defense: The Role of Nurses in Preventing Sentinel Events* (Oakbrook Terrace, IL: Joint Commission Resources, 2018); Joint Commission International, *Sentinel Event Policy* (Oakbrook Terrace, IL: Joint Commission Resources, June 2018); Joint Commission, *Understanding and Preventing Sentinel and Adverse Events in your Healthcare Organization* (Oakbrook, IL: Joint Commission Resources, 2008); Joint Commission, *Sentinel Event Data Summary* (Oakbrook, IL: Joint Commission Resource, September 2013), at www.jointcommission.org/sentinel_event_statistics_quarterly.

86 The Joint Commission publishes its Sentinel Event Alert and its Sentinel Alert Data Summary to provide information for organizations to reduce risk and improve effectiveness. See: Joint Commission, *Sentinel Event Alert Updates* (July 2019), at www.jointcommission.org/daily_update/joint_commission_daily_update.aspx?k=721; Joint Commission, *Sentinel Alert Data Summary* (2019), at www.jointcommission.org/sentinel_event_statistics_quarterly/.

87 B. J. Youngberg, *Principles of Risk Management and Patient Safety* (Burlington, MA: Jones & Bartlett, 2011).

88 Patient Safety Network, *Culture of Safety* (January 2019), at, https://psnet.ahrq.gov/primers/primer/5/Culture-of-Safety; Joint Commission, *The Essential Guide for Patient Safety Officers*, 2nd ed. (Oakbrook, IL: Joint Commission Resources, 2013), Chapter Two, "Assessing and Improving Mechanisms for Safety," 13–21.

89 See: G. Kaufman, D. McCaughan, "The Effect of Organizational Culture on Patient Safety," *Nursing Standard* 27 (43) (2013): 50–60; J. Braithwaite, et al., "Association Between Organizational and Workplace Cultures, and Patient Outcomes: Systematic Review," *BML Open* 7 (11) (November 8, 2017), at, https://doi.org/10.1136/bmjopen-2017–017708.

90 The Institute of Medicine, *To Err is Human: Building a Safer Health System* (Washington, DC: National Academies Press, 2000), "Creating Safety Systems in Healthcare Organizations," 155–201, at 166–197.

91 See: C. Argyris, *Organizational Traps: Leadership, Culture, Organizational Design* (New York: Oxford University Press, 2012).

92 See: Joint Commission, "The Essential Role of Leadership in Developing a Safety Culture," *Sentinel Event Alert* 57 (March 1, 2017); Joint Commission, "Effective Teamwork and Communication," *The Essential Guide for Patient Safety Officers*, 2nd ed. (Oakbrook, IL: Joint Commission Resources, 2013), Chapter Six, 53–68; E. Salas, K. Frush, eds., *Improving Patient Safety Through Teamwork and Team Training* (New York: Oxford University Press, 2012); A. C. Edmondson, *Teaming: How Organizations Learn, Innovate, and Compete in the Knowledge Economy* (San Francisco, CA: Jossey-Bass, 2012).

93 See: A. Joseph, et al., "Designing for Patient Safety: Developing Methods to Integrate Patient Safety Concerns in the Design Process," *Patient Safety Network* (September, 2012), at, https://psnet.ahrq.gov/resources/resource/25189/Designing-for-Patient-Safety-Developing-Methods-to-Integrate-Patient-Safety-Concerns-in-the-Design-Process; also published by The Center for Health Design, *Designing for Patient Safety: Developing Methods to Integrate Patient Safety Concerns in the Design Process* (2012), at, www.healthdesign.org/sites/default/files/chd416_ahrqreport_final.pdf.

94 See: Agency for Healthcare Research and Quality, *Advancing Patient Safety: A decade of Design and Implementation* (2009), at www.ahrq.gov/professionals/quality-patient-safety/patient-safety-resources/resources/advancing-patient-safety/index.html; J. F. Stichler, "A Priority for Healthcare and for Healthcare Design," *Health Environments Research &*

Design Journal (August 4, 2016), at, https://doi.org/10.1177/1937586716646648; Agency for Healthcare Research and Quality, *Transforming Hospitals: Designing for Safety and Quality* (2019), at www.ahrq.gov/professionals/systems/hospital/transform/index.html.

95 See: N. Dey, et al., eds., *Big Data Analytics for Intelligent Healthcare Management* (Cambridge, MA: Academic Press, 2019); S. Consoli, et al., eds., *Data Science for Healthcare* (Springer, 2019); S. Pestonik, V. Lemon, *How to Use Data to Improve Quality and Patient Safety* (HealthCatalyst, April 30, 2019), at www.healthcatalyst.com/insights/use-data-improve-patient-safety/; J. Bresnick, "Using Big Data Analytics for Patient Safety, Hospital Acquired Conditions" *Health IT Analytics* (August 6, 2018), at, https://healthitanalytics.com/features/using-big-data-analytics-for-patient-safety-hospital-acquired-conditions; HealthCatalyst, *The Top Seven Analytics-Driven Approaches for Reducing Diagnostic Error and Improving Patient Safety* (Health-Catalyst, October 13, 2016), at www.healthcatalyst.com/reducing-diagnostic-error-to-improve-patient-safety/; HealthCatalyst, *Improving Patient Safety: Machine Learning Targets an Urgent Concern* (HealthCatalyst, January 30, 2018), at www.healthcatalyst.com/machine-learning-patient-safety-improvement; Patient Safety Network, *Health Care Data Science for Quality Improvement and Patient Safety* (Patient Safety Network, October 2016), at, https://psnet.ahrq.gov/perspectives/perspective/208/health-care-data-science-for-quality-improvement-and-patient-safety.

96 See: Joint Commission, *The Joint Commission Journal on Quality and Patient Safety* (2019), at www.jcrinc.com/the-joint-commission-journal-on-quality-and-patient-safety/; Joint Commission, *The Joint Commission Perspectives* (2019), at www.jcrinc.com/the-joint-commission-perspectives/; Joint Commission, *The Source, Joint Commission* (2019), at www.jcrinc.com/the-source/; Joint Commission, *2019 National Patient Safety Goals* (October 2018), at www.jointcommission.org/hap_2017_npsgs/; Joint Commission, *Facts About the National Patient Safety Goals, Joint Commission* (November 30, 2018), at www.jointcommission.org/facts_about_the_national_patient_safety_goals/; Joint Commission, *Getting the Board on Board. What Your Boards Need to Know About Quality and Patient Safety*, 3rd ed. (Oakbrook, IL: Joint Commission Resources, 2016), Chapter 3, "The Board's Role in Improving Quality and Safety," 71–98.

97 Joint Commission, *Getting the Board on Board: What Your Boards Need to Know about Quality and Patient Safety*, 3rd ed. (Oakbrook, IL: Joint Commission Resources, 2016).

Select readings

Agency for Healthcare Research and Quality. 2019. *Transforming Hospitals: Designing for Safety and Quality*. Rockville, MD: Agency for Healthcare Research and Quality.

Al Hasmi, A. G. 2017. *Environment, Health and Safety Governance and Leadership*. United Kingdom: Routledge.

Allhoff, F. S., L. Borden, eds. 2019. *Ethics and Error in Medicine*. United Kingdom: Routledge.

Banja, J. D. 2019. *Patient Safety Ethics: How Vigilance, Mindfulness, Compliance, and Humility Can Make Healthcare Safer*. Baltimore, MD: Johns Hopkins University Press.

Joint Commission. 2017. *Root Cause Analysis in Healthcare*, 6th ed. Oakbrook Terrace, IL: Joint Commission Resources.

Joint Commission. 2018. *2019 National Patient Safety Goals, Joint Commission*. Oakbrook Terrace, IL: Joint Commission Resources.

Joint Commission. 2018. *Front Line of Defense: The Role of Nurses in Preventing Sentinel Events*. Oakbrook Terrace, IL: Joint Commission Resources.

Okes, D. 2019. *Root Cause Analysis: The Core Problem of Solving and Corrective Action*. Milwaukee, WI: ASQ Quality Press.

Pederson, K. Z. 2017. *Organizing Patient Safety*. United Kingdom: Palgrave MacMillan.

Prybil, L., et al. 2012. *Governance in Large Nonprofit Health Systems: Current Profile and Emerging Patterns*. Lexington, KY: Commonwealth Center for Governance Studies, Inc.

Quick, O. 2017. *Regulating Patient Safety*. New York: Cambridge University Press.

Tingle, J., et al., eds. 2018. *Global Patient Safety: Law, Policy and Practice*. United Kingdom: Routledge, 2018.

Wachter, R. M. 2017. *Understanding Patient Safety*, 2nd ed. New York: McGraw Hill.

Wears, R., K. Sutcliffe. 2019. *Still Not Safe: Patient Safety and the Middle-Managing of American Medicine*. New York: Oxford University Press.

9 Governance of conflicted collaborative arrangements

Introduction

This chapter continues the approach of applying the ethics paradigm to a pivotal problem for governance ethics: how boards of directors may permissibly navigate complex dilemmas involving conflicted collaborative arrangements in healthcare organizations. As boards pursue their governance responsibilities for communities (community benefit and community health, as discussed in Chapters 5 and 6) and for patients (patient care quality and patient safety, as discussed in Chapters 7 and 8), scenarios can arise in which collaborative arrangements can conflict with an organization's mission. The following discussion explains how to distinguish between wrongful complicity and legitimate cooperation with other institutions when there is a fundamental conflict over basic values related to an organization's mission. In such conflicted scenarios, the goal is to maintain quality care services in any new collaborative arrangement.

In the previous analysis, the concepts of the ethics paradigm organize core features of effective governance from landmark reports and the scholarly literature. The analysis in this chapter emphasizes the scholarly literature to explain the nuances of the ethical principle of cooperation that is discussed in this chapter. The purpose is to highlight hallmarks of governance ethics that denote associated moral imperatives. Because the hallmarks represent necessary moral attributes of governance ethics, they entail an obligation to be adopted by boards. In turn, the associated moral imperatives represent necessary endeavors to foster the hallmarks under consideration.

The ethics paradigm organizes multiple topics on board oversight of conflicted collaborative arrangements, as follows. First, the foundation component of the ethics paradigm deals with the *identity* of an organization, reflecting the leitmotif *who we are*, thereby highlighting board oversight of organizational reputation as a hallmark of governance ethics in conflicted collaborative arrangements. In turn, this hallmark denotes an associated moral imperative of board oversight of organizational flexibility. Second, the process component of the ethics paradigm addresses the *accountability* of the organization, reflecting the leitmotif *how we function*, thereby highlighting board oversight of institutional negotiations as a hallmark of governance ethics. In turn, this hallmark denotes an associated moral imperative regarding board oversight of the process of cooperation. Third, the

Table 1.1 Ethics paradigm

Components	Foundation component	Process component	Practice component
Context	Environment of healthcare	Organizational oversight	Organizational culture
Leadership	Identity: who we are	Accountability: how we function	Quality: what we do
Outcomes	Organizational stewardship of mission	Decision-making via participative deliberation	Best practices for standards of conduct

practice component of the ethics paradigm engages *quality* in an organization, reflecting the leitmotif *what we do*, thereby highlighting board oversight of collaborative arrangements as a hallmark of governance ethics. In turn, this hallmark denotes an associated moral imperative regarding board oversight of maintaining quality care services.

Each of the applied chapters begins with an explanation of the need for the pivotal topic under consideration, such as governance of conflicted collaborative arrangements here. Again, the concepts of *identity*, *accountability*, and *quality* provide a framework for the applied analysis. These concepts represent the foundation component (reflecting *who we are*), the process component (reflecting *how we function*), and the practice component (reflecting *what we do*) of the ethics paradigm (Table 1.1).

The need for collaborative arrangements has expanded exponentially in healthcare over recent decades. To begin the discussion, it is helpful to explain the need for the moral principle of cooperation.

Need for a moral principle of cooperation

Boards encounter occasions when their healthcare organization creates a collaborative arrangement with other institutions that undertake activities deemed to be immoral, even though such actions may be legal. As boards oversee their own organization based on the principle of stewardship, their focus is not merely to maintain the fiscal viability of the organization but also to nurture its mission. This duty of stewardship entails a serious responsibility to avoid what the organization deems to be wrong, that is, avoiding wrongful complicity with conflicting values in another institution. Nonetheless, in the complex arena of a secular and pluralistic democracy, there is a myriad of values that different organizations have. Surprisingly often, boards must navigate the difficult shoals of conflicting values between organizations to benefit from a variety of collaborative arrangements.

This dilemma in governance ethics raises a crucial distinction between wrongful complicity and legitimate cooperation. The following analysis explains two common circumstances. One situation is when the board of organization A becomes involved with actions that it deems to be immoral (but not illegal) in organization B. Another situation is when organization A is under duress, such as by government pressure, regarding the provision of services that are deemed by the organization to be immoral (such as some types of reproductive services). What should a board do in such situations to steward its own organizational values and mission?

Different analogies are discussed to shed light on these difficult scenarios. The chapter explains the ethical principle of cooperation to present options that boards can pursue. The principle is most explicitly used in Catholic healthcare that represents approximately 15 percent of acute care hospitals (owned by or affiliated with Catholicism).[1] Hence, the examples of conflicted collaborative arrangements that are considered deal with Catholic healthcare. The point is to use this religious tradition as an example of using this ethical principle when the values of any health system (religious or secular) become conflicted in collaborative arrangements.[2]

The discussion now applies the ethics paradigm to organize core features of effective governance regarding conflicted collaborative arrangements. The purpose is to highlight hallmarks of governance ethics that denote associated moral imperatives. The applied analysis begins with discussing hallmarks of governance ethics connected with the foundation component of the ethics paradigm.

Organizational reputation: foundation-related governance ethics hallmark

The foundation component of the ethics paradigm, in the context of the challenging environment of healthcare, focuses on stewardship to enhance an organization's mission as crucial for effective governance. This focus requires boards to be attentive to the healthcare environment as the context for meeting their responsibilities. This component depicts the *identity* of an organization, reflecting the leitmotif *who we are*. The concept of *identity* highlights board oversight of organizational reputation as a hallmark of governance ethics in conflicted collaborative arrangements. This concept draws attention to who the board is in relation with its organization. In turn, this hallmark denotes an associated moral imperative regarding board oversight of organizational flexibility that boards must have in conflicted collaborative arrangements involving conflicting mission or values. These are discussed in subsequent sections.

To understand board oversight of organizational reputation as a hallmark of governance ethics, it is helpful to consider how the ethical principle of cooperation pertains in a common example, bank robbery. This example clarifies who is or is not a thief, illustrating the reputation so to speak of the individuals involved. The point here is that when an institution undertakes actions in conflicted collaborative arrangements, its organizational reputation is at stake.

In a bank robbery, different reputations accrue to individuals who become involved. Naturally, the individuals who enact the robbery in a bank are thieves. That is who they are, that is their "reputation." However, what about a get-away driver? Of course, a get-away driver is complicit with the theft, even though the driver did not enter the bank. That sort of wrongful complicity occurs because the getaway driver intends the theft of the bank robber, participating in the crime albeit at some distance. The get-away driver also merits the "reputation" of being a thief.

However, another scenario can complicate this straightforward description of robbery. If the bank robber uses a gun to stop a passing car and forces the driver under duress to provide an escape, that innocent driver does not intend the theft. Nonetheless the beleaguered driver is involved in the robbery (that is, physically cooperating) by driving the car, albeit under duress of being shot. That sort of involvement or cooperation in the crime is not culpable because the driver is under unavoidable duress and does not intend the morally wrong action—despite the physical participation in the crime. This scenario is not morally wrong. In other words, the innocent driver does not merit the "reputation" of being a thief.

In ethics discourse, the distinction between these two situations has a specific terminology. In the first scenario, the planned getaway driver's action is described as illicit formal cooperation: the driver intends to participate in the crime, albeit without entering the bank vault. This driver merits the "reputation" of being a thief. In the second scenario, the action of the enforced passerby to drive the escape care is described as justified material cooperation: the passerby does not intend the theft but under duress is physically connected with the crime by driving the escape car. This driver does not merit the "reputation" of being a thief. The point to note is that formal cooperation cannot be morally justified, whereas material cooperation can be morally justified. No court would judge the unfortunate passerby as guilty of theft; nor does moral discourse construe guilt for this sort of physical involvement with immoral behavior (the bank robbery).

This straightforward example sheds light on how boards might use this ethical principle of cooperation to guide their oversight of organizational reputation in conflicted collaborative arrangements. For example, board members in a Catholic health organization may plan to expand their services via a collaborative arrangement with another healthcare provider who has services prohibited by Catholic teaching. The need for such an arrangement must be related to external pressure upon the Catholic organization, such as needing to provide permissible services to remain competitive, despite the other organization also providing services prohibited in Catholicism. Without external duress, conflicted collaborative arrangements should not be considered. Because the services of the other organization include activities prohibited by Catholic teaching (such as some reproductive services), the "reputation" of the Catholic organization is at stake. Hence, board members must have a valid motive for considering the collaborative arrangement. For example, there is a scenario (though unlikely) where board members of a Catholic organization consider the collaborative arrangement because they want to have access to the prohibited reproductive services in the other organization. This is unacceptable. Or, the board members may plan access to other collaborative arrangement services that are permissible in Catholicism, despite the other organization providing reproductive services that Catholicism prohibits. Again, the board's rationale to plan ahead is grounded in external duress that leads them to consider such a conflicted collaborative arrangement.

If board members intend the former (wanting the prohibited services), they intend the so-called wrongdoing. If board members intend the latter (seeking access to permissible services), they do not intend any perceived wrongdoing in the other organization. In these scenarios, the motive of the board members shapes the "reputation" of the organization.

Board oversight of organizational reputation constitutes a hallmark of governance ethics because board actions determine the ethical caliber of conflicted collaborative arrangements. That is, boards have a duty to protect the reputation of their organization when it considers conflicted collaborative arrangements with other institutions that may have conflicting values (providing services that are prohibited by the other organization). This discussion engages the challenging environment in healthcare where market pressures require organizations to make arrangements that raise the dilemma of a conflicted collaborative arrangement.

Moral imperative: board oversight of organizational flexibility

Board oversight of organizational reputation in conflicted collaborative arrangements is a hallmark of governance ethics. This hallmark denotes an associated moral imperative regarding oversight of organizational flexibility. This imperative refers to the flexibility that boards must have in conflicted collaborative arrangements. Boards need maneuvering room when involved with conflicting values.

Often, quandaries that emerge around conflicting organizational values in collaborative arrangement occur between secular and religiously affiliated institutions. Because Catholic healthcare holds the largest percentage of faith-based healthcare facilities in the USA, it can be useful to explore its use of the ethical principle of cooperation. This principle is useful not just for Catholic healthcare. Secular or other religiously affiliated healthcare systems may become involved with conflicted collaborative arrangements that can benefit from understanding this ethical principle. The flexibility permitted by the ethical principle of cooperation in Catholic healthcare is explained in the Ethical and Religious Directives for Catholic Health Care Services, referred to later as the Directives. These directives were revised in 2018 specifically to explain the nuances of this principle of cooperation.[3] The following discussion considers how the Catholic tradition uses this principle generally, while avoiding the multiple fine distinctions that the principle has generated over centuries of use.[4]

Boards must have organizational flexibility to avoid any arrangement that contributes to what Catholicism construes as the wrongdoing of other providers. The Directives explain that "Catholic health care services . . . should avoid, whenever possible, engaging in collaborative arrangements that would involve them in contributing to the wrongdoing of other providers."[5] Nonetheless, the Directives recognize that at times "in pursuit of the common good, the only available candidates for collaboration are institutions that do not operate in conformity with the Church's moral teaching."[6] The permissibility here refers to there being duress that requires such a collaborative arrangement and that it is undertaken to contribute to the common good.

The Directives refer to the ethical principle of cooperation when explaining that "the Catholic moral tradition provides principles for assessing cooperation with the wrongdoing of others."[7] This ethical principle provides boards with the organizational flexibility to plan appropriate collaborative arrangements. The purpose is specifically "to determine the conditions under which cooperation may or may not be morally justified, distinguishing between 'formal' and 'material' cooperation."[8] This principle provides organizational flexibility to clarify when instances of material cooperation are morally justified or not. This approach recognizes that collaborative arrangements between Catholic institutions and entities that do not share the Catholic moral tradition present both opportunities and challenges. This organizational flexibility emphasizes that "the challenges do not necessarily preclude all such arrangements on moral grounds," and urges "Catholic leaders to undertake careful analyses to ensure that . . . collaborative arrangements . . . abide by the principles governing cooperation."[9]

In sum, the foundation component of the ethics paradigm highlights board oversight of organizational reputation as a hallmark of governance ethics. By focusing on *identity* in the ethics paradigm (dealing with who the board is), this hallmark denotes an associated moral imperative regarding board oversight of organizational flexibility in collaborative arrangement. Boards need maneuvering room when involved with conflicting mission or values.

Institutional negotiations: process-related governance ethics hallmark

The concept of *accountability* in the ethics paradigm (reflecting the leitmotif *how we function*) emphasizes the importance of decision-making via participative deliberation. This focus requires boards to be attentive to organizational oversight as the context for overseeing their responsibilities. The concept of *accountability* highlights board oversight of institutional negotiations as a hallmark of governance ethics in conflicted collaborative arrangements. The concept draws attention to how the board functions in the organization. In turn, this hallmark denotes an associated moral imperative regarding board oversight of the process of cooperation. These are discussed in the next section.

To understand board oversight of institutional negotiations as a hallmark of governance ethics, it is helpful to consider an analogous scenario. The scenario deals with legislators undertaking negotiations about politics. The following discussion suggests options that boards can adopt in their institutional negotiations in conflicted collaborative arrangements.

The discussion deals with scenarios where Catholic legislators have to vote on abortion laws.[10] It would be illicit for Catholics to vote for abortion related to activities that they undertake. Yet, surprisingly, using the principle of cooperation, Catholics may legitimately vote in favor of an abortion law or for pro-abortion legislators as a form of licit cooperation. This may seem surprising given the strenuous opposition to abortion in this religious tradition.

However, the principle of cooperation in these conflicted situations can enlighten how boards of directors in healthcare may deal with their conflicted collaborative arrangements. Two related Catholic teachings can shed light on the complex deliberations around voting for legislation to permit abortion. The US bishops explain the nuanced Catholic stance in this way:

> Decisions about political life are complex and require the exercise of a well-formed conscience aided by prudence. . . . Sometimes morally flawed laws already exist. In this situation, the process of framing legislation to protect life is subject to prudential judgment and 'the art of the possible.' At times this process may restore justice only partially or gradually. Pope John Paul II taught that when a government official who fully opposes abortion cannot succeed in completely overturning a pro-abortion law, he or she may work to improve protection for unborn human life, 'limiting the harm done by such a law' and lessening its negative impact as much as possible. Such incremental improvements in the law are acceptable as steps toward the full restoration of justice.[11]

The key point being made here is that Catholic legislators may vote in favor of a law permitting abortion, provided the law decreases or diminishes the reach ("limiting the harm") of prior laws. The next quotation reiterates this stance referring to the principle of cooperation. The passage that the US bishops allude to is from the teaching of Pope John Paul II:

> A particular problem of conscience can arise in cases where a legislative vote would be decisive for the passage of a more restrictive law, aimed at limiting the number of authorized abortions, in place of a more permissive law already passed or ready to be voted on. Such cases are not infrequent. . . . In a case like the one just mentioned, when it is not possible to overturn or completely abrogate a pro-abortion law, an elected official, whose absolute personal opposition to procured abortion was well known, could licitly support proposals aimed at limiting the harm done by such a law and at lessening its negative consequences at the level of general opinion and public morality. This does not in fact represent an illicit cooperation with an unjust law, but rather a legitimate and proper attempt to limit its evil aspects.[12]

The key point here is to highlight that the US bishops rely on the principle of cooperation to permit Catholic legislators to vote in favor of an abortion law provided it limits a more permissive law. This means that a Catholic politician who is pro-life may support laws that, while continuing to permit abortion, limit the harm of previous laws. The renowned legal scholar John Finnis has argued, "even if there is cooperation of pro-life legislators with unjust legislators in enacting just restrictive legislation, this cooperation does not involve the pro-life legislator in the wrongdoing of the unjust legislator, or any other wrongdoing."[13]

The critical issue here is that the principle of cooperation permits Catholic politicians to support some types of legislation that permit abortion. Two crucial points must be noted. A Catholic politician must not intend the evil of abortion: that would constitute formal cooperation which is always illicit. Also, a Catholic politician may vote for an abortion law in such circumstances as a function of material connection with the abortion legislation. Here, the politician is under duress and the vote connects in a material way with the perceived wrongdoing of abortion, yet good can be achieved by voting for a law that limits the reach of prior legislation.

In this example, a Catholic politician may engage in the institutional negotiations that occur in the legislature. The politician can use the principle of cooperation to reach a collaborative arrangement (with fellow legislators), despite the law under discussion being connected with perceived wrongdoing (abortion). In this situation, the politician engages in justified material cooperation. Similarly, boards in Catholic healthcare may engage in institutional negotiations to establish a collaborative arrangement (with a fellow healthcare organization), despite the arrangement under discussion being connected with perceived wrongdoing (such as certain reproductive services). This analysis explains why board oversight of institutional negotiations constitutes a crucial hallmark of governance ethics.

Moral imperative: board oversight of the process of cooperation

Board oversight of institutional negotiations is a hallmark of governance ethics in conflicted collaborative arrangements. This hallmark denotes an associated moral imperative regarding board oversight of the process of cooperation. When boards in healthcare organizations find themselves in such conflicted collaborative arrangements, they must adopt the proper process of cooperation that is delineated by the principle of cooperation.

There is considerable discourse on the principle of cooperation to explain how to avoid wrongful complicity with conflicting values in collaborative arrangements.[14] The Directives of the US bishops explain how the process of cooperation functions in healthcare. To begin, any collaborative arrangement must avoid formal cooperation, such as intending the perceived wrongdoing of another organization. The Directives emphasize that to use the principle of cooperation, collaborative actions of the Catholic institution must be scrutinized carefully: "a Catholic institution must ensure neither its administration nor its employees will manage, carry out, assist in carrying out, make its facilities available for, make referrals for, or benefit from the revenue generated by immoral procedures."[15] Furthermore, the Directives emphasize that in such a process of cooperation the "acquisition, governance, or management" undertaken by a Catholic institution in conflicted collaborative arrangements require meticulous care in planning:

> It is not permitted to establish another entity that would oversee, manage, or perform immoral procedures. Establishing such an entity includes actions such as drawing up the civil bylaws, policies, or procedures of the entity, establishing the finances of the entity, or legally incorporating the entity.[16]

The point here is to avoid subtle or nuanced maneuvers that can entail formal cooperation. The explicit mention of governance here emphasizes the oversight responsibility of boards for these arrangements and their proper use of the process of cooperation in applying the principle of cooperation.

Another analogy can help to guide the process of cooperation. This analogy returns to the arena of voting that has elicited much attention with regard to the principle of cooperation. This analogy deals with Catholics voting for politicians who support legislative actions prohibited in Catholicism, such as abortion. The question is whether Catholic voters may vote for a pro-abortion politician who supports abortion legislation. The process of cooperation functions in this way. A Catholic voter may not directly support abortion legislation by intending it for its own sake: that would be formal cooperation and thereby immoral. The US bishops make this clear in their 2007 Pastoral Letter.

> A Catholic cannot vote for a candidate who takes a position in favor of an intrinsic evil, such as abortion or racism, if the voter's intent is to support that position. In such cases a Catholic would be guilty of formal cooperation in a grave evil.[17]

The nuanced question, then, is whether a Catholic voter may vote for a pro-abortion politician because of the politician's stance on other important issues. The principle of cooperation permits this. The US bishops explain that Catholic voters may evaluate the issue of abortion within a broader political landscape.

> A candidate's position on a single issue is not sufficient to guarantee a voter's support. Yet a candidate's position on a single issue that involves an intrinsic evil, such as support for legal abortion . . . may legitimately lead a voter to disqualify a candidate from receiving support.[18]

There is a subtle point being made here by the Bishops. A single issue dealing with a perceived harm like abortion "may legitimately lead a voter" to withdraw support. The single issue "may" but does not necessarily require a voter to withdraw support insofar as other issues can legitimately be considered in voting. That is, the process of cooperation can justify voting for a pro-abortion politician based on other relevant issues.

This point was made by Cardinal Joseph Ratzinger as Prefect of the Congregation of the Doctrine of the Faith (who later became Pope Benedict XVI) when he applied the principle of material cooperation. Cardinal Ratzinger explained that the justification of a vote like this would be an example of the process of cooperation. He explained: "A Catholic would be guilty of formal cooperation in evil . . . if he were to deliberately vote for a candidate precisely because of the candidate's permissive stand on abortion and/or euthanasia." On the other hand, he clarified: "When a Catholic does not share a candidate's stand in favor of abortion and/or euthanasia, but votes for that candidate for other reasons, it is considered remote material cooperation, which can be permitted in the presence of proportionate reasons."[19]

This analogy can clarify for boards how the process of cooperation functions when they are engaged with conflicted collaborative arrangements. On the one hand, a Catholic "voter's intent" may not support a candidate's stance on a prohibited action like abortion. Likewise, board members in a Catholic organization may not plan collaborative arrangements if they do so to gain access to prohibited services: that constitutes "formal cooperation in evil." On the other hand, it is permissible when a Catholic "votes for that candidate for other reasons" (distinct from the perceived wrongdoing like abortion). Similarly, in conflicted collaborative arrangements, board members may enact provisions that focus on "other reasons" in the collaboration that are distinct from the perceived wrongdoing: that constitutes "material cooperation." Briefly, the process of cooperation is designed to maintain a fundamental distinction between legitimate and wrongful complicity.

In sum, regarding conflicted collaborative arrangements the process component of the ethics paradigm indicates board oversight of institutional negotiations as a hallmark of governance ethics. By focusing on *accountability* in the ethics paradigm, this hallmark denotes an associated moral imperative concerning board oversight of the process of cooperation. Crucially, the process of cooperation must avoid wrongful complicity with conflicting values.

Collaborative arrangements: practice-related governance ethics hallmark

The concept of *quality* in the ethics paradigm (reflecting the leitmotif *what we do*) emphasizes the importance of best practices for standards of conduct. This focus requires boards to be attentive to organizational culture as the context for implementing their responsibilities. The concept of *quality* highlights board oversight of conflicted collaborative arrangements as a hallmark of governance ethics regarding this topic. In turn, this hallmark denotes an associated moral imperative regarding board oversight of maintaining quality care services. These are discussed in the next section.

To understand board oversight of conflicted collaborative arrangements as a hallmark of governance ethics, it is necessary to be attentive to the importance of external duress upon the Catholic organization. There numerous types of collaborative arrangements. At the foundation of collaborative arrangements when there are conflicting values between the institutions, the principle of cooperation cannot be adopted unless there is clear external duress. The different types of duress can range from financial stress to geographical distribution. In all cases, there must be external duress to justify a Catholic organization collaborating with another institution that does not follow Catholic teaching.

An example of the external duress that boards must endure is when Catholic organizations need to deal with a government mandate. For example, in 2010 healthcare reform was signed into law by President Barack Obama, achieving a goal of extending health insurance to most of the US population, many of whom previously lacked health insurance. The Patient Protection and Affordable Care Act was signed into law on March 23, 2010 by President Obama,[20] along with the Health Care and Education Reconciliation Act of 2010, signed on March 30,

2010.[21] Together these constituted the health care reform accomplishment of the Democratic 111th Congress.[22] This achievement of extending health care insurance and access to tens of millions of citizens who previously had none was consistent with Catholic teaching on social justice.[23]

The critical problem here deals with a government mandate regarding practices that conflict with Catholic teaching. The mandate was from the Department of Health and Human Services related to implementing the Affordable Care Act. The mandate required institutions, including health care organizations, to provide their employees with access to contraception services. However, for Catholic organizations, these services conflict with Catholic teaching.

The principle of cooperation can defuse the controversy by providing boards in Catholic organizations a way to plan collaborative arrangements to address this government mandate for contraception coverage. There are Catholic organizations that provide their employees with a health plan through an insurance company. Also, there are Catholic organizations that are self-insured, though they may use insurance companies to service their health plan and insurance claims. In both situations, the principle of cooperation can justify practices that resolve the problem related to the government's contraception mandate.

The resolution using the principle of cooperation can be described in this way. A Catholic organization informs a mandate-related authority that the organization cannot provide contraception services. The mandate-related authority informs the insurance company for the Catholic organization. Then the insurance company contacts the employees of the Catholic organization to provide contraception coverage separate from and not coordinated by the Catholic organization. This slightly convoluted arrangement means that the government mandate is honored without the Catholic organization having to engage in contraception related practices. This is an example of using the principle of cooperation in an effective manner. On the one hand, the Catholic organization remains at a distance, not intending the perceived wrongdoing. There is no formal cooperation. The organization simply informs the mandate-related authority of its stance against contraception. On the other hand, the Catholic organization remains materially connected insofar as contraception coverage is provided via the organization's insurance company. This is justified based on the principle of material cooperation in light of the external duress of the government mandate.

Moral imperative: board oversight of maintaining quality care services

This type of clean-hands arrangement between a Catholic organization and its insurance company underscores the importance of board oversight of conflicted collaborative arrangements. Board oversight of conflicted collaborative arrangements is a hallmark of governance ethics. This hallmark denotes an associated moral imperative regarding board oversight of maintaining quality care services.

When boards in health care become involved in conflicted collaborative arrangements, the measures that they pursue are designed to focus on maintaining quality care services. The rationale for dealing with other organizations that do not comport with Catholic teaching is to extend services that maintain and enhance the quality services already provided. The purpose of the principle of cooperation is to retain this focus while creating distance from prohibited services in the other institution.

It is important to note the various aspects of maintaining quality care services that are mentioned by the US bishops. The Directives acknowledge the contribution of collaborative arrangements between Catholic organizations and other institutions in health care. This contribution includes many issues: to further the mission of caring for the suffering and sick; to influence the healing profession; to provide a continuum of health care; to present a model of responsible stewardship of limited resources; to provide more equitable access to basic care; to enhance the quality of care; to continue a Catholic institution or the presence of a health care facility in a given area.[24]

Furthermore, the Directives emphasize that in using the principle of cooperation, leaders of health care organizations must ensure they protect the mission of health care (that is, maintaining quality care services):

> Even when there are good reasons for establishing collaborative arrangements that involve material cooperation with wrongdoing, leaders of Catholic healthcare institutions must assess whether becoming associated with the wrongdoing of a collaborator will risk undermining their institution's ability to fulfill its mission of providing health care.[25]

In sum, the practice component of the ethics paradigm highlights board oversight of conflicted collaborative arrangements as a hallmark of governance ethics. By focusing on *quality* in the ethics paradigm (dealing with what the board does), this hallmark denotes an associated moral imperative regarding board oversight of maintaining quality care services. It is crucial to maintain these services for quality in patient care when there are conflicting circumstances.

Conclusion

The chapter has identified hallmarks of governance ethics with associated moral imperatives regarding conflicted collaborative arrangements. The contribution of the ethics paradigm can be summarized in this manner.

First, in the context of the challenging health care environment, the foundation component of the ethics paradigm focuses on stewardship to enhance an organization's mission in health care as crucial for effective governance. This component deals with the *identity* of an organization, reflecting the leitmotif *who we are*, thereby identifying board oversight of organizational reputation as a hallmark of governance ethics in conflicted collaborative arrangements. In turn, this hallmark denotes an associated moral imperative concerning board oversight of organizational flexibility. Boards need this maneuvering room in conflicted collaborative arrangements involving conflicting mission or values.

Second, in the context of organizational oversight in health care, the process component of the ethics paradigm is to focus upon decision-making to foster participative deliberation in organizations. This component addresses the *accountability* of the organization, reflecting the leitmotif *how we function*, thereby identifying board oversight of institutional negotiations as a hallmark of governance ethics. In turn, this hallmark denotes an associated moral imperative concerning board oversight of the process of cooperation. The process of cooperation must avoid wrongful complicity with conflicting values.

Third, in the context of organizational culture in health care, the practice component of the ethics paradigm is to focus on best practices to develop standards of conduct. This component engages *quality* in an organization, reflecting the leitmotif *what we do*, thereby identifying board oversight of collaborative arrangements as a hallmark of governance ethics. In turn, this hallmark denotes associated moral imperatives concerning board oversight of maintaining quality care services. It is crucial to maintain these services for good quality patient care when there are conflicting circumstances.

The ethics paradigm clarifies an over-arching problem for boards of directors in health care when faced with conflicted collaborative arrangements: how to distinguish wrongful complicity and legitimate cooperation with other organizations when conflicting values are involved. The ethical principle of cooperation can resolve these complex dilemmas. The principle of cooperation enables boards of directors to robustly engage complex value dilemmas that arise and to astutely find solutions that foster their organizational mission, decision-making processes, and professional practices (reflecting the concepts of *identity*, *accountability*, and *quality* in the ethics paradigm). By upholding organizational integrity, especially in such difficult circumstances, boards can foster virtue in their organizations, as discussed in the next chapter.

Notes

1 See: Catholic Health Association, *U.S. Catholic Health Care: The Nation's Largest Group of Not-For-Profit Health Care Providers* (Washington, DC: Catholic Health Association, 2019); Catholic Health Association, *Facts-Statistics, Catholic Health Care in the United States* (January 2019), at www.chausa.org/about/about/facts-statistics.
2 This analysis develops discussions of this ethical principle by one of this book's authors in previous publications. See: G. Magill, "Complicity of Catholic Healthcare Institutions with Immoral Laws," in J. T. Eberl, ed., *Contemporary Controversies in Catholic Bioethics* (Springer 2017), Section VII: Healthcare Law and Policy; G. Magill, "Complicity," in H. ten Have & B. Gordijn, eds., *Encyclopedia of Global Bioethics* (Springer, 2016); D. F. Kelly, G. Magill, H. ten Have, *Contemporary Catholic Healthcare Ethics*, 2nd ed. (Washington, DC: Georgetown University Press, 2013), Chapter 24, "Organizational Ethics," at 278–290; G. Magill, "A Moral Compass for Cooperation with Wrongdoing," in N. F. Cafardi, ed., *Voting: Catholic Perspectives on Political Participation* (New York: Paulist, 2012), 135–157.
3 United States Conference of Catholic Bishops (USCCB), *Ethical and Religious Directives for Catholic Health Care Services* (Washington, DC: USCCB, 2018). Referred to as *Directives*.

4 J. F. Keenan, T. R. Kopfensteiner, "The Principle of Cooperation. Theologians Explain Material and Formal Cooperation," *Health Progress* 76 (3) (1995): 23–27.

5 *Directives*, Part Six, Introduction, page 30.

6 *Directives*, Part Six, Introduction, page 30.

7 *Directives*, Part Six, Introduction, page 30.

8 *Directives*, Part Six, Introduction, page 30.

9 *Directives*, Part Six, Introduction, page 32.

10 G. Magill, "A Moral Compass for Cooperation with Wrongdoing," in N. F. Cafardi, ed., *Voting: Catholic Perspectives on Political Participation* (New York: Paulist, 2012), 135–157.

11 United States Conference of Catholic Bishops, *Forming Consciences for Faithful Citizens* (USCCB: Washington, DC, 2009), #31.

12 Pope John Paul II, *The Gospel of Life* (Rome: Vatican City, 1995), #73.

13 See: J. Finnis, "Restricting Legalized Abortion Is Not Intrinsically Unjust," in H. Watt, ed., *Cooperation, Complicity & Conscience: Problems in Healthcare, Science, Law and Public Policy* (London: Linacre Centre, 2006), Chapter 12, 243; J. Finnis, "Helping Enact Unjust Laws without Complicity in Injustice," *American Journal of Jurisprudence* 49 (2004): 11–42.

14 For an analysis of the relation between cooperation and appropriation of evil with regard to this principle, see: M. C. Kaveny, *Law's Virtue: Fostering Autonomy and Solidarity in American Society* (Washington, DC: Georgetown University Press, 2012); C. Kutz, *Complicity: Ethics and Law for a Collective Age* (Cambridge: Cambridge University Press, 2000). Also see: M. C. Kaveny, "Tax Lawyers, Prophets and Pilgrims," in H. Watt, ed., *Cooperation, Complicity & Conscience: Problems in Healthcare, Science, Law and Public Policy* (London: Linacre Centre, 2006), Chapter 4, 75; M. C. Kaveny, "Appropriation of Evil: Cooperation's Mirror Image," *Theological Studies* 61 (2000): 280–313; M. C. Kaveny, J. F. Keenan, "Ethical Issues in Health-Care Restructuring," *Theological Studies* 56 (1) (1995): 136–150.

15 *Directives*, Part Six, number 73.

16 *Directives*, Part Six, number 74–75.

17 United States Conference of Catholic Bishops (USCCB), *Forming Consciences for Faithful Citizens* (Washington, DC: USCCB, 2009), #34. Also, Cardinal J. Ratzinger made a similar point in 2004: "A Catholic would be guilty of formal cooperation in evil . . . if he were to deliberately vote for a candidate precisely because of the candidate's permissive stand on abortion and/or euthanasia." See: Cardinal J. Ratzinger, "Worthiness to Receive Holy Communion," *The Wanderer Press* 137 (29) (July 15, 2004), final note.

18 Forming Consciences, #42: The US bishops also quote a Vatican doctrinal note: "It must be noted that a well-formed conscience does not permit one to vote for a political program or an individual law which contradicts the fundamental contents of faith and morals," Congregation for the Doctrine of the Faith, "Doctrinal Note on Some Questions Regarding the Participation of Catholics in Political Life," no. 4, in, United States Conference of Catholic Bishops, *Readings on Catholics in Political Life* (Washington, D.C: USCCB, 2006).

19 Cardinal Ratzinger, "Worthiness to Receive Holy Communion," *The Wanderer Press* 137 (29) (July 15, 2004), final note.

20 *H.R. 3590 – Patient Protection and Affordable Care Act*, 111th Congress (2009–2010), at www.congress.gov/bill/111th-congress/house-bill/3590.

21 *Public Law 111–152* (Washington, DC: Government Publishing Office, March 30, 2010).

22 U.S. House of Representatives, *Compilation of Patient Protection and Affordable Care Act*, 111th Congress, 2nd Session, at, http://housedocs.house.gov/energycommerce/ppacacon.pdf.

23 *Directives*, Part One, page 7.

24 *Directives*, Part Six, Introduction, pages 29.
25 *Directives*, Part Six, page 31.

Select readings

Kaveny, M. C. 2012. *Law's Virtue: Fostering Autonomy and Solidarity in American Society*. Washington, DC: Georgetown University Press.
Kutz, C. 2000. *Complicity: Ethics and Law for a Collective Age*. Cambridge: Cambridge University Press.
Watt, H. 2006. *Cooperation, Complicity & Conscience: Problems in Healthcare, Science, Law and Public Policy*. London: Linacre Centre.

10 Governance and virtuous organizations

The discussion in this book is designed to provide guidance regarding governance ethics in healthcare organizations. The content is both theoretical and applied. The goal is to foster greater board oversight, focusing on the need for continuous evaluation and evidence-based improvements. The theoretical chapters (chapters 1–3) explain the ethics paradigm designed for this book (Table 1.1). The ethics paradigm presents a framework to guide discourse by providing a structure that coalesces relevant data to interpret specific issues. The core structure of the ethics paradigm revolves around basic features of ethics: *who we are, how we function, what we do*. These features form a leitmotif throughout the study. These basic features generate the three components of the ethics paradigm. Each component is related to specific governance contexts. The foundation component (reflecting the leitmotif *who we are*) operates within the context of engaging the healthcare environment. The process component (reflecting the leitmotif *how we function*) operates within the context of undertaking organizational oversight. The practice component (reflecting the leitmotif *what we do*) operates within the context of fostering organizational culture.

The theoretical perspective presents the ethics paradigm as being in alignment with clinical ethics, organizational ethics, and professional ethics. The purpose of engaging the ethics paradigm with these established fields is to apply it to governance ethics as an emerging field in healthcare. The subsequent applied chapters begin with a discussion of the governance structure of boards, followed by board oversight of community-related issues (community benefit and community health) and patient-related issues (patient care quality and patient safety). These topics are pivotal for governance ethics because they have contributed in no small measure to undermining public confidence in healthcare organizations. In turn, these topics lead to an over-arching ethical problem for healthcare governance that deals with conflicted collaborative arrangements: how to distinguish wrongful complicity from legitimate cooperation with activities in other organizations.

In these applied chapters, the concepts of the ethics paradigm organize core features of effective governance from landmark reports and the scholarly literature. That is, the concepts of *identity*, *accountability*, and *quality* provide a framework for the applied analysis, representing the foundation, process, and practice

Table 1.1 Ethics paradigm

Components	Foundation component	Process component	Practice component
Context	Environment of healthcare	Organizational oversight	Organizational culture
Leadership	Identity: who we are	Accountability: how we function	Quality: what we do
Outcomes	Organizational stewardship of mission	Decision-making via participative deliberation	Best practices for standards of conduct

components of the ethics paradigm. The purpose of the applied analysis is to highlight hallmarks of governance ethics that denote associated moral imperatives. Because the hallmarks represent necessary moral attributes of governance ethics, they entail an obligation to be adopted by boards. In turn, the associated moral imperatives represent necessary endeavors to foster the hallmarks under consideration.

In this concluding chapter, it can be instructive to consider how governance ethics can foster virtuous organizations in healthcare. To grasp how organizations can be virtuous, it can be helpful to turn to discourse on virtue ethics. Basically, virtue ethics focuses on developing the moral character of individuals in terms of practical wisdom generating laudable actions that foster happiness.[1] Discussions about the theory and practice of virtue have a rich history,[2] especially celebrating respect for human nature.[3] This history typically focuses on vision rather than duty to foster moral education and to nurture positive character traits.[4] It is important to note that virtues, reasons and obligations are closely connected, highlighting the link between character, moral agency, and moral roles.[5] Virtues have become critical in understanding how to foster leadership in an organization, working effectively with others in the dynamics of a team-oriented group environment.[6] Ethics, and especially the virtue of prudence, are at the heart of effective leadership,[7] and virtue discourse provides a critical guide in defining moments.[8] Also, virtue ethics fostering character is crucial for leadership in organizational culture regarding both professional practice and policy development.[9] For example, humility is seen by many as a foundational virtue for successful decision-making in corporations.[10] Moreover, the virtue of prudence is crucial for decision making in healthcare and for the formation of health professionals.[11] Considerations about virtue ethics include social ethics,[12] business ethics,[13] and corporate governance,[14] each contribution different ways to foster a sense of virtuous organizations.[15] Referring to an organization as being virtuous denotes its institutional integrity.[16]

Organizations can be considered to be virtuous when they foster institutional integrity by applying the ethics paradigm. That is, the concept of individuals being virtuous can be transferred analogously to organizations being virtuous. The pathway for an individual to be virtuous connects moral character, practical wisdom, and laudable actions, as mentioned earlier. Similarly, the ethics paradigm can enable an organization to become virtuous in this manner: by connecting the focus on moral character with the concept of *identity*; by connecting the focus on practical wisdom as a decision making process with the concept of *accountability*; and by connecting the focus on laudable actions with the concept of *quality*.

The foundation component of the ethics paradigm helps to address a pervasive concern in healthcare organizations that was mentioned at the outset of the book, the destructive tension between margin and mission. The ethics paradigm emphasizes that stewardship of an organization requires enhancing its mission as a function of its *identity*, highlighting the moral character of the organization (thereby reflecting the leitmotif *who we are*). Governance ethics requires that margin should be calibrated in connection with the mission of the organization. Here, a virtuous organization will enable its mission to flourish in the context of the challenging environment of healthcare.

The process component of the ethics paradigm helps to address another pervasive concern in healthcare that was mentioned at the outset of the book, distrust of healthcare organizations, both public and private. The ethics paradigm emphasizes that decision-making in an organization requires enhancing participative deliberation as a function of its *accountability*, highlighting the practical wisdom of the organization (thereby reflecting the leitmotif *how we function*). Governance ethics requires that organizational success should be calibrated in connection with enhancing public trust in healthcare organizations. Here, a virtuous organization will encourage participative decision-making to cultivate public confidence in the context of its organizational oversight.

The practice component of the ethics paradigm helps to address an increasingly recurring concern in healthcare organizations, collaborative arrangements where values of the organization must be protected to uphold institutional integrity. The ethics paradigm emphasizes best practices to guide standards of conduct as a function of *quality*, highlighting the laudable actions of the organization (thereby reflecting the leitmotif *what we do*). Governance ethics requires that collaborative arrangements, especially when conflicted, respect the values of the organization. Here, a virtuous organization will implement standards of conduct to foster a healthy organizational culture.

These three components of the ethics paradigm clarify how an organization can be virtuous at a general level, by fostering mission, by cultivating public trust, and by pursuing collaborative arrangements with integrity. At a more practical level, organizations can be deemed to be virtuous by respecting the hallmarks and moral imperatives of governance ethics presented in the applied chapters. A summary of the pivotal topics in the applied chapters can provide a specific pathway for organizations to be virtuous. That is, by engaging these hallmarks and moral imperatives, boards can develop their healthcare institutions to be virtuous organizations.

In the applied chapters, the discussion begins by considering board structure as a pivotal topic for governance ethics. The analysis applies the foundation, process, and practice components of the ethics paradigm, as follows. The foundation component focusing on *identity* highlights two hallmarks with accompanying moral imperatives. Oversight of board competence is a hallmark of governance ethics with an associated moral imperative regarding oversight of term limits and board composition. Also, oversight of the board role is a hallmark of governance ethics with an associated moral imperative regarding oversight of defined responsibilities and board effectiveness. Furthermore, the process component focusing on *accountability* highlights two hallmarks with accompanying moral imperatives. Oversight of board evaluation is a hallmark of governance ethics with an associated moral imperative regarding oversight of fair evaluation processes. Also, oversight of succession planning is a hallmark of governance ethics with an associated moral imperative regarding oversight of system planning and continuous updating. Finally, the practice component focusing on *quality* highlights two hallmarks with accompanying moral imperatives. Oversight of leadership collaboration is a hallmark of governance ethics with an associated moral imperative regarding oversight of working relationships. Also, oversight of system-wide strategy is a hallmark of governance ethics with an associated moral imperative regarding oversight of transformational change and strategic planning.

The discussion continues in the applied chapters by considering board oversight of community benefit as a pivotal topic for governance ethics. Regarding the foundation component focusing on *identity*, oversight of board engagement is a hallmark of governance ethics. There is an associated moral imperative regarding oversight of the standing committee structure. Regarding the process component focusing on *accountability*, oversight of effective communication is a hallmark of governance ethics. There is an associated moral imperative regarding oversight of community needs assessment. Regarding the practice component focusing on *quality*, oversight of organizational performance is a hallmark of governance ethics. There is an associated moral imperative regarding oversight of continuous improvement.

Subsequently, when dealing with community issues, the discussion continues by considering board oversight of community health as a pivotal topic for governance ethics. Each of the three components of the ethics paradigm highlights a hallmark with an accompanying moral imperative. Regarding the foundation component focusing on *identity*, oversight of partnership engagement is a hallmark of governance ethics. There is an associated moral imperative regarding oversight of the mission and structure of community health partnerships. Regarding the process component focusing on *accountability*, oversight of partnership consensus is a hallmark of governance ethics. There is an associated moral imperative regarding oversight of collaboration with community health partnerships. Regarding the practice component focusing on *quality*, oversight of partnership performance is a hallmark of governance ethics. There is an associated moral imperative regarding oversight of performance improvement in community health partnerships.

After considering two community-related issues (community benefit and community health), the applied chapters then focus on patient-related issues (patient care quality and patient safety). The discussion begins by considering board oversight of patient care quality as a pivotal topic for governance ethics. Regarding the foundation component focusing on *identity*, oversight of board transparency is a hallmark of governance ethics. There is an associated moral imperative regarding oversight of the development of trust to support patient care quality. This support includes the assessment and continuous improvement of patient care quality. Regarding the process component focusing on *accountability*, oversight of board responsiveness is a hallmark of governance ethics. There is an associated moral imperative regarding oversight of factors contributing to support patient care quality. Regarding the practice component focusing on *quality*, oversight of board mechanisms for patient care quality is a hallmark of governance ethics. There is an associated moral imperative regarding oversight of the social contract for patient care quality.

In the next applied chapter on patient-related issues, the discussion continues by considering board oversight of patient safety as a pivotal topic for governance ethics. Regarding the foundation component focusing on *identity*, oversight of error prevention is a hallmark of governance ethics. There is an associated moral imperative regarding oversight of a systems approach for patient safety. Regarding the process component focusing on *accountability*, oversight of deliberative processes for patient safety is a hallmark of governance ethics. There is an associated moral imperative regarding oversight of proactive deliberations for patient safety. Regarding the practice component focusing on *quality*, oversight of practical mechanisms for patient safety is a hallmark of governance ethics. There is an associated moral imperative regarding oversight of a patient safety culture.

Having discussed community-related issues and patient-related issues regarding governance ethics, the applied chapters finish by considering board oversight of conflicted collaborative arrangements as a pivotal topic for governance ethics. Regarding the foundation component focusing on *identity*, oversight of organizational reputation is a hallmark of governance ethics. There is an associated moral imperative regarding oversight of organizational flexibility. Regarding the process component focusing on *accountability*, oversight of institutional negotiations is a hallmark of governance ethics. There is an associated moral imperative regarding oversight of the process of cooperation. Regarding the practice component focusing on *quality*, oversight of collaborative arrangements is a hallmark of governance ethics. There is an associated moral imperative regarding oversight of maintaining quality care services.

In sum, this concluding chapter explains that organizations can be deemed to be virtuous when they foster institutional integrity by applying the ethics paradigm. At a general level, the three components of the ethics paradigm clarify how an organization can be virtuous, by fostering mission, by cultivating public trust, and by pursuing collaborative arrangements with integrity. At a more practical level, by engaging the ethics paradigm in the applied chapters, boards can develop their healthcare institutions as virtuous organizations when they respect the hallmarks and moral imperatives of governance ethics.

This approach to governance ethics in healthcare organizations provides a practical guide for boards of directors in a manner that will enable patients and communities to respect their clinicians, their healthcare institutions, and the underlying fairness of the healthcare system.

Notes

1 L. van Zyl, *Virtue Ethics: A Contemporary Introduction* (New York: Routledge, 2019).
2 See: J. Budziszewski, *Commentary on Thomas Aquinas's Virtue Ethics* (New York: Cambridge University Press, 2018); M. Slote, L. Besser, eds., *The Routledge Companion to Virtue Ethics* (Routledge, 2018); D. C. Russell, *The Cambridge Companion to Virtue Ethics* (New York: Cambridge University Press, 2013); M. Rhonheimer, *The Perspective of Morality: Philosophical Foundations of Thomistic Virtue Ethics* (Washington, DC: Catholic University Press of America, 2011); A. McIntyre, *After Virtue: A Study in Moral Theory*, 3rd ed. (Notre Dame, IN: University of Notre Dame Press, 2003); R. J. Devettere, *Introduction to Virtue Ethics: Insights of the Ancient Greeks* (Washington, DC: Georgetown University Press, 2002).
3 J. J. Sanford, *Before Virtue: Assessing Contemporary Virtue Ethics* (Washington, DC: Catholic University Press of America, 2019).
4 G. C. Meilander, *The Theory and Practice of Virtue* (Notre Dame, IN: University of Notre Dame Press, 2017).
5 See: T. Dare, C. Swanton, eds. *Perspectives in Role Ethics: Virtues, Reasons, and Obligations* (Routledge, 2019); N. Borondo, S. S. Brown, eds., *Virtue's Reasons. New Essays on Virtue, Character and Reasons* (New York: Routledge, 2017).
6 P. Lencioni, *The Ideal Team Player. How to Recognize and Cultivate the Three Essential Virtues* (San Francisco, CA: Jossey-Bass, 2016).
7 J. B. Ciulla, ed., *Ethics: The Heart of Leadership* (Santa Barbara, CA: Praeger, 2014).
8 J. L. Badaracco, *Defining Moments. When Managers Must Choose Between Right and Right* (Boston, MA: Harvard Business Press Review, 1997).
9 See: D. Carr, *Cultivating Moral Character and Virtue in Professional Practice* (Routledge, 2019); M. Jinkins, D. B. Jinkins, *The Character of Leadership. Political Realism and Public Virtue in Nonprofit Organizations* (San Francisco, CA: Jossey-Bass, 1998).
10 J. C. Wright, ed., *Humility: The Virtues* (New York: Oxford University Press, 2019).
11 See: R. J. Deveterre, *Practical Decision Making in Health Care: Cases, Concepts, and the Virtue of Prudence* (Washington, DC: Georgetown University Press, 2016); E. D. Pellegrino, D. C. Thomasma, *The Virtues in Medical Practice* (New York: Oxford University Press, 1993).
12 B. Stiltner, *Toward Thriving Communities: Virtue Ethics as Social Ethics* (Anselm Academic, 2016).
13 A. Sison, et al., eds., *Handbook on Virtue Ethics in Business and Management* (New York: Springer, 2017).
14 A. Sison, *Corporate Governance and Ethics: An Aristotelian Perspective* (Gloucester, UK: Edward Elgar Publishing, 2010).
15 C. C. Manz, et al., eds., *The Virtuous Organization: Insights from Some of World's Leading Management Thinkers* (Singapore: World Scientific Publishing Co., 2008).
16 G. Moore, *Virtue at Work. Ethics for Individuals, Managers, and Organizations* (New York: Oxford University Press, 2017).

Select readings

Borondo, N., S. S. Brown, eds. 2017. *Virtue's Reasons: New Essays on Virtue, Character and Reasons*. United Kingdom: Routledge.
Carr, D. 2019. *Cultivating Moral Character and Virtue in Professional Practice*. United Kingdom: Routledge.
Ciulla, J. B., ed. 2014. *Ethics: The Heart of Leadership*. Santa Barbara, CA: Praeger.
Dare, T., C. Swanton, eds. 2019. *Perspectives in Role Ethics: Virtues, Reasons, and Obligations*. United Kingdom: Routledge.

Meilander, C. C. 2017. *The Theory and Practice of Virtue*. Notre Dame, IN: University of Notre Dame Press.

Moore, G. 2017. *Virtue at Work: Ethics for Individuals, Managers, and Organizations*. New York: Oxford University Press.

Slote, M., L. Besser, eds. 2018. *The Routledge Companion to Virtue Ethics*. United Kingdom: Routledge.

Stiltner, B. 2016. *Toward Thriving Communities: Virtue Ethics as Social Ethics*. Winona, MN: Anselm Academic.

van Zyl, L. 2019. *Virtue Ethics: A Contemporary Introduction*. United Kingdom: Routledge.

Wright, J. C., ed. 2019. *Humility: The Virtues*. New York: Oxford University Press.

Bibliography

ABA Coordinating Committee on Nonprofit Governance. 2007. *Guide to Nonprofit Corporate Governance in the Wake of Sarbanes-Oxley*. Chicago, IL: American Bar Association.

Abele, J. R., ed. 2011. *Medical Errors and Litigation*. Tucson, AR: Lawyers & Judges Publishing.

ACHE Code of Ethics. www.ache.org/ABT_ACHE/code.cfm.

ACHE Ethical Policy Statements. www.ache.org/policy/index_ethics.cfm.

ACHE Ethics Committee. www.ache.org/abt_ache/committee_function.cfm.

ACHE Mission and Vision. www.ache.org/abt_ache/facts.cfm.

ACHE Policy Statements. www.ache.org/policy/policy.cfm.

ACHE Social Responsibility. www.ache.org/abt_ache/socialresponsibility.cfm.

ACHE Strategic Plan. www.ache.org/abt_ache/planning.cfm.

Ackerman, T., et al. 1987. *Clinical Medical Ethics: Exploration and Assessment*. Lantham, MD: University Press of America.

Agency for Healthcare Research and Quality. 2009. *Advancing Patient Safety: A Decade of Design and Implementation*. www.ahrq.gov/professionals/quality-patient-safety/patient-safety-resources/resources/advancing-patient-safety/index.html.

Agency for Healthcare Research and Quality. 2010. *Medical Liability Reform and Patient Safety Initiative*. Rockville, MD: Agency for Healthcare Research and Quality.

Agency for Healthcare Research and Quality. 2012. *Hospital Survey on Patient Mechanisms for Safety*. Rockville, MD: Agency for Healthcare Research and Quality.

Agency for Healthcare Research and Quality. 2017. *National Healthcare Quality Report*. Washington, DC: Agency for Healthcare Research and Quality.

Agency for Healthcare Research and Quality. 2017. "Snapshot of U.S. Health Systems, 2016." *Comparative Health System Performance Initiative, Data Highlight No. 1* (September). Rockville, MD: Agency for Healthcare Research and Quality.

Agency for Healthcare Research and Quality. 2019. *Patient Safety Indicators Overview*. www.qualityindicators.ahrq.gov/Modules/psi_overview.aspx.

Agency for Healthcare Research and Quality. 2019. *Quality and Patient Safety*. www.ahrq.gov/professionals/quality-patient-safety/index.html.

Agency for Healthcare Research and Quality. 2019. *Systems Approach, Patient Safety Network*. https://psnet.ahrq.gov/primers/primer/21/systems-approach.

Agency for Healthcare Research and Quality. 2019. *Transforming Hospitals: Designing for Safety and Quality*. www.ahrq.gov/professionals/systems/hospital/transform/index.html.

Agency for Healthcare Research and Quality. 2019. *Understanding Quality Measurement*. www.ahrq.gov/professionals/quality-patient-safety/quality-resources/tools/chtoolbx/understand/index.html.

Agich, G. J. 1994. "Expertise in Clinical Ethics Consultation." *HEC Forum* 6: 379–383.

Agich, G. J. 2016. "Truth in Advertising: Reasonable Versus Unreasonable Claims About Improving Ethics Consultation." *American Journal of Bioethics* 16 (3): 25–26.

Agrawal, A., ed. 2014. *Patient Safety: A Case-Based Comprehensive Guide.* New York: Springer.

Albanese, J. S. 2015. *Professional Ethics in Criminal Justice: Being Ethical When No One Is Looking*, 4th ed. Pearson.

Alexander, P. 2015. *Corporate Social Irresponsibility.* Routledge.

Al Hasmi, A. G. 2017. *Environment, Health and Safety Governance and Leadership.* United Kingdom: Routledge.

Allen, J. 2012. *Health Law and Medical Ethics.* Pearson.

Allen, M. C., J. Norman. 2013. *Medical Error Prevention.* CME Resource/NetCE.

Allhoff, F. S., L. Borden, eds. 2019. *Ethics and Error in Medicine.* United Kingdom: Routledge.

Alliance for Advancing Nonprofit Healthcare. 2009. *Maximizing Community Benefit: A Six-Point Program.* Washington, DC: Alliance for Advancing Nonprofit Healthcare.

Alliance for Advancing Nonprofit Healthcare. 2011. *Great Governance: A Practical Guide for Busy Board Leaders and Executives of Nonprofit Healthcare Organizations.* Washington, DC: Alliance for Advancing Nonprofit Healthcare.

Altenburger, R., ed. 2018. *Innovation Management and Corporate Social Responsibility.* New York: Springer.

Altisent, R., et al. 2013. "Health Care Ethics Consultation. Individual Consultant or Committee Model? Pros and Cons." *American Journal of Bioethics* 13 (2): 25–27.

American Association for Marriage and Family Therapy. 2015. *User's Guide to the 2015 AAMFT Code of Ethics.* Alexandria, VA: American Association for Marriage and Family Therapy.

American College of Surgeons. 1918. "Standard of Efficiency for the First Hospital Survey of the College." *Bulletin of the American College of Surgeons* 3: 1–4.

American Hospital Association. 2006. *Strengthening Community Trust: Strategies for CEOs.* Chicago, IL: American Hospital Association.

American Hospital Association. 2007. *Community Accountability and Transparency: Helping Hospitals Better Serve their Communities.* Chicago, IL: American Hospital Association.

American Hospital Association. 2009. "Community Connections' Helps Keep Health System Close to Those It Serves." *AHA News* 45 (13): 7.

American Hospital Association. 2012. "AHA: Hospitals' Uncompensated Care Increased 82% Since 2000." *AHA News* (January 9): 7.

American Hospital Association. 2012. *Managing Population Health: The Role of the Hospital.* Chicago, IL: Health Research and Educational Trust.

American Hospital Association. 2016. *Triple Aim Strategies to Improve Behavioral Health Care.* Chicago, IL: American Hospital Association.

American Hospital Association. 2019. *2019 AHA Hospital Statistics.* Chicago, IL: American Hospital Association. www.aha.org/statistics/fast-facts-us-hospitals.

American Hospital Association. 2019. *2019 National Health Care Governance Survey Report.* Washington, DC: Center for Healthcare Governance.

American Hospital Association. 2019. *Tax-Exempt Hospitals' Schedule H Community Benefit Report.* Chicago, IL: American Hospital Association.

American Hospital Association. Center for Healthcare Governance. 2016. *Blue Ribbon Panel Report: Learnings on Governance from Partnerships that Improve Community Health.* Chicago, IL: American Hospital Association.

American Medical Association. 2008. *The Code of Medical Ethics*. Chicago, IL: American Medical Association.

American Nurses Association. 2010. *Social Policy Statement*. Silver Spring, MD: American Nurses Association.

American Nurses Association. 2015. *Code of Ethics for Nurses with Interpretative Statements*. Silver Spring, MD: American Nurses Association.

American Society for Bioethics and Humanities (ASBH). 2011. *Core Competencies for Health Care Ethics Consultation*, 2nd ed. Glenview, IL: ASBH.

American Society for Bioethics and Humanities (ASBH). 2014. *Code of Ethics and Professional Responsibilities for Healthcare Ethics Consultants*. Glenview, IL: ASBH.

American Society for Bioethics and Humanities (ASBH). 2015. *Improving Competencies in Clinical Ethics Consultation: An Education Guide*, 2nd ed. Glenview, IL: ASBH.

American Society for Bioethics and Humanities (ASBH). 2017. *Addressing Patient-Centered Ethical Issues in Health Care: A Case-Based Study Guide*. Glenview, IL: ASBH.

American Society for Bioethics and Humanities (ASBH), Clinical Ethics Consultation Affairs Committee. 2017. *Resources for Developing Advanced Skills in Ethics Consultation*. Glenview, IL: ASBH.

American Society of Anesthesiologists. 2001. *Ethical Guidelines for the Anesthesia Care of Patients with do-not-resuscitate Orders*. Park Ridge, IL: American Society of Anesthesiologists.

Andereck, W. S., W. J. McGaughey, A. R. Jonsen. 2012. "The Clinical Ethics Consultant. Verifying the Qualifications of a New Type of Practitioner in a Community Hospital." *Journal of Healthcare Management* 57 (4): 264–273.

Anderson, B., et al. 2010. *Root Cause Analysis and Improvement in the Healthcare Sector*. Quality Press.

Anderson, B., T. N. Fagerhaug. 2013. *The ASQ Pocket Guide to Root Cause Analysis*. ASQ Press.

Anderson, S. K., M. M. Handelsman. 2009. *Ethics for Psychotherapists and Counselors: A Proactive Approach*. Oxford: Wiley-Blackwell.

Anning, D., et al. 2010. *The Guide to Good Governance for Hospital Boards*. Chicago, IL: Center for Healthcare Governance.

Argenti, P. A. 2015. *Corporate Responsibility*. Sage.

Argyris, C. 2012. *Organizational Traps: Leadership, Culture, Organizational Design*. New York: Oxford University Press.

Arsalidou, D. 2018. *Rethinking Corporate Governance in Financial Institutions*. Routledge.

Aseni, P., et al., eds. 2016. *Multiorgan Procurement for Transplantation*. Springer.

Association for Community Health Improvement. 2013. *Trends in Hospital-Based Population Health Infrastructure*. Chicago, IL: Health Research and Educational Trust.

Aulisio, M. P., et al., eds. 2003. *Ethics Consultation: From Theory to Practice*. Baltimore, MD: Johns Hopkins University Press.

Badaracco, J. L. 1007. *Defining Moments: When Managers Must Choose Between Right and Right*. Boston, MA: Harvard Business Press Review.

Bader, B. 2009. "Culture: The Critical But Elusive Component of Great Governance." In *Governance Structure and Practices: Results, Analysis, and Evaluation. Biennial Survey of Hospitals and Healthcare Systems*. San Diego, CA: The Governance Institute.

Bader, B., E. Zablocki. 2008. "Evaluating and Improving Board Committees." *Great Boards* VIII (2): 1–19.

Bader, B., et al. 2006. *Emerging Standards for Institutional Integrity: A Tipping Point for Charitable Organizations*. San Diego, CA: The Governance Institute.

Baehr, A., et al. 2018. "Developing Data to Support Effective Coordination of Nonprofit Hospital Community Benefit Investment." *Journal of Healthcare Management* 63 (4) (July–August): 271–280.

Bagheri, A., J. M. Moreno, S. Semplici, eds. 2015. *Global Bioethics: The Impact of the UNESCO International Bioethics Committee*. Springer.

Bailey, J. S., M. R. Burch. 2016. *Ethics for Behavior Analysts*. Routledge.

Bajpai, G. N. 2016. *The Essential Book of Corporate Governance*. Sage.

Baker, E. 2003. *Caring for Ourselves: A Therapist's Guide to Personal and Professional Well-Being*. Washington, DC: American Psychological Association.

Ballard, M., et al. 2016. *Corporate Ethics for Big Data: A Group Project*. Amazon Digital Services.

Banja, J. D. 2019. *Patient Safety Ethics: How Vigilance, Mindfulness, Compliance, and Humility Can Make Healthcare Safer*. Baltimore, MD: Johns Hopkins University Press.

Bannow, T. 2019. "States Step in to Fill Regulatory Void Over Community Benefit." *Modern Healthcare* (August 5): 21–23.

Barker, K. N., et al. 2002. "Medication Errors Observed in 36 Healthcare Facilities." *Archives of Internal Medicine* 162 (16): 1897–1903.

Barnes, P., et al. 2014. "Measures of Highly Functioning Health Coalitions." *Frontiers in Public Health Services and Systems Research* 3: 1–5.

Barnett, P. 2001. *Ethics in Forensic Science: Professional Standards for the Practice of Criminalists*. Protocols in Forensic Science. CRC Press.

Barret, J. P., A. V. Tomasello. 2016. *Face Transplantation: Principles, Technique and Artistry*. Springer.

Barrett, D. H., et al., eds. 2016. *Public Health Ethics: Cases Spanning the Globe*. Springer.

Barry, R. 2017. *High-Reliability Healthcare*. Chicago, IL: Health Administration Press.

Barsky, A. E. 2009. *Ethics and Values in Social Work*. New York: Oxford University Press.

Barslou, M. A. 2014. *Root Cause Analysis: A Step-by-Step Guide*. Productivity Press.

Bart, C. 2006. "An Empirical Examination of the Content and Composition of Board Charters." *International Journal of Business Governance and Ethics* 2 (3/4): 198–216.

Baskett, L., et al. 2008. "Using the Dashboard Technology Properly." *Health Progress* 89 (5): 16–23.

Bass, K. H. 2008. "Should Physicians Serve on the Board?" *Healthcare Executive* 23 (4): 58–59.

Beatty, K., et al. 2015. "Collaboration among Missouri Nonprofit Hospitals and Local Health Departments." *American Journal of Public Health* 105: S237–S344.

Beauchamp, T. L., J. F. Childress. 2019. *Principles of Biomedical Ethics*, 8th ed. New York: Oxford University Press.

Beauchamp, T. L., L. Walters. 2013. *Contemporary Issues in Bioethics*, 8th ed. Belmont, CA: Wadsworth.

Bebchuk, L. A. 2005. "The Case for Increasing Shareholder Power." *Harvard Law Review* 118 (3): 835–914.

Beemsterboer, P. L. 2009. *Ethics and Law in Dental Hygiene*, 2nd ed. St. Louis, MO: Elsevier/Saunders.

Belmont, E., et al. 2011. "A New Quality Compass: Hospital Boards' Increased Role Under the Affordable Care Act." *Health Affairs* 30 (7): 1282–1289.

Benedict, J. 2017. *Covenant Consent: A Revised Consent Model for Vascularized Composite Allotransplantation*. New York: Springer.

Benjamin, M., J. Curtis. 2010. *Ethics in Nursing: Cases, Principles, and Reasoning*, 4th ed. New York: Oxford University Press.

Bennett, A. R. 2012. "Accountable Care Organizations." *Journal of Healthcare Management* 57 (4): 244–254.

Bennett, J., ed. 2016. *The Ethics of Biotechnology*. Ashgate.

Berkowitz, K. A., et al. 2016. "Quality Assessment of the Ethics Consultation Service at the Organizational Level: Accrediting Ethics Consultation Services." *American Journal of Bioethics* 16 (3): 42–44.

Bernheim, R. G., et al. 2015. *Essentials of Public Health Ethics*. Burlington, MA: Jones & Bartlett Learning.

Bersoff, D. N. 2008. *Ethical Conflicts in Psychology*. Washington, DC: American Psychological Association.

Berton, J. D. 2013. *Ethics for Addiction Professionals*. Oxford: Wiley.

Berwick, D. M. 2003. "Building Quality in the Healthcare Environment." *Quality and Safety in Healthcare* 12: 12–16. Reprinted in D. A. Shore. 2007. *The Trust Crisis in Healthcare*. New York: Oxford University Press, 49–59.

Bhagat, C., et al. 2011. "Governance Since the Economic Crisis: McKinsey Global Survey Results." *McKinsey Quarterly* (July 2011): 1–9.

Bhagat, C., et al. 2013. "Tapping the Potential of Boards." *McKinsey Quarterly* 1: 91–98.

Bhinekawati, R. 2016. *Corporate Social Responsibility and Sustainable Development*. Routledge.

Bhugra, D. 2014. "Medicine's Contract With Society." *Journal of the Royal Society of Medicine* 107 (4): 144–147.

Bialek, R., L. Beitsch, J. Moran. 2017. *Solving Population Health Through Collaboration*. Routledge.

Bismark, M., et al. 2014. "The Role of Governing Boards in Improving Patient Experience." *Patient Experience Journal* 1 (1): 144–152.

Black, J., C. Roberts. 2011. *Doing Ethics in Media: Theories and Practical Application*. Routledge.

Black, P. B. 2016. *Professional Nursing: Concepts & Challenges*, 8th ed. St. Louis, MO: Elsevier.

Blackwell, N., G. Durgan. 2017. *Essential Governance, Risk & Business Ethics*. Emile Woolf International.

Blum, J. D. 2010. "Great Boards Need Leaders, Not Followers. Turn Good Boards into High Performers." *Healthcare Executive* 25: 74–76.

Blum, J. D. 2010. "The Quagmire of Hospital Governance." *Journal of Legal Medicine* 35–57.

Bogan, C. E., M. J. English. 1994. *Benchmarking for Best Practices*. New York: McGraw Hill.

Bonnafous-Boucher, M., J. D. Rendorff. 2016. *Stakeholder Theory: A Model for Strategic Management*. Springer Briefs in Ethics. Springer.

Bonnie, R., Bernheim, R. G. 2015. *Public Health Law, Ethics, and Policy*. St. Paul, MN: University Casebook Series, West Academic.

Borondo, N., S. S. Brown, eds. 2017. *Virtue's Reasons: New Essays on Virtue, Character and Reasons*. United Kingdom: Routledge.

Boubaker, S., D. K. Ngyuen, eds. 2014. *Corporate Governance in Emerging Markets*. Springer.

Bou-Karroum, L., et al. 2017. "Using Media to Impact Health Policy-Making: An Integrative Systematic Review." *Implementation Science* 12 (18 April): Article no. 52. https://implementationscience.biomedcentral.com/articles/10.1186/s13012-017-0581-0

Bowen, R. T. 2009. *Ethics and the Practice of Forensic Science*. CRC Press.

Bradley, J. T. 2013. *Brutes of Angels: Human Possibility in the Age of Biotechnology*. Tucaloosa, AL: University of Alabama Press.

Bradley, N. 2004. "Corporate Governance Scoring and the Link Between Corporate Governance and Performance Indicators: In Search of the Holy Grail." *Corporate Governance* 12: 8–10.

Brainbridge, S. M. 2002. "Why a Board? Group Decision Making in Corporate Governance." *Vanderbilt Law Review* 55 (1): 1–55.

Brainerd, M., et al. 2013. "Doing Well by Doing Good: A Leader's Guide." *McKinsey Quarterly*. https://www.mckinsey.com/industries/social-sector/our-insights/doing-well-by-doing-good-a-leaders-guide.

Braithwaite, J., et al. 2017. "Association Between Organizational and Workplace Cultures, and Patient Outcomes: Systematic Review." *BML Open* 7 (November 8): e017708. https://doi.org/10.1136/bmjopen-2017-017708.

Braswell, M. C., B. L. McCarthy, B. J. McCarthy. 2014. *Justice, Crime, and Ethics*, 8th ed. New York: Routledge.

Brenkert, G. G., T. L. Beauchamp, eds. 2012. *The Oxford Handbook of Business Ethics*. New York: Oxford University Press.

Brennan, T. A. 2000. "The IOM Report on Medical Error: Could it Do Harm?" *New England Journal of Medicine* 342: 1123–1125.

Brennan, T. A., et al. 1991. "Incidence of Adverse Events and Negligence in Hospitalized Patients: Results of the Harvard Medical Practice Study." *New England Journal of Medicine* 324: 370–376.

Bresnick, J. 2018. "Using Big Data Analytics for Patient Safety, Hospital Acquired Conditions." *Health IT Analytics* (August 6). https://healthitanalytics.com/features/using-big-data-analytics-for-patient-safety-hospital-acquired-conditions.

Briggle, A., ed. 2010. *A Rich Bioethics: Public Policy, Biotechnology, and the Kass Council*. Notre Dame, IN: University of Notre Dame Press.

Brooks, L. J. 2014. *Business & Professional Ethics for Directors, Executives & Accountants*, 7th ed. Stamford, CT: Cengage Learning.

Brown, F., ed. 2011. *Journalism Ethics: A Casebook of Professional Conduct for News Media*, 4th ed. Marion Street Press.

Brown, J. 2010. *The Imperfect Board Member: Discovering the Seven Disciplines of Governance Excellence*. Wiley.

Browning, P. 2016. *The Director's Manual: A Framework for Board Governance*. Wiley.

Bruce, C., et al. 2011. "A Systematic Review of Activities at a High-Volume Ethics Consultation Service." *Journal of Clinical Ethics* 22 (2): 151–164. Bruce, C., et al. 2015. *A Practical Guide to Developing & Sustaining a Clinical Ethics Consultation Service*. Baylor College of Medicine.

Bruce, C., et al. 2016. "Practical Guidance for Charting Ethics Consultation." *American Journal of Bioethics* 16 (3): 48–50.

Bruce, C., et al. 2018. "Building a Vibrant Clinical Ethics Consultation Service." *The National Catholic Bioethics Quarterly* 18 (1) (Spring): 29–38.

Bryan, V., S. Sanders, L. Kaplan. 2015. *The Helping Professional's Guide to Ethics: A New Perspective*. New York: Oxford University Press.

Bryson, J. B., et al., eds. 2015. *Public Value and Public Administration*. Washington, DC: Georgetown University Press.

Budziszewski, J. 2018. *Commentary on Thomas Aquinas's Virtue Ethics*. New York: Cambridge University Press.

Buell, J. M. 2010. "Trust & Confidence: Does Your Board Have These in You?" *Healthcare Executive* 25 (5): 18–25.

Buerki, R. A., L. D. Vottero. 2002. *Ethical Responsibility in Pharmacy Practice*, 2nd ed. American Institute of the History of Pharmacy.

Buerki, R. A., L. D. Vottero. 2013. *Pharmacy Ethics: A Foundation for Professional Practice*. American Pharmacists Association.

Burkhardt, M. A., A. Nathaniel. 2013. *Ethics and Issues in Contemporary Nursing*, 4th ed. Boston, MA: Cengage Learning.

Butts, J. B., K. L. Rich. 2015. *Nursing Ethics: Across the Curriculum and into Practice*, 4th ed. Jones & Bartlett.

Bynum, T. W., S. Rogerson, eds. 2003. *Computer Ethics and Professional Responsibility*. Oxford: Wiley-Blackwell.

Byrnes, J., S. Teman. 2017. *The Safety Playbook: A Healthcare Leader's Guide to Building a High-Reliability Organization*. Chicago, IL: Health Administration Press.

Cafardi, N. F., ed. 2012. *Voting: Catholic Perspectives on Political Participation*. New York: Paulist.

Caldero, M. A., J. P. Crank. 2010. *Police Ethics: The Corruption of Noble Cause*, 3rd. ed. Routledge.

Callender, A. N., et al. 2007. *Corporate Responsibility and Healthcare Quality: A Resource for Healthcare Boards of Directors*. Washington, DC: U.S. Department of Health and Human Services.

Camarow, A. 2003. "Jesica's Story: One Mistake didn't Kill Her – the Organ Donor System Was Fatally Flawed." *US News & World Report* 51–54.

Cameron, K. S., et al. 2004. "Exploring the Relationships Between Organizational Virtuousness and Performance." *American Behavioral Scientist* 47: 766–790.

Camilieri, M. A. 2017. *Corporate Sustainability, Social Responsibility, and Environmental Management*. Springer.

Campbell, L., et al. 2009. *APA Ethics Code Commentary and Case Illustrations*. American Psychological Association.

Cannon, T. 2013. *Ethics and Professional Responsibility for Paralegals*, 7th ed. Philadelphia, PA: Wolters and Kluwer.

Capaldi, N., et al., eds. 2017. *Dimensional Corporate Governance: An Inclusive Approach*. Springer.

Caplan, A. L., J. J. McCartney, D. P. Reid. 2015. *Replacement Parts: The Ethics of Procuring and Replacing Organs in Humans*. Washington, DC: Georgetown University Press.

Caplea, G. 2019. "Taking a Systems Approach to Patient Safety." *Health IT & CEO Report* (March 11). www.beckershospitalreview.com/ehrs/taking-a-systems-approach-to-improve-patient-safety.html.

Capron, A. M. 2004. "When Experiments Go Wrong: The U.S. Perspective." *Journal of Clinical Ethics* 15 (1): 22–29.

Carman, A., L. Prybil, M. Totten. 2013. "Partners for Public Health: Hospitals and Health Departments Can Collaborate on Community Health Needs Assessments." *Trustee* 66 (May): 26–27.

Carr, D. 2019. *Cultivating Moral Character and Virtue in Professional Practice*. United Kingdom: Routledge.

Carroll, A. 2014. "The Social Contract and Health Care Reform." *The Incidental Economist* (July 18). https://theincidentaleconomist.com/wordpress/more-on-the-social-contract-and-health-care-reform/.

Carroll, A. 2017. "The High Costs of Unnecessary Care." *JAMA Forum* (November 14): 1748– 1749. https://doi.org/10.1001/jama.2017.16193.

Casalino, L., et al. 2015. "Accountable Care Organizations and Population Health Organizations." *Journal of Health Politics, Policy, and Law* 40: 819–821.

Cassidy, B., A. D. Blessing. 2007. *Ethics and Professionalism: A Guide for the Physician Assistant*. Philadelphia, PA: Davis Company.

Catholic Health Association. 2008 and 2017. *A Guide for Planning & Reporting Community Benefit*. St. Louis, MO: Catholic Health Association.

Catholic Health Association. 2009. *The IRS Form 990, Schedule H*. St. Louis, MO: Catholic Health Association.

Catholic Health Association. 2009. *"What Board Members Should Know About the Organization's Community Benefit Program."* St. Louis, MO: Catholic Health Association.

Catholic Health Association. 2013. *Assessing and Addressing Community Health Needs*. Washington, DC: Catholic Health Association.

Catholic Health Association. 2014. *Striving for Excellence in Ethics: A Resource for the Catholic Health Ministry*, 2nd ed. Washington, DC: Catholic Health Association.

Catholic Health Association. 2019. *Facts-Statistics, Catholic Health Care in the United States* (January). www.chausa.org/about/about/facts-statistics.

Catholic Health Association. 2019. *U.S. Catholic Health Care: The Nation's Largest Group of Not-For-Profit Health Care Providers*. Washington, DC: Catholic Health Association.

Celie, K.-B., K. Prager. 2016. "Health Care Ethics Consultation in the United States." *AMA Journal of Ethics* 18 (5): 475–478.

Center for Healthcare Governance. 2007. *Building an Exceptional Board: Effective Practices for Healthcare Governance*. Chicago, IL: Center for Healthcare Governance.

Center for Healthcare Governance. 2009. *Competency-Based Governance: A Foundation for Board and Organizational Effectiveness*. Chicago, IL: Center for Healthcare Governance.

Center for Healthcare Governance. 2010. "Board Member Evaluation Incorporates Core Competencies." *Healthcare Executive* 25 (5): 70–71.

Center for Healthcare Governance. 2012. *Governance Practices in an Era of Healthcare Transformation*. AHA's Center for Healthcare Governance.

Center for Healthcare Governance. 2013. "Governance in Transformational Times." *Healthcare Executive* 28 (1): 80–83.

The Center for Health Design. 2012. *Designing for Patient Safety: Developing Methods to Integrate Patient Safety Concerns in the Design Process*. www.healthdesign.org/sites/default/files/chd416_ahrqreport_final.pdf

Centers for Disease Control and Prevention. 2017. *Infant Mortality*. www.cdc.gov/reproductivehealth/maternalinfanthealth/infantmortality.htm

Centers for Medicare & Medicaid Services. 2019. *National Health Expenditure Data*. www.cms.gov/research-statistics-data-and-systems/statistics-trends-and-reports/nationalhealthexpenddata/nationalhealthaccountshistorical.html.

Centers for Medicare & Medicaid Services. 2019. *Quality Measure and Quality Improvement*. www.cms.gov/Medicare/Quality-Initiatives-Patient-Assessment-Instruments/MMS/Quality-Measure-and-Quality-Improvement-.html.

CEO Survey. 2010. "CEO Survey, Board Role and Succession Plans." *Healthcare Executive* 25 (6): 92.

Chambers, N., C. Cornforth. 2010. "The Role of Corporate Governance and Boards in Organizational Performance." In K. Walsh, G. Harvey, P. Jas, eds., *Connecting Knowledge and Performance in Public Service: From Knowing to Doing*. New York: Cambridge University Press, 99–127.

Chao, J., et al. 2014. "Avoiding Blind Spots in Your Next Joint Venture." *McKinsey on Finance* 48: 25–30.

Charney, W. 2012. *Epidemic of Medical Errors and Hospital-Acquired Infections: Systemic and Social Causes*. Taylor and Francis, CRC Press.

Cheeseman, K., et al., eds. 2015. *Everyday Ethics for the Criminal Justice Professional*, 2nd ed. Durham, NC: Carolina Academic Press.

Chen, M., et al. 2016. *The Role of Hospitals in Improving Non-Medical Determinants of Community Population Health*. New York, NY: New York State Health Foundation.

Chiarenza, G., ed. 2014. "Embracing a Collective Action Approach to Community Development." *Community Investments* 26 (1): 2–4.

Childress, J. F., et al., eds. 2005. *Belmont Revisited: Ethical Principles for Research with Human Subjects*. Washington, DC: Georgetown University Press.

Christians, C. G., et al. 2011. *Media Ethics: Cases and Moral Reasoning*, 9th ed. Routledge.

Churchill, L. R., A. W. Cross. 1986. "Moralist, Technician, Sophist, Teacher/Learner: Reflections on the Ethicist in the Clinical Setting." *Theoretical Medicine* 7: 3–12.

Cigarini, A., et al. 2018. "Quantitative Account of Social Interactions in a Mental Health Care Ecosystem: Cooperation, Trust and Collective Action." *Nature: Scientific Reports* 28 (8): 3794. www.nature.com/articles/s41598-018-21900-1.

Ciulla, J. B., ed. 2014. *Ethics: The Heart of Leadership*. Santa Barbara, CA: Praeger.

Clarke, T. 2017. *International Corporate Governance: A Comparative Approach*, 2nd ed. Routledge.

Classen, D. C., et al. 2011. "'Global Trigger Tool' Shows that Adverse Events in Hospitals May Be Ten Times Higher than Previously Measured." *Health Affairs* 30 (3): 581–589.

Cliff, B. 2012. "Patient-Centered Care: The Role of Healthcare Leadership." *The Journal of Healthcare Management* 57 (6): 381–383.

Coggan, C., et al. 2016. *Public Health Law: Ethics, Governance, and Regulation*. United Kingdom: Routledge.

Cohen, J. R. 2004. "Future Research on Disclosure of Medical Errors." *Annals of Internal Medicine* 141 (6): 481.

Cohen, K. R. 2008. *Best Practices for Developing Effective and Enduing Board/CEO Relationships*. Chicago, IL: American Hospital Association, Center for Healthcare Governance.

Collins, D. 2011. *Business Ethics: How to Design and Manage Ethical Organizations*. Oxford: Wiley.

Committee on the Costs of Medical Care. 1932. *Medical Care for the American People*. Chicago, IL: The University of Chicago Press.

Comstock, G., ed. 2014. *Life Sciences Ethics*, 2nd ed. Springer.

Congregation for the Doctrine of the Faith. 2006. "Doctrinal Note on Some Questions Regarding the Participation of Catholics in Political Life." In NCCB, ed., *Readings on Catholics in Political Life*. Washington, DC: USCCB.

Congressional Budget Office. 2006. *Nonprofit Hospitals and the Provision of Community Benefit*. Washington, DC: Congressional Budget Office.

Connelly, M., L. Prybil. 2017. "Charting a Course to Community Health: A Governance Priority." *Health Progress* 98 (September–October): 71–72.

Consoli, S., et al., eds. 2019. *Data Science for Healthcare*. Springer.

Cooper, D. E. 2003. *Ethics for Professionals in a Multicultural World*. Pearson.

Corey, G., M. S. Corey. 2015. *Codes of Ethics for the Helping Professions*, 5th ed. Stamford, CT: Cengage Learning.

Corey, G., M. S. Corey, P. Callahan. 2014. *Issues and Ethics in the Helping Professions.* Boston, MA: Cengage Learning.

Cornforth, C., ed. 2003. *The Governance of Public and Non-Profit Organizations: What Do Boards Do?* New York: Routledge.

Corrigan, J., et al. 2015. "Hospital Community Benefit Programs: Increasing Benefits to Communities." *JAMA* 313 (12): 1211–1121.

Cottone, R. R., V. M. Tarvydas. 2016. *Ethics and Decision Making in Counseling and Psychotherapy*, 4th ed. New York: Springer.

Council for Exceptional Children. 2016. *What Every Special Educator Must Know: Ethics, Standards, and Guidelines*, 7th ed. Council for Exceptional Children.

Cowan, J. 2007. "Good Medical Practice Should Improve Patient Safety." *Clinical Governance: An International Journal* 12 (2): 136–141.

Cranford, R. E., et al. 1984. *Institutional Ethics Committees and Health Care Decisionmaking.* Ann Arbor, MI: Health Administration Press.

Cressy, R., et al., eds. 2016. *Entrepreneurship, Finance, Governance and Ethics.* Springer.

Cribb, A., P. Duncan, eds. 2002. *Health Promotion and Professional Ethics.* Oxford: Wiley-Blackwell.

Croskerry, P., ed. 2009. *Patient Safety in Emergency Medicine.* Philadelphia, PA: Wolters Kluwer.

Crosson. F. J., L. A. Tollen. 2010. *Partners in Health: How Physicians and Hospitals Can be Accountable Together.* San Francisco, CA: Jossey-Bass.

Crowther, D., et al., eds. 2018. *Responsibility and Governance: The Twin Pillars of Sustainability.* New York: Springer.

Crystal, N. M. 2011. *Professional Responsibility: Problems of Practice & Profession*, 5th ed. Aspen Publishers.

Culica, D., E. Prezio. 2009. "Hospital Board Infrastructure and Functions: The Role of Governance in Financial Performance." *International Journal of Environmental Research and Public Health* 6 (3): 862–873.

Cureatr. 2019. *There's Much Work to be Done: 8 Medical Error Statistics to Know.* https://blog.cureatr.com/theres-much-work-to-be-done-8-medical-errors-statistics-to-know.

Dallas, L. L. 2002. "The New Managerialism and Diversity on Corporate Boards of Directors." *Tulane Law Review* 76: 1363–1391.

Dallas, L. L. 2004. "Corporate Ethics in the Healthcare Marketplace." *Seattle Journal for Social Justice* 3 (1): 213–227.

Daniels, N. 2008. *Just Health: Meeting Health Needs Fairly.* New York: Cambridge University.

Daniels, N., J. E. Sabin. 2008. *Setting Limits Fairly.* New York: Oxford University Press.

Dare, T., C. Swanton, eds. 2019. *Perspectives in Role Ethics: Virtues, Reasons, and Obligations.* United Kingdom: Routledge.

Darr, K. 2018. *Ethics in Health Services Management*, 6th ed. Baltimore, MD: Health Professions Press.

Davis, K. 2012. *Ethics of Big Data: Balancing Risk and Innovation.* O'Reilly Media.

Davis, K., et al. 2014. *Mirror, Mirror on the Wall: How the Performance of the U.S. Health Care Systems Compares Internationally.* New York: The Commonwealth Fund.

Dawson, A., ed. 2011. *Public Health Ethics: Key Concepts and Issues in Policy and Practice.* New York: Cambridge University Press.

Day, L. A. 2005. *Ethics in Media Communications: Cases and Controversies.* Belmont, CA: Wadsworth.

Decker, S. 2011. *Drift into Failure: From Hunting Broken Components to Understanding Complex Systems*. Farnham, UK: Ashgate.

Decker, S. 2011. *Patient Safety: A Human Factors Approach*. Taylor and Francis, CRC Press.

DeGeorge, R. T. 2009. *Business Ethics*, 7th ed. Pearson.

Dekker, S. 2011. *Patient Safety: A Human Factors Approach*. Taylor & Francis.

Deloitte. 2018. *2018 Global Health Care Outlook: The Evolution of Smart Health Care*. https://www2.deloitte.com/global/en/pages/life-sciences-and-healthcare/articles/global-health-care-sector-outlook.html.

Department of Health and Human Services. 2010. *Office of the Inspector General, Adverse Events in Hospitals*. National Incidence Among Medicare Beneficiaries. Washington, DC: DHHS.

Department of Health and Human Services. 2014. *HHS Data Shows Major Strides Made in Patient Safety*. https://innovation.cms.gov/files/reports/patient-safety-results.pdf.

Department of Health and Human Services. Agency for Healthcare Research and Quality. *National Healthcare Quality Report*. Washington, DC: Agency for Healthcare Research and Quality.

Department of Health and Human Services, Office of the Surgeon General. 2019. *Surgeon General Priority: Community Health and Economic Prosperity*. www.hhs.gov/surgeongeneral/priorities/community-health-economic-security/index.html.

DesJardins, J. 2013. *An Introduction to Business Ethics*, 5th ed. McGraw-Hill.

Devettere, R. J. 2002. *Introduction to Virtue Ethics: Insights of the Ancient Greeks*. Washington, DC: Georgetown University Press.

Devettere, R. J. 2016. *Practical Decision Making in Health Care Ethics*, 4th ed. Washington, DC: Georgetown University Press.

Devlin, B., G. Magill. 2006. "The Process of Ethical Decision-Making." In W. E. Scott, *Current Ethical Thinking in Anaesthesia and Intensive Care*, special issue of the journal, *Best Practice & Research Clinical Anaesthesiology* 20 (4): 493–506.

DeVore, S., R. W. Champion. 2011. "Driving Population Health Through Accountable Care Organizations." *Health Affairs* 30 (1): 41–50.

Dey, N., et al., eds. 2019. *Big Data Analytics for Intelligent Healthcare Management*. Cambridge, MA: Academic Press.

Dhillon, D. S. 2003. *Human Reliability and Error in Medical System*. Hackensack, NJ: World Scientific Publishing.

Dicker, A. P. 2016. *Quality and Safety in Radiation Oncology*. New York: Springer.

Diehl, S., et al., eds. 2016. *Handbook of Integrated Corporate Social Responsibility Communication*. New York: Springer.

Dixon, N. 2009. *Review of Ethical Issues Related to Clinical Audit and Quality Improvement Activities: A Guide for NHS Organizations*. United Kingdom: Healthcare Quality Improvement Partnership, 1–41.

Dlugacz, Y. D. 2017. *Introduction to Health Care Quality: Theory, Methods, and Tools*. Plano, TX: Jossey-Bass.

Dodd-Frank Wall Street Reform and Consumer Protection Act. 2010. www.congress.gov/bill/111th-congress/house-bill/4173/text.

Dolan, T. C. 2011. "The CEO Turnover and Succession Planning Crisis." *Healthcare Executive* 26 (5): 6.

Dolan, T. C. 2013. "Increasing Diversity in Governance and Management." *Journal of Healthcare Management* 58 (2): 84–86.

Donchin, Y., D. Gopher, eds. 2013. *Around the Patient Bed: Human Factors and Safety in Healthcare*. Taylor and Francis, CRC Press.

Dranove, D., et al. 2015. *A Floor-and-Trade Proposal to Improve the Delivery of Charity-Care by U.S. Nonprofit Hospitals*. Washington, DC: The Hamilton Project at the Brookings Institute.

Dubler, N. N., C. B. Liebman. 2004. *Bioethics Mediation: A Guide to Shaping Shared Solution*. New York: United Hospital Fund.

Dukes, M. N. G. 2005. *The Law and Ethics of the Pharmaceutical Industry*. Elsevier.

Durkeim, E. 2003 (1957). *Professional Ethics and Civic Morals*, 3rd ed. New York: Routledge, 2003.

Duska, R., et al. 2011. *Accounting Ethics*, 2nd ed. Oxford: Wiley-Blackwell.

Dutelle, A. W. 2011. *Ethics for the Public Service Professional*. CRC Press.

DuVal, G., et al. 2004. "A National Survey of US Internists' Experiences With Ethical Dilemmas and Ethics Consultation." *Journal of General Internal Medicine* 19 (3): 252–258.

Dyson, A., J. Harris. 2014. *Ethics & Biotechnology*. Routledge.

Dzienkowski, J. 2016. *Professional Responsibility, Standards, Rules and Statutes*. West Academic Publishing.

Eberl, Jason T., ed. 2017. *Contemporary Controversies in Catholic Bioethics*. Springer.

Edmondson, A. C. 2012. *Teaming: How Organizations Learn, Innovate, and Compete in the Knowledge Economy*. San Francisco, CA: Jossey-Bass.

Elsevier Publishing. 2014. *Legal and Ethical Issues for Health Professionals*, 3rd ed. Elsevier Saunders.

Emerson K., T. Nabatchi. 2015. *Collaborative Governance Regimes*. Washington, DC: Georgetown University Press.

Entin, F., et al. 2006. *The Board's Fiduciary Role: Legal Responsibilities of Health Care Governing Boards*. Chicago, IL: Center for Healthcare Governance.

Erford, B. T. 2013. *Orientation to the Counseling Profession: Advocacy, Ethics, and Essential Professional Foundations*, 2nd ed. Pearson.

Ermann, M. D., M. S. Shauf, eds. 2002. *Computers, Ethics, and Society*. New York: Oxford University Press.

Evashwick, C. J. 2013. *Hospitals & Community Benefit: New Demands and New Approaches*. Chicago, IL: Health Administration Press.

Evashwick, C. J., K. Gautam. 2008. "Governance and Management of Community Benefit." *Health Progress* 89 (5): 10–15.

Faden, R. R., et al. 2011. "Learning Healthcare Systems and Justice." *Hastings Center Report* 41 (4): 3.

Farber Post, L., et al. 2007. *Handbook for Health Care Ethics Committees*. Baltimore, MD: The Johns Hopkins University Press.

Federal Interagency Workgroup. 2020. *Healthy People 2020*. Federal Interagency Workgroup.

Feigal, D., et al. 2003. "Ensuring Safe and Effective Medical Devices." *New England Journal of Medicine* 348 (3): 191–192.

Fernandez-Lynch, H. 2008. *Conflicts of Conscience in Healthcare: An Institutional Compromise* Cambridge, MA: MIT Press.

Ferrell, O. C., J. Fraedrich, L. Ferrell. 2016. *Business Ethics: Ethical Decision Making and Cases*, 11th ed. Boston, MA: Cengage Learning.

Field, R. I. 2007. *Healthcare Regulation in America: Complexity, Confrontation, and Compromise*. New York: Oxford University Press.

Filerman, G. L., et al., eds. 2014. *Managerial Ethics in Healthcare: A New Perspective*. Chicago, IL: Health Administration Press.

Fines, B. G. 2013. *Professional Responsibility: A Context and Practice Casebook*. Durham, NC: Carolina Academic Press.

Finnis, J. 2004. "Helping Enact Unjust Laws Without Complicity in Injustice." *American Journal of Jurisprudence* 49: 11–42.

Finnis, J. 2006. "Restricting Legalized Abortion Is Not Intrinsically Unjust." In Helen Watt, ed., *Cooperation, Complicity & Conscience: Problems in Healthcare, Science, Law and Public Policy*. London: Linacre Centre, Chapter 12.

Fins, J. J., et al. 2016. "A Pilot Evaluation of Portfolios for Quality Attestation of Clinical Ethics Consultants." *American Journal of Bioethics* 16 (3): 3–14.

Fisher, C. B. 2012. *Decoding the Ethics Code: A Practical Guide for Psychologists*. Sage.

Fitzpatrick, K. R. 2016. *Ethics in Public Relations: responsible Advocacy*. Sage.

Fleming, H.-K. 2018. "Improving Quality and Lowering Cost Through Community Care Teams." *Journal of Healthcare Management* 63 (4): 242–250.

Fletcher, J. C., et al. 1989. *Ethics Consultation in Health Care: Rationale and History*. Ann Arbor, MI: Health Administration Press.

Fletcher, J. C., M. Siegler. 1996. "What Are the Goals of Ethics Consultations? A Consensus Statement." *Journal of Clinical Ethics* 7: 122–126.

Flores, A. 1987. *Professional Ideals*. Wadsworth.

Folkemer, D. C., et al. 2011. "Hospital Community Benefits After the ACA: The Emerging Federal Framework." *The Hilltop Institute – Issue Brief* (January).

Ford-Eickhoff, K., et al. 2011. "Hospital Boards and Hospital Strategic Focus: The Impact of Board Involvement in Strategic Decision-Making." *Healthcare Management Review* 36 (2): 145–154.

Forehand, A. 2000. "Mission and Organizational Performance in the Healthcare Industry." *Journal of Healthcare Management* 45 (4): 267–277.

Forman, L., J. C. Kohler. 2012. *Access to Medicines as a Human Right: Implications for Pharmaceutical Industry Responsibility*. Toronto, Canada: University of Toronto Press.

Forrer, J. 2014. *Governing Cross-Sector Collaboration*. Wiley.

Forrestal, E. J., L. W. Cellucci. 2016. *Ethics and Professionalism for Healthcare Managers*. Chicago, IL: Health Administration Press.

Foster, I. R., J. Lasser. 2010. *Professional Ethics in Midwifery Practice*. Jones and Bartlett.

Fox, E. 2013. "Evaluating Ethics Quality in Health Care Organizations: Looking Back and Looking Forward." *American Journal of Bioethics* 4 (1): 71–77.

Fox, E. 2014. "Developing a Certifying Examination for Health Care Ethics Consultants." *American Journal of Bioethics* 14 (1): 1–4.

Fox, E. 2016. "The Road to Certification for Clinical Ethics Consultants: Finding Our Bearings." *American Journal of Bioethics* 16 (3): 33–35.

Fox, E. 2016. "Strategies to Improve Health Care Ethics Consultation: Bridging the Knowledge Gap." *AMA Journal of Ethics* 18 (5) (May): 528–529.

Fox, E., et al. 2007. "Ethics Consultation in United States Hospitals: A National Survey." *American Journal of Bioethics* 7 (2): 13–25.

Fox, E., et al. 2010. "An Innovative Program to Improve Ethics Quality in Health Care." *Innovation Journal* 15 (2): 1–36.

Fox, M., et al. 1998. "Paradigms for Clinical Ethics Consultation Practice." *Cambridge Quarterly of Healthcare Ethics* 7: 308–314.

Framption, S., P. Charmel. 2009. *Putting Patients First: Best Practices in Patient Centered Care*, 2nd ed. San Francisco, CA: Jossey-Bass.

Frankel, A. S., et al. 2006. "Fair and Just Culture, Team Behavior, and Leadership Engagement: The Tools to Achieve High Reliability." *Health Services Research* 41 (4): 1690–1709.

Freeman, R. E. 2010. *Strategic Management: A Stakeholder Approach.* New York: Cambridge University Press.

Freeman, R. E., et al. 2010. *Stakeholder Theory: The State of the Art.* New York: Cambridge University Press.

Freeman, R. E., et al. 2017. *Stakeholder Engagement: Clinical Research Cases.* New York: Springer.

Fremgen, B. F. 2015. *Medical Law and Ethics,* 5th ed. Pearson.

Friberg, E. E., J. L. Creasia. 2016. *Conceptual Foundations: The Bridge to Professional Nursing Practice.* St. Louis, MO: Elsevier.

Friedman, A. L., S. Miles. 2006. *Stakeholders: Theory and Practice.* New York: Oxford University Press.

Fritz, J. H. 2012. *Professional Civility: Communicative Virtue at Work.* Peter Lang.

Fry, S. T., R. M. Veatch. 2010. *Case Studies in Nursing Ethics.* Jones & Bartlett.

Fulton, B. T. 2017. "Health Care Market Concentration Trends in the United States: Evidence and Policy Responses." *Health Affairs* 36: 9. https://doi.org/10.1377/hlthaff.2017.0556.

Furrow, B., et al. 2018. *Law and Health Care Quality, Patient Safety, and Liability.* St. Paul, MN: West Academic Publishing.

Future Health Index. 2018. *Trust in Healthcare: Aligning HCPs and Patients* (July). www.futurehealthindex.com/2018/07/17/trust-healthcare-aligning-hcps-patients-long-term-partnership.

Gabard, D. L., M. W. Martin. 2011. *Physical Therapy Ethics,* 2nd ed. Davis Company.

Gage, L. 2012. *Transformational Governance: The Challenges Facing Trustees of Nonprofits and Public Hospitals.* Chicago, IL: Center for Healthcare Governance.

Gallagher, C., et al. 2018. "A Retrospective Review of Clinical Ethics Consultations Requested by Nurses for Oncology Patients." *Journal of Nursing* 7 (1): 1–7.

Garcia, A., et al. 2013. "U.S. Health Care is Moving Upstream." *Health Progress* 94: 7–13.

Gasparetto, A., R. J. Jox, M. Picozzi. 2018. "The Notion of Neutrality in Clinical Ethics Consultation." *Philosophy, Ethics, and Humanities in Medicine* 13 (1): 3.

Gazley, B. 2015. *Transformational Governance: How Boards Achieve Extraordinary Change.* Hoboken, NJ: Wiley.

Gefanus, E. 2011. "Clinical Ethics Committee and Ethics Support Infrastructure: A European Perspective." *Asian Bioethics Review* 3 (3): 293–298.

Gert, B. 2007. *Common Morality: Deciding What To Do.* New York: Oxford University Press.

Gert, B., et al. 2006. *Bioethics: A Systematic Approach,* 2nd ed. New York: Oxford University Press.

Geuras, D., C. Garafalo. 2010. *Practical Ethics in Public Administration,* 3rd ed. Vienna, VA: Management Concepts Inc.

Ghandi, T. K., et al. 2003. "Adverse Drug Events in Ambulatory Care." *New England Journal of Medicine* 348 (16): 1556–1564.

Gilbert, J. A. 2013. "A Reflection on Everyday Ethics." *Healthcare Executive* 28 (1): 60–63.

Gillespie, K. N., et al. 2008. "Measuring the Impact of Community Benefit." *Health Progress* 89 (5): 29–33.

Gittell, J., et al. 2013. "Interprofessional Collaborative Practice and Relational Coordination." *Journal of Interprofessional Care* 27: 210–213.

Glied, S., et al. 2016. "Where the Money Goes: The Evolving Expenses of the US Health Care System." *Health Affairs* 35: 1197–1203.

Goeschel, C. A. 2008. "Monitoring Patient Safety and Quality: A Simple Framework." *Trustee* 61 (3): 34–35.

Goeschel, C. A. 2010. *Quality, Patient safety, and Boards of Trustees: Implications for Creating Safer Healthcare*. Dr. Sci. Dissertation, Tulane University School of Public Health and Tropical Medicine.

Goldberg, D. S. 2017. *Public Health Ethics and Social Determinants of Health*. Springer.

Goodman, R. A., et al. 2014. "What Is Community Health? Examining the Meaning of an Evolving Field in Public Health." *Preventive Medicine* 67 (Suppl. 1) (October): S58–S61.

Goodspeed, S. W. 1998. *Community Stewardship*. Chicago, IL: AHA Press.

Gordon, J.-S., J. Schildmann, J. Vollmann, eds. 2010. *Clinical Ethics Consultation*. Routledge.

Gordon, S., et al. 2013. Beyond the Checklist: What Else Healthcare Can Learn Beyond *Teamwork and Safety*. Ithaca, NY: Cornell University Press.

Gorka, C., et al. 2017. "Growing an Ethics Consultation Service: A Longitudinal Study Examining Two Decades of Practice." *American Journal of Bioethics, Empirical Bioethics* 8 (2) (April): 116–127.

Gosbee, J. W., L. L. Gosbee, eds. 2010. *Using Human Factors Engineering to Improve Patient Safety*, 2nd ed. Oakbrook, IL: Joint Commission Resources.

Gostin, L. O., ed. 2010. *Public Health and Law Ethics: A Reader*, 2nd ed. Berkeley, CA: University of California Press.

Gouillart, F., D. Billings. 2013. "Community-Powered Problem Solving." *Harvard Business Review* 71–77.

Governance Institute. 2002. *Striving for Excellence: Health System Governance at the Dawn of the New Millennium*. The Governance Institute.

Governance Institute. 2009. *Governance Structure and Practices: Results, Analysis, and Evaluation*. Biennial Survey of Hospitals and Healthcare Systems. San Diego, CA: The Governance Institute.

Governance Institute. 2010. "Enhancing Quality Oversight." *Healthcare Executive* 25 (2): 80–81.

Governance Institute. 2010. "Great Boards Need Leaders, Not Followers." *Healthcare Executive* 25 (6): 74–76.

Governance Institute. 2010. *Intentional Governance: Advancing Boards Beyond the Conventional*. Chicago, IL: The Governance Institute.

Governance Institute. 2011. *Dynamic Governance: An Analysis of Board Structure and Practices in a Shifting Industry*. San Diego, CA: The Governance Institute.

Governance Institute. 2017. *2017 Governance Institute Biennial Survey Shows Positive Governance Evolution*. San Diego, CA: The Governance Institute.

Governance Institute. 2019. *Subsidiary and Local Boards*. www.governanceinstitute.com/page/SubLocalBoards

Graber, G., et al., eds. 1987. *Clinical Medical Ethics: Exploration and Assessment*. Lanham, MD: University Press of America.

Grace, P. M., ed. 2014. *Nursing Ethics and Professional Responsibility*, 2nd ed. Burlington, MA: Jones and Bartlett, 3rd ed. 2017.

Gram, L., et al. 2018. "Understanding Participation Dilemmas in Community Mobilization: Can Collective Action Theory Help?" *Journal of Epidemiology and Community Health* 1–7. https://jech.bmj.com/content/73/1/90.

Grant Thornton. 2009. *National Board Governance Survey for Not-for-Profit Organizations*. Chicago, IL: Grant Thornton, LLP.

Greenberg, R. A., et al., eds. 2016. *Ethical Issues in Pediatric Organ Transplantation*. Springer.

Greenleaf, R. K. 1991. *The Servant as Leader*. Atlanta, GA: Greenleaf Center.

Guido, G. W. 2013. *Legal and Ethical Issues in Nursing: Challenges and Opportunities*, 6th ed. Pearson.

Gula, R. M. 2010. *Just Ministry: Professional Ethics for Pastoral Ministers*. Paulist.

Gutman, A., J. D. Moreno. 2019. *Bioethics and the Transformation of Health Care in America*. New York: Liveright.

Guy, D. M., D. R. Carmichael, A. A. Lach. 2003. *Ethics for CPAs: Meeting Expectations in Challenging Times*. Oxford: Wiley.

Haga, S. B., W. Burke. 2004. "Using Pharmacogenetics to Improve Drug Safety and Efficacy." *Journal of the American Medical Association* 291 (23): 2869–2871.

Halbert, T. 2014. *Law and Ethics in the Business Environment*, 8th ed. Boston, MA: Cengage Learning.

Hall, M. A. 2004. "A Corporate Ethics of 'Care' in Healthcare." *Seattle Journal for Social Justice* 3 (1): 417–428.

Hamilton, R. 2000. "Corporate Governance in America: Major Changes But Uncertain Benefits." *Journal of Corporate Law* 349–373.

Handy, F., A. R. Russell. 2018. *Ethics for Social Impact: Ethical Decision-Making in Nonprofit Organizations*. United Kingdom: Palgrave MacMillan.

Hanefield, J., et al. 2017."Understanding and Measuring Quality of Care: Dealing with Complexity." *Bulletin of the World Health Organization* 95: 368–374. http://doi.org/10.2471/BLT.16.179309.

Haniyeh, S. S., et al. 2012. "Does Transfer of Hospital Governance to Board of Trustees per se Lead to Improved Hospital Performance?" *International Journal of Hospital Research* 1 (2): 97–102.

Hann, A. 2016. *Applied Public Health Ethics: Making Ethical Decision*. United Kingdom: Routledge.

Hansen, K. 2016. *Corporate Social Responsibility and Diversity Management*. Springer.

Harman, L. B. 2006. *Ethical Challenges in the Management of Health Information*. Jones & Bartlett.

Harris, C. E., et al. 2013. *Engineering Ethics: Concepts and Cases*, 5th ed. Boston, MA: Cengage Learning.

Hartmann, L., J. DesJardins, C. MacDonald. 2013. *Business Ethics: Decision Making for Personal Integrity and Social Responsibility*, 3rd ed. McGraw-Hill.

Health Care Cost Institute. 2017. *2017 Health Care Cost and Utilization Report*. www.healthcostinstitute.org/images/easyblog_articles/276/HCCI-2017-Health-Care-Cost-and-Utilization-Report-02.12.19.pdf.

Health Grades Quality Study. 2004. *Patient Safety in American Hospitals*. Denver, CO: Health Grades Inc.

Health Policy Center. 2011. *What Directions for Public Health Under Affordable Care Act?* Washington, DC: Urban Institute.

Health Research and Educational Trust. 2014. *Hospital-Based Strategies for Creating a Culture of Health*. Chicago, IL: Health Research and Educational Trust.

Health Research and Educational Trust. 2014. *The Second Curve of Population Health*. Chicago, IL: Health Research & Educational Trust. Also in *Trustee* 67: 17–20.

Health Research and Educational Trust. 2016. *Creating Effective Hospital–Community Partnerships to Build a Culture of Health*. Chicago, IL: Health Research and Educational Trust.

Health Research and Educational Trust. 2016. *Creating Effective Partnerships to Build a Culture of Trust*. Chicago, IL: Health Research and Educational Trust.

Health Research and Educational Trust. 2016. *Engaging Patients and Communities in the Community Health Needs Assessment Process*. Chicago, IL: Health Research and Educational Trust.

HealthCatalyst. 2016. "The Top Seven Analytics-Driven Approaches for Reducing Diagnostic Error and Improving Patient Safety." *HealthCatalyst* (October 13). www.healthcatalyst.com/reducing-diagnostic-error-to-improve-patient-safety/.

HealthCatalyst. 2018. "Improving Patient Safety: Machine Learning Targets an Urgent Concern." *HealthCatalyst* (January 30). www.healthcatalyst.com/machine-learning-patient-safety-improvement.

HealthCatalyst. 2019. "Engaging Health System Boards of Trustees in Quality and Safety: Six Must-Know Guidelines." *HealthCatalyst* (June 5). www.healthcatalyst.com/insights/healthcare-boards-quality-safety-pivotal-role.

Hébert, P.C. 2009. *Doing Right: A Practical Guide to Ethics for Medical Trainees and Physicians*. New York: Oxford University Press.

Hecker, L. 2009. *Ethics and Professional Issues in Couple and Family Therapy*. Routledge.

Heiman, H. J., S. Artiga. 2014. *Beyond Health Care: The Role of Social Determinants in Promoting Health and Health Equity*. The Kaiser Commission on Medicaid and the Uninsured: Issue Brief. Menlo Park, CA: The Henry J. Kaiser Family Foundation.

Herald, L., et al. 2013. "Decision-Making Fairness and Consensus-Building in Multisector Community Alliances." *Nonprofit Management and Leadership* 24: 159–161.

Herlihy, B., G. Corey. 2014. *ACA Ethical Standards Casebook*, 7th ed. American Counseling Association – ACA.

Hester, M. D., et al., eds. 2012. *Guidance for Healthcare Ethics Committees*. New York: Cambridge University Press.

Higgins, C. 2011. *The Good Life of Teaching: An Ethics of Professional Practice*. Oxford: Wiley-Blackwell.

Ho, D. 2017. *Philosophical Issues in Pharmaceuticals: Development, Dispensing, Use*. Springer.

Hoffmaster, C., B. Freedman, G. Fraser, eds. 1989. *Clinical Ethics: Theory and Practice*. Clifton, NJ: Humana Press.

Hofmann, P. B. 2010. "Addressing Racial and Ethnic Disparities in Healthcare." *Healthcare Executive* 25 (5): 46–50.

Holland, S. 2015. *Public Health Ethics*, 2nd ed. Cambridge, UK: Polity.

Homan, M. E. 2018. "Factors Associated with the Timing and Patient Outcomes of Clinical Ethics Consultation in a Catholic Health System." *The National Catholic Bioethics Quarterly* 18 (1) (Spring): 71–92.

Homer, J., et al. 2016. "Combined Regional Investments Could Substantially Enhance Health System Performance and Be Financially Affordable." *Health Affairs* 35: 1135–1143.

Honore, P., et al. 2012. "Bridging the Quality Chasm Between Health Care and Public Health." *Journal of Public Health Management and Practice* 18 (1): 1–2.

Horwitz, J. R. 2003. "Why We Need the Independent Sector: The Behavior, Law, and Ethics of Not-for-Profit Hospitals." *UCLA Law Review* 50: 6. www.inova.org/upload/docs/Quality/ILH/Inova-Loudoun-Hospital-Quality-Compact.pdf; www.healthypeople.gov/2020.

Horwitz, J. R. 2006. "Nonprofit Ownership, Private Property, and Public Accountability." *Health Affairs* W308–W311.

Hotchkiss, D. 2016. *Governance and Ministry: Rethinking Board Leadership*, 2nd ed. Rowman & Littlefield.

Houser, R., S. J. Thoma. 2012. *Ethics in Counseling and Therapy: Developing an Ethical Identity*. London: Sage.

Howard, J. 2019. *Cognitive Errors and Diagnostic Mistakes: A Case-based Guide to Critical Thinking in Medicine*. New York: Springer.

Huston, C. J. 2016. *Professional Issues in Nursing*, 4th ed. Wolters Kluwer.

Huynh, T. N., et al. 2013. "The Frequency and Cost of Treatment Perceived to be Futile in Critical Care." *JAMA Internal Medicine* 173 (20): 1887–1894.

Ide, B. 2011. "Moving Beyond Quality: Growing Regulations and Enforcement Are Expanding Trustees' Oversight Responsibilities." *Trustee* 64 (6): 29.

Idowu, S. O., et al., eds. 2018. *A Standardized View on Corporate Social Responsibility*. New York: Springer.

Idowu, S. O., et al., eds. 2019. *Corporate Social Responsibility in Times of Crisis*. New York: Springer.

Iedema, R., et al. 2015. *Communicating Quality and Safety in Health Care*. New York: Cambridge University Press, 2015.

Independent Sector. 2015. *Principles for Good Governance and Ethical Practice: A Guide for Charities and Foundations*. Washington, DC: Independent Sector.

Institute for Healthcare Improvement. 2011. *How to Improve*. Cambridge, MA: Institute for Healthcare Improvement.

Institute for Healthcare Improvement. 2012. *The Power of Having the Board on Board*. Cambridge, MA: Institute for Healthcare Improvement.

Institute for Healthcare Improvement. 2017. *New Survey Finds 21 Percent of Americans Report Personal Experience with Medical Errors* (September 28). www.ihi.org/about/news/Documents/IHIPressRelease_Patient_Safety_Survey_Sept28_17.pdf.

Institute for Healthcare Improvement. 2019. *CPPS, Certified Professional in Patient Safety*. www.ihi.org/education/cpps-certified-professional-in-patient-safety/Pages/default.aspx.

Institute for Healthcare Improvement. 2019. *Quality, Cost and Value*. www.ihi.org/Topics/QualityCostValue/Pages/default.aspx.

Institute for Healthcare Improvement. 2019. *Universal Patient Compact*. www.npsf.org/page/patientcompact.

Institute of Medicine. 2002. *Committee on Enhancing Federal Healthcare Quality Programs*. Leadership by Example: Coordinating Government Roles in Improving Healthcare Quality. Washington, DC: National Academy Press.

Institute of Medicine. 2004. Healthcare Quality Initiative, *Keeping Patients Safe: Transforming the Work Environment of Nurses*. Washington, DC: National Academy Press.

Institute of Medicine. 2004. *Patient Safety: Achieving a New Standard of Care*. Washington, DC: National Academies Press.

Institute of Medicine. 2006. *Preventing Medication Errors*. Washington, DC: National Academies Press.

Institute of Medicine. 2011. *Committee on Patient Safety and Health Information Technology, Health IT and Patient Safety: Building Better Systems for Better Care*. Washington, DC: National Academies Press.

Institute of Medicine. 2011. *The Future of Nursing: Leading Change, Advancing Health*. Washington, DC: The National Academies Press.

Institute of Medicine. 2012. *For the Public's Health: Investing in a Healthy Future*. Washington, DC: National Academy of Science.

Institute of Medicine. 2013. *Best Care at Lower Cost*. Washington, DC: National Academies Press.

Institute of Medicine. 2013. *Toward Quality Measures for Population Health and the Leading Indicators*. Washington, DC: National Academy of Sciences.

Institute of Medicine. 2015. *Collaboration Between Health Care and Public Health.* Washington, DC: The National Academies Press.

Institute of Medicine. 2015. *Spread, Scale, and Sustainability in Population Health.* Washington, DC: The National Academies Press.

Institute of Medicine. 2015. *Vital Signs: Core Metrics for Health and Health Care Progress.* Washington, DC: The National Academies Press.

Institute of Medicine, Committee on Quality of Health Care in America. 2000. *To Err Is Human: Building a Safer Health System.* Washington, DC National Academy Press.

Institute of Medicine, Committee on Quality of Health Care in America. 2001. *Crossing the Quality Chasm: A New Health System for the 21st Century.* Washington, DC: National Academy.

Institute of Medicine of the National Academies. 2012. *Primary Care and Public Health: Exploring Integration to Improve Population Health.* Washington, DC: The National Academies Press.

International Council of Nurses. 2012. *Code of Ethics for Nurses.* Geneva, Switzerland: International Council of Nurses.

IRS. 1969. *Revenue Ruling 69–545, 1969–2, C.B 117.* www.irs.gov/charities-non-profits/charitable-hospitals-general-requirements-for-tax-exemption-under-section-501c3.

IRS. 2008. *Governance and Related Topics: 501(c)(3) Organizations.*" www.irs.gov/pub/irs-tege/governance_practices.pdf.

IRS. 2009. *Form 990. Instructions for Schedule H.* www.irs.gov/instructions/i990sh.

IRS. 2009. *IRS Exempt Organizations Hospital Study. Final Report.* www.irs.gov/pub/irs-tege/execsum_hospprojrept.pdf.

IRS. 2010. *New Requirements for 501(c)3 Hospitals Under the Affordable Care Act.* www.irs.gov/charities-non-profits/charitable-organizations/new-requirements-for-501c3-hospitals-under-the-affordable-care-act.

IRS. 2016. *Form 990. Return of Organization Exempt from Income Tax. For accompanying instructions.* www.irs.gov/pub/irs-pdf/i990.pdf.

Islam, R., et al. 2016. "Clinical Complexity in Medicine: A Measurement Model of Task and Patient Complexity." *Methods of Information in Medicine* 55 (1): 14–22.

Jacob, S., et al. 2016. *Ethics and Law for School Psychologists,* 7th ed. Oxford: Wiley.

Jacobsen, K. H. 2016. *Introduction to Health Research Methods: A Practical Guide,* 2nd ed. Jones & Bartlett.

Jecker, N. S., et al. 2007. *Bioethics: An Introduction to the History, Methods, and Practice,* 2nd ed. Jones & Bartlett.

Jennings, B., et al. 2004. *The Ethics of Hospital Trustees.* Washington, DC: Georgetown University Press.

Jennings, B., et al., eds. 2016. *Emergency Ethics: Public Health Preparedness and Response.* New York: Oxford University Press.

Jha, K., A. Epstein. 2010. "Hospital Governance and the Quality of Care." *Health Affairs* 29 (1): 182–187.

Jiang, H. J., et al. 2012. "Enhancing Board Oversight on Quality of Hospital Care: An Agency Theory Approach." *Healthcare Management Review* 37 (2): 144–153.

Jinkins, M., D. B. Jinkins. 1998. *The Character of Leadership: Political Realism and Public Virtue in Nonprofit Organizations.* San Francisco, CA: Jossey-Bass.

John, J. 2013. "A New, Evidence-based Estimate of Patient Harms Associated with Hospital Care." *Journal of Patient Safety* 9 (3): 122–128.

Johns Hopkins University, Johns Hopkins Medicine. 2016. *Study Suggests Medical Errors Now Third Leading Cause of Death in the U.S.* www.hopkinsmedicine.org/news/media/releases/study_suggests_medical_errors_now_third_leading_cause_of_death_in_the_us.

Johnson, C. E. 2018. *Organizational Ethics: A Practical Approach.* Washington, DC: Sage Publications.

Johnson, D. G. 2009. *Computer Ethics*, 4th ed. Pearson.

Johnson, L. S., et al. 2012. "Use of the Medical Ethics Consultation Service in a Busy Level 1 Trauma Center: Impact on Decision-Making and Patient Care." *American Surgeon* 78 (7): 735–740.

Johnson, M. 1993. *Moral Imagination.* Chicago, IL: University of Chicago Press.

Johnson, R. W. 2013. *Collaborations to Build Healthier Communities.* Princeton, NJ: Robert Wood Johnson Foundation.

Johnson, R. W. 2014. *Time to Act: Investing in the Health of our Children and Communities.* Princeton, NJ: Robert Wood Johnson Foundation.

Johnson, S. 2014. "Diagnosing a Community Health Needs: Non-For-Profit Hospitals Target Health Improvement Efforts Under Reform Law." *Modern Healthcare* 44: 14–16.

Johnson, W. B., C. R. Ridley. 2008. *The Elements of Ethics for Professionals.* New York: Palgrave MacMillan.

Joint Commission. 2008. *Advanced Lean Thinking: Proven Methods to Reduce Waste and Improve Quality in Healthcare.* Oakbrook, IL: Joint Commission Resources.

Joint Commission. 2008. *Understanding and Preventing Sentinel and Adverse Events in your Healthcare Organization.* Oakbrook, IL: Joint Commission Resources.

Joint Commission. 2010. *Patient Safety in the Intensive Care Unit.* Oakbrook, IL: Joint Commission Resources.

Joint Commission. 2010. *Pediatric Patient Safety in the Emergency Department.* Oakbrook, IL: Joint Commission Resources.

Joint Commission. 2010. *The Value of Close Calls in Improving Patient Care: Learning How to Avoid and Mitigate Patient Harm.* Oakbrook Terrace, IL: Joint Commission Resources.

Joint Commission. 2011. *From the Front Office to the Front Line: Essential Issues for Healthcare Leaders*, 2nd ed. Oakbrook, IL: Joint Commission Resource.

Joint Commission. 2011. *Speak Up: Help Prevent Errors in Your Care.* Oakbrook, IL: Joint Commission Resources.

Joint Commission. 2011. *The Value of Close Calls in Improving Patient Care: Learning How to Avoid and Mitigate Patient Harm.* Oakbrook Terrace, IL: Joint Commission Resources.

Joint Commission. 2013. *The Essential Guide for Patient Safety Officers*, 2nd ed. Oakbrook, IL: Joint Commission Resources.

Joint Commission. 2013. *Sentinel Event Data Summary.* Oakbrook, IL: Joint Commission Resource. www.jointcommission.org/sentinel_event_statistics_quarterly.

Joint Commission. 2016. *Getting the Board on Board: What Your Boards Need to Know About Quality and Patient Safety*, 3rd ed. Oakbrook, IL: Joint Commission Resources.

Joint Commission. 2017. "The Essential Role of Leadership in Developing a Safety Culture." *Sentinel Event Alert* 57 (March 1).

Joint Commission. 2017. *Root Cause Analysis in Healthcare*, 6th ed. Oakbrook Terrace, IL: Joint Commission Resources.

Joint Commission. 2018. *2019 National Patient Safety Goals, Joint Commission.* Oakbrook Terrace, IL: Joint Commission Resources.

Joint Commission. 2018. *Comprehensive Accreditation Manual*. CAMH for Hospitals Effective January 1, 2019. Oakbrook, IL: Joint Commission Resources.

Joint Commission. 2018. *Facts About the National Patient Safety Goals, Joint Commission* (November 30). www.jointcommission.org/facts_about_the_national_patient_safety_goals/.

Joint Commission. 2018. *Front Line of Defense: The Role of Nurses in Preventing Sentinel Events*. Oakbrook Terrace, IL: Joint Commission Resources.

Joint Commission. 2018. *Inspiring Health Care Excellence*. Oakbrook Terrace, IL: Joint Commission Resources. www.jointcommission.org/assets/1/6/General_brochure.pdf.

Joint Commission. 2018. *Sentinel Event Policy*. Oakbrook Terrace, IL: Joint Commission Resources. Joint Commission. 2018. *2019 Hospital Accreditation Standards*. Oakbrook, IL: Joint Commission Resources.

Joint Commission. 2019. *The Joint Commission Journal on Quality and Patient Safety*. www.jcrinc.com/the-joint-commission-journal-on-quality-and-patient-safety/.

Joint Commission. 2019. *The Joint Commission Perspectives*. www.jcrinc.com/the-joint-commission-perspectives/.

Joint Commission. 2019. *Sentinel Alert Data Summary*. www.jointcommission.org/sentinel_event_statistics_quarterly/

Joint Commission. 2019. *Sentinel Event Alert Updates*. www.jointcommission.org/daily_update/joint_commission_daily_update.aspx?k=721.

Joint Commission. 2019. *The Source*. www.jcrinc.com/the-source/.

Jonsen, A. R., et al. 2015. *Clinical Ethics*, 7th ed. New York: McGraw-Hill.

Joseph, A., et al. 2012. "Designing for Patient Safety: Developing Methods to Integrate Patient Safety Concerns in the Design Process." *Patient Safety Network* (September). https://psnet.ahrq.gov/resources/resource/25189/Designing-for-Patient-Safety-Developing-Methods-to-Integrate-Patient-Safety-Concerns-in-the-Design-Process.

Joshi, M. S., B. Horak. 2009. *Healthcare Transformation: A Guide for the Hospital Board Member*. Taylor & Francis.

Jungers, C., J. Gregoire, eds. 2012. *Counseling Ethics: Philosophical and Professional Foundations*. New York: Springer.

Kabcenell, A. 2012. "Creating a Culture of Excellence." *Healthcare Executive* 27 (4): 68–71.

Kane, N. M., et al. 2009. "The Internal Processes and Behavioral Dynamics of Hospital Boards: An Exploration of Differences Between High- and Low-Performing Hospitals." *Healthcare Management Review* 34 (1): 80–91.

Kang, H., et al. 2007. "Corporate Governance and Board Composition: Diversity and Independence of Australian Boards." *Corporate Governance: An International Review* 15 (2): 194–207.

Kanie, J., et al. 2013. "Embracing Emergence: How Collective Impact Addresses Complexity." *Stanford Social Innovation Review* 54 (4): 36–41.

Kaplan, G. S. 2018. "Building a Culture of Transparency in Health Care." *Harvard Business Review* (November 9). https://hbr.org/2018/11/building-a-culture-of-transparency-in-health-care.

Kaplan, R., et al. 2010. "Managing Alliances With the Balanced Scorecard." *Harvard Business Review* 88: 114–120.

Kassirer, J. P. 2005. *On the Take: How Medicine's Complicity with Big Business Can Endanger Your Health*. New York: Oxford University Press.

Kaufman, A. L., D. B. Wilkins. 2009. *Problems in Professional Responsibility for a Changing Profession*, 5th ed. Durham, NC: Carolina Academic Press.

Kaufman, G., D. McCaughan. 2013. "The Effect of Organizational Culture on Patient Safety." *Nursing Standard* 27 (43): 50–60.

Kaveny, M. C. 2000. "Appropriation of Evil: Cooperation's Mirror Image." *Theological Studies* 61: 280–313.

Kaveny, M. C. 2006. "Tax Lawyers, Prophets and Pilgrims." In Helen Watt, ed., *Cooperation, Complicity & Conscience: Problems in Healthcare, Science, Law and Public Policy*. London: Linacre Centre, Chapter 4.

Kaveny, M. C. 2012. *Law's Virtue: Fostering Autonomy and Solidarity in American Society*. Washington, DC: Georgetown University Press.

Kaveny, M. C., J. F. Keenan. 1995. "Ethical Issues in Health-Care Restructuring." *Theological Studies* 56 (1): 136–150.

Keenan, J. F., and T. R. Kopfensteiner. 1995. "The Principle of Cooperation. Theologians Explain Material and Formal Cooperation." *Health Progress* 76 (3): 23–27.

Keith, K. M. 2015. *The Case for Servant Leadership*. Atlanta, GA: Greenleaf Center.

Kelly, D. F., G. Magill, H. ten Have. 2013. *Contemporary Catholic Health Care Ethics*, 2nd ed. Washington, DC: Georgetown University Press.

Kenney, M. R. 2018. "A System Approach to Proactive Ethics Integration." *The National Catholic Bioethics Quarterly* 18 (1) (Spring): 93–122.

Kepler, M. O. 1981. *Medical Stewardship: Fulfilling the Hippocratic Legacy*. Santa Barbara, CA: Praeger.

Kerns, C. D. 2000. "Loyalty in Managed Care: A Leadership System." *Journal of Healthcare Management* 45 (3): 158–169.

Khoury, C. M., et al. 2011. "Nursing Leadership from Bedside to Boardroom: A Gallup National Survey of Opinion Leaders." *Journal of Nursing Administration* 41 (7–8): 299–305.

Killian, R., L. Prybil. 2015. "Improving Community Health through Multi-Sector Partnerships." *Governance Institute Boardroom Press* 26 (August): 5–11.

Kim, B., et al. 2009. "The Strategic Role of the Board." *Corporate Governance: An International Review* 17 (6): 728–743.

Kimbrough-Walls, V., C. Lautar. 2011. *Ethics, Jurisprudence and Practice Management in Dental Hygiene*, 3rd ed. Pearson.

King, J. G., E. Moran. 2006. *Trust Counts Now: Hospitals and their Communities: A Report to the American Hospital Association*. American Hospital Association.

King, M. 2017. *A Spirit of Charity: Restoring the Bond Between America and Its Public Hospitals*. Salisbury, MD: Secant Publishing.

Kirby, J. 2012. "Trust in the Age of Transparency." *Harvard Business Review* 89: 158–159.

Kirk, E., T. Nabatchi. 2015. *Collaborative Governance Regimes*. Washington, DC: Georgetown University Press.

Klein, G. 2015. *Ethics in Accounting: A Decision-Making Approach*. Oxford: Wiley.

Knapp, S. J., L. VandeCreek. 2012. *Practical Ethics for Psychologists: A Positive Approach*, 2nd ed. American Psychological Association.

Knecht, P. R., K. Bass. 2012. "Why Board Culture Matters. Interpersonal and Group Dynamics Can Affect the Entire Organization." *Trustee* 65 (5): 21–24.

Kockler, N. J., K. M. Dirksen. 2014. "Competencies Required for Clinical Ethics Consultation as Coaching." *Health Care Ethics USA* 23 (4) (Fall): 25–33.

Kockler, N. J., K. M. Dirksen. 2018. "Integrating Ethics Services in a Catholic Health System." *The National Catholic Bioethics Quarterly* 18 (1) (Spring): 113–134.

Kodish, E., et al. 2013. "Quality Attestation for Clinical Ethics Consultants. A Two-Step Model From the American Society for Bioethics and Humanities." *Hastings Center Report* 43 (5): 26–36.

Koepsell, D. 2017. *Scientific Integrity and Research Ethics*. New York: Springer.

Koocher, G. P., P. Keith-Spiegel. 2016. *Ethics in Psychology and the Mental Health Professions: Standards and Cases*, 4th ed. New York: Oxford University Press.

Kovner, A. R., et al., eds. 2009. *Evidence-Based Management in Healthcare*. Chicago, IL: Health Administration Press.

Kuhse, H., et al., eds. 2015. *Bioethics: An Anthology*, 3rd ed. Wiley-Blackwell.

Kutz, C. 2000. *Complicity: Ethics and Law for a Collective Age*. Cambridge: Cambridge University Press.

Laake, P., et al., eds. 2015. *Research in Medical and Biological Sciences*. London: Academic Press.

Ladikas, M., et al., eds. 2016. *Science and Technology Governance and Ethics: A Global Perspective from Europe, India and China*. Springer.

Lake, C. B. 2013. *Prophets of the Posthuman: American Fiction, Biotechnology, and the Ethics of Personhood*. Notre Dame, IN: University of Notre Dame Press.

La Puma, J., D. L. Schiedermayer. 1991. "Ethics Consultation: Skills, Roles and Training." *Annals of Internal Medicine* 112: 155–160.

Largent, E. A., et al. 2011. "Can Research and Care Be Ethically Integrated?" *Hastings Center Report* 41 (4): 37–46.

Lasker, R., the Committee on Medicine and Public Health. 1997 *Medicine and Public Health: The Power of Collaboration*. New York: New York Academy of Medicine.

Latino, R. J., et al. 2016. *Root Cause Analysis: Improving Performance for Bottom-Line Results*, 4th ed. CRC Press, Taylor & Francis.

Lawner, B. J., et al. 2012. *Avoiding Common Prehospital Errors*. Wolters Kluwer.

Lazarus, I. R. 2012. "On the Road to Find Out . . . Transparency and Just Culture Offer Significant Return on Investment." *Journal of Healthcare Management* 56 (4): 223–228.

Leach, M. M., et al., eds. 2012. *The Oxford Handbook of International Psychological Ethics*. New York: Oxford University Press.

Leape, L. L. 1994. "Error in Medicine." *Journal of the American Medical Association* 272: 1851–1857.

Leape, L. L. 2002. "Patient Safety: Reporting of Adverse Events." *New England Journal of Medicine* 347: 1633–1638.

Leape, L. L. 2006. *Disclosing Medical Errors: A Guide to an Effective Explanation and Apology*. Chicago, IL: Joint Commission Resources.

Leape, L. L. 2006. "Medical Errors and Patient Safety." In D. A. Shore, ed., *The Trust Crisis in Healthcare*. New York: Oxford University Press, 60–69.

Leape, L. L., et al. 1993. "Preventing Medical Injury." *Quality Review Bulletin* 19: 144–149.

Leape, L. L., et al. 1995. "Systems Analysis of Adverse Drug Events." *Journal of the American Medical Association* 274: 35–43.

Leape, L. L., et al. 1998. "Promoting Patient Safety by Preventing Medical Error." *Journal of the American Medical Association* 280: 1444–1447. www.leapfroggroup.org

Lebacqz, K., J. Driskall. 2000. *Ethics and Spiritual Care: A Guide for Pastors and Spiritual Directors*. Nashville, TN: Abingdon Press.

LeBlanc, R., ed. 2016. *The Handbook of Board Governance: Public, Private, and Not-for-Profit Board Members*. Wiley.

Lencioni, P. 2016. *The Ideal Team Player: How to Recognize and Cultivate the Three Essential Virtues*. San Francisco, CA: Jossey-Bass.

Lerman, L. G. 2016. *Ethical Problems in the Practice of Law*. Philadelphia, PA: Wolters Kluwer.

Lesandrini, J., A. Muster. 2018. "Practical Steps for Integrating an Ethics Program." *The National Catholic Bioethics Quarterly* 18 (1) (Spring): 39–47.

Leslie, M. B. 2010. "The Wisdom of Crowds? Groupthink and Nonprofit Governance." *Florida Law Review* 62: 1179–1226.

Lessig, L. 2013. "Institutional Corruption Defined." *Journal of Law, Medicine and Ethics* 41 (3): 553–545.

Letourneau, R. 2014. "Partnering for Better Population Health Management." *HealthLeaders* 17: 48–51.

Levinson, W., et al. 2016. "Disclosure of Medical Error." *JAMA Professional* (August 16): 764–765. https://doi.org/10.1001/jama.2016.9136.

Levitt, D. H., H. J. Moorhead, eds. 2013. *Values and Ethics in Counseling: Real-Life Ethical Decision Making*. United Kingdom: Routledge.

Lewis, M. A., C. D. Tamparo, B. M. Tatro. 2012. *Medical Law, Ethics & Bioethics, for the Health Professions*, 7th ed. Philadelphia, PA: Davis Company.

Light, D. W., A. F. Maturo. 2015. *Good Pharma: The Public Health Model*. Palgrave MacMillan.

Lloyd, R. 2017. *Quality Health Care: A Guide to Developing and Using Indicators*. Burlington, MA: Jones and Bartlett.

Lo, B. 2013. *Resolving Ethical Dilemmas: A Guide for Clinicians*, 5th ed. Baltimore, MD: Lippincott Williams & Wilkins.

Long, D. G., Z. Inbar. 2017. *The Ethical Kaleidoscope: Values, Ethics and Corporate Governance*. Routledge.

Lynch, H. F. 2010. *Conflicts of Conscience in Health Care: An Institutional Compromise*. Cambridge, MA: MIT Press.

Lyu, H., et al. 2017. "Overtreatment in the United States." *PLos One* 12 (9) (September 6). https://doi.org/10.1371/journal.pone.0181970.

Mack, K. E., et al. 2013. "The Search for Quality and Outcomes: Strategic Physician Alignment is Key to Improving Care While Reducing Costs." *Healthcare Executive* 28 (3): 86–88.

Mackiewicz, B. S. 2018. "Essential Goals of Ethics Committees and the Role of Professional Ethicists." *The National Catholic Bioethics Quarterly* 18 (1) (Spring): 49–57.

Magelssen, M., R. Pedersen, R. Førde. 2016. "Four Roles of Ethical Theory in Clinical Ethics Consultation." *American Journal of Bioethics* 16 (9): 26–33.

Magill, G., ed. 2004. *Genetics and Ethics: An Interdisciplinary Study*. Saint Louis, MO: Saint Louis University Press.

Magill, G. 2006. "Ethical and Policy Issues Related to Medical Error and Patient Safety." In S. A. M. McLean, ed., *First Do No Harm: Law, Ethics, and Healthcare*. London: Ashgate, Chapter 7, 101–116.

Magill, G. 2012. "A Moral Compass for Cooperation with Wrongdoing." In N. F. Cafardi, ed., *Voting: Catholic Perspectives on Political Participation*. New York: Paulist, 135–157.

Magill, G. 2013. "Quality in Ethics Consultation." *Medicine, Health Care and Philosophy* 16 (4): 761–774.

Magill, G. 2015. *Religious Morality in John Henry Newman: Hermeneutics of the Imagination*. New York: Springer.

Magill, G., ed. 2016. "Clinical Ethics: Accreditation." In H. ten Have, B. Gordijn, eds., *Encyclopedia of Global Bioethics*. New York: Springer.

Magill, G., eds. 2016. "Complicity." In H. ten Have, B. Gordijn, eds., *Encyclopedia of Global Bioethics*. New York: Springer.

Magill, G., eds. 2016. "Patient Safety." In H. ten Have, B. Gordijn, eds., *Encyclopedia of Global Bioethics*. New York: Springer.

Magill, G. 2017. "Complicity of Catholic Healthcare Institutions with Immoral Laws." In J. T. Eberl, ed., *Contemporary Controversies in Catholic Bioethics.* Section VII: Health-care Law and Policy. New York: Springer, 523–536.

Magill, G., L. Prybil. 2001. "Guidelines for Organizational Ethics." *Health Progress* (July–August): 12–14.

Magill, G., L. Prybil. 2004. "Stewardship and Integrity in Health Care: A Role for Organizational Ethics." *Journal of Business Ethics* 50: 225–238.

Magill, G., L. Prybil. 2011. "Board Oversight of Community Benefit: A Moral Imperative." *Kennedy Institute of Ethics Journal* 21 (1): 25–50.

Magnus, D. 2016. "Finding the Right Tools for Assessing Quality in Clinical Ethics Consultation." *American Journal of Bioethics* 16 (3): 1–2.

Makary, M. 2013. *Unaccountable: What Hospitals Won't Tell You and How Transparency Can Revolutionize Healthcare.* New York: Bloomberg Press.

Makely, S. 2012. *Professionalism in Health Care: A Primer for Career Success,* 4th ed. Pearson.

Makely, S., S. Badasch, D. Chesebro. 2013. *Becoming a Health Care Professional.* Pearson.

Mallin, A. 2016. *Corporate Governance,* 5th ed. New York: Oxford University Press.

Mannion, R., et al. 2017. "Do Hospital Boards Matter for Better, Safer, Patient Care?" *Social Science & Medicine* 177 (March): 278–287.

Manz, C. C., et al., eds. 2008. *The Virtuous Organization: Insights from Some of World's Leading Management Thinkers.* Singapore: World Scientific Publishing Co.

Marchant, G. E. 2016. *Emerging Technologies: Ethics, Law and Governance.* Ashgate.

Marcucci, C., et al., eds. 2007. *Avoiding Common Anesthesia Errors.* Philadelphia, PA: Wolters Kluwer.

Marsha, D. M. 2015. *Guide to the Code of Ethics for Nurses: Interpretation and Application.* American Nurses Association.

Marshall, D. 2010. *Crew Resource Management: From Patient Safety to High Reliability.* Littleton, CO: SaferHealthcare.

Martin, C., W. Vaught, R. S. Solomon. 2009. *Ethics Across the Professions: A Reader for Professional Ethics.* New York: Oxford University Press.

Martin, M. L. et al., eds. 2018. *Diversity and Inclusion in Quality Patient Care: A Case-Based Compendium.* New York: Springer.

Martin, M. W. 2000. *Meaningful Work: Rethinking Professional Ethics.* New York: Oxford University Press.

Mascalzoni, D., ed. 2016. *Ethics, Law and Governance of Biobanking.* Springer.

Mason, D. J., et al. 2012. "The Representation of Health Professionals on Governing Boards of Healthcare Organizations in New York City." *Journal of Urban Health* 90 (5): 888–901.

May, T. 2001. "The Breadth of Bioethics: Core Areas of Bioethics Education for Hospital Ethics Committees." *Journal of Medicine and Philosophy* 26: 101–118.

Mayer, L. H. 2016. "The Rising of the States in Nonprofit Oversight." *Nonprofit Quarterly.* https://nonprofitquarterly.org/rising-states-nonprofit-oversight/.

Mays, G., F. D. Scutchfield. 2010. "Improving Public Health System Performance Through Multiorganizational Partnerships." *Preventing Chronic Disease* 7 (6): 1–8.

Mazor, K. M., et al. 2004. "Communicating With Patients About Medical Errors: A Review of the Literature." *Archives of Internal Medicine* 164 (15): 1690–1697.

McBride, K., T. Rosentiel. 2013. *The New Ethics of Journalism: Principles for the 21st Century.* CQ Press.

McClimans, L., et al. 2012. "Can UK Clinical Ethics Committees Improve Quality of Care?" *HEC Forum* 24 (2): 139–47.

McCruden, P. 2012. "The Affordable Care Act and Community Benefit: A Mandate Catholic Health Care Can (Partly) Embrace." *Kennedy Institute of Ethics Journal* 23 (3): 229–248.

McDonagh, K., L. Prybil, L., M. Totten. 2013. "Leadership Succession Planning: A Governance Imperative." *Trustee* 66 (April): 15–18.

McDonald, C. J., et al. 2000. "Deaths Due to Medical Errors Are Exaggerated in Institute of Medicine Report." *Journal of the American Medical Association* 284: 93–95.

McDonald, P. A., et al. 2015. "The Employer-led Health Care Revolution." *Harvard Business Review* 93: 39–50.

McDonough, M. J. 2007. *Can A Healthcare Market Be Moral?* Washington, DC: Georgetown University Press.

McGee, G., et al. 2002. "Successes and Failures of Hospital Ethics Committees: A National Survey of Ethics Committee Chairs." *Cambridge Quarterly of Healthcare Ethics* 11 (2): 87–93.

McGuire, J. 2016. *Population Health Investments by Health Plans and Large Provider Organizations: Exploring the Business Case.* Boston, MA: Northeastern University.

McIntyre, A. 2003. *After Virtue: A Study in Moral Theory*, 3rd ed. Notre Dame, IN: University of Notre Dame Press.

McIver, S., R. Wyndham. 2013. *After the Error: Speaking out About Patient Safety to Save Lives.* Toronto: ECW Press.

McLean, S. A. M. ed. 2006. *First Do No Harm: Law, Ethics, and Healthcare.* London: Ashgate.

McNeil, B. J. 2001. "Shattuck Lecture: Hidden Barriers to Improvement in the Quality of Care." *New England Journal of Medicine* 345 (22): 1612–1620.

McSherry, R., P. Pearce. 2007. *Clinical Governance: A Guide to Implementation for Healthcare Professionals*, 2nd ed. London: Blackwell Publishing.

McWay, D. C. 2014. *Legal and Ethical Aspects of Health Information Management*, 4th ed. Clifton Park, NY: Cengage Learning.

Mead, J. 2008. "Confidence in the Non-Profit Sector Through Sarbanes-Oxley Style Reforms." *Michigan Law Review* 106: 881–900.

Meilander, C. C. 2017. *The Theory and Practice of Virtue.* Notre Dame, IN: University of Notre Dame Press.

Meyers, C. ed. 2010. *Journalism Ethics: A Philosophical Approach.* New York: Oxford University Press.

Micklethwait, A., P. Dimond. 2017. *Driven to the Brink: Why Corporate Governance, Board Leadership and Culture Matter.* United Kingdom: Palgrave MacMillan.

Miller, F. J., R. D. Truog. 2016. *Death, Dying, and Organ Transplantation: Reconstructing Medical Ethics at the End of Life.* New York: Oxford University Press.

Miller, L. B. 2001. *Boards Under Fire: Are Not-for-Profit Institutions Being Held to a New Standard of Accountability.* Washington, DC: Volunteer Trustee Foundation and the Governance Institute.

Miller, R., et al. 2015. "Hospital Board Oversight of Quality and Safety: A Stakeholder Analysis." *BMC Health Services Research* 15 (June 16): 196. https://doi.org/10.1186/s12913-015-0771-x.

Miller, T., M. Triana. 2009. "Demographic Diversity in the Boardroom: Mediators of the Board Diversity: Firm Performance Relationship." *Journal of Management Studies* 46 (5): 755–786.

Minich, L., et al. 2006. "Can Community Change Be Measured for Outcome-Based Initiative?" *American Journal of Community Psychology* 38: 182–190.

Mitchell, C. B., D. J. Riley. 2014. *Christian Bioethics: A Guide for Pastors, Health Care Professionals, and Families*. Nashville, TN: B & H Academics.

Mitchell, L. E., ed. 2018. *Corporate Governance: Values, Ethics and Leadership*. United Kingdom: Routledge.

Mittelstadt, B., L. Floridi, eds. 2016. *The Ethics of Biomedical Data*. Springer.

Moeller, J. R., et al. 2012. "Functions and Outcomes of a Clinical Medical Ethics Committee: A Review of 100 Consults." *HEC Forum* 24(2) (June): 99–114.

Moini, J. 2013. *Law and Ethics for Pharmacy Technicians*. Stamford, CT: Cengage Learning.

Moliterno, J. E. 2016. *Crunch Time: Professional Responsibility*, 5th ed. Philadelphia, PA: Wolters Kluwer.

Moore, G. 2017. *Virtue at Work: Ethics for Individuals, Managers, and Organizations*. New York: Oxford University Press.

Moreno, J. D. 1995. *Deciding Together: Bioethics and Moral Consensus*. New York: Oxford University Press.

Morgan, T., R. Rotunda, J. Dzienkowski. 2014. *Professional Responsibility*, 12th ed. Foundation Press.

Morreim, E. H. 2011. *Holding Healthcare Accountable*. New York: Oxford University Press. 2011.

Morrison, E. E. 2015. *Ethics in Health Administration: A Practical Approach for Decision Makers*, 3rd ed. Jones & Bartlett.

Morrissey, J. 2003. "Quality vs. Quantity. IOM Report: Hospitals Must Cut Back Workload and Hours of Nurses to Maintain Patient Safety." *Modern Healthcare* 8: 11.

Munson, R. 2011. *Intervention and Reflection: Basic Issues in Medical Ethics*, 9th ed. Belmont, CA: Wadsworth.

Murphy, M. J. 2016. *Ethics and Professional Issues in Couple and Family Therapy*, 2nd ed. Routledge.

Murphy, P. 2017. *Biotechnology, Education and Life Politics*. Routledge.

Murray, C., A. Lopez. 2013. "Measuring the Global Burden of Disease." *New England Journal of Medicine* 369: 448–457.

Murray, E. 2017. *Nursing Leadership and Management for Patient Safety and Quality Care*. Philadelphia, PA: F. A. Davis Company.

Nagy, T. F. 2010. *Essential Ethics for Psychologists*. American Psychological Association.

Nash, D. B., et al., eds. 2008. *Governance for Healthcare Providers: The Call to Leadership*. New York: Taylor & Francis.

National Academies of Science, Engineering, and Medicine. 2013. *Toward Quality Measures for Population Health and the Leading Health Indicators*. Washington, DC: The National Academies Press.

National Academies of Science, Engineering, and Medicine. 2015. *Vital Signs: Core Metrics for Health and Health Care Progress*. Washington, DC: The National Academies Press.

National Academies of Science, Engineering, and Medicine. 2017. *Human Gene Editing: Science, Ethics, and Governance*. Washington, DC: The National Academies Press.

National Academies of Science, Engineering, and Medicine. 2019. *Criteria for Selecting the Leading Health Indicators for Healthy People 2030*. Washington, DC: The National Academies Press.

National Association for Healthcare Quality (NAHQ). 2012. *Call to Action: Safeguarding the Integrity of Healthcare Quality and Safety Systems*. Washington, DC: NAHQ.

National Association of Corporate Directors (NACD). 2011. *NACD Public Company Governance Survey*. Washington, DC: National Association of Corporate Directors.

National Association of Corporate Directors (NACD). 2012. *Governance Challenges: 2012 and Beyond*. Washington, DC: NACD.

National Association of Corporate Directors. 2019. *2018–2019 NACD Public Company Governance Survey*. www.nacdonline.org/analytics/survey.cfm?ItemNumber=63801.

National Association of Corporate Directors. 2019. *NACD Directorship 2020: Dynamics and Culture in the Boardroom*. www.nacdonline.org/insights/publications.cfm?Item Number=8838.

National Association of Social Workers. 2015. *Code of Ethics*. NASW Press.

National Center for Ethics in Health Care. 2015. *Ethics Consultation: Responding to Ethics Questions in Health Care*, 2nd ed. Washington, DC: U.S. Department of Veterans Affairs.

National Coalition on Healthcare and the Institute for Healthcare Improvement. 2000. *Reducing Medical Errors and Improving Patient Safety*. Washington, DC: National Coalition on Healthcare, 1–31.

National Council of Nonprofits. 2019. *Finding the Right Board Member for Your Nonprofit*. www.councilofnonprofits.org/tools-resources/finding-the-right-board-members-your-nonprofit.

National Quality Forum. 2008. *Aligning Our Efforts to Transform America's Healthcare: National Priorities and Goals*. Washington, DC: National Quality Forum.

National Quality Forum. 2016. *Improving Population Health by Working with Communities*. Washington, DC: National Quality Forum.

National Quality Forum. 2016. *Multistakeholder Input on a National Priority: Improving Population Health by Working with Communities*. Washington, DC: National Quality Forum.

National Research Council. 1997. *Aviation Safety and Pilot Control: Understanding and Preventing Unfavorable Pilot/Vehicle Interactions*. National Academies Press.

NEJM Catalyst. 2018. *Taking Healthcare Governance to the Next Level*. https://catalyst.nejm.org/healthcare-governance-next-level-quality-committee/.

Nelson, G., et al. 2014. *Hospital Community Benefits after the ACA: Addressing Social and Economic Factors that Shape Health*. Baltimore, MD: The Hilltop Institute.

Nelson, W. A. 2008. "Addressing Organizational Ethics." *Healthcare Executive* 23 (2): 43–44.

Nelson, W. A. 2010. "Comparing Ethics and Compliance Programs." *Healthcare Executive* 27 (4): 46–49.

Nelson, W. A. 2011. "Ethics: A Foundation for Quality." *Healthcare Executive* 26 (6): 46–49.

Nelson, W. A., J. Donnellan. 2009. "An Executive-Driven Ethical Culture." *Healthcare Executive* 24 (6): 44–46.

Nelson, W. A., P. B. Hofmann. 2015. *Managing Healthcare Ethically: An Executive's Guide*, 2nd ed. Chicago, IL: Health Administration Press.

New York State Department of Health. 2014. *Community Health Report*. www.health.ny.gov/prevention/prevention_agenda/2013-2017.

Nimita, L., I. B. Carol. 2014. "The Modern Social Contract between the Patient, the Healthcare Provider, and Digital Medicine." *Journal of Socialomics* 3: 1. https://doi.org/10.4172/2167-0358.1000105.

Noble, A. A., T. A. Brennan. 2001. "Managing Care in the Era of Systems-Think: Organizational Liability and Patient Safety." *Journal of Law, Medicine, & Ethics* 29: 290–304.

Nollkaemper, A., I. Plakokefalos, eds. 2017. *The Practice of Shared Responsibility in International Law*. New York: Cambridge University Press.

Norris, T., T. Howard. 2015. *Can Hospitals Heal America's Communities?* Cleveland, OH: Democracy Collaborative.

Nunnery, R. K. 2015. *Advancing Your Career: Concepts in Professional Nursing.* Philadelphia, PA: David Company.

Nygren, D. 2013. "Competitors as Collaborators." *Trustee* 66: 13–27.

O'Brien, J., ed. 2005. *Governing the Corporation: Regulation and Corporate Governance in an Age of Scandal and Global Markets.* John Wiley & Sons.

O'Connor, M. A. 2003. "The Enron Board: The Perils of Groupthink." *University of Cincinnati Law Review* 71: 1233–1320.

Okes, D. 2019. *Root Cause Analysis: The Core Problem of Solving and Corrective Action.* Milwaukee, WI: ASQ Quality Press.

Oliva, J., M. Totten. 2007. *A Seat at the Power Table: The Physician's Role on the Hospital Board.* Chicago, IL: Center for Healthcare Governance.

Olsen, L. et al., eds. 2007. *The Learning Healthcare System: Workshop Summary.* Washington, DC: National Academies Press.

Oneview. 2015. *Principles of Patient-Centered Care.* www.oneviewhealthcare.com/the-eight-principles-of-patient-centered-care.

Orlik, D. K. 2013. *Ethics for the Legal Profession,* 8th ed. Pearson.

Orr, R. D., et al. 1996. "Evaluation of An Ethics Consultation Service: Patient and Family Perspective." *American Journal of Medicine* 101: 135–141.

Oster, C., J. Braaten. 2016. *High Reliability Organizations: A Healthcare Handbook for Patient Safety and Quality.* Nursing Knowledge.

Ozar, D. T., D. S. Sokol. 2002. *Dental Ethics at Chairside: Professional Principles and Practical Applications,* 2nd ed. Washington, DC: Georgetown University Press.

Page, A. 2009. "Unconscious Bias and the Limits of Director Independence." *University of Illinois Law Review* 1: 237–294.

Parsons, P. J. 2016. *Ethics in Public Relations: A Guide to Best Practice,* 3rd. ed. Philadelphia, PA: Kogan Page.

Parsons, R. D. 2000. *The Ethics of Professional Practice.* Pearson.

Patient Protection and Affordable Care Act. 2010. *H. R. 3590.* www.congress.gov/bill/111th-congress/house-bill/3590.

Patient Safety Network. 2016. *Health Care Data Science for Quality Improvement and Patient Safety* (October). https://psnet.ahrq.gov/perspectives/perspective/208/health-care-data-science-for-quality-improvement-and-patient-safety.

Patient Safety Network. 2019. *Culture of Safety* (January). https://psnet.ahrq.gov/primers/primer/5/Culture-of-Safety.

Patterson, P., L. Wilkins. 2013. *Media Ethics: Issues & Cases.* McGraw-Hill.

Pearce, R., et al. 2013. *Professional Responsibility: A Contemporary Approach,* 2nd ed. West Academic Publishing.

Pearl, S. 2017. *Face/On: Face Transplants and the Ethics of the Other.* Chicago, IL: University of Chicago Press.

Pearlman, R. A., et al. 2016. "Ethics Consultation Quality Assessment Tool." *American Journal of Bioethics* 16 (3): 3–14.

Pearson, S. D., et al. 2003. *No Margin, No Mission: Health-Care Organizations and the Quest for Ethical Excellence.* New York: Oxford University Press.

Peck, L. E., G. S. Reel, eds. 2016. *Media Ethics at Work: True Stories from Young Professionals,* 2nd ed. CQ Press.

Pederson, K. Z. 2017. *Organizing Patient Safety.* United Kingdom: Palgrave MacMillan.

Peirce, A. G., J. Smith, eds. 2013. *Ethical and Legal Issues for Doctoral Nursing Students.* Lancaster, PA: Destech Publications.

Peisert, K. 2013. *Governing the Value Journey: A Profile of Structure, Culture, and Practices of Boards in Transition*. San Diego, CA: The Governance Institute.

Pellegrino, E. D., D. C. Thomasma. 1993. *The Virtues in Medical Practice*. New York: Oxford University Press.

Pellegrino, E. D., R. M. Veatch, J. P. Langan, eds. 2001. *Ethics, Trust, and the Professions: Philosophical and Cultural Aspects*. Washington, DC: Georgetown University Press.

Pence, G. E. 2014. *Medical Ethics: Accounts of Ground-Breaking Cases*, 7th ed. McGraw-Hill.

Perry, F., ed. 2014. *Ethics and Management Dilemmas in Healthcare*. Chicago, IL: Health Administration Press.

Pestonik, S., V. Lemon. 2019. "How to Use Data to Improve Quality and Patient Safety." *HealthCatalyst* (April 30). www.healthcatalyst.com/insights/use-data-improve-patient-safety/.

Pestronk, R., et al. 2013. "Public Health's Role: Collaborating for Healthy Communities." *Health Progress* 94: 21–25.

Peterson-Kaiser. 2019. *Health Care Tracker, How Does Health Spending in the US Compare to Other Countries?* www.healthsystemtracker.org/chart-collection/health-spending-u-s-compare-countries/#item-start.

Petryana, A., A. Lakoff, A. Kleinman, eds. 2006. *Global Pharmaceuticals: Ethics, Markets, Practices*. Duke University Press.

Plaisance, P. L. 2013. *Media Ethics: Key Principles for Responsible Practice*, 2nd ed. Sage.

Pollock, J. M. 2013. *Ethical Dilemmas and Decisions in Criminal Justice*, 8th ed. Boston, MA: Cengage Learning.

Pope John Paul II. 1995. *The Gospel of Life*. Rome: Vatican City.

Pope, K. S., M. J. T. Vasquez. 2016. *Ethics in Psychotherapy and Counseling: A Practical Guide*, 5th ed. Oxford: Wiley.

Porterfield, R., et al. 2015. "Measuring Public Health Practice and Outcomes in Chronic Disease: A Call for Coordination." *American Journal of Public Health* 105 (Suppl. 2): S180–S188.

Post, L. F., J. Blustein. 2015. *Handbook for Health Care Ethics Committees*, 2nd ed. Baltimore, MD: Johns Hopkins University Press.

Pozen, R. 2010. "The Case for Professional Boards." *Harvard Business Review* 88: 51–58.

Pozgar, G. D. 2014. *Legal and Ethical Issues for Health Professionals*, 4th ed. Jones & Bartlett.

Prybil, L. 2007. "Nursing Involvement in Hospital Governance." *Journal of Nursing Care Quality* 22 (1): 1–3.

Prybil, L. 2008. "What's Your Board's Culture." *Trustee* 61 (6): 16–24.

Prybil, L. 2009. "Engaging Nurses in Governing Hospitals and Health Systems." *Journal of Nursing Care Quality* 24 (1): 5–9.

Prybil, L. 2013. "Nurses in Health Care Governance: Is the Picture Changing?" *Journal of Nursing Care Quality* 28 (2): 103–107.

Prybil, L. 2016. "Nursing Engagement in Governing Health Care Organizations: Past, Present, and Future." *Journal of Nursing Care Quality* 31 (4): 299–303.

Prybil, L. 2017. *The Leadership Role of Nonprofit Health Systems in Improving Community Health*. Advances in Healthcare Governance Series. Chicago, IL: American Hospital Association.

Prybil, L., et al. 2005. *Governance in High-Performing Organizations: A Comparative Study of Governing Boards in Not-for-Profit Hospitals*. Chicago, IL: Health Research and Educational Trust.

Prybil, L., et al. 2008. *Governance in Nonprofit Community Health Systems: An Initial Report on CEO Perspectives*. Chicago, IL: Grant Thornton LLP.

Prybil, L., et al. 2009. *Governance in High-Performing Community Health Systems: A Report on Trustee and CEO Views*. Chicago, IL: Grant Thornton LLP.

Prybil, L., et al. 2009. *Governance in High-Performing Organizations: A Comparative Study of Governing Boards in Not-for-Profit Hospitals*. Chicago, IL: Health Research and Educational Trust.

Prybil, L., et al. 2009. "Transforming CEO Evaluation in a Multi-Unit Organization." In A. R. Kovner et al., eds., *Evidence-Based Management in Healthcare*. Chicago, IL: Health Administration Press, 153–159.

Prybil, L., et al. 2012. "Board Oversight of Patient Care in Community Health Systems." *American Journal of Medical Quality* 25 (1): 34–41.

Prybil, L., et al. 2012. *Governance in Large Nonprofit Health Systems: Current Profile and Emerging Patterns*. Lexington, KY: Commonwealth Center for Governance Studies, Inc.

Prybil, L., et al. 2013. *The Evolving Accountability of Nonprofit Health System Boards*. Chicago, IL: American Hospital Association, Center for Healthcare Governance.

Prybil, L., et al. 2014. "Board Oversight of Patient Care Quality in Large Nonprofit Health Systems." *American Journal of Medical Quality* 29 (1): 39–43.

Prybil, L., et al. 2014. *Improving Community Health Through Hospital–Public Health Collaboration: Insights and Lessons Learned from Successful Partnerships*. Lexington, KY: Commonwealth Center for Governance Studies, Inc.

Prybil, L., et al. 2014. "Nurses on Boards: The Time Has Come." *Nurse Leader* 12 (4): 48–52.

Prybil, L., et al. 2015. *A Perspective on Public–Private Collaboration in the Health Sector*. Washington, DC: National Academy of Medicine.

Prybil, L., et al. 2016. "The Evolution of Public Health–Hospital Collaboration in the United States." *Public Health Reports* 131 (July–August): 522–525.

Prybil, L., et al. 2019. "Building the Case for Including Nurse Leaders on Healthcare Organization Boards." *Nursing Economics* 37 (4) (July): 169–197.

Prybil, L., et al. 2019. "Involving Nurse Leaders in Governance Roles." *BoardRoom Press* 30 (4): 4 and 14.

Prybil, L., J. Benton. 2009. "Community Benefit: The Nonprofit Community Health Perspective." In D. B. Nash et al., eds., *Governance for Healthcare Providers: The Call to Leadership*. Boca Raton, FL: CRC Press, Taylor and Francis Group, 267–283.

Prybil, L., R. Killian. 2013. "Community Benefit Needs Board Oversight." *Health Progress* 94 (July–August): 90–94.

Prybil, L., M. Totten. 2016. "Better Community Health: Hospital, Health System Boards Need to Find, Work with Multiple Partners to Achieve Their Goals." *Trustee* 69 (March): 26–27.

Public Health Accreditation Board. 2013. *Standards: An Overview*. www.phaboard.org/wp-content/uploads/2019/01/PHAB-Standards-Overview-Version-1.5.pdf.

Public Health Accreditation Board. 2019. *Standards and Measures for Initial Accreditation*. www.phaboard.org/standards-and-measures-for-initial-accreditation/.

Public Health Institute. 2004. *Advancing the State of the Art of Community Benefit*. Oakland, CA: Public Health institute.

Purtilo, R. 2005. *Ethical Dimensions in the Health Professions*, 4th ed. Philadelphia, PA: Elsevier.

Purtilo, R., et al. 2014. *Health Professional and Patient Interaction*, 8th ed. St. Louis, MO: Elsevier.

Quick, O. 2017. *Regulating Patient Safety*. New York: Cambridge University Press.

Quinn, J. F. 2002. "Revisioning the Nursing Shortage: A Call to Caring for Healing the Healthcare System." *Frontiers of Health Services Management* 19 (2): 3–21.

Quinn, M. J. 2014. *Ethics for the Information Age*, 6th ed. Pearson.

Radley, D., et al. 2016. *Rising to the Challenge: The Commonwealth Fund Scoreboard on Local Health System Performance*. New York: The Commonwealth Fund.

Rajan, K. S., ed. 2012. *Lively Capital: Biotechnologies, Ethics, and Governance in Global Markets*. Durham, NC: Duke University Press.

Ransome, W., C. Sampford. 2016. *Ethics and Socially Responsible Investment*. Routledge.

Rao, K. V., G. N, Raju. 2017. *Business Ethics and Corporate Governance*. New Delhi: International Publishing House.

Rapoport, N. B., B. G. Dharan, eds. 2004. *Enron: Corporate Fiascos and Their Implications*. New York: Foundation Press.

Rasche, A., et al., eds. 2017. *Corporate Social Responsibility: Strategy, Communication, Governance*. New York: Cambridge University Press.

Ratzinger, Cardinal J. 2004. "Worthiness to Receive Holy Communion." *The Wanderer Press* 137: 29.

Reamer, F. G. 2006. *Ethical Standards in Social Work: A Review of the NASW Code of Ethics*. NASW Press.

Reamer, F. G. 2013. *Social Work Values and Ethics*, 4th ed. New York: Columbia University Press.

Reason, J. T. 1990. *Human Error*. Cambridge: Cambridge University Press.

Reason, J. T. 1997. *Managing the Risk of Organizational Accidents*. Aldershot: Ashgate.

Rebore, R. W. 2013. *The Ethics of Educational Leadership*, 3rd ed. Pearson.

Reinersten, J. L. 2007. *Hospital Boards and Clinical Quality: A Practical Guide*. Toronto, ON: Ontario Hospital Association.

Remley, T. P., B. P. Herlihy. 2015. *Ethical, Legal, and Professional Issues in Counseling*, 5th ed. Pearson.

Rendtorff, J. D. 2017. *Perspectives on Philosophy of Management and Business Ethics*. Springer.

Repenshek, M. 2018. "Examining Quality and Value in Ethics Consultation Services." *The National Catholic Bioethics Quarterly* 18 (1) (Spring): 59–68.

Resnick, D. 2003. "The Jesica Santillan Tragedy: Lessons Learned." *Hastings Center Report* 33 (4): 12–20.

Resnick, J. 2014. "Leading the Way to Population Health." *Hospitals and Health Network* 88.

Reyes, M. G., ed. 2011. *Nonprofit Hospitals and the Community Benefit Standard*. Hauppauga, NY: Nova Science Publications.

Reynolds, G. 2014. *Ethics in Information Technology*, 5th ed. Cengage.

Rhonheimer, M. 2011. *The Perspective of Morality: Philosophical Foundations of Thomistic Virtue Ethics*. Washington, DC: Catholic University Press of America.

Ritvo, R. A., et al. 2004. *Ethical Governance in Healthcare: A Board Leadership Guide for Building an Ethical Culture*. Chicago, IL: Health Forum, Inc.

Rivkin, S., F. Seitel. 2011. *Transparency: How Much of a Good Thing?* Chicago, IL: Center for Healthcare Governance.

Roberson, C., S. Mire. 2009. *Ethics for Criminal Justice Professionals*. CRC Press.

Robert Wood Johnson. 2014. *Building a Culture of Health: 2014 President's Message*. Princeton, NJ: Robert Wood Johnson Foundation.

Robert Wood Johnson Foundation. 2015. *From Vision to Action: A Framework and Measures to Mobilize a Culture of Health*. Princeton, NJ: Robert Wood Johnson Foundation.

Roberts, L. W. 2016. *A Clinical Guide to Psychiatric Ethics*. American Psychiatric Publishing.

Roberts, L. W., C. Geppert, eds. 2008. *The Book of Ethics: Expert Guidance for professionals Who Treat Addiction*. Center City, MN: Hazelden Publishing.

Rodwin, M. A. 2011. *Conflicts of Interest and the Future of Medicine*. New York: Oxford University Press.

Rosenbaum, S., et al. 2015. "The Value of the Nonprofit Hospital Tax Exemption." *Health Affairs* 34: 1–9.

Rosiek-Kryszweska, A., ed. 2017. *Healthcare Administration for Patient Safety and Engagement*. Medical Information Science References.

Rothman, J. C. 2013. *From the Front Lines: Student Cases in Social Work Ethics*, 4th ed. Pearson.

Rowan, R. R., S. Zinaich. 2002. *Ethics for the Professions*. Wadsworth Thomson Learning.

Rubin, D. B., et al. 2015. "Tax-Exempt Hospitals and Community Benefit: New Directions in Policy and Practice." *Annual Review of Public Health* 36 (1): 545–557.

Rubin, S. B., L. Zoloth, eds. 2000. *Margin of Error: The Ethics of Mistakes in the Practice of Medicine*. Hagerstown, MD: University Publishing Group.

Rudnick, A., et al. 2014. "Informal Ethics Consultations in Academic Health Care Settings: A Quantitative Description and a Qualitative Analysis With a Focus on Patient Participation." *Clinical Ethics* 9 (1) (March): 28–25.

Rudolf, L., J. Caplan. 2014. *Health in All Policies: A Guide to State and Local Government*. Oakland, CA: Public Health Institute.

Ruger, J. P. 2010. *Health and Social Justice*. New York: Oxford University Press.

Russell, D. C. 2013. *The Cambridge Companion to Virtue Ethics*. New York: Cambridge University Press.

Sage, W. M. 2003. "Medical Liability and Patient Safety." *Health Affairs* 22 (4): 26–36.

Salas, E., K. Frush, eds. 2013. *Improving Patient Safety Through Teamwork and Team Training*. New York: Oxford University Press.

Salcines, J. L. P., K. Babiak, G. Walters, eds. 2015. *Routledge Handbook of Sport and Corporate Social Responsibility*. Routledge Handbooks.

Salek, S., A. Edgar, eds. 2008. *Pharmaceutical Ethics*. Wiley.

Sanford, J. J. 2019. *Before Virtue: Assessing Contemporary Virtue Ethics*. Washington, DC: Catholic University Press of America.

Santoro, M. A., T. M. Gorrie. 2007. *Ethics and the Pharmaceutical Industry*. New York: Cambridge University Press.

Sarbanes-Oxley Act. 2008. *The Public Company Accounting Reform and Investor Protection Act*. www.soxlaw.com.

Sarra, J., ed. 2005. *Corporate Governance in Global Capital Markets*. British Columbia, Canada: University of British Columbia Press.

Sasso, P. 2003. "Searching for Trust in the Not-for-Profit Boardroom: Looking Beyond Duty of Obedience to Ensure Accountability." *UCLA Law Review* 50: 6.

Schildmann, J., et al., eds. 2016. *Clinical Ethics Consultation: Theories and Methods, Implementation, Evaluation*. New York: Routledge, 2016.

Schlesinger, M., B. Gray. 2006. "How Nonprofits Matter in American Medicine, and What To Do About It." *Health Affairs* 25: 287–303.

Schneider, R. C. 2008. *Ethics of Sports and Athletics: Theory, Issues, and Application*. Philadelphia, PA: Walters Kluwer.

Schulz, R. 2015. *A New Model for Private Sector Partnerships to Improve Economic Well-being and Community Outcomes*. Washington, DC: Institute of Medicine.

Scott, R. W. 2008. *Promoting Legal and Ethical Awareness: A Primer for Health Professionals*. Mosby.

Scott, W. E. 2006. "Current Ethical Thinking in Anaesthesia and Intensive Care." Special Issue of *Best Practice & Research Clinical Anaesthesiology* 20 (4): 493–506.

Scutchfield, F. D., L. Prybil, et al. 2016. "Public Health and Hospitals: Lessons Learned From Partnerships in a Changing Healthcare Environment." *American Journal of Public Health* 106 (January): 45–48.

Scutchfield, F. D., L. Prybil, R. Dixon. 2017. "Entering a New Era in Hospital and Public Health Collaboration for Community Benefit." In R. Bialek, L. Beitsch, J. Moran, eds., *Solving Population Health Through Collaboration*. Routledge, Chapter 25.

Seifi, S., D. Crowther, eds. 2018. *Stakeholders, Governance and Responsibility*. United Kingdom: Emerald Publishing.

Self, D. J., et al. 1993. "A Comparison of the Moral Reasoning of Physicians and Clinical Medical Ethicists." *Academic Medicine* 68: 840–855.

Senthil, K., et al. 2015. "Preserving the Social Contract in Health Care: A Call to Action." *American Journal of Public Health* 105 (12): 2404.

Shapiro, J. P., J. A. Stefkovich, 2010. *Ethical Leadership and Decision Making in Education*, 3rd ed. Routledge.

Sharp, B. S., G. Aguirre, K. Kicklam. 2010. *Managing in the Public Sector: A Casebook in Ethics and Leadership*. Routledge.

Sharpe, V. A., A. I. Faden. 1998. *Medical Harm: Historical, Conceptual, and Ethical Dimensions of Iatrogenic Illness*. New York: Cambridge University Press, 1–14.

Shaw, W. H. 2016. *Business Ethics: A Textbook with Cases*, 9th ed. Boston, MA: Cengage Learning.

Shelton, W., B. D. White. 2016. "The Process to Accredit Clinical Ethics Fellowship Programs Should Start Now." *American Journal of Bioethics* 16 (3): 28–30.

Shore, D. A. 2007. *The Trust Crisis in Healthcare: Causes, Consequences, and Cures*. New York: Oxford University Press.

Sidebottom, A. C., et al. 2018. "Assessing the Impact of the Health of New Ulm Project on Cardiovascular Risk Factors: A Population-Based Program to Reduce Cardiovascular Disease." *Preventive Medicine* 112 (July): 216–221.

Silverman, H. J., E. Bellavance, B. H. Childs. 2013. "Ensuring Quality in Clinical Ethics Consultations: Perspectives of Ethicists Regarding Process and Prior Training of Consultants." *American Journal of Bioethics* 13 (2): 29–31.

Singh, S. R., et al. 2015. "Analysis of Hospital Community Benefit Expenditures' Alignment with Community Health Needs: Evidence from a National Investigation of Tax-Exempt Hospitals." *American Journal of Public Health* 105 (5): 914–921.

Singh, S. R., et al. 2015. "Hospital Community Benefit in the Context of the Larger Public Health System: A State-Level Analysis of Hospital and Governmental Public health Spending Across the United States." *Journal of Public Health management and Practice* 22 (2): 164–174.

Sipe, J. W., D. M. Frick. 2015. *Seven Pillars of Servant Leadership*. Mahwah, NJ: Paulist Press.

Sison, A., et al., eds. 2017. *Handbook on Virtue Ethics in Business and Management*. New York: Springer.

Slote, M., L. Besser, eds. 2018. *The Routledge Companion to Virtue Ethics*. United Kingdom: Routledge.

Slowther, A., et al. 2012. "Development of Clinical Ethics Services in the UK: A National Survey." *Journal of Medical Ethics* 38 (4): 210–224.

Sokol, D. K. 2012. *Doing Clinical Ethics: A Hands-on Guide for Clinicians and Others.* Dordrecht and New York: Springer.

Sondheim, S. E., et al. 2017. "Governance Practices in an Era of Healthcare Transformation." *Journal of Healthcare Management* 62 (5): 316–326.

Soto, M. 2013. *Population Health in the Accountable Care Era.* Washington, DC: Academy Health.

Souryai, S. S. 2014. *Ethics in Criminal Justice: In Search of the Truth,* 6th ed. Routledge.

Sox, H. 2013. "Resolving the Tension Between Population and Individual Health." *Journal of the American Medical Association* 310: 1933–1934.

Spears, L., ed. 1998. *Insights on Leadership: Service, Stewardship, Spirit, and Servant Leadership.* New York: John Wiley and Sons, Inc.

Spencer, E. M., et al. 2000. *Organization Ethics in Health Care.* New York: Oxford University Press.

Sperry, L. 2007. *The Ethical and Professional Practice of Counseling and Psychotherapy.* Pearson.

Spielman. B. 2001. "Has Faith in Health Care Ethics Consultants Gone Too Far? Risks of an Unregulated Practice and a Model Act to Contain Them." *Marquette Law Review* 85: 161–221.

Spike, J. 2016. "Baby Steps Toward the Professionalization and Accreditation of Ethics Consultation Services." *American Journal of Bioethics* 16 (3): 52–54.

Spitzeck, H., C. Lins. 2018. *Talking Sustainability in the Boardroom.* United Kingdom: Routledge.

Squazzo, F. D. 2010. "Today's Leader: Committed to Core Values." *Healthcare Executive* 25 (6): 8–18.

Stader, D. L. 2012. *Law and Ethics in Educational Leadership,* 2nd ed. Pearson.

Stanfield, P. S., N. Cross. 2008. *Introduction to the Health Professions,* 5th ed. Jones & Bartlett.

Stanford, C. C., V. J. Connor. 2014. *Ethics for Health Professionals.* Burlington, MA: Jones & Bartlett.

Statista. 2019. *National Per Capita Health Expenditures in the United States From 1960–2019.* www.statista.com/statistics/184955/us-national-health-expenditures-per-capita-since-1960/.

Stichler, J. F. 2016. "A Priority for Healthcare and for Healthcare Design." *Health Environments Research & Design Journal* 9 (4) (August 4): 10–15. https://doi.org/10.1177/1937586716646648.

Stiltner, B. 2016. *Toward Thriving Communities: Virtue Ethics as Social Ethics.* Winona, MN Anselm Academic, 2016.

Stoto, M. 2013. *Population Health in the Accountable Care Era.* Washington, DC: Academy Health.

St. Pierre, M., et al. eds. 2011. *Crisis Management in Acute Care Settings: Human Factors, Team Psychology, and Patient Safety in a High Stakes Environment.* New York: Springer.

Stranberg, K. M. 2011. *Essentials of Law and Ethics for Pharmacy technicians,* 3rd ed. CRC Press, Taylor & Francis.

Strech, D., I. Hirschberg, G. Markermann, eds. 2013. *Ethics in Public Health and Health Policy.* New York: Springer.

Stretch, D., M. Mertz, eds. 2016. *Ethics and Governance of Biomedical Research: Theory and Practice.* New York: Springer.

Strike, K. A., E. J. Haller, J. F. Soltis. 2005. *The Ethics of School Administration,* 3rd ed. Teachers College Press.

Strom-Gottfried, K. 2014. *Straight Talk About Professional Ethics*, 2nd ed. New York: Oxford University Press.

Stuart, S. 2011. "Vision Statement. Corporate Boards: Now and Then." *Harvard Business Review* 89: 39.

Studdart, D. M., et al. 2004. "Medical Malpractice." *New England Journal of Medicine* 350 (3): 283–292.

Sugarman, J., D. P. Sulmasy, eds. 2010. *Methods in Medical Ethics*, 2nd ed. Washington, DC: Georgetown University Press.

Sundaramurthy, C., M. Lewis. 2003. "Control and Collaboration: Paradoxes of Governance." *Academy of Management Review* 28: 397–415.

Sundean, L., K. White, L. Thompson, L. Prybil. 2019. "Governance Education for Nurses: Preparing Nurses for the Future." *Journal of Professional Nursing* 35 (Sept–Oct, 2019): 346–352.

Surbone, A., M. Rowe. 2015. *Clinical Oncology and Error Reduction*. Wiley-Blackwell.

Svara, J.H. 2014. *The Ethics Primer for Public Administrators in Government and Nonprofit Organizations*, 2nd ed. Jones & Bartlett.

Swetz, K. M., et al. 2007. "Report on 255 Clinical Ethics Consultations and Review of the Literature." *Mayo Clinic Proceedings* 82 (6): 686–691.

Szekendi, M., L. Prybil, et al. 2015. "Governance Practices and Performance in U.S. Academic Medical Centers." *American Journal of Medical Quality* 30 (6): 520–525.

Taleff, M. J. 2009. *Advanced Ethics for Addiction Professionals*. Springer.

Tarzian, A. J. 2013. "Health Care Ethics Consultation: An Update on Core Competencies and Emerging Standards from the American Society for Bioethics and Humanities' Core Competencies Update Task Force." *American Journal of Bioethics* 13 (2): 3–13.

Tarzian, A. J., et al. 2015. "A Code of Ethics for Health Care Ethics Consultants." *American Journal of Bioethics* 15 (5): 38–51.

Taylor, H. A., et al. 2010. "Ethics, Oversight and Quality Improvement Initiatives." *Quality and Safety in Healthcare* 19 (4): 271–274.

Taylor, H. A., et al. 2010. *The Ethical Review of Healthcare Quality Improvement Initiatives: Findings from the Field*. New York: The Commonwealth Fund, 1–9.

Taylor, L., et al. 2015. *Leveraging the Social Determinants of Health*. New Haven, CT: Yale Global Health Leadership Institute.

Ten Have, H., B. Gordijn. 2016. *Encyclopedia of Global Bioethics*. New York: Springer.

Ten Have, H., M. S. Jean. 2009. *The UNESCO Declaration on Bioethics and Human Rights*. Paris, France: UNESCO Publishing.

Territo, L., R. Matteson, eds. 2011. *The International Trafficking of Human Organs: A Multidisciplinary Approach*. CRC/Taylor & Francis.

Teutsch, S., J. Fielding. 2011. "Applying Comparative Effectiveness Research to Public and Population Health Initiatives." *Health Affairs* 30: 349–355.

Thomas, E. J., et al. 2000. "Incidence and Types of Adverse Events and Negligent Care in Utah and Colorado." *Medical Care* 38: 261–271.

Thomas, J. T. 2010. *Ethics of Supervision and Consultation: Practical Guidance for Mental Health Professionals*. American Psychological Association.

Thomas, M. 2018. *Best of Boards: Sound Governance and Leadership for Nonprofit Organizations*, 2nd ed. Wiley.

Thomasma, D. C. 1987. "Legitimate and Illegitimate Roles for the Medical Ethicist." In T. Ackerman et al., eds., *Clinical Medical Ethics: Exploration and Assessment*. Lanham, MD: University Press of America, 83–94.

Thornton, G. 2010. *Succeeding at Succession: establishing your goals and objectives*. Chicago, IL: Grant Thornton LLP.

Thornton, P. K., et al. 2011. *Sports Ethics for Sports Management Professionals.* Jones and Bartlett Learning.

Tierney, W. M. 2003. "Adverse Outpatient Drug Events: A Problem and an Opportunity." *New England Journal of Medicine* 348 (16): 1587–1589.

Tingle, J., et al., eds. 2018. *Global Patient Safety: Law, Policy and Practice.* Routledge.

Tio, R. 2014. "Moving Towards Population Health." *Hospitals and Health Networks* 88 (May).

Tipton, D. 2013. *Professionalism, Work, and Clinical Responsibility in Pharmacy.* Jones & Bartlett.

Tomlinson, T. 2012. *Methods in Medical Ethics.* New York: Oxford University Press.

Totten, M. K. 2012. "Transforming Care Delivery to Focus on Patient Outcomes." *Healthcare Executive* 27 (5): 68–69.

Totten, M. K. 2012. "Transforming Healthcare: The Board's Role." *Healthcare Executive* 27 (1): 74–77.

Totten, M. K., L. Prybil, 2017. "Building Community Health." *Trustee*, 70 (February): 26–27.

Trochio, J., C. Evashwick. 2009. "The Future of Evidence-Based Community Benefit." *Health Progress* 89: 5.

Trull, J. E., J. E. Carter. 2014. *Ministerial Ethics: Moral Formation for Church Leaders.* Grand Rapids, MI: Baker Academic.

Truog, R. D., et al. 2011. *Talking with Patients and Families about Medical Error: A Guide for Education and Practice.* Baltimore, MD: Johns Hopkins University Press.

United States Conference of Catholic Bishops (USCCB). 2006. *Readings on Catholics in Political Life.* Washington, DC: USCCB.

United States Conference of Catholic Bishops (USCCB). 2009. *Ethical and Religious Directives for Catholic Healthcare Services*, 5th ed. Washington, DC: USCCB.

United States Conference of Catholic Bishops (USCCB). 2009. *Forming Consciences for Faithful Citizens.* Washington, DC: USCCB.

United States Conference of Catholic Bishops (USCCB). 2018. *Ethical and Religious Directives for Catholic Healthcare Services*, 6th ed. Washington, DC: USCCB.

United States Congress. 2010. *Medical Errors.* BiblioGov.

United States House of Representatives. 2010. *Compilation of Patient Protection and Affordable Care Act, 111th Congress, 2nd Session.* http://housedocs.house.gov/energy-commerce/ppacacon.pdf.

Upadhyay, R. 2018. *Ethics, Integrity, and Aptitude in Governance.* Thousand Oaks, CA: Sage.

U.S. Centers for Disease and Prevention. 2013. *Community Health Assessment for Population Health Improvement: Resources of Most Frequently Recommended Health Outcomes and Determinants.* Atlanta, GA: Office of Surveillance, Epidemiology, and Laboratory Services.

U.S. Department of Health and Human Services. 2012. *Annual Progress Report to Congress, National Strategy for Quality Improvement in Healthcare.* www.ahrq.gov/working forquality/nqs/nqs2012annlrpt.pdf.

U.S. Department of Health and Human Services. 2013. Agency for Healthcare Research and Quality. *National Healthcare Quality Report.* Washington, DC: Agency for Healthcare Research and Quality.

U.S. Department of Health and Human Services. 2015. *Practical Guidelines for Health Care Governing Boards on Compliance Oversight.* Washington, DC: U.S. Department of Health and Human Services.

U.S. Department of Labor. 1970. *OSH Act of 1970*. www.osha.gov/laws-regs/oshact/ completeoshact.

Useem, M. 2006. "How Well-Run Boards Make Decisions." *Harvard Business Review* 84 (11): 130–138.

U.S. News and World Report. 2018. *Health Care Access Rankings* (July). www.usnews. com/news/best-states/rankings/health-care/healthcare-access

Uttling, P., J. Marques, eds. 2013. *Corporate Social Responsibility and Regulatory Governance: Towards Inclusive Development*. Palgrave-MacMillan.

Vagelos, P. R., L. Galambos. 2006. *The Moral Corporation: Merck Experiences*. New York: Cambridge University Press.

Vallabhaneni, S. R. 2008. *Corporate Management, Governance, and Ethics Best Practices*. Wiley.

Vanden Heuvel, L. N., et al. 2014. *Root Cause Analysis Handbook*. Rothstein Publishing.

Van de Poel, I., L. Royakkers. 2011. *Ethics, Technology, and Engineering*. Wiley-Blackwell.

van Zyl, L. 2019. *Virtue Ethics: A Contemporary Introduction*. United Kingdom: Routledge.

Veatch, R. M. 1989. "Clinical Ethics, Applied Ethics, and Ethical Theory." In C. Hoffmaster, B. Freedman, G. Fraser, eds., *Clinical Ethics: Theory and Practice*. Clifton, NJ: Humana Press.

Veatch, R. M. 2014. *Transplantation Ethics*, 2nd ed. Washington, DC: Georgetown University Press.

Veatch, R. M., A. Haddad, ed. 2008. *Case Studies in Pharmacy Ethics*, 2nd ed. New York: Oxford University Press.

Verschoor, C. S. 2003. "Ethical Corporations Are Still More profitable." *Strategic Finance* 22–23.

Verulava, T., et al. 2018. "The Role of Non-Profit Organizations in Health Care Systems." *Georgian Medical News* 274: 174–178.

Voges, N. D. 2012. "The Ethics of Mission and Margin." *Healthcare Executive* 27 (5): 30–38.

Volpp, K. G. M., D. Grande. 2003. "Residents' Suggestions for Reducing Errors in Teaching Hospitals." *New England Journal of Medicine* 348 (9): 851–855.

Wachter, R. M. 2017. *Understanding Patient Safety*, 2nd ed. New York: McGraw Hill.

Walker, L. L. 2012. "The Supporting Cast. Strong, Focused Committees and Task Forces Are Essential to Overall Governance Excellence." *Trustee* 65–67.

Wasson, K. 2016. "A Call for Multiple Means of Assessing Quality in Clinical Ethics Consultation." *American Journal of Bioethics* 16 (3): 44–45.

Wasson, K., et al. 2015. "Developing an Evaluation Tool for Assessing Clinical Ethics Consultation Skills in Simulation Based Education." *HEC Forum* 27 (1): 1–22.

Watt, H. ed. 2006. *Cooperation, Complicity & Conscience: Problems in Healthcare, Science, Law and Public Policy*. London: Linacre Centre.

Wears, R., K. Sutcliffe. 2019. *Still Not Safe: Patient safety and the Middle-Managing of American Medicine*. New York: Oxford University Press.

Weber, J., D. M. Wasielski, eds. 2018. *Corporate Social Responsibility*. United Kingdom: Emerald Publishing.

Webley, S., E. More. 2003. *Does Business Ethics Pay? Ethics and Financial Performance*. London: The Institute of Business Ethics.

Weeks, K., et al. 2012. *Reducing Medical Errors and Adverse Events*. Amazon Digital Services.

Weeks, W. B., et al. 2001. "Tort Claims Analysis in the VHA for Quality Improvement." *Journal of Law, Medicine, & Ethics* 29: 335–45.

Weil, P. A. 2009. "A Racial/Ethnic Comparison of Career Attainments in Healthcare Management." *Healthcare Executive* 24 (6): 22–31.

Weil, P. A. 2014. "It Takes a Community." *Health Affairs* 33: 1886.

Weimer, D. L. 2010. *Medical Governance: Values, Expertise, and Interests in Organ Transplantation.* Washington, DC: Georgetown University Press.

Welfel, E. R. 2015. *Ethics in Counseling & Psychotherapy*, 6th ed. Boston, MA: Cengage Learning.

Wells, A. L. 2004. "Reevaluating the Social Contract in American Medicine." *Virtual Mentor* 6 (4): 194–196. https://journalofethics.ama-assn.org/article/reevaluating-social-contract-american-medicine/2004-04.

Wendel, W. B. 2016. *Professional Responsibility: Examples & Explanations*, 5th ed. Philadelphia, PA: Wolters Kluwer.

Werhane, P. H. 1999. *Moral Imagination and Management Decision Making.* New York: Oxford University Press.

Werhane, P. H. 2002. "Moral Imagination and Systems Thinking." *Journal of Business Ethics* 13 (1–2): 33–42.

Werhane, P. H. 2014. "The Healthcare Organization, Business Ethics, and Stakeholder Theory." In G. L. Filerman, A. E. Mills, P. M. Shyve, eds., *Managerial Ethics in Healthcare: A New Perspective.* Chicago, IL: Health Administration Press, Chapter 4.

Westrick, S. J. 2013. *Essentials of Nursing Law and Ethics*, 2nd ed. Jones & Bartlett.

Wheeler, D. 2012. *Servant Leadership for Higher Education: Principles and Practice.* San Francisco, CA: Jossey-Bass.

Whincop, M. J. 2016. *Corporate Governance in Government Corporations.* Routledge.

White, B., et al. 2014. "Structuring a Written Examination to Assess ASBH Healthcare Ethics Consultation Core Knowledge Competencies." *American Journal of Bioethics* 14 (1): 5–17.

Wicclair, M. R. 2011. *Conscientious Objection in Health Care.* New York: Cambridge University Press.

Wieland, J. 2014. *Governance Ethics: Global Value Creation, Economic Organization and Normativity.* New York: Springer.

Wiist, W. H. 2010. *The Bottom Line or Public Health.* New York: Oxford University Press.

Wilcoxon, A. P., et al. 2013. *Ethical, Legal, and Professional Issues in the Practice of Marriage and Family Therapy*, 5th ed. Pearson.

Williams, C. R., B. A. Arrigo. 2011. *Ethics, Crime, and Criminal Justice*, 2nd ed. Pearson.

Willmott, C., S. Macip. 2016. *Where Science and Ethics Meet: Dilemmas at the Frontiers of Medicine and Biology.* Praeger.

Wilson, K., et al. 2014. "Describing the Continuum of Collaboration among Local Health Departments With Hospitals Around the Community Health Assessments." *Journal of Public Health Management and Practice* 20: 617–624.

Windt, P., et al. 1989. *Ethical Issues in the Professions.* Prentice Hall [Pearson].

Winstone, K. 2015. *Ethics in Public Life.* United Kingdom: Palgrave-MacMillan.

Wocial, L. D., E. Molnar, M. A. Ott. 2016. "Values, Quality, and Evaluation in Ethics Consultation." *AJOB Empirical Bioethics* 7 (4): 227–234.

Wolfson, D. 2019. "Commentary: Erosion of Trust Threatens Essential Element of Practicing Medicine." *Modern Healthcare* (March 9). www.modernhealthcare.com/opinion-editorial/commentary-erosion-trust-threatens-essential-element-practicing-medicine.

World Health Organization. 2004. *World Alliance for Patient Safety.* www.who.int/patientsafety/worldalliance/en/.

Wright, J. C. ed. 2019. *Humility: The Virtues.* New York: Oxford University Press.

Wright, M., et al., eds. 2014. *The Oxford Handbook of Corporate Governance*. Oxford University Press.

Wueste, D. E. 1994. *Professional Ethics and Social Responsibility*. Rowman & Littlefield.

Wynland, M. 2014. "The Role of Nonprofits in Healthcare: A Trends Summary." *Nonprofit Quarterly* (February). https://nonprofitquarterly.org/the-role-of-nonprofits-in-health-care-a-trends-summary/.

Yarmolinsky, R. 2016. "Ethics for Ethicists? The Professionalization of Clinical Ethics Consultation." *AMA Journal of Ethics* 18 (5): 506–513.

Yeo, M. 1993. "Prolegomena to Any Future Code of Ethics for Bioethicists." *Cambridge Quarterly of Healthcare Ethics* 2: 403–415.

Yingjie, L., et al. 2017. "Understanding Health Care Social Media Use from Different Stakeholder Perspectives: A Content Analysis of an Online Health Community." *Journal of Medical Internet Research* 19 (4) (April): e109. https://doi.org/10.2196/jmir.7087.

Yonek, J., et al. 2010. *A Guide to Achieving High Performance in Multi-Hospital Health Systems*. Chicago, IL: Hospital Research and Educational Trust.

Young, G., et al. 2013. "Provision of Community Benefits by Tax-Exempt U.S. Hospitals." *New England Journal of Medicine* 368: 1519–1527.

Youngner, S. J., et al. 1983. "A National Survey of Hospital Ethics Committees." *Critical Care Medicine* 11 (11): 902–905.

Zaner, R. M. 2015. *A Critical Examination of Ethics in Health Care and Biomedical Research*. Springer.

Zuckerman, A. M. 2000. "Creating a Vision for the Twenty-First Century Healthcare Organization." *Journal of Healthcare Management* 45 (5): 294–305.

Zuckerman, D. 2013. *Hospitals Building Healthier Communities: Embracing the Anchor Mission*. Takoma Park, MD: The Democracy Collaborative.

Index